BIRDFINDER

A BIRDER'S GUIDE TO PLANNING NORTH AMERICAN TRIPS

BIRDFINDER

A BIRDER'S GUIDE TO PLANNING NORTH AMERICAN TRIPS

by
Jerry A. Cooper

American Birding Association, Inc.

Library of Congress Catalog Number: 95-075100
ISBN Number: 1-878788-10-8
First Edition
   1   2   3   4   5   6   7   8   9
Printed in the United States of America
Publisher
    American Birding Association, Inc.
    George G. Daniels, Publications Committee
Series Editor
    Paul J. Baicich
Associate Editors
    Cindy Lippincott and Bob Berman
Copy Editor
    Hugh Willoughby
Layout, Typography, and Maps
    Cindy Lippincott; using CorelVENTURA, Windows ver 5.0 and
        CorelDRAW ver 5.0
Cover Photography
    front cover: Brown Pelican, Least Grebe, Gambel's Quail
                   Jerry A. Cooper
    author photo: Kristi L. Cooper
Cover Design
    Terry O'Nele
Illustrations

Georges Dremeaux	David A. Sibley
Shawneen E. Finnegan	Gail Diane Yovanovich
Dan Kilby	Louise Zemaitis

Distributed by
    American Birding Association Sales
    PO Box 6599
    Colorado Springs, Colorado 80934-6599 USA
    tel: (800) 804-0056; fax: (800) 590-2473
European and UK Distribution
    Subbuteo Natural History Books, Ltd.
    Treuddyn, Mold, Clwyd
    CH7 4LN   UK   tel: 0352-770581; fax: 0352-771590

This book is dedicated to my wife Betty,

who for thirty-five years

has been the wind beneath my wings.

ACKNOWLEDGEMENTS

It would be impossible for me to name the original sources of much of the information in this book. I do want to thank all of the birders who have shared their knowledge of particular locations with me and all of the authors of birdfinding guides and articles. I acknowledge a debt of gratitude to all of these individuals because they have made my travels and my birding education so enjoyable.

A special thanks must go to the following people who reviewed important parts of this book or otherwise have had a direct influence on me and on this book:

Ben Anderson, Gwenda Anderson, Robert Andrle, Michelle Axtell, Sharon Bartels, Gordon Berkey, Stacy Cooper Boyles, Jean Brandt, Gus Daniels, Charles D. Duncan, Kim Eckert, Eve Feeberg, William J. Graber III, Joseph A. Grzybowski, Bruce Hallett, Stuart Healy, Ken Hollinga, Liz Hutson, Deloris Isted, David Lambeth, Greg W. Lasley, Mark Lockwood, Blake Maybank, Bill Maynard, Virginia Maynard, Robert W. Morse, Gary Nielsen, Kayo Roy, Kevin Sarsfield, Joan Scott, Debi Shearwater, Arnold Small, David Sonneborn, Rich Stallcup, the late George M. Sutton, Theodore G. Tobish, Jr., Michael Toochin, Michael Tove, Bill Tweit, and Noel Wamer.

Also, Paul Lehman, the editor of ABA's *Birding*, gave generously of his time to comment on so many aspects of traveling birding. The artists—Georges Dremeaux, Shawneen E. Finnegan, Dan Kilby, David A. Sibley, Gail Diane Yovanovich, and Louise Zemaitis—provided wonderful works to accompany this book.

The regular ABA birdfinding guide staff was essential in putting this book into shape: Paul J. Baicich, the series editor; Cindy Lippincott, associate editor and map-maker, Bob Berman, associate editor and computer whiz, and Hugh Willoughby, the copy editor and master of the misplaced modifier.

Jerry A. Cooper
October 1995

TABLE OF CONTENTS

PREFACE

The pleasures of birding are numerous. It is one of the best excuses a person will ever find to travel both the populated and the unpopulated areas of the world. It is a marvelous way to see North America, and to see it thoroughly. One cannot be a traveling birder for long without meeting new and interesting people, birders and non-birders alike. Some will become your friends, and some you will meet again and again over the years at various birding hotspots.

Birders, for the most part, are friendly, helpful, and generous with fellow enthusiasts. Birding is a very democratic pastime. Lawyers and college professors bird happily alongside unemployed vagabonds and hourly wage-earners of all types. No one cares what your income is when you are birding. You are a birder, a kindred spirit, and that is enough.

For me, one of the real pleasures of birding is to see at a birding hotspot someone whom I have met on a previous birding trip. Maybe this is someone I birded with for a single day with or met in a campground. A few minutes reminiscing and catching-up may not pass for a close personal relationship, but it is hard to beat for camaraderie.

Birding has afforded me many experiences in life that I would have missed otherwise. My desire to see new and different bird species has led me to hike in the mountain snow, camp in the desert heat, and sail the ocean in good weather and bad. I have met new people and made good friends. I have birded with jobless drifters and professional people whose enthusiasm and birding expertise made it impossible to guess their different backgrounds. I have shared my food, drink, shelter, and birding information, and have had others share theirs with me. I have looked through a stranger's spotting scope on many occasions and have slept on the floor in a friend of a distant friend's home more than once. I have talked on the phone for an hour getting directions and guidance from people whom I have never met. I have had others drop what they were doing to come along to guide me. I have watched the sun set through the "window" at Big Bend National Park, Texas. I have been the first person in the U.S. to see the new day's sunrise from the top of Cadillac Mountain in Maine. I have seen snowstorms in Yosemite and flash floods in the desert. I have been on the ocean where rain squalls frightened me one minute and rainbows elated me the next. What I am saying is that being a traveling birder, being a birdfinder, is a magnificent adventure; you would do well to give it a try.

INTRODUCTION

This book is a working journal of birding trips. Using it as a trip planning guide, you can take nineteen separate trips over a period of years or spend a very jam-packed, exciting, or frantic calendar year doing them all in rapid succession. The trips are chronologically arranged to enable you to be in the right place at the right time to maximize the number of bird species seen and at the same time experience much of the beauty of varied areas in the continental U.S. and Canada—otherwise known to birders as the American Birding Association (ABA) Area.

However, if you are making these trips over a period of years you certainly don't have to do them in chronological order. Simply make the trip or trips each year that will fit into your personal schedule; the eventual outcome will be the same. Moreover, with a little adjustment, you should be able to open this book at any chapter, at any location, and start your birding afresh.

And while discussing adjustment, not only can this book help you to build a significant life list or a wonderful year list, but it can also assist you in fashioning multiple state or province lists.

Whichever way you elect to see the birds in North America, these trips will do much more than provide the traveling birder a chance to see the 650-odd listed species. You can make friends that will last a lifetime, have experiences that will become priceless memories, and vastly improve the quality time and level of satisfaction in your life.

OBJECTIVES

Each chapter/trip in the book covers a well-known (to birders at least) birding location. Most, if not all, of these places are described in great detail in the appropriate birdfinding guides. *This book is not intended as a replacement for these guides but as a supplement to them.* It is intended to help the birdfinder maximize the number of species seen for the time spent. Each chapter will list (in chronological order) the guidebooks that I have found to be most useful. Included are not only the original guides pioneered by Jim Lane, and continued through the work of his dedicated co-worker, Harold Holt, but also many of the best local birdfinding guides that have emerged over the past two decades. I highly recommend that you buy these useful books. They are, by design, much more detailed than this book of routes and plans. Some of these guides go out of print from time to time but can usually be found with a little effort through nature stores and from other experienced birders.

Birding trips do not need to be expensive. If a trip is well-planned and a birder is willing to undergo a few minor hardships, the trip can be a very inexpensive, rewarding vacation. This is another important aim of this book—to help you to get the most enjoyment from your birding time and money.

Many birders regularly travel with one or more other birders. Having a travel partner allows each person a further reduction in expenses such as travel costs, car rentals, fuel, and lodging. I have made very few trips without a traveling companion. Birders will benefit in many ways other than saving on expenses. Sharing time with others with similar interests, seeing in the field with four eyes instead of two, and having safety in numbers while in remote areas are all good reasons for traveling with a partner. Above all, the joy of pointing out your find to someone else and possibly showing him or her a new species is a reward in itself.

My partner for many trips over the years has been Ben Anderson. I have been extremely fortunate to have found and kept a friend who is as avid a birdfinder as myself. Additionally, we share a love of travel and new experiences. I have been doubly blessed because we live in the same town and have proved to be compatible over the years on trips both short and long. If I could wish any one thing for the reader, it would be to find a partner like Ben. With a good birding companion and sufficient time in the field, the bird species will come, but more importantly the quality time in your life will expand.

This book provides general itineraries, general timing of trips, and other useful bits of information. It will help you to plan your North American birding trips the way Ben and I have found to be the most successful.

PLANNING TOOLS

As an aid to your planning, each chapter provides a reasonable itinerary for that particular trip. Obviously, since the readers live in widely varying locations, I cannot plan your trip from door-to-door, so to speak. Each itinerary by necessity will start in the area of the trip and concern itself with the immediate trip area only. It also follows that the readers will be from all economic levels; therefore, I can deal only in general with modes of travel and the luxury or the lack thereof concerning accommodations. Additionally, if my plan calls for a seven-day trip to an area, some birders may be able to stay a month if they desire; others cannot. The time allowed for each birding itinerary is a *minimal amount* necessary to cover the trip. While it is always good to add a number of extra days to cover the sites reasonably, the itinerary should work well as outlined. Any additional time should be considered a bonus. The trip plans will work regardless of mode of travel with slight alterations in route and/or timing for such factors as weather.

AMERICAN BIRDING ASSOCIATION

Good planning starts at home prior to each trip. My single most important aid to planning any trip is my membership in the American Birding Association. This affiliation is inexpensive and indispensable to any birder who travels or ever plans to do so.

In way of explanation, for the last quarter century the American Birding Association has existed to promote recreational birding, to contribute to the development of bird identification and population study, and to help foster public appreciation of birds and their vital role in the environment. All of this depends on a diverse and viable avifauna, and the ABA strongly supports and encourages efforts to protect wild birds and their habitats. Everyone who shares these pleasures and purposes is invited to join the association; as of this writing, a individual membership is only $36 per year. (An ABA membership application can be found at the back of this book.)

By joining the ABA you are automatically connected to a birding network which provides as least four vital resources: *Birding*, the *ABA Membership Directory*, the *ABA Sales Catalog*, and *Winging It*.

How do these resources aid in trip planning? As a member you receive six issues a year of the association journal *Birding*. It consists primarily of bird identification and birdfinding articles, photos, reviews, and technical information. It covers the state-of-the-art in birding, bird identification, birdfinding information, birding equipment, and bird conservation.

ABA also provides members with a yearly *ABA Membership Directory* that gives you contacts almost anywhere you may travel. I have used this listing extensively prior to trips, establishing contacts for local help. The directory is coded so that you know whom you can call and when you can call. Some members do not make themselves available for phone calls but will answer letters. More and more birders are reached through e-mail and the Internet. It is amazing what you can learn by asking the right questions using any of these three modes of communication. Please respect the members' wishes concerning calls and letters, though. Have questions ready if you call, and don't waste the contact's time. Remember that he or she is doing you the favor! Using the *ABA Membership*

Directory prior to a trip aids greatly in your planning. Usually it is no problem to make good contacts, new friends, and a local backup should you need more information. I find that most of the time one new contact leads to another contact, and so on.

Through ABA you will also receive twice yearly an *ABA Sales Catalog* listing more bird books, birdfinding guides, birding equipment, and birding-related items than you ever dreamed existed. Using ABA Sales' toll-free number you can within days have the items you order. For me, this is the most important source of books on birdfinding. The overwhelming majority of birdfinding guides cited in this book can be bought at ABA Sales.

The association's monthly newsletter, *Winging It*, contains birdfinding articles, classified advertisements, bird tour information, and regular pelagic trip information. One issue per year—the January issue—is devoted almost exclusively to pelagic tour information. It contains a rather complete listing of dates and contacts for pelagic trips ABA Area-wide. *Winging It* also keeps you current on all state, provincial, area, and regional rare bird alert "hotlines." Each issue of *Winging It* has a one-page article entitled "Bird Sightings from the Hotlines." This is a listing of rare or unusual sightings ABA Area-wide from the previous month.

RARE BIRD ALERTS/HOTLINES

A "hotline" or "rare bird alert" (RBA) is a phone number that you can call for the cost of only the call and hear a frequently updated tape of bird sightings for that particular state, province, area, or region. The hotlines are usually run by local bird clubs, nature centers, or dedicated individuals. Occasionally, these numbers will change. I use the hotline or lines once or twice in the week prior to traveling to a new area. The information on these tapes has made me change the sequence of my travels on more than one occasion and has resulted in my seeing many birds that I might otherwise have missed. Additionally, I again call when I arrive in the area and depending on how long I am there may use it several times on a trip. On some trips you will be in several rare bird alert areas; calling each of them is of great value.

Before leaving the subject of rare bird hotlines, nearly all hotlines make provisions for the caller to leave a message concerning rarities discovered. Birding is a cooperative venture; please report to the hotlines you use any unusual sighting you may have made. And reporting on the status of the existing rarity which you pursued—if it is still there, if it has moved, or if it has left altogether—is also important. This kind of follow-up will help those calling after you to see unusual or rare species, just as the hotlines originally helped you.

Much of the summary of "Bird Sightings from the Hotlines" in *Winging It* is gleaned from the most comprehensive of all hotlines—the North American Rare Bird Alert (NARBA). Most of this information is prepared by Mike Austin and others at Houston Audubon Society, sponsors of NARBA. For the most timely access to this information you can subscribe to NARBA for $25 per year. For subscription information write to NARBA, Suite 6A, 807 S. Friendswood Drive, Friendswood, TX 77546.

BIRDERS ON-LINE

A new planning tool for birders is the growing enthusiasm for on-line information. You can connect with your fellow birders through Internet discussions and get "hotline" reports through the National Birding Hotline Cooperative (NBHC). This last service includes the transcripts of many of the hotlines throughout North America. If you are connected to the Internet with a computer and a modem, you can receive the hotline transcripts as e-mail. This kind of computer networking is a growing phenomenon. For more information on NBHC, contact Chuck Williamson by e-mail at Listserv@Listserv.Arizona.EDU, or by regular mail at 7309 E. Princeton Drive, Tucson, AZ 85710 (include a SASE).

BIRDING TOURS

Another planning tool that is available is the packaged birding tour. There are any number of tour companies and/or guides who lead small groups, large groups, or even individuals for the specific purpose of birding. There are times when trips are much more likely to be successful with a guide than going by yourself. Examples of trips where access to certain areas is limited or cost prohibitive to do alone are trips to the Dry Tortugas, some areas in Alaska, and pelagic trips. Tour companies are run professionally by extremely competent birders. Going with a tour package leaves the planning to the tour company and leaves the birder to just enjoy the results. This method of birding appeals to a lot of birders but is more expensive as a rule than doing it all yourself. Still, there are times when you may want to use these services. One thing that works well is to combine birding on your own in an area—such as South Florida—with joining a tour group for two or three days (e.g., the Dry Tortugas) of your trip. Three of the most widely known tour companies are as follows:

Field Guides Incorporated, P.O. Box 160723, Austin, TX 78716
512/327-4953

Victor Emanuel Nature Tours, Inc., P.O. Box 33008, Austin, TX 78764
800/328-8368

WINGS, Inc., P.O. Box 31930, Tucson, AZ 85751
520/749-1967

Each of these tour companies publishes an extensive catalog of tours, costs, dates, species expected, and other information. Many other excellent tour companies advertise in birding magazines, and many are listed in the Yellow Pages section of the *ABA Membership Directory.* All birders should take a packaged tour at least occasionally to see how the pros do it. They are very good, and they do make your trip easy.

Sandhill Crane
Dan Kilby

Note: See Chapter 20, Trip B for crane-watching along the Platte River.

DEVELOPING A TRIP PLAN

With all of the preceding information to work with, my basic twelve stages to developing a good trip plan are fairly simple:

1. Decide where you want to go.
2. Find out the best times to visit the selected area.
   > (Most places will yield completely different birds at different seasons. Sometimes these are very desirable species for the different seasons, necessitating more than one trip to the same location.)
3. Settle on what mode or modes of transportation you will use.
4. Buy the latest editions of the ever-important birdfinding guides that exist for the area and study these guides carefully.
5. Develop a set of lists of birds to be seen on the trip by using the birdfinding guides and field guides. Make four lists that include a list of "key species," a list of "probable species," a list of "possible species," and finally a fourth list of birds that are "remotely possible."

   - Your *key species* are the primary reason for that particular trip. These are species that can be seen only in that specific area or species that are worth an extra effort to see because there are few opportunities to see them on later planned trips.

   - Your *probable species* are birds that will be seen with minimal effort, and if they are not seen on one trip you should have many chances on other trips.

   - Your *possible species* are birds that take extra effort and/or extra luck but are real possibilities.

   - The *remotely possible species* are those that may take real luck, but you should be alert to that chance. The purpose of all four lists is to make you aware of all possibilities.

6. Use these lists, birdfinding guides, and a good map to develop a route, a possible itinerary, and a timetable that will allow you to see the birds on your lists.
7. Use the *ABA Membership Directory* or other contacts that you have established in the past to touch base with birders in the area. Get all the information on key species that you possibly can.
8. Check the rare bird alerts/hotlines for the target area.

9. Always add at least one extra day onto your schedule. This day can be used at any point during the trip to pursue rarities reported on the hotline or discovered through contacts made on the trip. The day can be used to catch up if bad weather has interfered with your birding plans. The extra day can also be used simply to enjoy a location that you've just discovered and wish to savor. Stay flexible.

10. Make all needed reservations for lodging, pelagic trips, tours, guides, car rentals, flights, etc.

11. Pack for your trip. I keep a checklist to help me pack and I can pack in thirty minutes for any trip. This checklist has been developed over several years and may seem ridiculous to some, but this way I never overlook packing an item that I may need. Each person's list must be tailored to his/her own needs. Here is my own personal packing list:

Clothes	_Toiletries_	_Birding & Photo Gear_
socks	razor	field guides
shoes	razor blades	guide books
underwear	shaving cream	bird list records
pants	aftershave	binoculars
T-shirts	toothbrush	camera
long johns	toothpaste	camera bag
shirts	shampoo	lenses
belt	comb	tripod
gloves	deodorant	film
rain coat	soap	spotting scope
jacket & coat	soap dish	spotlight
hiking boots	scissors	tape player/recorder
hat	clippers	bird tapes
		day pack

Medicine	_Miscellaneous_	_Camping Gear_
prescription medicines	sunglasses	sleeping bag
vitamins	travelers checks	one-man tent
sinus medicine	trash bags (2)	canteen
aspirin	flashlight	camp stove
seasickness preventive	tick/insect repellents	
sunscreen	bathing suit	

12. Take into account any potential field hazards: snow, excessive heat, Poison Ivy, chiggers, ticks, poisonous snakes, bears, rabies.... Fortunately, you won't be plagued by all of these at once!

Then you can leave for the trip, using all the information and contacts available to you. Work hard at it, and the plan will work just as you hoped that it would.

The advantage of this book is that I have already provided for you most of these dozen planning elements for nineteen important trips in the pages that follow. This pre-planning can make for uncomplicated final planning and some fine birding.

THE BIRDFINDER

Most of the trips in this book have been made at least once by Ben Anderson and me. God willing, we will make them again and again. No trip is ever the same and no trip is entirely predictable, but by using this trip guide and the general itineraries provided, the numbers of species cited are achievable and have been accomplished by numerous birders in the past. The itineraries can obviously be varied. Trips can be made longer or shorter as your schedule allows. Transportation and lodging may be as varied as you can afford. Nothing here is carved in stone, but this system has worked extremely well for Ben and me.

The trips and species outlined in this book are realistic goals, but (as we all know!) there are no birding guarantees. If you put a reasonable amount of effort into seeing the birds, use the rare bird alerts, use the existing birdfinding guides, and allow the local birders to impart some of their knowledge to you, no more than five percent of the 650-odd species should be missed. This five percent can be offset to some degree by staying tuned to the birders' grapevine, by subscribing to the North American Rare Bird Alert, and simply by spending time in the field.

KEY SPECIES — AN EXPLANATION

Within each trip description there are featured your crucial "key" species. Some explanations on these "key" species are necessary. When I devised this system, I decided that if a bird appeared on these nineteen trips as "probable" only three times (sometimes four times, or for some pelagic species up to five times), then it should almost certainly be marked as a "key" species at the first "probable" opportunity. **The premise is that a "key" species should be pursued with some determination.** However, some of the "key" species might not be "key" to *you* depending on where *you* live. For example, if you are from Kentucky, tracking down a Wood Thrush as a "key" species along the Texas Coast during spring migration may seem strange to you. After all, you happen to live in the center of the Wood Thrush's range, and you will surely see one around home later in the season. Running after Common Eider in Alaska or Purple Sandpiper at Niagara Falls may not make sense to you if you live along the New England coast, where you are likely to find these species without much effort in winter. Likewise, if you live along the the central or southern California coast, you may not have to pursue a "key" Heermann's Gull with any more effort than checking the closest beach at the beginning of the year. Therefore, if you factor out your own "home range," the "key" birds will make more sense.

PROBABLE, POSSIBLE, AND REMOTELY POSSIBLE SPECIES

Also featured in each chapter in side-bars are almost all the "probable," "possible," and "remotely possible" species that I could think of. **These lists can assist you with a running count of species, virtually a working checklist, seen on each trip.** Using a slim highlighting pen, for example, you can mark right on the side-bar list those species which you have found. I have also put in **boldface** the species in the side-bars that appear as "probable" usually four times or fewer. This device will help you to focus additional attention on these birds wherever you may travel. (The boldfaced species in the side-bar are particularly helpful if you begin picking and choosing the trips out of sequence in the book.)

Putting the species into the four categories for the nineteen trips was mostly a practical decision, but some of it was problematic. One could quibble with my decisions, especially in terms of the "possible" or "remotely possible" categories. Moreover, some species are included in the "remotely possible" category simply because they have been seen a few times at the periphery of the ABA Area, e.g., Texas, Florida, Southern California, or Arizona. The alternative would be to neglect them altogether. Finally, the "remotely possible" category could actually have been much longer in each case, but I had to keep the list within some bound. (Outside of the personal decision of putting a species in one or another category, clearly some outright errors will have crept into this text. I would certainly appreciate hearing from users of this book on this issue: Jerry Cooper, c/o ABA Birdfinding Guides, P.O. Box 6599, Colorado Springs, CO 80934.)

SUMMARY OF SPECIES SEEN ON TRIPS

Near the close of each chapter, there is a hypothetical summary of the bird species seen on the trip described in that chapter. The potential species numbers are arrived at by totaling the lists in that chapter of key, probable, possible, and remotely possible species. **The expected species numbers show the total species in each of those categories that you can**

reasonably expect to see by following that chapter's trip plan. Totals of species actually seen cannot be predicted for obvious reasons, but I feel that the totals in these summaries will prove to be reasonably accurate.

In addition, there is a cumulative total of the species that you could expect to see if the trips were taken in the sequence in which they appear in the book. This number is arrived at by assuming that on each trip you will see all of the key species and the probable species. While this result is not likely on most of the trips, you still should not miss more than five percent of the total species. This cumulative number will allow you a fairly accurate running total throughout the book. Following the running list of species, some 650-odd species of birds are possible. If you are able to include visiting Alaskan outposts (i.e., Attu, Gambell, Barrow, and the Pribilofs) and a few of the extra places that are mentioned in Chapter 20, you could approach 700 species and might, with a little luck, even surpass that number.

SUMMARY OF POTENTIAL EXPENSES

At the end of each of the nineteen trips/chapters you will also find a summary of potential expenses. You can write in your own potential or actual costs in the spaces provided. I have tried to be economical in my estimates, stressing regular camping and what I often call the "ice-chest and supermarket method" for meals during trips. Of course, if you are not as frugal as I, you will insert your own adjusted numbers, reflecting your own style of spending in the field.

Using these features, plus the section at the end of each chapter for "personal notes," you can further individualize this book, and adapt it to your own birding style and speed. Use "personal notes" to write in names, addresses, phone numbers, ID notes, or new/changed hotline numbers, for example. (As a matter of fact, I suggest that you read each chapter as a whole before leaving on any trip so that you can write in other details, and add to the travel schedule as necessary.)

THE BIRDFINDER CHART AND THE ABA CODES

A practical summary chart is presented at the end of the book. This birdfinder chart will help you to track your progress from trip to trip and aid you in alternate planning. This chart also includes a place to write in the date and place of your first sighting for each bird. It incorporates the "ABA code numbers," a system which may need some explanation. Code 1 and 2 are species that occur routinely and are easily found. (Code 2 species are simply a bit more difficult to find than are Code 1 birds because of their distribution or habitat.) Code 3 birds occur annually in

CONTENTS OF EACH OF THE NINETEEN BIRDFINDER CHAPTERS

General—a summary of the trip, goals, and places to visit.

Birdfinding Guides—a short listing of the birdfinding guides covering the trip area.

Rare Bird Alert Numbers—hotlines for the area.

Special Equipment—hints on what to bring.

Accommodations—a brief indication on the status of motels and camp-grounds in the area.

Key Species—an annotated listing of the birds that are the primary purpose of the trip.

Side-bars—a listing on the sides of the pages of *Probable* species, *Possible* species, and *Remotely Possible* species for the area. (**Boldface** *Probables* are those which appear infrequently in the book's itineraries.)

Itinerary—a suggested route to cover the area in the allotted days while still seeing all the *Key* species.

Bird Numbers—a summary of the potential species and expected species for the trip covered by the chapter. Also a running total of the cumulative list for the trips in sequence.

This Trip's Mileage and Expenses—an estimate of the costs involved, in addition to a place to tabulate your own expenses.

Personal Notes—a space to write in additional notes.

the ABA Area but are extremely local, are difficult to see, or have a very short season when they may be readily observed. Code 4 species probably occur more-or-less regularly, but either there is no place in our area where they can be expected or their regular North American range is so remote that getting to it is very difficult to accomplish. Code 5—a code used rarely in the body of this book—indicates that the species are true accidentals, with little predictability of occurrence again.

TIME AFIELD

The nineteen trips as outlined from Chapters 1 to 19 would require you to spend a minimum of 128 days in the field. If you travel by air to each of the trip areas, this schedule will require a maximum of 38 more days. This addition would make your total time 166 days.

Depending on your particular "home range," you may elect to drive (to at least some of the areas) to eliminate airfare and car rental expenses. This method can certainly be more economical but will, of course, eat up more of your time. The deciding factor must be whether time or money is the greater consideration to the individual birder.

OVERALL EXPENSES

The approximate expenses outlined in this book are only the expenses incurred in the nineteen immediate trip areas. These expenses are based on being in the trip area for the suggested number of days and staying reasonably close to the itinerary as outlined. Of course, some birders will spend more on food and less on lodging, or vice versa. Overall, the cost of the trip will come close to the projected expense. If you have a traveling companion to share these expenses, it would cost each of you about $5,675 to do all nineteen trips. (This figure is estimated in 1995 dollars.) This number also excludes the major expenses of traveling to and from the individual trip areas and that of renting a car, if necessary, while in the trip area.

There are many ways to approach these expenses, but in the final analysis their allocation must be dictated by the individual birder and his or her circumstances. Some birders travel extensively while pursuing their worklives and can schedule in birding time. Some are retired and can take the leisurely route; others are busy, and air travel is the only way in which they can fit birding into their lives. There are many variables that go into determining this expense for each individual birder, so there is no possible way for me to calculate it for you.

I can, however, provide you with an example that will put this discussion into some kind of perspective. We can look at a single frantic year of dedicated birding. For the example, let's assume that you live in mid-America, have a traveling companion to share expenses with, and that both of you can spend a busy year pursuing birding. Let's further assume that you do not mind camping or traveling in a small, economical vehicle. If you elected to drive to each of the areas (excluding the Alaska trip), you would make the following trade-off. You would not have to pay airfares or car rental costs, but you would have the expense of gasoline and the added expense of food and lodging (or camping) on your travel days. Your travel expenses in this example would be approximately $4,500. The $4,500 figure also includes round-trip airfare and car rental for the Alaska trip. This total means of course that when your travel expenses ($4,500) are added to your trip area expenses ($5,675), the nineteen trips would cost you approximately $10,175.

Unfortunately, most of us do not fit into the above circumstances, and our trips must be made now and then as our busy schedules allow. For many birders it is possible to plan these trips over, say, four years, to maximize bird variety, to build on previously acquired identification skills and knowledge of bird distribution, and to get the most out of savoring the varied birds and habitats in North America. Whatever your options and limitations, the best approach to each trip is to plan ahead and do what works best for you as an individual. For the average birder, a good mix of traveling by car when circumstances allow and traveling by air when they do not, is the best solution.

One further note about expenses: if Attu, Gambell, Barrow, and the Pribilofs are added to your travels, they will cost an additional $9,000. (This expansion would also tighten up your schedule enough to make it absolutely necessary to use air travel on some of the other trips if you were doing them all in one year.)

Don't think that doing a "Big Year" is impossible. The classic book on the subject was *Wild America* (1955), by Roger Tory Peterson and James Fisher, recounting their 30,000-mile adventure in 1953. The Peterson and Fisher story was mild compared to the pace and expense of later Big Year tales. A number of other books have been written by practitioners of this financial and organizational masochism: Jim Vardaman in his *Call Collect, Ask for Birdman* (1980), Steve Perry in his aptly titled *The Loonatic Journals* (1989), Sandy Komito in his *Birding's Indiana Jones* (1990), and Bill Rydell in *A Year for the Birds* (1995). For a more mellow account of a calm, instructive, and entertaining Big Year, see Pete Dunne's *The Feather Quest* (1992). Each of these books has some good things to say about planning for trips and seeing great birds in one year.

BIRDING ETHICS

The basis of birding ethics is nothing but a combination of common sense and human decency. There are many published lists of rules that birders should follow; the American Birding Association Code of Ethics is probably the best and was created after much thought and member input. A copy of the ABA Code of Ethics is reproduced on this book's inside front cover. This code basically says that a birder must not endanger or harm birds, other wildlife, or the natural environment. A birder must respect property-owners, their property, and other birders. While this simple statement may seem to fall under the category of common sense and simple courtesy, there always seem to be the gray areas.

The largest gray area concerns the use of a tape player and bird tapes in the field. There are several schools of thought on this subject, and each has merit. They range from absolutely not using tapes to using tapes extensively. This problem has been recently eased by the ABA with its acceptance of the philosophy that identified *heard* birds can be counted on all lists. Remember, identification by ear can be as valid as identification by sight.

I personally use tapes in the field. I have good friends who do not, and I respect their views; I hope that they also respect mine. I feel that tapes do little, if any, harm *if used properly.* This means using tapes sparingly, and not using them in heavily birded areas or repeatedly in the same area. Never use them in any area where they are prohibited. Never use them in stake-out areas—such as the popular Buff-collared Nightjar site in McCleary Wash in Arizona. Never use them for officially endangered species. *Do* use them in your car between stops, especially to familiarize yourself with the songs of expected species. I follow these general rules and use tapes with a clear conscience.

SOME FINAL THOUGHTS AND REMINDERS

This book is not a standard birdfinding guide. It is a planning guide and should be used in tandem with the detailed birdfinding guides that exist for many birding areas throughout North America. Linger at each of the better sites if you have the time. Moreover, if you use only my book, you will certainly drive right by some wonderful birding places by following the text's somewhat rapid pace. Besides, this book cannot describe in any detail the fascinating habitats which you will be visiting. These are additional reasons why using the standard birdfinding guides is suggested.

Some birders might view this book as only a book of numbers. Some birders feel that listing is somehow "improper." Others feel that the list is all-important. There may, in fact, be as many types of birders as there are bird species. My feeling is that even though there are many different approaches to birding, we all share one common goal: to enjoy the birds and to improve our lives without harming the very thing from which we derive so much pleasure.

I hope that all of us can remember that amassing a large birdlist is not nearly as important as having quality time in our lives. Remember that new birds on our lists are not as long-lasting as new friends met and enjoyed. Remember that our particular way of birding is not the only way, nor is it the only "proper" way. Remember that tolerance of fellow birders who either do not understand or do not agree with the above points is a key ingredient to successful birding. Remember that making the most of your North American birding trips means enjoying the natural world and appreciating why it should be preserved for future generations. If we can remember these things, then we will all be "world class" birders regardless of the size or even the absence of any list.

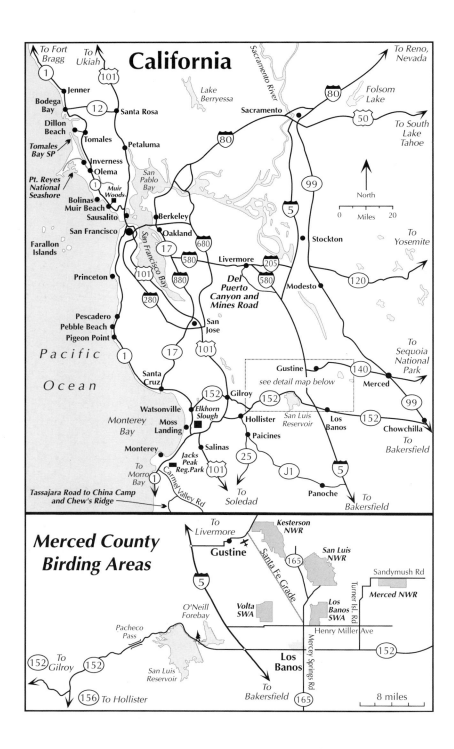

California

To Fort Bragg
To Ukiah
Jenner
1
101
Bodega Bay
12
Santa Rosa
Dillon Beach
Tomales
Petaluma
Tomales Bay SP
Inverness
Olema
San Pablo Bay
Pt. Reyes National Seashore
1
Muir Woods
Bolinas
Muir Beach
Sausalito
Berkeley
San Francisco
Oakland
Farallon Islands
San Francisco Bay
17
680
Lake Berryessa
Sacramento River
Sacramento
80
Folsom Lake
50
To Reno, Nevada
To South Lake Tahoe
99
North
0 Miles 20
5
Princeton
101
880
580
Livermore
205
580
Stockton
Modesto
To Yosemite
280
Del Puerto Canyon and Mines Road
San Jose
120
Pescadero
Pebble Beach
Pigeon Point
Pacific
17
101
To Sequoia National Park
Ocean
1
Santa Cruz
Gustine
see detail map below
140
Merced
99
Watsonville
152
Gilroy
152
Monterey Bay
Elkhorn Slough
Moss Landing
Hollister
San Luis Reservoir
Los Banos
152
Chowchilla
Paicines
To Bakersfield
Monterey
Salinas
Jacks Peak Reg.Park
25
To Morro Bay
101
J1
5
1
Carmel Valley Rd
Panoche
To Bakersfield
Tassajara Road to China Camp and Chew's Ridge →
To Soledad

Merced County Birding Areas

To Livermore
Kesterson NWR
Gustine
Santa Fe Grade
165
San Luis NWR
Sandymush Rd
5
Merced NWR
O'Neill Forebay
Volta SWA
Turner Isl. Rd
Los Banos SWA
Pacheco Pass
Henry Miller Ave
152
San Luis Reservoir
Los Banos
Mercey Springs Rd
152
To Gilroy
152
To Bakersfield
165
8 miles
156
To Hollister

Chapter 1

NORTHERN AND CENTRAL CALIFORNIA IN WINTER

January—9 Days

General

Essential to this trip's success—and critical to its scheduling—are two pelagic birding trips. Most California pelagic trip operators publish their schedules and rates in the American Birding Association's annual directory of pelagic trips (January issue of *Winging It*). Because you need to make your reservations in December *or even earlier*, ask ABA for a free copy of the previous January's directory. It will give you a good indication of the range of trips offered, as well as providing you with contact addresses and phone numbers. Fares vary (between $55 and $95) depending on the departure point and duration of the trip.

In January, pelagic birding trips are always scheduled out of Monterey, usually out of Bodega Bay, and rarely out of San Francisco Bay (Sausalito). If possible, reserve space for two separate day-trips. Even if both trips depart the same port, the bird species and their abundance will vary, and one trip is never a repeat of the previous day's outing. Be aware that inclement weather may force the cancellation of some January trips, but if your schedule is flexible, you might be able to arrange alternate dates.

Debra Love Shearwater of Shearwater Journeys is recognized as the premier organizer of pelagic birding trips in California (call 408/688-1990 or write to P.O. Box 1445, Soquel, California 95073). She also sends out more boats than all other operators combined. If you can book only one pelagic trip, a Monterey Bay trip with Shearwater Journeys is probably the best choice.

Whale-watching boats that take tourists to see Gray Whales, which migrate fairly close to shore, provide another option. They have frequent departure times, and reservations are not needed in most cases. There are two drawbacks to these trips: they seldom get far from shore, and they focus on whales, making it likely that nobody on board will be able to help you resolve seabird identification predicaments.

Probable Species
Total of 139 Species
Common Loon
Pied-billed Grebe
Horned Grebe
Eared Grebe
Brown Pelican
Double-crested
   Cormorant
American Bittern
Great Blue Heron
Great Egret
Snowy Egret
Black-crowned
   Night-Heron
Snow Goose
Canada Goose
Wood Duck
Green-winged Teal
Mallard
Northern Pintail
Blue-winged Teal
Cinnamon Teal
Northern Shoveler
Gadwall
American Wigeon
Canvasback
Redhead
Ring-necked Duck
Lesser Scaup
Common Goldeneye
Bufflehead
Hooded Merganser
Common Merganser
Red-breasted Merganser
Ruddy Duck
Turkey Vulture
Osprey
Northern Harrier
Sharp-shinned Hawk
Cooper's Hawk
Red-shouldered Hawk
Red-tailed Hawk
Ferruginous Hawk
Golden Eagle
American Kestrel
Merlin
Peregrine Falcon
Prairie Falcon
Ring-necked Pheasant
Virginia Rail
Sora
American Coot
Sandhill Crane
Black-bellied Plover
Snowy Plover
Semipalmated Plover
Killdeer
Black-necked Stilt
American Avocet
Greater Yellowlegs
Willet
Spotted Sandpiper
Whimbrel
Long-billed Curlew
Marbled Godwit
Ruddy Turnstone
Sanderling
Western Sandpiper
Least Sandpiper
Dunlin

After you finalize your pelagic trip reservations, build the rest of the itinerary around those dates. This trip includes birding at Bodega Bay, Point Reyes, the San Francisco area, San Mateo County, Monterey Bay, Monterey Peninsula, Panoche Valley, Merced County, and Del Puerto Canyon.

Note: You could add on The Klamath Basin trip
described in Chapter 20, Trip A.

Birdfinding Guides

The following books are extremely helpful.

California Birds: Their Status and Distribution by Arnold Small (1994) is technically not a birdfinding guide, but can be an important aid in planning.

Birders Guide to Northern California by LoLo and Jim Westrich (1991).

Ocean Birds of the Nearshore Pacific by Rich Stallcup (1990).

Birding Northern California by Jean Richmond (1985).

Monterey Birds by Don Roberson (1985). This out-of-print book had many details on the birds and birding sites in Monterey County. Ask a friend to loan it to you.

Pelagic Birds of Monterey Bay, California, by Rich Stallcup (1981). This out-of-print booklet is actually a reprint of a very helpful article from *Western Birds* (Volume 7, Number 4, 1976).

Rare Bird Alert Numbers

Monterey 408/375-9122
   and for updates . . *408/375-2577*
Northern California . . 510/524-5592
   and for reporting . . *510/528-0288*

Special Equipment

A scope is an absolute must for birding the bays and coastal waters. Though tripods are not allowed on boats, a gunstock mount can be used with some success. Waterproof clothes (raingear) are highly recommended for pelagic trips. Seasickness preventives are also advised for all pelagic trips.

Accommodations

In California motels are plentiful and campgrounds abound. Accommodations should not be a problem, though in the Monterey area advance reservations are recommended in any season.

Key Species — Total of 57 Species

This list catalogs the birds that are the primary purpose of this January trip.

1. **Red-throated Loon**—Fairly common; can be anywhere along coastline, bays, or estuaries. Most likely at Bodega Bay, Point Reyes, Elkhorn Slough.

2. **Pacific Loon**—A little harder to locate than other loons because they tend to stay farther offshore. Look closely at all loons, and you will eventually locate one. Easily found on a pelagic trip.

3. **Red-necked Grebe**—Bodega Bay, Drake's Beach at Point Reyes, and Monterey Harbor are the best locations. It is somewhat uncommon; you may encounter it anywhere along the coast—the farther north, the better the likelihood.

4. **Western Grebe**—Very common along the entire coast; hard to miss.

5. **Clark's Grebe**—Check out all Western Grebes and you will ultimately find a Clark's. Bolinas Lagoon, the "Fish Docks" at Point Reyes, and Elkhorn Slough are all good locations.

6. **Northern Fulmar**—Monterey Bay from whale-watching boats or any pelagic trip. Fairly common offshore most years. Can be seen at times (usually following storms) from coastal points.

7. **Sooty Shearwater**—Common in this area during most years; regularly seen on pelagic trips.

8. **Short-tailed Shearwater**—Seen on pelagic trips, with winter being the best time. Be careful with identification—this species is very similar to Sooty Shearwater. See Rich Stallcup's *Ocean Birds of the Nearshore Pacific* for identification pointers.

Probable Species
(continued)

Short-billed Dowitcher
Long-billed Dowitcher
Common Snipe
Bonaparte's Gull
Ring-billed Gull
California Gull
Herring Gull
Western Gull
Forster's Tern
Rock Dove
Band-tailed Pigeon
Mourning Dove
Greater Roadrunner
White-throated Swift
Belted Kingfisher
Acorn Woodpecker
Downy Woodpecker
Hairy Woodpecker
Northern Flicker
Black Phoebe
Say's Phoebe
Horned Lark
Tree Swallow
Steller's Jay
Western Scrub-Jay
American Crow
Common Raven
Plain Titmouse
Bushtit
Red-breasted Nuthatch
White-breasted
  Nuthatch
Pygmy Nuthatch
Brown Creeper
Rock Wren
Bewick's Wren
Winter Wren
Marsh Wren
Golden-crowned
  Kinglet
Ruby-crowned Kinglet
Western Bluebird
Mountain Bluebird
Hermit Thrush
American Robin
Northern Mockingbird
American Pipit
Cedar Waxwing
Loggerhead Shrike
European Starling
Hutton's Vireo
Orange-crowned
  Warbler
Yellow-rumped
  Warbler
Townsend's Warbler
Common Yellowthroat
Spotted Towhee
Rufous-crowned
  Sparrow
Lark Sparrow
Savannah Sparrow
Fox Sparrow
Song Sparrow
Lincoln's Sparrow
White-crowned
  Sparrow
Dark-eyed Junco
Red-winged Blackbird

Probable Species
(continued)

Western Meadowlark
Brewer's Blackbird
Brown-headed Cowbird
Purple Finch
House Finch
Pine Siskin
Lesser Goldfinch
American Goldfinch
House Sparrow

Note: The species in **boldface** appear no more than four times in the itineraries as *key* or *probable* species. Watch for them on this trip. It is very unlikely that you will see *all* of the probable species inasmuch as you will be focusing on the initial key species. However, for the purposes of this book and because all of the probables are Codes 1 or 2 (see *Introduction* and *Birdfinder*) assume that you'll see 100%. If not seen on this trip, they will be seen on another trip with no special effort.

Possible Species
Total of 26 Species
Black-footed Albatross
Pink-footed Shearwater
Cattle Egret
Green Heron
White-faced Ibis
Greater White-fronted
    Goose
White-tailed Kite
Bald Eagle
Wild Turkey
Clapper Rail
Mountain Plover
Red Knot
Pomarine Jaeger
Ancient Murrelet
Barn Owl
Western Screech-Owl
Great Horned Owl
Northern Pygmy-Owl
Burrowing Owl
Long-eared Owl
Short-eared Owl
Violet-green Swallow
Canyon Wren
Phainopepla
White-throated Sparrow
Yellow-headed
    Blackbird

Note: On this trip you should see at least 2 of the above possibles.

9. **Black-vented Shearwater**—Encountered on pelagic trips and often seen from whale-watching boats. Seen from shore most years. Curiously, abundant some years and absent other years.

10. **Brandt's Cormorant**—Common all along the coast, primarily in rocky areas; often found with Double-crested and Pelagic Cormorants. This is the most frequently seen cormorant on pelagic trips.

11. **Pelagic Cormorant**—Fairly common along the coast in rocky areas. Feeds near cliffs and rocks.

12. **Tundra Swan**—Might be found at Elkhorn Slough some years, but the best bet by far is Merced County as described in Day 8 of the trip plan.

13. **Ross's Goose**—Check in same areas as Tundra Swan. Best bet is Merced County.

14. **Brant**—Scarce but can usually be located. Try Bodega Bay, Moss Landing, or Monterey area.

15. **Eurasian Wigeon**—Scan all American Wigeons; if you keep looking long enough, you will find an Eurasian. One viable location is Bolinas Lagoon (8 miles south of Olema along Highway 1.)

16. **Tufted Duck**—Virtually always found somewhere in this area in January. Point Reyes, Rodeo Lagoon, and Sutro Bath Ruins at Golden Gate Park in San Francisco are all good possibilities.

17. **Greater Scaup**—Common in harbors and estuaries, such as Tomales Bay at Point Reyes, Moss Landing, and Elkhorn Slough.

18. **Harlequin Duck**—The rocky shore north of Bodega Bay and the "Fish Docks" at Point Reyes are reliable locations. Some years you can try the area north of Coast Guard Pier in Monterey. The farther north you are, though, the better the prospects.

19. **Oldsquaw**—Bodega Bay, Point Reyes, Monterey Bay, Moss Landing, and Elkhorn Slough. Rare, but more frequently encountered the farther north you go.

20. **Black Scoter**—North of Bodega Bay and the "Fish Docks" at Point Reyes are two reasonable places to look. Rarer than other scoters, but usually not difficult to locate.

21. **Surf Scoter**—Common along coastlines and bays from Bodega Bay to Monterey Bay.

22. **White-winged Scoter**—Fairly common along coastlines and bays from Bodega Bay to Monterey Bay.

23. **Barrow's Goldeneye**—Most easily found on the north segment of this trip at Bolinas Lagoon or on Lake Merritt in Oakland. Be prepared to carefully scan goldeneye flocks.

24. **California Quail**—Common; spend time in oak and chaparral woodland and you will locate it.

25. **Mountain Quail**—May be difficult; might be found on Day 7 at Chew's Ridge or China Camp.

26. **Pacific Golden-Plover**—Regular, but very local, in January. Reliable locations are the pastures on Spaletta Plateau on Point Reyes and the pasture at Lawson's Landing near Dillon Beach on the northeast edge of Tomales Bay.

27. **Black Oystercatcher**—Rocky seacoast areas throughout; Pigeon Point and Point Pinos are likely sites.

Remotely Possible Species
Total of 25 Species
Yellow-billed Loon
Laysan Albatross
Flesh-footed Shearwater
Fork-tailed Storm-Petrel
Ashy Storm-Petrel
Emperor Goose
King Eider
Broad-winged Hawk
Rough-legged Hawk
Chukar
Common Moorhen
Rock Sandpiper
Ruff
Red-necked Phalarope
Parasitic Jaeger
Glaucous Gull
Thick-billed Murre
Xantus's Murrelet
Tufted Puffin
Horned Puffin
Allen's Hummingbird
American Dipper
Northern Shrike
Palm Warbler
Lawrence's Goldfinch
Note: On any given trip you will probably see only 1 of the remote possibilities.

28. **Wandering Tattler**—Could be observed along any rocky coastal area, such as Pigeon Point, Monterey Peninsula, or Bodega Bay.

29. **Black Turnstone**—Found on rocky coasts throughout.

30. **Surfbird**—Easy to locate on rocky coasts at Pigeon Point or Monterey.

31. **Red Phalarope**—Anywhere along the coast from whale-watching boats or on pelagic trips. Absent some winters.

32. **Heermann's Gull**—Fairly common from San Francisco south along the coast. More common the farther south you go.

33. **Mew Gull**—Common all along the coast.

34. **Thayer's Gull**—Uncommon throughout the coastal area, and may take some serious searching. Be careful identifying this species—Glaucous-winged Gull x Western Gull hybrids are fairly common and can be mistaken for Thayer's Gull. (Be aware that most of the Thayer's Gulls seen here are first-winter individuals.)

35. **Glaucous-winged Gull**—Very common throughout the coastal area, but more numerous the farther north you go.

36. **Black-legged Kittiwake**—Status varies annually, ranging from common to rare. Should see on pelagic birding trips and from whale-watching boats during years of high abundance.

37. **Common Murre**—Commonly seen on boat trips up to 10 or 12 miles offshore. Frequently seen from shore on Monterey Bay (try scoping from Coast Guard Pier).

38. **Pigeon Guillemot**—This species stays very close to shore. Scarce in January but can be found year round at some locations. Try Bodega Head and near Hopkins Marine Station on south side of Monterey Bay.

39. **Marbled Murrelet**—Fairly common, sometimes seen from whale-watching boats; best seen from land, especially if you scope for it off Pigeon Point.

40. **Cassin's Auklet**—Common; sometimes seen from whale-watching boats and regularly on pelagic trips. Sometimes seen flying west at daybreak from Point Pinos.

41. **Rhinoceros Auklet**—Commonly seen from whale-watching boats and pelagic trips. Sometimes seen from the Coast Guard Pier in Monterey, and, like Cassin's, is seen at dawn from Point Pinos.

42. **Spotted Owl**—Resident at Point Reyes, particularly Tomales Bay State Park; also resident at Muir Woods National Monument. Seek local advice to avoid unintentionally disturbing this sensitive species.

43. **Northern Saw-whet Owl**—Fairly common throughout, but difficult to locate. You need local help, or you will probably miss it. Robinson Canyon, Chew's Ridge, and Point Reyes are all known sites.

44. **Anna's Hummingbird**—Common throughout the trip area; will be seen numerous times.

45. **Lewis's Woodpecker**—Can be found with some luck in Panoche Valley, but best bet is the Mines Road and Del Puerto Canyon route described on Day 8.

46. **Red-breasted Sapsucker**—Fairly common throughout, and easy to locate at Point Reyes or in Golden Gate Park.

47. **Nuttall's Woodpecker**—Common resident of oak woodland in Point Reyes area, Panoche Valley, Carmel Valley, and residential areas.

48. **Yellow-billed Magpie**—Favors the drier outlying portions of the Monterey area. Easy to see in Panoche Valley and in many other areas.

49. **Chestnut-backed Chickadee**—Common from Point Reyes to Monterey in parks, residential areas, and riparian, coniferous, and oak woodlands.

50. **Varied Thrush**—Numbers vary from year to year. Usually can be located in forested areas at Point Reyes. May be present in any forested lowlands on the west slopes of the coastal ranges.

51. **Wrentit**—Common but hard-to-see resident of chaparral and coastal scrub throughout, from Point Reyes to Monterey.

52. **California Thrasher**—Uncommon and local in chaparral and scrub away from coast throughout. Best bets are Mines Road, Del Puerto Canyon, Upper Carmel Valley, and Panoche Valley.

53. **Hermit Warbler**—Small numbers are present every winter in conifers, rarely in oaks. Most reliable location is Jack's Peak in Monterey. Usually takes time to spot the bird high in the pines, but don't give up.

54. **California Towhee**—Extremely common resident in parks, chaparral, brush, and residential areas. If you miss this one, you are not trying.

55. **Sage Sparrow**—Uncommon and local in the proper habitat—large areas of chaparral. Best bet is Mines Road on Day 8.

56. **Golden-crowned Sparrow**—Common in winter throughout, especially in brushy areas and chaparral along the coast. Often flocks with White-crowned Sparrows.

57. **Tricolored Blackbird**—Common at Point Reyes, fairly easy to find in San Mateo County, and also in the Moss Landing area and at Elkhorn Slough. Found in many other locations on this trip.

Note: You would be very lucky to find all 57 key species, but it is possible to do so using this trip plan.

Itinerary

Note: Trip begins and ends in San Francisco.

Day 1 — Bodega Bay Area

The town of Bodega is about a one-hour drive north of San Francisco's Golden Gate Bridge. Follow Highway 101 across the bridge and north to Santa Rosa. Exit west onto Highway 12 and follow the signs to Bodega. This is a superb area for many species because of its diversity of habitat. It can be particularly productive for species with more "northern" affinities, such as Red-necked Grebe, Black Scoter, Oldsquaw, Eurasian Wigeon, Barrow's Goldeneye, Harlequin Duck, and more. It is best to arrive early and plan to spend a full day here.

You will find excellent, specific directions for Bodega Bay in Jean Richmond's *Birding Northern California*. A spotting scope is essential to help you identify often-distant Red-throated and Pacific Loons, Western and Clark's Grebes, Northern Fulmar, Brandt's and Pelagic Cormorants, Brant, Surf and White-winged Scoters, Black Oystercatcher, Wandering Tattler, gulls, and alcids.

Include a short excursion to the small town of Dillon Beach (less than a 20-mile drive each way) in your birding plans for Day 1. Pacific Golden-Plovers regularly winter in small numbers on the pasture at nearby Lawson's Landing.

(If you are joining a pelagic trip from Bodega Bay, you will have scheduled an extra day here. The standard pelagic destination, Cordell Bank, often teems with an excellent variety of open-ocean birds. On January trips, it is conceivable that a rare Laysan Albatross will float in.)

Locate a motel or campsite in the evening.

Days 2 and 3 — Point Reyes Area

Point Reyes is only a one-hour drive south on Highway 1 from Bodega Bay. Whether you camp or stay at a motel, make sure to get an early start. Allow two full days to explore the varied habitats at Point Reyes National Seashore and the surrounding area; this is one of California's premier, and most enjoyable, birding locations. If you plan your forays around the sites detailed in *Birding Northern California*, you won't accidently miss any of the best ones.

Of the approximately 440 species recorded at Point Reyes, about half have been rarities or out-of-range species. Be alert for a steady stream of birders coming in to chase vagrants (that they learned about by calling the Northern California hotline).

You will add many key or sought-after species to your list at Point Reyes: Red-throated and Pacific Loons, Red-necked, Western, and Clark's Grebes, Brandt's and Pelagic Cormorants, Tundra Swan, Brant, Eurasian Wigeon, Tufted Duck, Greater Scaup, Harlequin Duck, Old-squaw, all three scoters, Barrow's Goldeneye, and California Quail. Shorebird possibilities are Pacific Golden-Plover, Black Oystercatcher, Wandering Tattler, Black Turnstone, and Surfbird. Sift through the gulls and alcids for Mew, Thayer's, and Glaucous-winged Gulls, Common Murre, Marbled and Ancient Murrelets, and Cassin's and Rhinoceros Auklets. If you spend time owling, you may see Barn Owl, Western Screech-Owl, Northern Pygmy-Owl, Spotted Owl, and Northern Saw-whet Owl. Other likely species include Anna's Hummingbird, Nuttall's Woodpecker, Red-breasted Sapsucker, Chestnut-backed Chickadee, Varied Thrush, Wrentit, California Towhee, Golden-crowned Sparrow, and Tricolored Blackbird.

A small flock of Pacific Golden-Plovers winters on the pastures of Spaletta Plateau at Point Reyes. The usual way to locate this flock is to park along Sir Francis Drake Highway 0.8 mile past Spaletta Ranch. Walk through the gate on the left and scan fields to locate the golden-plovers.

Tomales Bay State Park is one of the best locations in California for Spotted Owl. However, it is best to ask for local advice to prevent disturbing this species. The park rangers, who keep very close tabs on these owls, can be helpful. *Do not use a tape recorder here.*

Point Reyes almost always produces one or two unexpected species in any season. Birding here is often so outstanding, that two days in this area alone should yield 60 percent of the key species for this trip!

Day 4 — Down the Coast: Bolinas Lagoon to Monterey Bay

You can make it from Point Reyes to Monterey Bay in about 4 hours by driving straight through on Highway 1. Instead, plan on spending a long, interesting day with many excellent birding stops.

Your first stop is Bolinas Lagoon, which holds many of the same species you found at Point Reyes. Both the eastern and western shores of the lagoon are accessible, so drive around a bit to sample all of the good vantage points. *Please do not trespass on posted property.*

Next, drive to Muir Woods National Monument, an impressive example of Coast Redwood forest. Of primary interest here is Spotted Owl, especially if you missed it at Tomales Bay State Park. A park ranger can tell you whether it's possible to see an owl today.

Return to Highway 1 and continue south to Golden Gate Park in San Francisco. Key species normally found in this urban park include all of the winter gulls, Anna's Hummingbird, Red-breasted Sapsucker, Varied Thrush, Wrentit, California Quail, and Golden-crowned Sparrow. Eurasian Wigeon and Tufted Duck often overwinter here with the flocks of less-exotic waterfowl.

Tufted Duck
Georges Dremeaux

San Mateo County coastline, farther south on Highway 1, offers many birding opportunities: Pillar Point Harbor at Princeton, Pescadero Beach and Marsh, Pebble Beach, and Pigeon Point are among the best sites in winter. Pillar Point Harbor is fairly reliable for Rock Sandpiper. You will need a spotting scope at Pescadero Beach for pelagic species, grebes, and ducks. Pebble Beach is practically a cinch for Wandering Tattler, Black Turnstone, and Surfbird. Pigeon Point with a scope has excellent potential for pelagic species plus good looks at Black Oystercatcher, Wandering Tattler, Black Turnstone, Surfbird, and Tricolored Blackbird.

Spend the night in Monterey.

Day 5 — Monterey Bay Area

Get out early on a whale-watching boat. These trips can yield Common Murre, Cassin's and Rhinoceros Auklets, and Red Phalarope. Of course, anything might fly by, but other legitimate possibilities are Northern Fulmar, Black-vented Shearwater, and Marbled Murrelet.

Whale-watching boats are available with frequent departures from Fisherman's Wharf. These short (two-hour) trips are excellent for developing your "sea-legs," if you have little or no pelagic experience. Unless you are already adept at seabird identification, Rich Stallcup's *Pelagic Birds of Monterey Bay, California,* is indispensable for getting the most out of your boat trip on Monterey Bay.

Spent the remainder of the day sampling sites chosen from Jean Richmond's *Birding Northern California* and Don Roberson's *Monterey Birds,* both excellent guides to this area.

Go to Jack's Peak Regional Park for Pygmy Nuthatch, Varied Thrush, Wrentit, Hutton's Vireo, and Hermit Warbler. Visit Municipal Wharf to see Red-necked, Western, and Clark's Grebes, gulls, and possibly wintering alcids. Coast Guard Wharf is productive for loons, grebes, cormorants, and wintering alcids. Crespi Pond has rails, shorebirds if the water is low, and gulls. (*Birders must yield to golfers here.*) Drive the road along the bay to Point Pinos, stopping at the pull-outs to look for Black Oystercatcher, Wandering Tattler, turnstones, Surfbird, gulls, and other coastal birds. Scope the bay from Point Pinos for loons, grebes, shearwaters, scoters, jaegers, and gulls.

Just before dawn or after dusk a trip to Robinson Canyon might yield the local owls: Barn, Northern Saw-whet, Western Screech-, Northern Pygmy-, Great Horned, and Spotted Owls are regular here. See *Monterey Birds* for specific locations. *Please do not use owl tapes here and bird only from the road since this area is all private property.*

Spend the night in Monterey again.

Day 6 — Pelagic Trip out of Monterey

Your entire California trip revolves around this exhilarating event. Rich Stallcup's guides, *Ocean Birds of the Nearshore Pacific* and *Pelagic Birds of Monterey Bay, California*, are the best books to study for this trip.

Pelagic birding trips are usually seven hours long, so be sure to pack your lunch and snacks; most boats sell drinks and nibbles. Be ready to see Black-footed and Laysan Albatrosses, Northern Fulmar, Pink-footed, Sooty, Short-tailed, and Black-vented Shearwaters, Fork-tailed Storm-Petrel, Red Phalarope, Pomarine Jaeger, lots of gulls (including Black-legged Kittiwake), Forster's Tern, Common and Thick-billed Murres, Pigeon Guillemot, Ancient Murrelet, Cassin's and Rhinoceros Auklets, and Tufted Puffin. Not many trips will produce all these species, since some occur only rarely, but several will be seen on a normal excursion.

Spend the night in Monterey again.

Day 7 — Chew's Ridge, Moss Landing, Elkhorn Slough, Panoche Valley

Start your day southwest of Monterey at Chew's Ridge and China Camp. Be there at dawn; it will take you a good hour-and-a-half to drive there from Monterey. (If you don't get an early start, you will not finish today's itinerary.) Your primary goals in this area are owls and montane species. You should see Mountain Quail, and have a good chance at Northern Pygmy-Owl, Western Screech-Owl, and Northern Saw-whet Owl. *Do not use tapes here.*

On the way back to Monterey, search for Yellow-billed Magpie, particularly in the fields along the lower part of Tassajara Road. At Monterey, turn north onto Highway 1 for approximately 15 miles to Moss Landing, good for ducks, shorebirds, gulls, and grebes. Greater Scaup is likely; Harlequin Duck and Oldsquaw are possible.

Your next stop is Elkhorn Slough, an excellent birding area with a large variety of waterbirds and winter raptors. Rarely, you will find Tundra Swan and Ross's Goose. All of the above locations are well covered in Don Roberson's *Monterey Birds*.

Take Highway 1 to Hollister, then Highway 25 south to Paicines. Turn east onto Panoche Road (secondary road J-1) to enter Panoche Valley. Jean Richmond covers this route in *Birding Northern California*. Use the map in the guide, but reverse the directions in the text, because the book describes the route from east to west and you will be driving it from west to east. The drive through Panoche Valley to Interstate 5 provides an excellent opportunity to pick up some of the key species missed thus far. Yellow-billed Magpie, California Thrasher, and Nuttall's Woodpecker are easy to find. Chukars are rare here, but they have been seen. Mountain Plovers are a possibility.

When you reach Interstate 5, drive north to Los Banos for the night.

Day 8 — Merced, Alameda, Santa Clara, and Stanislaus Counties

Merced County is the best area on this itinerary for several key species. Use routes described in *Birding Northern California* to tour Los Banos Wildlife Management Area, San Luis Wildlife Refuge, and Merced National Wildlife Refuge.

Key species easily located in Merced County are Tundra Swan, Ross's Goose, Yellow-billed Magpie, and Tricolored Blackbird. In addition, you might snag several species on the "possible" and "remotely possible" lists: Cattle Egret, Green Heron, White-faced Ibis, Greater White-fronted Goose, Mountain Plover, Rough-legged Hawk, Common Moorhen, Barn, Burrowing, Long-eared, and Short-eared Owls, and Yellow-headed Blackbird.

Return to Interstate 5, drive north about 40 miles to Interstate 580, and then travel west on I-580 to Livermore. At Livermore follow the directions for Mines Road and Del Puerto Canyon in *Birding Northern California*. This route winds through varied habitat on its way to Interstate 5.

Key species along the way include California Quail, Anna's Hummingbird, Lewis's Woodpecker, Red-breasted Sapsucker, Nuttall's Woodpecker, Yellow-billed Magpie, Varied Thrush, Wrentit, California Thrasher, California Towhee, Sage and Golden-crowned Sparrows, and Tricolored Blackbird. You may also see Barn Owl, Western Screech-Owl, Rough-legged Hawk, and Lawrence's Goldfinch.

When you return to Interstate 5, you will be approximately 75 miles from San Francisco. Spend the night somewhere between this point and the city.

Day 9 — Extra Day

This is the extra day included in the trip for chaser species. (However, you might have used up this day for a pelagic trip out of Bodega Bay; see Day 1.) If you're still enthusiastic about finding new and wonderful birds, call the hotlines to see what's around, and figure out whether you can get there and back before your departure time. Did you miss any key or other species that you *really* wanted to see? *Birding Northern California* might list locations for them other than those you have already visited. With an early start, you can reach anywhere in central California in just a few hours, so go for it! If you don't want to bird, remember—it's not possible to spend a boring day in the Bay Area.

Bird Numbers This Trip

	Potential	Expected	Actual
Key Species	57	57	
Probable Species	139	139	
Possible Species	26	2	
Remotely Possible Species	25	1	
Totally Unexpected Species	?	1	
TOTAL	247	200	

Cumulative List

Total key and probable species after this trip - 196 species

This Trip's Mileage and Expenses

Approximate miles traveled, San Francisco to San Francisco: 1,050

- Fuel: $75; sharing $37.50 $_____
- Lodging: 8 nights at motels $400; sharing $200 $_____
-   OR camping 8 nights $50; sharing $25   or $_____
- Food: Ice-chest/supermarket for most meals $90 $_____
- Monterey pelagic outing: under $75 $_____

  *The total per person cost of the above items with a companion
  to share expenses should come to under $350.*

- Add to this the cost of any additional pelagic trip: $_____
- Add to this car rental expenses, if any: $_____
- Add to this your expense to/from San Francisco: $_____

  This will give you a good idea of the cost of this trip.

- TOTAL $_____

Personal Notes

_____

_____

_____

_____

Chapter 2

OKLAHOMA IN WINTER

January—3 Days

General

You won't find a winter trip to Oklahoma recommended in any other compilation of North American birding hotspots. Don't let this oversight stop you from seriously considering the benefits of this three-day adventure! Though none of the 10 key species you will seek is particuarly rare (all are either Code 1 or Code 2 birds), no other location of which I (your Oklahoma-born author) am aware offers these 10 species all in the same season. Search for them elsewhere and you might find yourself making several separate trips—possibly even a journey to far northern Canada. This short trip is a unique opportunity.

If you are lucky enough to visit central and western Oklahoma following a snowfall, it will simplify your work finding these key species, especially the longspurs and Lesser Prairie-Chicken.

This trip includes Oklahoma City, Norman, Wichita Mountains Wildlife Refuge, Altus, Arnett, and Washita National Wildlife Refuge.

Birdfinding Guides

Guide to Birding in Oklahoma, published by the Tulsa Audubon Society (1986), covers our sites as well as the remainder of the state.

Rare Bird Alert Numbers

Statewide 918/669-6646
Oklahoma City 405/373-4531

Special Equipment

January's weather in western Oklahoma is unpredictable. It may be very mild, but it can be bitterly cold. Low temperatures combined with high winds create extremely low wind-chills. Be prepared for the cold.

A spotting scope can be useful, especially at Foss Reservoir in Washita National Wildlife Refuge.

Probable Species
Total of 70 Species
Pied-billed Grebe
Great Blue Heron
Canada Goose
Wood Duck
Green-winged Teal
Mallard
Northern Pintail
Gadwall
American Wigeon
Redhead
Ring-necked Duck
Lesser Scaup
Common Goldeneye
Bufflehead
Hooded Merganser
Common Merganser
Bald Eagle
Northern Harrier
Sharp-shinned Hawk
Red-tailed Hawk
Ferruginous Hawk
American Kestrel
Wild Turkey
Northern Bobwhite
American Coot
Killdeer
Ring-billed Gull
Herring Gull
Rock Dove
Mourning Dove
Greater Roadrunner
Great Horned Owl
Belted Kingfisher
Red-headed
   Woodpecker
Red-bellied
   Woodpecker
Downy Woodpecker
Hairy Woodpecker
Northern Flicker
Horned Lark
Blue Jay
American Crow
Tufted Titmouse
Brown Creeper
Carolina Wren
Bewick's Wren
Golden-crowned
   Kinglet
Ruby-crowned Kinglet
Eastern Bluebird
American Robin
Northern Mockingbird
Cedar Waxwing
Loggerhead Shrike
European Starling
Yellow-rumped
   Warbler
Northern Cardinal
Spotted Towhee
Rufous-crowned
   Sparrow
Field Sparrow
Savannah Sparrow
Song Sparrow
White-crowned
   Sparrow
Dark-eyed Junco
Red-winged Blackbird

Accommodations

Motels for under $40 per night are readily available in Oklahoma City, Lawton, and Elk City as well as many other locations along the route.

Key Species — Total of 10 Species

1. **Greater White-fronted Goose**—Winters at Washita National Wildlife Refuge in good numbers. Scan the flocks and you will find it.

2. **Rough-legged Hawk**—Winters in open country throughout Oklahoma in small numbers. If you check all Buteos, you will have little problem locating this bird.

3. **Lesser Prairie-Chicken**—In winter this species can be found feeding in grain fields or on acorns near the booming grounds that they use in spring. The Arnett area is the most likely location; however, they are also seen regularly in suitable habitat in Roger Mills County and in the Texas Panhandle.

4. **Carolina Chickadee**—Common to abundant throughout the trip area in any wooded location.

5. **American Tree Sparrow**—Common throughout; easy to find at Washita National Wildlife Refuge.

6. **Harris's Sparrow**—Common throughout. Should be seen easily everywhere but Wichita Mountains Wildlife Refuge.

7. **McCown's Longspur**—Look for this longspur on short-grass prairie, overgrazed pasture, and plowed fields; it often flocks with Horned Larks. Can show up anywhere in western Oklahoma, but the best possibility is in the Altus area and to the south and west of Altus. In scarce years it may be necessary to drive into the Texas Panhandle to find one.

8. **Lapland Longspur**—Look on winter wheat fields, overgrazed pasture, burned fields, prairie-dog towns, and air fields. Often flocks with Horned Larks. Best bets are the Arnett area, the Oklahoma City area, and Washita National Wildlife Refuge. Lapland Longspur, like McCown's, can also be seen in the Texas Panhandle around Amarillo.

9. **Smith's Longspur**—Search in open fields with short grass, especially Aristids, and around air strips. Less common the farther west you go. You will need to locate this bird in the Oklahoma City or Norman areas. Local birders can guide you to several good areas inside these cities.

10. **Chestnut-collared Longspur**—Look on mixed- or short-grass prairies and air strips. Common at Wichita Mountains Wildlife Refuge.

Note: You should see all 10 key species without too much difficulty.

Itinerary

Note: Trip begins and ends in Oklahoma City.

Day 1 — Oklahoma City, Norman, Wichita Mountains Wildlife Refuge, and Altus Area

Drive from Oklahoma City to the Norman area via Interstate 35 south, a less than thirty-minute drive. Bird the Norman area, particularly around the air strips and any short-grass prairie area, for Smith's Longspur. Local birders will be able to tell you the current best locations.

Return to Interstate 35 and continue south to Highway 9. After you turn onto Highway 9, start watching for mixed flocks of Horned Larks and longspurs, which might occur anywhere. Go west to near Chickasha and take the H. E. Bailey Turnpike (Interstate 44) south to Highway 49. Wichita Mountains Wildlife Refuge, run by the U.S. Fish and Wildlife Service, is west on Highway 49. Total driving time is about one-and-one-half hours.

Wichita Mountains Wildlife Refuge is covered in *Guide to Birding in Oklahoma*. Chestnut-collared Longspur is common in winter with Lapland Longspur being seen occasionally. Carolina Chickadee and American Tree Sparrow are both common and should be easily located. Harris's Sparrow may be difficult to locate in this area but is common at most other stops on this trip. Rough-legged Hawk is seen on an occasional basis. Winter waterfowl are

---

Probable Species
(continued)

Eastern Meadowlark
Western Meadowlark
Brewer's Blackbird
Common Grackle
Brown-headed Cowbird
American Goldfinch
House Sparrow

Note: The species in **boldface** appear no more than four times in the itineraries as *key* or *probable* species. Watch for them on this trip. Assume that you will see all of the probable species. Most of them will have been seen on the previous trip. You should gain 14 new species not seen on the California trip.

Possible Species
Total of 32 Species
Double-crested
  Cormorant
Snow Goose
Ross's Goose
Northern Shoveler
Canvasback
Ruddy Duck
Cooper's Hawk
Prairie Falcon
Common Snipe
Bonaparte's Gull
Barn Owl
Eastern Screech-Owl
Burrowing Owl
Barred Owl
Long-eared Owl
Short-eared Owl
Ladder-backed
  Woodpecker
White-breasted
  Nuthatch
Rock Wren
Canyon Wren
Mountain Bluebird
Hermit Thrush
Brown Thrasher
American Pipit
Rufous-sided Towhee
Lark Bunting
Fox Sparrow
Lincoln's Sparrow
White-throated Sparrow
Great-tailed Grackle
Purple Finch
Pine Siskin

Note: On this trip you should see at least 10 of the above possibles.

Remotely Possible Species
Total of 23 Species
Horned Grebe
Eared Grebe
Blue-winged Teal
Greater Scaup
Harris's Hawk
Golden Eagle
Merlin
Ring-necked Pheasant
Sandhill Crane
American Woodcock
Golden-fronted
    Woodpecker
Yellow-bellied
    Sapsucker
Verdin
Red-breasted Nuthatch
House Wren
Winter Wren
Townsend's Solitaire
Sage Thrasher
Curve-billed Thrasher
Sprague's Pipit
Le Conte's Sparrow
Swamp Sparrow
Rusty Blackbird

Note: You will probably see at least 3 of these species.

plentiful, and Rufous-crowned Sparrow can usually be found on Mount Scott along with Rock and Canyon Wrens.

Upon leaving the refuge, take Highway 62 west, about an hour's drive, to the Altus area. This area is covered in *Guide to Birding in Oklahoma* as the Eldorado area. The prairie-dog town 9.5 miles west and 2 miles north of Altus should be checked for Ferruginous and Rough-legged Hawks and McCown's Longspur.

Note: This part of the state provides the best chance for McCown's Longspur. If time allows, traveling south to the Eldorado area or even into Texas may be necessary to locate this species.

Proceed west on Highway 62 to Highway 34, then north on Highway 34 to Elk City. All open country should be scanned for McCown's Longspur. If you walk the fields, the possibility of Sprague's Pipit does exist.

Spend the night in Elk City.

Day 2 — Elk City, Arnett, and Washita National Wildlife Refuge

Take Highway 6 west 14 miles from Elk City to Highway 283. Turn north to Arnett. This is about an hour's drive. The Arnett area is covered in *Guide to Birding Oklahoma*. The Arnett specialty is Lesser Prairie-Chicken. Although easier to find in the spring, it can be seen in the same areas in the winter. Lapland Longspur frequents the sparse overgrazed pastures both west and north of Arnett.

Return south on Highway 283 to the Highway 33 intersection. Turn east onto Highway 33 to Washita National Wildlife Refuge. You'll want to take your time to sort through the huge flocks of geese wintering at this refuge. Canada Geese are abundant; Greater White-fronted Geese and Snow Geese, though not so numerous, are well-represented. Ross's Geese are usually present, and a spotting scope will help you to positively identify them. Longspurs are seen on the fields and pastures. Small flocks of winter-plumaged Lark Buntings are around. Carolina Chickadee and Harris's Sparrow are common, and Rough-legged Hawks winter here most years. Return to Elk City to find lodging for the night.

Day 3 — Extra Day

If any of the 10 key species has been missed, this day should be used to concentrate on finding it. If not, a stop at Red Rock Canyon near Hinton on the way back to Oklahoma City is always worthwhile. Another pleasant birding site is Lake Hefner in northern Oklahoma City, an excellent place to observe winter ducks and gulls. Don't forget to check the Oklahoma City area hotline if you bird Lake Hefner.

DAS 1995

Harris's Sparrows
David A. Sibley

Bird Numbers This Trip

	Potential	Expected	Actual
Key Species	10	10	
Probable Species	70	70	
Possible Species	32	10	
Remotely Possible Species	23	3	
Totally Unexpected Species . . . . ?		1	
TOTAL	135	94	

Cumulative List

Total key and probable species seen after 2 trips

Previous trip	196	species
Winter Oklahoma	24	species
TOTAL	220	species

This Trip's Mileage and Expenses

Approximate miles traveled, Oklahoma City to Oklahoma City: 580

- Fuel : $42; sharing $21 $_____
- Lodging: 2 nights at motels $70; sharing $35 $_____
- Food: Assuming restaurants for most meals - $40 $_____
  *The total per person cost for the above items with a companion
  to share expenses should be less than $100*
- Add to this your car rental expenses, if any: $_____
- Add to this expenses to/from Oklahoma City: $_____
  This will give you a good idea of the cost of this trip.
- TOTAL $_____

Personal Notes

_____

_____

_____

_____

_____

_____

_____

_____

_____

_____

_____

_____

_____

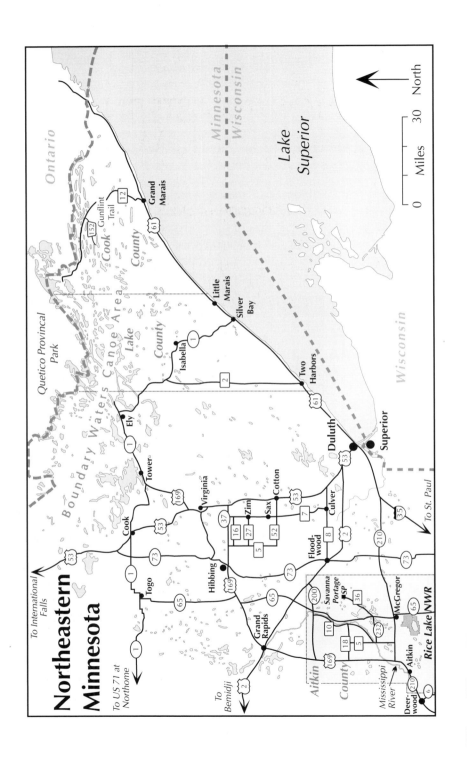

Northeastern Minnesota

To US 71 at
Northome

To International
Falls

To Bemidji

Ontario

Quetico Provincal
Park

Boundary Waters Canoe Area

Cook County

Lake County

Minnesota
Wisconsin

Lake
Superior

Grand
Marais

Gunflint
Trail

Little
Marais

Silver
Bay

Isabella

Ely

Tower

Two
Harbors

Duluth

Superior

To St. Paul

Wisconsin

Virginia

Cotton

Zim

Sax

Culver

Cook

Flood-
wood

Togo

Hibbing

Grand
Rapids

Savanna
Portage
SP

McGregor

Aitkin
County

Aitkin

Rice Lake NWR

Mississippi
River

Deer-
wood

0   Miles   30

North

Chapter 3

NORTHEASTERN MINNESOTA IN WINTER

February—4 Days

General

A face-to-face encounter with a Great Gray Owl can take the chill off the coldest of Minnesota winter days, or so it seems. The same can be said of a winter meeting with a Snowy, Boreal, or Northern Hawk Owl. These are incidents which can truly boost your birding spirits.

These northern owls lure many a birder to Duluth at a time of year when temperatures can be brutally cold. With a good plan and local networking you have a very good chance of seeing Snowy Owl, Northern Hawk Owl, and Great Gray Owl. Boreal Owl is usually present but is much harder to locate. The Duluth area is probably the only location in the Lower 48 to offer a reasonable possibility of seeing all 4 species. (There are a few accessible locations in southern Ontario where northern owls gather, but their occurrence there seems to be more dependent on whether or not it is an invasion winter. Duluth's owls are, on the whole, more reliable.)

Minnesota's birders keep close tabs on their owls. Their willingness to help you and many others to find these birds is commendable, and you should not hesitate to tap into local resources as your trip plans progress. Call the excellent Duluth hotline periodically to get a feel for the numbers and types of owls moving into the region. Buy a copy of Kim R. Eckert's *A Birder's Guide to Minnesota*, which you'll need if you plan to go beyond Duluth city limits. Kim lists regional contacts—birders willing to pass along current status and locations for species you want to see. Other birders you can write or phone for advice are listed in the *ABA Membership Directory*. (Please don't ask them to rewrite the birdfinding guide for you, though; most of the information that you need to plan a great birding trip is clearly spelled out in the book.)

You will want to schedule your visit to maximize your chances of seeing the winter owls, of course, but there are 7 other key species to

39

Probable Species
Total of 19 species
Mallard
Common Goldeneye
Common Merganser
Rock Dove
Great Horned Owl
Downy Woodpecker
Hairy Woodpecker
Pileated Woodpecker
Gray Jay
Blue Jay
American Crow
Common Raven
Black-capped
   Chickadee
Red-breasted Nuthatch
White-breasted
   Nuthatch
European Starling
Pine Siskin
Evening Grosbeak
House Sparrow

Note: The species in **boldface** appear no more than four times in the itineraries as *key* or *probable* species. Watch for them on this trip. As on all of the trips assume that you will see all birds on the probable-species list. You will gain 4 new species not seen on previous trips.

Possible Species
Total of 20 species
Oldsquaw
Northern Goshawk
Rough-legged Hawk
Gyrfalcon
Ring-necked Pheasant
Spruce Grouse
Sharp-tailed Grouse
Herring Gull
Thayer's Gull
Glaucous Gull
Eastern Screech-Owl
Barred Owl
Golden-crowned
   Kinglet
American Robin
Cedar Waxwing
Dark-eyed Junco
Purple Finch
Red Crossbill
White-winged Crossbill
Hoary Redpoll

Note: You will probably see only 5 of the 20 species on this list.

find: Ruffed Grouse, Black-backed Woodpecker, Boreal Chickadee, Bohemian Waxwing, Northern Shrike, Snow Bunting, Pine Grosbeak, and Common Redpoll. Finding the finches may be tricky, because they wander around and, some years, are present only in small numbers, but you will have opportunities to see them on other birding trips if you don't find them here. Your likelihood of finding the owls together in any other location is very, very remote.

This trip covers the Duluth area with side trips to Sax-Zim Bog, northern Aitkin County, Lake County Road 2, and the Gunflint Trail in Cook County.

Birdfinding Guides

The guide for this area is *A Birder's Guide to Minnesota* by Kim R. Eckert (1994). It is very thorough, with maps for the entire state and a large amount of bird identification information.

Another extremely helpful book is *Birds in Minnesota* by Robert B. Janssen (1987). This is a handbook, not a birdfinding guide, showing the distribution of 400 species in Minnesota; you will find its range maps to be very useful. Published by the University of Minnesota Press, Minneapolis, it is currently out of print, but copies can still be located with a little effort.

Rare Bird Alert Numbers

Statewide 612/780-8890
Duluth 218/525-5952

Special Equipment

Temperatures in northeastern Minnesota often plunge below zero, and the frigid air mass might stall in the region for the duration of your brief visit. You must come with clothing (including footwear) suitable for this weather.

In addition, if you are driving to Minnesota instead of renting a local car, be sure that your car's anti-freeze tests 30 to 40 degrees below zero. Ask your local auto mechanic about a battery blanket or other simple devices designed to help your vehicle survive a below-zero night. It is not unwise to stow a full complement of winter survival gear (for you *and* for your vehicle) in your trunk. If you don't need it, you might happen upon someone who does.

Remotely Possible Species
Total of 5 species
Harlequin Duck
Iceland Gull
Boreal Owl
Northern Saw-whet Owl
Three-toed Woodpecker
Note: Unless you are very lucky you will miss all 5 of these species on this short trip.

Accommodations

You will need motel or hotel accommodations each night. Camping is certainly not practical in these temperatures. Prices range from $50 to $60 for two at most area motels.

Key Species — Total of 11 species

1. **Ruffed Grouse**—Primarily found in deciduous and mixed forests throughout the trip area. In winter they are frequently seen in poplar and birch trees feeding on the buds. Usually easier to see at dusk. Sax-Zim Bog provides one of the better chances on this trip.

2. **Snowy Owl**—Active in the daytime but commonly seen at dusk or dawn. Usually present in the grain-elevator area at Duluth Harbor. May be present throughout the trip area in invasion years.

3. **Northern Hawk Owl**—The two best locations are northern Aitkin County and Sax-Zim Bog. Hunts in the daylight hours, usually in open areas. This is one owl that frequents the same area long enough to be staked out.

4. **Great Gray Owl**—Resident year round. Local advice is important. Hunts at dusk and dawn in open meadows. The best two areas are northern Aitkin County and Sax-Zim Bog.

5. **Black-backed Woodpecker**—Resident; try at all stops along Lake County Road 2 and Gunflint Trail in Cook County. Favors burned areas. Black-backs go about their business quietly, so be patient and give them a chance to resume tapping before you drive off empty-handed.

6. **Boreal Chickadee**—Resident throughout northeastern Minnesota. Prefers to feed in spruce trees so is usually hard to see. Try Sax-Zim Bog or northern Aitkin County.

7. **Bohemian Waxwing**—Feeds on fruit trees throughout the area. Most easily found in towns. Usually not too hard to locate, but can be difficult to find in years of scarce food.

8. **Northern Shrike**—Common in open areas throughout; Sax-Zim Bog is usually a good location. Any shrike seen in the trip area in this season will be a Northern.

9. **Snow Bunting**—Uncommon and local throughout the region with the exception of heavily wooded areas. Usually found in large flocks in open country. Sax-Zim Bog, Aitkin County, and Highways 2 and 210 between Duluth and Aitkin County can all be good.

10. **Pine Grosbeak**—Varies from abundant, in invasion years, to uncommon and local. Usually can be found at feeders. Both the Gunflint Trail in Cook County and Lake County Road 2 should be productive.

11. **Common Redpoll**—In most years this finch can easily be found in fields of weeds or at feeders, typically in large flocks; scarce some years. Carefully sort through every redpoll flock you find—Hoary Redpolls, when found, are usually traveling with Common Redpolls.

> Note: On the average trip it will be tough to find all of the key species.
> However, if the owling is good, you could see all 11.

Itinerary

> Note: This trip begins and ends in Duluth. Your itinerary will be influenced to
> some degree by current locations for Great Gray Owl, Northern Hawk Owl,
> and the remotely possible Boreal Owl.

Day 1 — Duluth, Northern Aitkin County, and Sax-Zim Bog

Leave Duluth early enough to make the one-hour drive to Aitkin County by daylight. Head south on Interstate 35 for about 12 miles to Highway 210. Turn west onto this road and drive approximately 41 miles to the Highway 65 intersection. Turn south onto Highway 65 for a short drive to Rice Lake National Wildlife Refuge.

As you slowly tour the accessible refuge roads, your prospects are good for finding 3 key species: Ruffed Grouse, Northern Shrike, and Snow Bunting. Other species of interest here are Rough-legged Hawk and Sharp-tailed Grouse.

Return to Highway 210, turn left, and drive through McGregor. Continue on Highway 210 for about 8 miles to County Road 5, where you will turn right (north). Spend the morning driving all the Aitkin County back roads that lie north of Highway 210. This area is one of the better places to find both Northern Hawk Owl and Great Gray Owl. Other possible key species in the vicinity are Ruffed Grouse, Snowy Owl (rare), Boreal Chickadee, Northern Shrike, Snow Bunting, Pine Grosbeak, and Common Redpoll. You may run across Northern Goshawk, Rough-legged Hawk, and Sharp-tailed Grouse, too. Aitkin County is well covered in *A Birder's Guide to Minnesota*.

When you leave, take Highway 200 east to Highway 2, and then turn right to go 9 miles to Floodwood. Get on County Road 8, drive east to Culver, and turn north onto County Road 7, which passes through the two small villages of Sax and Zim. This is the Sax-Zim Bog, one of Minnesota's most rewarding birding destinations. Consult Kim Eckert's book for suggestions about how to cover it well.

Your basic approach is to drive every open road, searching for each key species in its appropriate habitat. In Sax-Zim's spruce/tamarack bogs, deciduous woods, and meadows you will be looking for Ruffed Grouse, Northern Hawk Owl, Great Gray Owl, Boreal Chickadee, Northern Shrike, Snow Bunting, Pine Grosbeak, and Common Redpoll.

Return to Duluth to spend the night.

Day 2 — Duluth Harbor, Lake County Road 2, and Grand Marais

Start the day at dawn looking for Snowy Owls around Duluth Harbor, usually the surest place to locate this beautiful owl. It is also the most likely place to see a Gyrfalcon in the years when it occurs in Duluth. Although the entire Duluth/Superior Harbor area can be good for both raptors, concentrate your efforts in the vicinity of the grain elevators off Garfield Avenue. Snowy Owls are accustomed to a definite lack of high perches on their far northern breeding grounds. You might find one standing around on the ground or, perhaps, perched on the ice in Duluth's harbor.

When you leave the harbor, cruise around the eastern sections of the city looking for flocks of Bohemian Waxwings. You'll generally find them stripping the small red berries from American Mountain Ash trees, a planted species which is plentiful in the eastern half of Duluth.

Leave Duluth on scenic Highway 61 (watch for Ruffed Grouse in the aspens alongside the road) and drive 20 miles to Two Harbors in Lake County. Turn north onto Lake County Road 2. It is about 50 miles from Two Harbors to the Highway 1 intersection.

As you drive through the various habitats, including areas of fine coniferous forest, stop to bird any likely-looking place. Forest birds commonly mix in small feeding flocks, so linger a while to make sure you've noticed all the species these little groups contain. This route might produce several of your key species, such as Great Gray Owl, Black-backed Woodpecker, Northern Shrike, Snow Bunting, Pine Grosbeak, and Common Redpoll. Other possibilities are Northern Goshawk, Spruce Grouse, and Gray Jay.

When you reach Highway 1, turn right and bird this highway for the same species as listed for County Road 2. Follow Highway 1 back to Highway 61, then turn left for the drive to Grand Marais. Bird the park areas along Highway 61 as time allows.

Overnight in Grand Marais, after checking the harbor for waterfowl and gulls.

Day 3 — Grand Marais Harbor and the Gunflint Trail

Visit the harbor again before leaving Grand Marais; you might discover one of the Oldsquaws that occasionally shows up, or other out-of-range waterfowl or gulls.

Go north from Grand Marais on Cook County Road 12. This good, paved road, known as the Gunflint Trail, winds north and then northwest for about 50 miles. Bird all of it that you can, sampling some of the side roads, especially the first 5 miles of Forest Road 152, reliable for Black-backed Woodpecker in past years.

The Gunflint Trail may be the place you finally get satisfying looks at Black-backed Woodpecker, Boreal Chickadee, Pine Grosbeak, and Common Redpoll, all key species. Sometimes Spruce Grouse and Three-toed Woodpecker are found here, too. Though seeing one is unlikely, it should be noted that Boreal Owl has nested in the vicinity. It is here in winter, but is seldom seen.

Return to Highway 61 at Grand Marais. Depending on what key species you have missed, if any, decide whether you want to spend a second night in Grand Marais for another try at Cook County or return to Duluth.

Day 4 — Extra Day

If you still need some of the key species, try the most productive areas again. Consult A Birder's Guide to Minnesota, the Duluth hotline, or your local contacts for suggestions about where to spend the day.

Trip ends in Duluth in the evening.

Bird Numbers This Trip

	Potential	Expected	Actual
Key species	11	11	
Probable species	19	19	
Possible species	20	5	
Remotely possible species	5	0	
Totally unexpected species	?	1	
TOTAL	55	36	

Cumulative List

Total key and probable species seen after 3 trips.

Previous trips . . . . 220 species
Winter Northeastern Minnesota . . . . . . 15 species
TOTAL . . . . 235 species

This Trip's Mileage and Expenses

Approximate miles traveled, Duluth to Duluth: 750

- Fuel: $54; sharing $27 $_____
- Lodging: 3 nights at motels $240; sharing $120 $_____
- Food: Assuming restaurants for all meals - $60 $_____
  The total per person cost for the above items with a companion to share expenses should be less than $210.
- Add to this car rental expenses, if any: $_____
- Add to this your expenses to/from Duluth: $_____
  This will give you a good idea of the cost of this trip.
- TOTAL $_____

Personal Notes

_____

_____

_____

_____

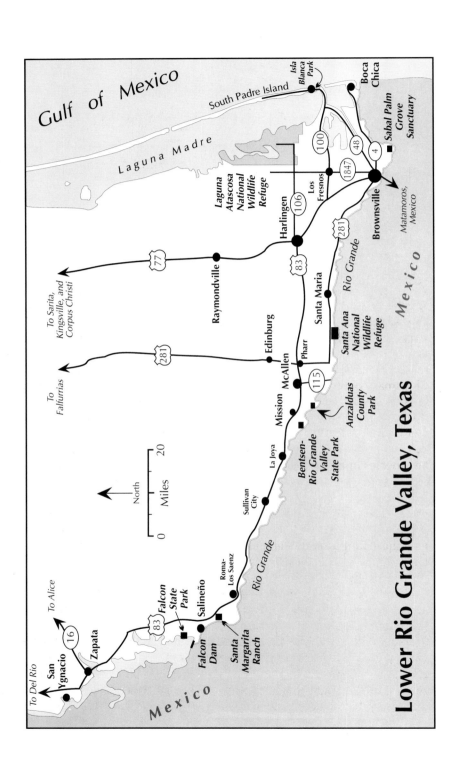

Lower Rio Grande Valley, Texas

Chapter 4

LOWER RIO GRANDE VALLEY OF TEXAS

February—8 Days

General

A birder's definition of paradise might sound suspiciously like January in the Lower Rio Grande Valley of Texas to "normal" people. The weather is mild enough (most nights) to making camping out a pleasure. Lots of other birders are around—new and old friends. You'll soon be swapping bird stories, directions to refuges, parks, and street corners, and talking shop with people who care as much about birds as you do. And there's no lack of birds—really good birds—at this time of year. The Christmas counters will have just completed their work, never failing to uncover a rarity or two or more. Be prepared to be very busy!

The Valley is the northern range limit for over two dozen species of "Mexican" birds that occur regularly in South Texas, but never or rarely ever occur elsewhere in the ABA Area. You will find a number of your key species (many of them with Mexican affinities) to be common, fairly predictable, and basically routine to find at their regular, published locations. Into this category fall Least Grebe, Neotropic Cormorant, White-faced Ibis, Mottled Duck, White-tailed Kite, Harris's Hawk, White-tailed Hawk, Crested Caracara, Plain Chachalaca, White-tipped Dove, Pauraque, Ringed and Green Kingfishers, Golden-fronted Woodpecker, Great Kiskadee, Green Jay, Mexican Crow, Chihuahuan Raven, Long-billed Thrasher, Olive Sparrow, and Altamira Oriole.

The remaining key species—Muscovy Duck, Hook-billed Kite, Red-billed Pigeon, Red-crowned Parrot, Ferruginous Pygmy-Owl, Buff-bellied Hummingbird, Brown Jay, Clay-colored Robin, Sprague's Pipit, Tropical Parula, White-collared Seedeater, and Audubon's Oriole—are usually present, but might require you to spend more time, exert more effort, or gather more information before you are able to locate them. Aside from the unanticipated vagrants, though, these are the very species that *every* birder here is looking for. You won't have any difficulty

Probable Species
Total of 130 Species
Pied-billed Grebe
Eared Grebe
American White
  Pelican
Double-crested
  Cormorant
Great Blue Heron
Great Egret
Snowy Egret
Tricolored Heron
Reddish Egret
Cattle Egret
Black-crowned
  Night-Heron
**Greater White-fronted
  Goose**
Snow Goose
Canada Goose
Green-winged Teal
Northern Pintail
Blue-winged Teal
Cinnamon Teal
Northern Shoveler
Gadwall
American Wigeon
Canvasback
Redhead
Ring-necked Duck
Lesser Scaup
Bufflehead
Hooded Merganser
Red-breasted Merganser
Ruddy Duck
Black Vulture
Turkey Vulture
Northern Harrier
Sharp-shinned Hawk
Cooper's Hawk
Red-shouldered Hawk
Red-tailed Hawk
American Kestrel
Merlin
Wild Turkey
Northern Bobwhite
Scaled Quail
Sora
Common Moorhen
American Coot
Black-bellied Plover
Snowy Plover
Semipalmated Plover
Killdeer
Black-necked Stilt
American Avocet
Greater Yellowlegs
Lesser Yellowlegs
Willet
Spotted Sandpiper
Long-billed Curlew
Marbled Godwit
Ruddy Turnstone
Sanderling
Western Sandpiper
Least Sandpiper
Dunlin
Long-billed Dowitcher
Common Snipe
Laughing Gull
Ring-billed Gull

learning where to see each one, providing it's around. Sharing information is one of the most satisfying aspects of birding—from the giving or from the receiving end. There are few places where this custom is practiced with such enthusiasm as in the Lower Rio Grande Valley of Texas.

The Valley should be birded in two seasons—winter and spring—to catch all of its specialties and to maximize your opportunities for seeing the rarities that sporadically occur. On your January trip you may be fortunate enough to see one or more of the "summer" species that you won't officially target until your April trip. You also may not find some of this trip's key species but might locate them on the April trip described in Chapter 7.

The Lower Rio Grande Valley regularly plays host to species that are real rarities in the ABA Area. It is important at this point to recognize that 5 of the key birds are Code 3 species and 3 are Code 4 species. Your persistence in using the hotlines and communicating with other birders will make the difference in missing or seeing these species.

This trip begins in Brownsville, with stops at Sabal Palm Grove Sanctuary, Brownsville City Dump, Gladys Porter Zoo, Boca Chica, Santa Ana National Wildlife Refuge, Anzalduas County Park, Bentsen-Rio Grande Valley State Park, Santa Margarita Ranch, Salineño, Falcon State Park, Falcon Dam, Zapata, San Ygnacio, Highway 77 from Raymondville to Kingsville, and Laguna Atascosa National Wildlife Refuge.

Birdfinding Guides

The birdfinding guides that have set the standard are the "Lane Guides" pioneered 30 years ago by James A. Lane. The American Birding Association now owns and publishes this popular series; they are systematically updating and expanding the original guides. The two books that I have found most useful in the Valley are both from that series:

A Birder's Guide to the Texas Coast by Harold R. Holt (1993).

A Birder's Guide to the Rio Grande Valley of Texas by Harold R. Holt (1992).

Not as detailed, yet still very helpful, is Ed Kutac's *Birder's Guide to Texas* (1989).

Rare Bird Alert Numbers

Statewide 713/992-2757
Lower Rio Grande . . 210/969-2731

Special Equipment

A spotting scope is useful at Laguna Atascosa, Falcon Dam, and the Red-billed Pigeon roost north of Zapata. Bird song/call tapes may be helpful, though their use is prohibited in some areas.

Accommodations

At this time of year the days are generally warm, while the nights can be cool, but you can usually camp comfortably with a sleeping bag and a tent. (Some years periods of rain and wind blow in during January, but these conditions don't last long.) You will find campgrounds with hot showers at Bentsen-Rio Grande Valley State Park, Falcon State Park, and South Padre Island. In addition, there are many other primitive campsites in the Valley. If you prefer motels, they are plentiful throughout the trip area at reasonable prices. Motels may be busy in winter, so advance reservations are advised.

Key Species — Total of 33 Species

1. **Least Grebe**—Resident on small ponds throughout the Lower Rio Grande Valley from Laguna Atascosa at least to Falcon Reservoir. Most easily found at Santa Ana National Wildlife Refuge, Sabal Palm Grove Sanctuary, and Bentsen-Rio Grande Valley State Park.

2. **Neotropic Cormorant**—Usually easy to locate at Laguna Atascosa and Santa Ana National

Probable Species
(continued)

Herring Gull
Gull-billed Tern
Caspian Tern
Forster's Tern
Black Skimmer
Rock Dove
White-winged Dove
Mourning Dove
Inca Dove
Common Ground-Dove
Greater Roadrunner
Eastern Screech-Owl
Great Horned Owl
Belted Kingfisher
Ladder-backed
    Woodpecker
Northern Flicker
Eastern Phoebe
Tree Swallow
Northern Rough-
    winged Swallow
Tufted Titmouse
Cactus Wren
Carolina Wren
Bewick's Wren
House Wren
Golden-crowned
    Kinglet
Ruby-crowned Kinglet
Blue-gray Gnatcatcher
Eastern Bluebird
Hermit Thrush
American Robin
Gray Catbird
Northern Mockingbird
Curve-billed Thrasher
American Pipit
Cedar Waxwing
Loggerhead Shrike
European Starling
White-eyed Vireo
Solitary Vireo
Orange-crowned
    Warbler
Nashville Warbler
Yellow-rumped
    Warbler
Black-and-white
    Warbler
Common Yellowthroat
Northern Cardinal
Pyrrhuloxia
Rufous-sided Towhee
Field Sparrow
Vesper Sparrow
Lark Sparrow
Black-throated Sparrow
Savannah Sparrow
Grasshopper Sparrow
Song Sparrow
Lincoln's Sparrow
Swamp Sparrow
White-throated Sparrow
Red-winged Blackbird
Eastern Meadowlark
Western Meadowlark
Brewer's Blackbird
Great-tailed Grackle
Brown-headed Cowbird

Probable Species
(continued)
American Goldfinch
House Sparrow

Note: The species in **boldface** appear no more than four times in the itineraries as *key* or *probable* species. Watch for them on this trip. On all the trips assume that you will see all of the probable species. This outcome is not likely, but the ones that you miss will be seen on subsequent trips without extra effort. On this trip you will gain 36 new species from the probable list not seen on the previous trips.

Possible Species
Total of 50 Species
Western Grebe
Anhinga
American Bittern
Little Blue Heron
Green Heron
Roseate Spoonbill
Black-bellied
    Whistling-Duck
Mallard
Osprey
Bald Eagle
Gray Hawk
King Rail
Sandhill Crane
Wilson's Plover
Piping Plover
Solitary Sandpiper
Red Knot
Stilt Sandpiper
Short-billed Dowitcher
Bonaparte's Gull
Royal Tern
Sandwich Tern
Groove-billed Ani
Barn Owl
Elf Owl
Burrowing Owl
Ruby-throated
    Hummingbird
Black-chinned
    Hummingbird
Rufous Hummingbird
Yellow-bellied
    Sapsucker
Say's Phoebe
Vermilion Flycatcher
Couch's Kingbird
Horned Lark
Cave Swallow
Verdin
Rock Wren
Sedge Wren

Wildlife Refuges, Bentsen-Rio Grande Valley State Park, or Falcon State Park. At this time of year it is more likely to be found on fresh water.

3. **White-faced Ibis**—Present year round; may be difficult to locate at this season, but try Laguna Atascosa and Santa Ana National Wildlife Refuges.

4. **Muscovy Duck**—Sightings are primarily along the Rio Grande between the Falcon Dam spillway and the Roma area, with most records coming from Salineño and Santa Margarita Ranch.

5. **Mottled Duck**—Common year round at Laguna Atascosa National Wildlife Refuge.

6. **Hook-billed Kite**—Usually present year round at Bentsen-Rio Grande Valley State Park, Santa Ana National Wildlife Refuge, or Anzalduas County Park. One good strategy is to drive west down the levee near the entrance to Bentsen-Rio Grande Valley State Park in early morning. From this vantage point you can survey a large area and have a good chance at a fly-by.

7. **White-tailed Kite**—Resident from the Gulf to Falcon Dam. Should be seen at Santa Ana and Laguna Atascosa National Wildlife Refuges, Bentsen-Rio Grande Valley State Park, fields near Sabal Palm Grove Sanctuary, and at Falcon State Park.

8. **Harris's Hawk**—Resident throughout, but easier to locate the farther west you go. Common at Falcon State Park and on the drive north along Highway 77.

9. **White-tailed Hawk**—Drive Highway 77 north from Raymondville to Kingsville. Check all hawks; you should see a half-dozen White-tails. Operating chicken ranches near Kingsville are also good places to try.

10. **Crested Caracara**—You'll see these handsome scavengers along Highway 77—standing around in a field, perched on a fence post, or snatching bites of roadkill at considerable risk to their own safety. Or check the chicken ranches near Kingsville.

11. **Plain Chachalaca**—Common, noisy, and conspicuous resident of the Lower Valley. Hard to miss at Bentsen-Rio Grande Valley State Park or Santa Ana National Wildlife Refuge.

12. **Red-billed Pigeon**—Can show up anywhere from San Ygnacio to the Gulf. Most commonly found below Falcon Dam spillway (scope the tree-tops) and at the roadside roost north of Zapata.

13. **White-tipped Dove**—Common at Bentsen-Rio Grande Valley State Park and Santa Ana National Wildlife Refuge. Easy to locate throughout most of trip area.

14. **Red-crowned Parrot**—A traditional location has been in Brownsville on both sides of Central Boulevard between Boca Chica Boulevard and Los Ebanos Boulevard. Easiest to find in early morning or at dusk when the parrots are coming from or going to a roost. They are noisy and not hard to locate if you are close to the right area. If this attempt fails, there are also roost sites in McAllen.

15. **Ferruginous Pygmy-Owl**—For several years the most consistent place to locate this bird has been the woodland around the old campground below Falcon Dam. It is also seen occasionally at Bentsen-Rio Grande Valley State Park, Santa Ana National Wildlife Refuge, and at wooded rest-stops along Highway 77.

16. **Pauraque**—Common resident; most birders find it by driving the park roads at Bentsen-Rio Grande Valley State Park at dusk. (Now you must be registered in the campground to have access to these roads from 10 pm to 7 am.)

17. **Buff-bellied Hummingbird**—Believed to be resident on the grounds at Gladys Porter Zoo in Brownsville. It is often seen at Sabal Palm Grove Sanctuary. Your best bet other than these locations is to check with local birders for the current reliable spots, generally at someone's feeder.

18. **Ringed Kingfisher**—Usually found just below Falcon Dam. Can be found downriver to Salineño and the Santa Margarita Ranch. Occa-

Possible Species
(continued)

Marsh Wren
Yellow-throated Vireo
Palm Warbler
Green-tailed Towhee
Spotted Towhee
Botteri's Sparrow
Cassin's Sparrow
Clay-colored Sparrow
Lark Bunting
Le Conte's Sparrow
Bronzed Cowbird
Pine Siskin

Note: You will probably see at least 7 species on the possible list during this trip.

Remotely Possible Species
Total of 42 Species
Common Loon
Yellow-crowned
    Night-Heron
White Ibis
Fulvous Whistling-Duck
Ross's Goose
Wood Duck
Common Goldeneye
Common Merganser
Masked Duck
Common Black-Hawk
Roadside Hawk
Zone-tailed Hawk
Aplomado Falcon
Peregrine Falcon
Prairie Falcon
Mountain Plover
Northern Jacana
Whimbrel
White-rumped
    Sandpiper
Pectoral Sandpiper
American Woodcock
Ruddy Ground-Dove
Short-eared Owl
Northern Beardless-
    Tyrannulet
Black Phoebe
Ash-throated Flycatcher
Tropical Kingbird
Scissor-tailed Flycatcher
Mountain Bluebird
Northern Parula
Black-throated Gray
    Warbler
Black-throated Green
    Warbler
Yellow-throated
    Warbler
Pine Warbler
Gray-crowned
    Yellowthroat
Golden-crowned
    Warbler
Crimson-collared
    Grosbeak

Remotely Possible Species
(continued)

Blue Bunting
Nelson's Sharp-tailed
Sparrow
Seaside Sparrow
Bullock's Oriole
Lesser Goldfinch

Note: You will probably see only 2 of the species on the remotely possible list on this trip. Some of these species are extremely rare in the ABA Area—these are Code 4 and Code 5 species. They are on the list because most have appeared at least a few times and are well worth the extra effort expended in pursuing them. Among these is Aplomado Falcon; this species is being reintroduced at Laguna Atascosa, making identification of free-flying, wild birds in South Texas a problem.

sional at Santa Ana National Wildlife Refuge and Bentsen-Rio Grande Valley State Park.

19. **Green Kingfisher**—Usually sits on a limb very low over water, making it hard to spot until it changes perches. Best bets are in the wooded area below Falcon Dam (anywhere along the Rio Grande to at least Salineño), at ponds in Santa Ana National Wildlife Refuge, and at Bentsen-Rio Grande Valley State Park.

20. **Golden-fronted Woodpecker**—Common and easily seen at Sabal Palm Grove Sanctuary, Santa Ana and Laguna Atascosa National Wildlife Refuges, Bentsen-Rio Grande Valley State Park, or in the Falcon Dam area.

21. **Great Kiskadee**—Easily seen in proper habitat at Sabal Palm Grove Sanctuary, Santa Ana National Wildlife Refuge, or Bentsen-Rio Grande Valley State Park.

22. **Green Jay**—Common at Sabal Palm Grove Sanctuary, Santa Ana National Wildlife Refuge, and Bentsen-Rio Grande Valley State Park.

23. **Brown Jay**—Usually seen along the river or at feeders at Salineño. Frequently found below Falcon Dam and at Santa Margarita Ranch.

24. **Mexican Crow**—Numerous and easy to locate at the Brownsville City Dump.

25. **Chihuahuan Raven**—Common at the Brownsville City Dump. Easily located at Falcon State Park.

26. **Clay-colored Robin**—May be present at Bentsen-Rio Grande Valley State Park, Santa Ana National Wildlife Refuge, or Anzalduas County Park. This is a hotline bird.

27. **Long-billed Thrasher**—Fairly common throughout the Lower Valley. Normally easy to find at feeders on the trailer loop at Bentsen-Rio Grande Valley State Park or at Salineño.

28. **Sprague's Pipit**—Can be located at Laguna Atascosa National Wildlife Refuge. See Day 6 of itinerary for a possible location near Ricardo.

29. **Tropical Parula**—Generally present in very low numbers in the Lower Valley or at one of the rest-stops along Highway 77 between Raymondville and Kingsville.

30. **Olive Sparrow**—Shy but common species at Sabal Palm Grove Sanctuary, Santa Ana National Wildlife Refuge, below Falcon Dam, and

at many other locations. It forages on the ground so intently that you might almost step on it before it flies off.

31. **White-collared Seedeater**—Can show up anywhere, but most frequently seen at San Ygnacio, and sometimes at Zapata.

32. **Altamira Oriole**—Common at Sabal Palm Grove Sanctuary, Bentsen-Rio Grande Valley State Park, and Santa Ana National Wildlife Refuge. Really hard to miss.

33. **Audubon's Oriole**—Best spots are the Salineño area, Santa Margarita Ranch, and below Falcon Dam. Any feeder in this area offering fruit is a good bet.

Note: Assume that you will see all 33 key species. (You will have another chance at those you miss, if you follow the April trip plan in Chapter 7.)

Itinerary
Note: Trip begins and ends in Brownsville.

Day 1 — Brownsville, Sabal Palm Grove Sanctuary, and Boca Chica
It's hard to imagine that this tiny 32-acre plot is all that remains of the Lower Valley's once extensive Sabal Palm forest. Though there's precious little land available for these graceful palms to stage a comeback, the immediate future of this grove is assured thanks to fierce protection by the National Audubon Society. The old farm fields surrounding the palm grove comprise the balance of the sanctuary's 172 acres. A small admission fee is charged—consider doubling it. The sanctuary is open 8 am to 5 pm Thursday through Monday from November 1 to the end of April. (The remainder of the year it is open only on weekends.) Remember this schedule when you're planning your trip.

To reach the sanctuary from Brownsville go southeast from International Boulevard on Farm Road 1419 for 5.5 miles to the entrance road.

Green Jay
Louise Zemaitis

Sabal Palm Grove is a delightful place to start your Rio Grande Valley trip. You will discover many new species here, but most will be found again during the coming week. The exceptions might be Buff-bellied Hummingbird (a habitual visitor to the feeders by the shop) and any real rarities present (such as Gray-crowned Yellowthroat or Crimson-collared Grosbeak) that you'll quickly learn about from fellow birders. In the grove or around the fields you can expect to find White-tailed Kite, Plain Chachalaca, Pauraque (dawn or dusk), White-winged and White-tipped Doves, Common Ground-Dove, Golden-fronted Woodpecker, Great Kiskadee, Green Jay, Olive Sparrow, and Altamira Oriole. Least Grebe is usually seen around the resaca (oxbow lake); sometimes Black-bellied Whistling-Ducks are there, too. Tropical Parula is located here fairly often.

Return to Farm Road 1419, turn right, and follow 1419 until it turns back north. From this point, until 1419 meets Highway 4, check the fields for possible Botteri's and Cassin's Sparrows.

Your next stop is the huge Brownsville City Dump, for over 20 years the best place for Mexican Crow. Chihuahuan Ravens and Great-tailed Grackles abound here, and you'll want to spend time sorting through the scavenging gulls. For directions to the dump see *A Birder's Guide to the Rio Grande Valley of Texas.*

Return to Highway 4 and drive east for about 20 miles to Boca Chica. The mudflats along the way are usually loaded with shorebirds. From Boca Chica you can drive south (or north) on the beach for miles—to the mouth of the Rio Grande—getting close looks at shorebirds, terns, gulls, and wading birds.

Return to Brownsville and make a stop at the Gladys Porter Zoo. Buff-bellied Hummingbird is believed to be resident on the grounds. In the last hour or so of daylight, cruise along Central Boulevard between Boca Chica Boulevard and Los Ebanos Boulevard. Small groups of chattering Red-crowned Parrots head to roost at this time of day and, with luck, you'll be able to keep up with some until you see where they land. Of course, it's less hazardous just to ask around for the location of a roost site.

Inexpensive motels are plentiful in Brownsville and Harlingen, although you will be better positioned for tomorrow's birding if you spend tonight in the McAllen area. If you prefer camping, it is a one-and-a-half-hour drive to Bentsen-Rio Grande Valley State Park near Mission. Advance reservations, particularly on weekends, are recommended.

Day 2 — Santa Ana National Wildlife Refuge and Anzalduas County Park

Get an early start at Santa Ana National Wildlife Refuge. Unless you arrive on a day when vehicle access is allowed, a good part of your day will be required to cover the area even lightly. Pack a light lunch in case you become too absorbed to tear yourself away. The refuge trail system through the various habitats is well covered in *A Birder's Guide to the Rio Grande Valley of Texas.*

You will have great opportunities to pursue many of your key species here: Least Grebe, Neotropic Cormorant, White-faced Ibis, Mottled Duck, Hook-billed Kite, White-tailed Kite, Harris's Hawk, Plain Chachalaca, Red-billed Pigeon, White-tipped Dove, Pauraque (dawn or dusk), Buff-bellied Hummingbird, Ringed Kingfisher, Green Kingfisher, Golden-fronted Woodpecker, Great Kiskadee, Green Jay, Long-billed Thrasher, Olive Sparrow, and Altamira Oriole.

In addition, White-tailed Hawk, Crested Caracara, Red-crowned Parrot, Clay-colored Robin, Tropical Parula, and Audubon's Oriole are found occasionally. Vague possibilities to be alert for are Muscovy Duck, Masked Duck, Common Black-Hawk, Gray Hawk, Zone-tailed Hawk, Northern Jacana, Ruddy Ground-Dove, Gray-crowned Yellowthroat, Golden-crowned Warbler, Crimson-collared Grosbeak, and Blue Bunting.

Anzalduas County Park normally will have little that you can't see at Santa Ana or Bentsen-Rio Grande Valley State Park, but nevertheless it should be thoroughly birded. An uncommonly large number of Mexican rarities has been recorded here over the past few years.

Return to your McAllen motel or Bentsen-Rio Grande Valley State Park for the night.

Day 3 — Bentsen-Rio Grande Valley State Park, Santa Margarita Ranch, and Salineño

Bentsen-Rio Grande Valley State Park offers the same habitats and many of the same species as Santa Ana, but the tour roads, trailer-loop, picnic area, and boat ramp give the birding experience here a very different tone. There are more edges here, longer views, and perfect vantage points for scoping both sides of the Rio Grande. In some years Bentsen has had Roadside Hawk, Blue Bunting, Clay-colored Robin, or White-collared Seedeater wintering in the park. Spend time walking around the trailer-loop—it's a rare camper who doesn't put out fruit or other goodies, and some of the birds attracted are the key species you are looking for.

Bentsen is a good place to find Hook-billed Kite. A worthwhile way to start your day is to drive west on the levee near the park entrance for about one-quarter mile. Spend an hour or two identifying raptors; one of them might be a Hook-billed Kite.

Next, follow the directions in *A Birder's Guide to the Rio Grande Valley of Texas* to find Santa Margarita Ranch (a one-hour drive from Bentsen). This is private property, and a small fee must be paid to bird here. The area along the river is good for Plain Chachalaca, Red-billed Pigeon, White-tipped Dove, Pauraque, Ringed and Green Kingfishers, Golden-fronted Woodpecker, Great Kiskadee, Green and Brown Jays, Long-billed Thrasher, Olive Sparrow, and Audubon's and Altamira Orioles.

Muscovy Duck is sometimes seen on the river and should be watched for from here to Falcon Dam and beyond. A scope is very useful for getting a decent look at this species.

Proceed to Salineño, where the road dead-ends at the Rio Grande. Most of the area here is posted against trespassing, and this circumstance doesn't leave a very large area to bird. Even with these limitations this has been a consistently good place to see Brown Jay, Audubon's Oriole, and Muscovy Duck. Check the sign on the gate of the Salineño Birders Colony a short distance from the river. If it invites you to enter, do so—Brown Jay and Audubon's Oriole are a cinch at the feeders.

Continue to Falcon State Park for camping with showers. There are no motels in this area, though you will find a few upriver at Zapata.

Day 4 — Falcon State Park, Falcon Dam, Zapata, and San Ygnacio

The old campground below Falcon Dam, a 1-mile hike below the spillway, is a good place to start the day. The area may yield Neotropic Cormorant, Harris's Hawk, Plain Chachalaca, Red-billed Pigeon, White-tipped Dove, Pauraque, Ringed and Green Kingfishers, Golden-fronted Woodpecker, Great Kiskadee, Green and Brown Jays, Long-billed Thrasher, Olive Sparrow, and Audubon's and Altamira Orioles.

Most birders who see (or hear) Ferruginous Pygmy-Owl in South Texas have lucked upon the same little family of owls that you might find here. *Please don't play tapes in this area.*

Do search carefully under the overhanging vegetation along the riverbanks for shy Muscovy Ducks.

Return to Falcon State Park; the road into and around the camp area is good for some of the same species as those found below the dam. In addition, Chihuahuan Raven is common in winter and Bronzed Cowbird and Cassin's Sparrow are definite possibilities.

When you leave Falcon Dam, turn northwest onto Highway 83. Zapata is a thirty-minute drive away and is an excellent place to locate White-collared Seedeater. Fourteen miles farther upriver another small town, San Ygnacio, has been the spot where many birders have seen their first White-collared Seedeater. In addition, the river at San Ygnacio is a good place for Red-billed Pigeon. Audubon's Oriole and Brown Jay have also been observed here occasionally. For a number of years there has been a Red-billed Pigeon roost on Highway 83, 5 miles north of Zapata. If your local inquiries determine that the roost is still in use, the best times to visit it are at sunset or sunrise.

Overnight in Zapata or at Falcon State Park.

Day 5 — Falcon Dam, Salineño, Santa Margarita Ranch, and Bentsen-Rio Grande Valley State Park

The secret to locating the rarer species along the Lower Rio Grande is putting in lots of time in the field. The more visits you make to each of the good birding sites, the better your chances of seeing all of the key species. Spend Day 5 birding your way downriver from Zapata or Falcon Dam to Bentsen. You will have plenty of time at each unique location.

Overnight at McAllen or Bentsen-Rio Grande Valley State Park.

Day 6 — Anzalduas County Park, Santa Ana National Wildlife Refuge, and Highway 77 north

Go back to Anzalduas County Park and Santa Ana National Wildlife Refuge this morning. It's a particularly good opportunity to explore different parts of beautiful Santa Ana.

Plan on driving to Harlingen around noon, and then head north on Highway 77 toward Kingsville. At Raymondville slow down and start birding again in earnest. Driving this corridor through the immense King Ranch and other private ranchland is the best way to locate White-tailed Hawk and Crested Caracara in South Texas. If you keep checking the circling and perched hawks, you should see 4 to 6 White-tails during this drive. Crested Caracaras are as likely to be seen picking at roadkill on the highway or standing around in the fields as they are to be seen flying. If you miss either raptor, you can drive the chicken-ranch route described in *A Birder's Guide to the Texas Coast.* (These ranches have fluctuating levels of operation—sometimes active, sometimes not.)

Tropical Parula is often seen at one of the rest-stops along Highway 77. The one south of Sarita on the west side of the highway has been fairly reliable for several years.

Spend the night at Kingsville.

Day 7 — Highway 77 and Laguna Atascosa National Wildlife Refuge

Leave Kingsville and head south on Highway 77. Two miles south of Ricardo turn east onto Farm Road 772. Follow 772 for 4.1 miles, until it merges with Farm Road 1118 and turns south. Continue 0.5 mile south and stay on 772 as it turns back east. Approximately 1 mile later you will arrive at a small triangular area of grass that was created when the highway department replaced a square turn with a curve. If it has been recently mowed, this area might hold a Sprague's Pipit or two.

Return to Highway 77 and proceed south to Laguna Atascosa National Wildlife Refuge, a two-hour drive. The refuge is well covered in both *A Birder's Guide to the Rio Grande Valley of Texas* and *A Birder's Guide to the Texas Coast.* You can practically count on seeing Mottled Duck, White-tailed Kite, Harris's Hawk, Plain Chachalaca, White-tipped Dove, Pauraque, Golden-fronted Woodpecker, Great Kiskadee, Green Jay, Long-billed Thrasher, and Olive Sparrow of the key species, although you would need to remain until nightfall for the Pauraque. The main attraction is the huge concentration of many species of waterbirds and shorebirds on the loop roads along both Laguna Atascosa and Laguna Madre. Many sparrows (including Le Conte's, Cassin's, and Botteri's) are present in winter. Sprague's Pipit and Groove-billed Ani are possibilities.

An Aplomado Falcon reintroduction program, in operation since 1985, has apparently not yet resulted in an established breeding population of these exquisite birds. Keep your eyes open, though, because it's not uncommon to see one in the region.

If you are camping, try Isla Blanca Park on South Padre Island.

Day 8 — Extra Day

If you haven't used this day already, check your birdfinding guides for ideas. Or just go back to your favorite places. With hundreds of birders around, it's likely that the hotline or the grapevine will have at least one report that you want to investigate.

Trip ends at Brownsville in the evening.

Bird Numbers This Trip

	Potential	Expected	Actual
Key Species	33	33	
Probable Species	130	130	
Possible Species	50	7	
Remotely Possible Species	42	2	
Totally Unexpected Species	?	2	
TOTAL	255	174	

Cumulative List

Total key and probable species seen after 4 trips.

Previous trips . . . . 235 species
Winter Rio Grande . . . . 69 species
TOTAL . . . . 304 species

This Trip's Mileage and Expenses

Approximate miles traveled, Brownsville to Brownsville: 1,050

- Fuel: $75; sharing $37.50 $_____
- Lodging: 2 nights at motels and other
  nights paying a camping fee $130; shared $65 $_____
- Food: Using ice-chest/supermarket method for
  most meals, your food will cost less than $80 $_____
  *The total per person cost for the above items with a companion
  to share expenses should be less than $185.*
- Add to this car rental expenses, if any: $_____
- Add to this your expenses to/from Brownsville: $_____
  This will give you a good idea of the cost of this trip.
- TOTAL $_____

Personal Notes

_____

_____

_____

_____

_____

_____

_____

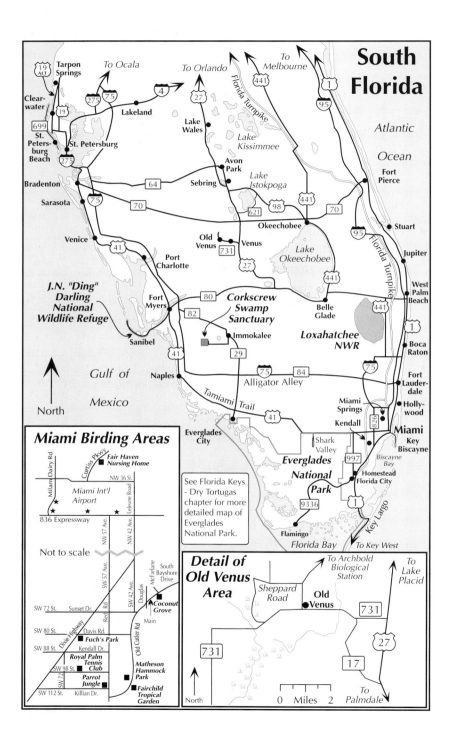

South Florida

To Ocala

To Orlando

To Melbourne

Tarpon Springs

Clearwater

Lakeland

Lake Wales

Lake Kissimmee

Avon Park

Sebring

Lake Istokpoga

Fort Pierce

St. Peters-burg Beach

St. Petersburg

Bradenton

Sarasota

Venice

Okeechobee

Stuart

Atlantic

Ocean

Old Venus

Venus

Lake Okeechobee

Jupiter

Port Charlotte

J.N. "Ding" Darling National Wildlife Refuge

Fort Myers

Corkscrew Swamp Sanctuary

Belle Glade

West Palm Beach

Loxahatchee NWR

Boca Raton

Sanibel

Immokalee

Fort Lauder-dale

Gulf of

Naples

Mexico

Alligator Alley

Miami Springs

Hollywood

North

Kendall

Miami

Tamiami Trail

Key Biscayne

Everglades City

Shark Valley

Biscayne Bay

Everglades National Park

See Florida Keys - Dry Tortugas chapter for more detailed map of Everglades National Park.

Homestead Florida City

Flamingo

Florida Bay

To Key West

Key Largo

Miami Birding Areas

Curtiss Pkwy

Miami Dairy Rd

Fair Haven Nursing Home

NW 36 St.

Miami Int'l Airport

Lejeune Road

836 Expressway

Not to scale

NW 57 Ave.

NW 42 Ave.

South Bayshore Drive

McFarlane

Douglas

SW 72 St.

Sunset Dr.

Red Rd

SW 42 Ave.

Coconut Grove

Main

SW 80 St.

Davis Rd.

Old Cutler Rd

Dixie Highway

Fuch's Park

SW 88 St.

Kendall Dr.

Royal Palm Tennis Club

SW 98 St.

Parrot Jungle

SW 72

Matheson Hammock Park

SW 112 St.

Killian Dr.

Fairchild Tropical Garden

Detail of Old Venus Area

To Archbold Biological Station

Sheppard Road

Old Venus

731

To Lake Placid

731

27

North

17

0 Miles 2

To Palmdale

Chapter 5

SOUTH FLORIDA IN WINTER

Mid-March—6 days

General

There are so many outstanding birds in South Florida—and so much territory in South Florida to bird—that you might find it impossible to fit it all into a one-week tour. Almost all of the key species listed for this trip can be seen in South Florida at any time of year. This suggests that this chapter's itinerary might be combined with the late April or early May visit to the Keys and the Dry Tortugas (see Chapter 8) to create a longer, very productive trip. However, if you are planning to travel elsewhere for spring migration (or actually trying to see 600+ species in a calendar year), you won't have time for a lengthy trip to Florida at the peak of migration.

The purpose, then, for this March trip is to see the year-round South Florida specialties at a time when birding is slow elsewhere, and yet do it at a time when the weather is mild enough to enjoy both the birding and the camping.

It is important for the success of this trip to have up-to-date information on some of the Miami-area specialties. You could reach local birders or contact Tropical Audubon Society (5530 Sunset Drive, Miami, FL 33143) for a sheet on current locations for the exotic birds of Dade County and vicinity. (Include a self-addressed stamped envelope for this information sheet.)

This trip includes Miami, Miami Springs, Kendall, Homestead, Everglades National Park, Tamiami Trail, Corkscrew Swamp Sanctuary, Sanibel Island, St. Petersburg, the Lake Placid area, Old Venus, West Palm Beach, and Loxahatchee National Wildlife Refuge.

Birdfinding Guides

A Birder's Guide to Florida by Harold R. Holt (1989) (currently being updated by Bill Pranty for release in 1996) covers South Florida in detail.

61

Probable Species
Total of 132 Species
Common Loon
Pied-billed Grebe
Horned Grebe
American White
Pelican
Brown Pelican
Double-crested
Cormorant
American Bittern
Great Blue Heron
Great Egret
Snowy Egret
Little Blue Heron
Tricolored Heron
Reddish Egret
Cattle Egret
Green Heron
Black-crowned
Night-Heron
Wood Duck
Green-winged Teal
Mottled Duck
Mallard
Blue-winged Teal
Northern Shoveler
Gadwall
American Wigeon
Canvasback
Ring-necked Duck
Lesser Scaup
Red-breasted Merganser
Ruddy Duck
Black Vulture
Turkey Vulture
Osprey
Bald Eagle
Northern Harrier
Sharp-shinned Hawk
Red-shouldered Hawk
Red-tailed Hawk
Crested Caracara
American Kestrel
Peregrine Falcon
Northern Bobwhite
Sora
Common Moorhen
American Coot
Sandhill Crane
Black-bellied Plover
Snowy Plover
Semipalmated Plover
Killdeer
Black-necked Stilt
American Avocet
Greater Yellowlegs
Lesser Yellowlegs
Solitary Sandpiper
Willet
Spotted Sandpiper
Whimbrel
Marbled Godwit
Ruddy Turnstone
Sanderling
Western Sandpiper
Least Sandpiper
Dunlin
Short-billed Dowitcher
Long-billed Dowitcher
Common Snipe

Rare Bird Alert Numbers

Statewide 813/657-4442
Miami 305/667-7337

Special Equipment

A spotting scope will be appreciated at many locations on this trip. Bird call tapes are helpful for Bachman's Sparrow. (*Tape recorder use, however, is forbidden at Everglades National Park.*) Do not even consider this trip, especially Snake Bight Trail, without a tough insect repellent. (Permethrin is an effective alternative.) A powerful spotlight makes owling easy along the roads at night. You will need to take, and use, sunscreen.

Accommodations

There is no shortage of motels in all price ranges. Camping facilities are also plentiful; most require payment of a small fee, but there are numerous places to camp without facilities that can be used without charge.

Key Species — Total of 33 Species

1. **Anhinga**—Abundant and easy to locate. Best location is Anhinga Trail in Everglades National Park, but it can easily be found at most marshy areas on the Tamiami Trail. Occurs even around Miami Springs along the canals.

2. **Yellow-crowned Night-Heron**—Commonly seen in salt marshes in the evening hours. Probably easiest to find at ponds in Everglades National Park or on beaches and marshes along the Gulf Coast.

3. **White Ibis**—Common resident of marshes and swamps throughout. For example, you can't miss it at Eco Pond at Flamingo in the evening.

4. **Glossy Ibis**—Resident of wet prairies and marshes throughout. Not as common as White Ibis. Best location is along Highway 70 on Day 5.

5. **Roseate Spoonbill**—Will be seen at numerous locations. Usually a cinch at Eco Pond at Flamingo or Ding Darling National Wildlife Refuge on Sanibel.

6. **Wood Stork**—Common throughout. Should see at Everglades National Park, Tamiami Trail, Corkscrew Swamp Sanctuary, and other locations.

7. **American Swallow-tailed Kite**—Easy to locate in Everglades National Park, along the Tamiami Trail, and at Corkscrew.

8. **Snail Kite**—Populations apparently shift to find snail-rich areas. Reliable north of Tamiami Trail in the 4 miles just west of the Miccosukee Restaurant. Another good spot is the landfill at West Palm Beach on Day 5. If this spot fails to produce, try Loxahatchee National Wildlife Refuge, also on Day 5.

9. **Short-tailed Hawk**—Can be located with patience just outside the entrance to Everglades National Park. Also, along Highway 29 around Copeland just off Tamiami Trail.

10. **Purple Gallinule**—Small numbers winter in South Florida. Most likely on the Anhinga Trail at Everglades National Park or at Loxahatchee National Wildlife Refuge. Seen frequently on small marshy ponds along Highway 29 north of Copeland.

11. **Limpkin**—Best locations are along Tamiami Trail and at Loxahatchee National Wildlife Refuge.

12. **Wilson's Plover**—Fairly common in coastal areas, especially on the Gulf Coast. Your best chances are on Day 3 and Day 4 on Sanibel and in St. Petersburg.

13. **Piping Plover**—Uncommon on sandy beaches throughout coastal Florida. Best bet is along the causeway to Sanibel Island on Day 3. There are other good locations in St. Petersburg on Day 4.

14. **American Oystercatcher**—Common on both coasts, but becoming increasingly uncommon the farther south you go. Best chances will be the causeway to Sanibel Island and the beaches in the St. Petersburg area.

15. **Royal Tern**—Easy to locate in any beach area. On this trip it will be the most common tern.

Probable Species
(continued)

Laughing Gull
Bonaparte's Gull
Ring-billed Gull
Herring Gull
Gull-billed Tern
Caspian Tern
Forster's Tern
Black Skimmer
Rock Dove
White-winged Dove
Mourning Dove
Common Ground-Dove
Eastern Screech-Owl
Great Horned Owl
Ruby-throated
    Hummingbird
Belted Kingfisher
Red-headed
    Woodpecker
**Red-bellied
    Woodpecker
Yellow-bellied
    Sapsucker**
Downy Woodpecker
Northern Flicker
Pileated Woodpecker
Eastern Phoebe
Great Crested
    Flycatcher
Eastern Kingbird
Purple Martin
Tree Swallow
Barn Swallow
Blue Jay
American Crow
Carolina Wren
House Wren
Ruby-crowned Kinglet
Blue-gray Gnatcatcher
Eastern Bluebird
Hermit Thrush
American Robin
Gray Catbird
Northern Mockingbird
Brown Thrasher
American Pipit
Cedar Waxwing
Loggerhead Shrike
European Starling
White-eyed Vireo
Solitary Vireo
Orange-crowned
    Warbler
Northern Parula
Yellow-rumped
    Warbler
Black-and-white
    Warbler
Ovenbird
Common Yellowthroat
Northern Cardinal
Rufous-sided Towhee
Chipping Sparrow
Field Sparrow
Savannah Sparrow
Grasshopper Sparrow
Song Sparrow
Swamp Sparrow
Red-winged Blackbird

16. **Eurasian Collared-Dove**—The center of population used to be in Homestead, but the species is spreading quickly in the greater Miami area. James Archer Park in Homestead is always good. It is established in the St. Petersburg and Clearwater areas, too.

17. **Budgerigar**—Primary location is Bradenton north to Tarpon Springs. Watch for it in mixed flocks with European Starlings. Check near beaches in St. Petersburg area. This species is declining.

18. **Monk Parakeet**—Best current location is in trees on the front lawn of Fair Haven Nursing Home in Miami Springs, just a short distance north of Miami International Airport (see inset map). Also found in St. Petersburg/Clearwater area.

19. **Canary-winged Parakeet**—This bird may actually be two distinct species rather than one. The birds shown in most field guides (*versicolurus*) have an obvious white wing-patch, but there are as many, if not more, of the birds in the field that do not have this white patch (*chiriri*). The variety with the white wing patch seems to be declining. Many of the birds found around Coconut Grove have this wing-patch, while birds seen in the Miami Springs area are almost exclusively of the variety without the wing-patch. Some of the better locations to see this bird are along Bay Shore Drive at dawn in the Dinner Key Auditorium area, the parking lot at Parrot Jungle, Matheson Hammock County Park, and Miami Springs.

20. **Smooth-billed Ani**—The Bailey Tract of Ding Darling National Wildlife Refuge and Loxahatchee National Wildlife Refuge are good locations. Eco Pond at Flamingo has been a reliable spot.

21. **Barn Owl**—Easiest to locate by driving Highway 27 from Florida City to Everglades National Park well after dark and using a spotlight on fence-posts and utility poles.

22. **Burrowing Owl**—Check the south side of Miami International Airport (Day 1). There are also several good locations in the Lake Placid and Okeechobee areas (see Days 4 and 5).

23. **Barred Owl**—Easy to find in daylight hours. Common at Corkscrew Swamp Sanctuary and Mahogany Hammock in Everglades National Park.

24. **Red-cockaded Woodpecker**—The small stand of pines near Old Venus has been a good place for years. Other sites to the north are covered in *A Birder's Guide to Florida.*

25. **Florida Scrub-Jay**—Fairly common in central Florida, at a number of disjunct locations of low-growing oak scrub. Two suggestions are Archbold Biological Station (along Highway 70) and Jonathan Dickinson State Park.

26. **Fish Crow**—Common in a large part of the trip area. Usually easy to locate by its raspy nasal call, which is quite different from that of American Crow.

27. **Red-whiskered Bulbul**—Best spot is vicinity of Royal Palms Tennis Courts at SW 98th Street and SW 72nd Avenue in Kendall.

28. **Pine Warbler**—Common resident in pine forests throughout. Long Pine Key Campground in Everglades National Park and Old Venus pinewoods area are both good locations.

29. **Prairie Warbler**—Common resident of mangrove swamps. Easy to find in Everglades National Park and Ding Darling National Wildlife Refuge.

30. **Palm Warbler**—Common throughout; difficult to miss.

31. **Bachman's Sparrow**—Can be located at pine woods near Old Venus. They respond readily to a tape of their call.

32. **Boat-tailed Grackle**—Abundant; no way to miss it.

33. **Spot-breasted Oriole**—Currently limited to suburban areas, particularly around Miami and Fort Lauderdale. You might run into it in Miami Springs, Coconut Grove, or Matheson Hammock. Or in the 6900 block of SW 96th street in Kendall.

Note: With luck you will see all 33 key species.

Possible Species
(continued)

Yellow-throated Warbler
American Redstart
Northern Waterthrush
Louisiana Waterthrush
Wilson's Warbler
Indigo Bunting
Painted Bunting
Vesper Sparrow
Lark Sparrow
Shiny Cowbird
Baltimore Oriole

Note: You will probably see 6 birds on the possible list.

Remotely Possible Species
Total of 34 Species
Greater Flamingo
American Black Duck
White-cheeked Pintail
Hooded Merganser
Masked Duck
White-tailed Kite
Swainson's Hawk
Yellow Rail
Black Rail
Ruff
American Woodcock
Lesser Black-backed Gull
Great Black-backed Gull
Roseate Tern
Common Tern
Zenaida Dove
Key West Quail-Dove
Mangrove Cuckoo
Short-eared Owl
Least Flycatcher
La Sagra's Flycatcher
Western Kingbird
Bahama Swallow
Cliff Swallow
Black-whiskered Vireo
Stripe-headed Tanager
Clay-colored Sparrow
Salt-marsh Sharp-tailed Sparrow
Seaside Sparrow
Lincoln's Sparrow
White-throated Sparrow
White-crowned Sparrow
Bronzed Cowbird
Bullock's Oriole

Note: You will probably be lucky to see 2 of the species on the remotely possible list. Some are extremely rare and are worth spending a lot of time on.

Itinerary

Note: Trip begins and ends in Miami.

Day 1 — Miami, Miami Springs, Kendall, Homestead, and Everglades National Park

Get an early start to Miami Springs. Take the 826 (Palmetto) Expressway to the N.W. 36th Street exit eastbound. Continue east for about 2 miles and turn left onto Curtiss Parkway. Watch for Fair Haven Nursing Home on the right. Monk Parakeets nest in the trees both in front of the nursing home and in the wide median of Curtiss Parkway. Their huge bulky nests are easy to locate, and the birds easy to see.

Spot-breasted Oriole may also be seen in this neighborhood, and by driving the streets you should be able to locate Canary-winged Parakeet (*chiriri*, or green flight-feathered form). *A Birder's Guide to Florida* gives directions to other sites in the Miami Springs area.

When you finish in Miami Springs, you can work your way around to the southwest corner of the airport if you would like to see Burrowing Owls. Where Milam Dairy Road swings around the west end of the runway and where Perimeter Road runs along the south end of the airport, there are at least four traditional burrow sites.

Then drive eastward to U.S. Highway 1 and turn south. Pass the exit for Key Biscayne, then exit onto South Miami Boulevard, which soon becomes South Bayshore Drive. Check the palm trees that line Pan American Drive to the City Hall on Dinner Key. Canary-winged Parakeets use these palms to roost and are easy to see at dawn and dusk. You may arrive here too late for the parakeets; if so, take Main Highway (Ingraham Highway) south from Coconut Grove for about 2 miles, turn left at Le Jeune Road, and then go around the traffic circle to Old Cutler Road. Follow Old Cutler Road south for about 2 miles to Matheson Hammock County Park, another good spot for Canary-winged Parakeet and Spot-breasted Oriole. Hill Mynas (not on the ABA list, but interesting nonetheless) have hung around this park for a number of years.

If you still want Canary-winged Parakeet (*versicolurus*, or white wing-patch variety), continue on Old Cutler Road to Red Road and turn right onto S.W. 112th Street. A short stop at the Parrot Jungle parking lot often produces free-flying Canary-winged Parakeets (both types). Try your hand at identifying some of the other free-flying parrots that you might see. Hurricane Andrew in 1992 released untold numbers of cage-birds, and the reason for some to congregate here is obvious.

When you leave Parrot Jungle, drive west on Killian Drive to S.W. 72nd Avenue and turn right onto S.W. 98th Street. The tennis courts at this intersection are the center of Red-whiskered Bulbul territory. Drive the neighborhood streets looking for wire-perched bulbuls. If you pass by the 6900 block of S.W. 96th Street, check feeding stations for resident Spot-breasted Orioles. You can pick up Palm Warbler in the neighborhood; it is often seen feeding on the ground like a sparrow.

When you leave Kendall, continue south to Homestead, the center of South Florida's population of Eurasian Collared-Doves. If you do not see one sitting on a highline, go to James Archer Park, where it is very common. Stay alert for Shiny Cowbirds in this area; they are often found in or around Homestead (e.g., near S.W. 209th Street).

Follow signs to Everglades National Park, but don't rush right in. The entry road is one of the best places to see Short-tailed Hawk, so pull over and spend a little time searching for this often hard-to-locate raptor. Scan the distant trees for perching hawks, and check all hawk-sized birds flying over the hammock.

After a quick stop at the visitor center to get oriented, head straight over to bird the Anhinga Trail. The elevated boardwalk loops through a small area of the swamp, giving you fantastic portraits of its namesake and numerous other wading birds, all so accustomed to human traffic that you can get very close for a good look. On your walk you will probably find Purple Gallinule, Least Bittern, Smooth-billed Ani, Boat-tailed Grackle, and wintering warblers, too.

Gumbo Limbo Trail is usually good for Northern Parula, Ovenbird, and other wintering warblers. Watch overhead throughout this area for Short-tailed Hawk, frequently seen here.

Stop at Long Pine Key Campground to camp for the night. Resident Pine Warblers are fairly easy to find here.

At dusk and after dark drive the roads, both in the park and between the park and Florida City, searching for owls and nightjars. A hand-held spotlight or powerful flashlight will help you to illuminate utility and fence poles where Barn and Barred Owls as well as Great Horned Owl and Eastern Screech-Owl might be perched. Whip-poor-wills and Chuck-will's-widow are also possible at this time of year.

Day 2 — Everglades National Park

You will be surprised at how much time you can spend checking out each of Everglades National Park's birding sites. Cover Paurotis Pond, Nine Mile Pond, and West Lake in early morning. These ponds can be reliable for a number of the key species: Anhinga, Yellow-crowned Night-Heron, White Ibis, Roseate Spoonbill, American Swallow-tailed Kite, Purple Gallinule, and Limpkin. Numerous other herons, egrets, coots, and ducks will pleasantly distract you.

Throughout the day keep in mind that White-cheeked Pintail, Black Rail, White-crowned Pigeon, Mangrove Cuckoo, and Shiny Cowbird have all been seen at this season, if only occasionally.

Not every birder tackles Snake Bight Trail, but you should plan to hike the 2-mile path to the boardwalk on Florida Bay. You will find many shorebirds and waders, but more importantly this is one of the few locations in the United States that is accessible without a boat where you might see Greater Flamingo. It is worth the effort to carry your spotting scope with you. (Be sure to use a mighty insect repellent prior to this hike.)

Mrazek and Coot Bay Ponds are both excellent for herons and egrets. Yellow-crowned Night-Herons are seen here in early morning or late evening. Bear Lake Trail holds wintering warblers, including common Northern Parulas and Ovenbirds.

Limpkin
Gail Diane Yovanovich

At Flamingo be sure to visit Eco Pond (another great spot for mosquitoes). A viewing platform and the path circling this small pond give you many vantage points from which to glimpse its many resident birds. White Ibises and Roseate Spoonbills congregate here in numbers, mainly in the evening. Smooth-billed Ani might be found teetering around in the small trees. Scan all blackbird flocks working the lawns for Shiny Cowbird, a good possibility at Flamingo.

Depending on the time of day, either stay at the motel (advance reservation recommended), camp at Flamingo, or bird your way back to Long Pine Key Campground for the night.

Day 3—Tamiami Trail, Corkscrew Swamp Sanctuary, and Sanibel Island

Leave Everglades National Park early, return to Homestead, and take Highway 997 north to Highway 41 (Tamiami Trail). Follow Highway 41 westward across South Florida.

The Tamiami Trail and Tamiami Canal run side-by-side, making it convenient to spot most of South Florida's waders as you cruise along sandwiched between tractor-trailers. You can pull well off the road practically anywhere, though, and it's a good idea to do so if you want good looks at White Ibis, Glossy Ibis, Wood Stork, and Limpkin; the latter is always present but is not easy to find.

To find wintering Snail Kites, you need to budget more time and look in the right spots. Just past the intersection for Shark Valley you will see the Miccosukee Restaurant. The next 3.5 to 4 miles to the west are prime Snail Kite viewing areas. Stop anywhere along the highway to scan the everglades to the north thoroughly. Snail Kites will be found either flying over the marsh or perching in the low scrubby trees. A spotting scope is a real asset when a perching bird is located, but even then the heat waves may distort your view.

One other worthwhile birding stop is Kirby S. Storter Wayside Park, which is usually dependable for wintering warblers.

At the Highway 29 intersection, turn north for a one-hour drive to Corkscrew Swamp Sanctuary, a National Audubon Society property. This drive can be productive for several of the key species. Short-tailed Hawk is often seen, especially in the Copeland area. Wood Stork, American Swallow-tailed Kite, and Fish Crow can show up anywhere, and Purple Gallinule is often spotted in the small ponds and marshy areas along the highway.

Corkscrew Swamp Sanctuary is designed to give its many visitors intimate looks at swamp life in South Florida. The boardwalk and trails wind through pine woods, too, where you can study woodpeckers, warblers, and many other species. You might find Yellow-crowned Night-Heron, Wood Stork, or Limpkin on your own, but ask the board-walk-docents to point out a perched Barred Owl.

Tear yourself away, drive to Fort Myers, and then take Highway 867 to Sanibel Island. Bird the causeway to the island for shorebirds, terns, and gulls. Wilson's and Piping Plovers, American Oystercatcher, and Royal Tern should be easy to locate among the many other species present.

The first stop on Sanibel Island is the Bailey Tract of J.N. Ding Darling National Wildlife Refuge, where the attractions are Smooth-billed Ani, small landbirds, and rails. If you have decided to spend the night on Sanibel, make those arrangements now before starting the wildlife drive at the main tract of Ding Darling; motels at this season fill quickly at Sanibel.

The spectacle of herons, egrets, ibises, and Roseate Spoonbills sailing in to their nighttime roosts might make you neglect to look for small passerines, but they are here, too. Prairie Warbler is easy to find; other wintering warblers (if you're lucky, Cape May Warbler) and a variety of sparrows are dependable.

If you're not staying on Sanibel, you will find a choice of motels in Fort Myers. Campers can try Koreshan State Park, 17 miles south of Fort Myers, just off Highway 41.

Day 4 — St. Petersburg and Highlands Hammock State Park

Using Interstate 75 to avoid traffic, make the two-and-a-half-hour drive north to Interstate 275 and St. Petersburg. The primary purpose of a trip to St. Petersburg is to see Budgerigar. This established but declining introduced cage-bird flocks with European Starlings and is often found along Highway 699 between St. Petersburg Beach and Clearwater. There should also be Monk Parakeets and Eurasian Collared-Doves along 699.

All of the beach areas are likely spots for shorebirds, including Wilson's and Piping Plovers, American Oystercatcher, and Royal Tern. In addition, Lesser and Great Black-backed Gulls are seen occasionally at St. Petersburg Beach.

Return south on Interstate 275, and near Bradenton take Highway 64 east to the Avon Park area. At this point you can find a motel in Avon Park or Sebring or camp at Highlands Hammock State Park just west of Sebring. This park is good for Pine Warbler and sometimes for Brown-headed Nuthatch.

You should have some daylight left and you are only a few miles from a good location for Burrowing Owl. Approximately 5 miles south of

Sebring, take Highway 98 east around Lake Istokpoga, turn south onto Cow House Road, and then back west on Boat Ramp Road. Scope the field to the northwest of this intersection for owls. If you miss them, check *A Birder's Guide to Florida* for other nearby locations. Return to your motel or campsite for the night.

Day 5 — Highway 70, Old Venus, and Loxahatchee National Wildlife Refuge

Take Highway 27 south to where it intersects with Highway 70. You can turn west onto U.S. 70 for 1.0 mile to Old SR 8, where you turn left to reach Archbold Biological Station, 1.8 miles down old SR 8. Archbold has a self-guided nature trail (open weekdays only), where you can find Florida Scrub-Jay. (Until very recently, this bird was considered a subspecies of the Scrub Jay of the West.)

You can travel east along Highway 70, and for the next 30 miles you will pass through areas productive for White Ibis, Glossy Ibis, Wood Stork, Crested Caracara, and Burrowing Owl. If you still need any of these species, take this detour and then return to this intersection. You should also be aware that this stretch is a another good place to see Florida Scrub-Jay.

After this short side trip, or if you skip it, go south on Highway 27 to SR-731. Turn west through Venus to Old Venus and then north to the pine woods northwest of Old Venus (see inset map).

This area has been consistent for Swallow-tailed Kite, Red-cockaded Woodpecker, Pine Warbler, and Bachman's Sparrow. Stay alert for Brown-headed Nuthatch since this is a good area for it also, but not reliably so. A sure way to locate Bachman's Sparrow is to use a tape of its call. *Use it sparingly, however.*

Leave Old Venus and return to Highway 27. Take Highway 27 south and then east to Belle Glade. Take Highway 441 east from Belle Glade for 30 miles. At this point Highway 441 turns south toward the entrance to Loxahatchee National Wildlife Refuge. Prior to turning south, there are two other options which you can consider. First, you might want to make a side trip to Jonathan Dickinson State Park (7 miles north of Jupiter on Highway 1). Finding a Red-cockaded Woodpecker now is a long-shot (it used to nest here), but this is another chance to see Florida Scrub-Jays. Second, if you missed Snail Kite, it is only a short drive into West Palm Beach, where they can be found at a landfill located at the west end of 45th Street (North Jog Road and 45th Street intersect on the edge of the landfill). Park outside the landfill and view the kites from there. Local birders say that this location is best at dusk.

After the side trip, return to Highway 441 and drive south to Loxa-hatchee National Wildlife Refuge. Here you will have a good shot at several key species; besides, it is the most consistent place in South Florida to find a rare Masked Duck. Of course, you would have to be *very* lucky to locate a Masked Duck, but the possibility exists. There are two nature trails through the area, both worth a visit. Purple Gallinule, Limpkin, Smooth-billed Ani, Barred Owl, and numerous other species are regularly seen here. Snail Kite is possible.

After birding the refuge, you can drive south to the Miami area for the night.

Day 6 — Extra Day

This day should be used to locate any key species that you have missed. If your list is already complete, bird the Bill Baggs Cape Florida State Park on Key Biscayne. It's an interesting spot, where West Indian vagrants have been found with regularity. You might also consider using the rest of the day to chase exotics in the Miami area; most of them will probably be "countable" sooner or later.

Trip concludes in Miami in the evening.

Bird Numbers This Trip

	Potential	Expected	Actual
Key Species	33	33	
Probable Species	132	132	
Possible Species	50	6	
Remotely Possible Species	34	2	
Totally Unexpected Species	?	1	
TOTAL	249	174	

Cumulative List

Total key and probable species seen after 5 trips.

Previous trips	304	species
South Florida in Winter	46	species
TOTAL	350	species

This Trip's Mileage and Expenses

Approximate miles traveled, Miami to Miami: 1,025

- Fuel: $74; sharing $37 $_____
- Lodging: 2 nights at motels, 4 nights
  camping $110; sharing $55 $_____
- Food: Ice-chest/supermarket for most meals - $72 $_____
  *The total per person cost for the above items with a companion
  to share expenses should be less than $165.*
- Add to this car rental expenses, if any: $_____
- Add to this your expenses to/from Miami: $_____
  This will give you a good idea of the cost of this trip.
- TOTAL $_____

Personal Notes

_____

_____

_____

_____

_____

_____

_____

_____

_____

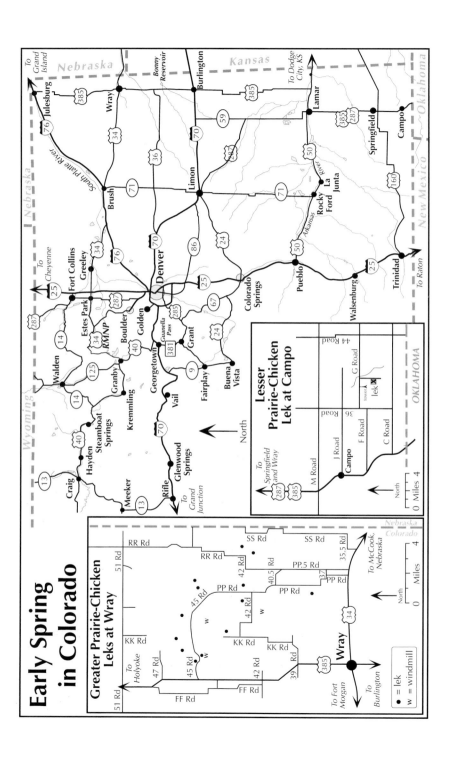

Early Spring in Colorado

Greater Prairie-Chicken Leks at Wray

● = lek
w = windmill

Lesser Prairie-Chicken Lek at Campo

Chapter 6

EARLY SPRING IN COLORADO

Late March or Early April—5 Days

General

There is no way to predict whether Colorado's fickle springtime weather will snow all over your carefully crafted trip, but don't let that possibility dissuade you from embarking on this unique Colorado adventure. The grouse that you are looking for will go right on with their strutting and displaying, despite a thin layer of snow.

Breeding populations of 4 species of grouse are active at this season. The best time to view them on their leks is at sunrise. The catch is that each species is located in a different region of this large state, so you will be spending substantial time moving between these scattered sites.

Although the trip is planned around grouse locations, your travels will take you through prime areas for several other species, and you will have sufficient daylight to search for them. With luck and cooperative weather conditions, you should be able to find all 12 of the key species targeted.

Many bird tour companies offer spring grouse trips to Colorado. Though this choice is not as economical as making an independent trip, it relieves you of handling the somewhat complicated logistics. Another option is to check well in advance with Denver Field Ornithologists (DFO Field Trip Coordinator, Zoology Department, Denver Museum of Natural History, 2001 Colorado Boulevard, Denver, CO 80205) and Colorado Field Ornithologists to see if their inexpensive prairie-chicken and grouse trips will fit into your travel plans. The Colorado Division of Wildlife runs Greater Prairie-Chicken and Sage Grouse tours in conjunction with the Watchable Wildlife Program. For further information on these CDOW tours, write to Prairie-Chicken Tours, c/o Wray Museum, 205 East 3rd, Wray, CO 80758, phone 970/332-5063 or Sage Grouse Tours, c/o North Park Chamber of Commerce, 491 Main Street, Walden, CO 80480, phone 970/723-4600. Alternately, *A Birder's Guide to Colorado* will give you information to find the leks in Wray and Campo—*please note*

Probable Species
Total of 77 Species
Pied-billed Grebe
Eared Grebe
Double-crested
 Cormorant
Great Blue Heron
Snow Goose
Canada Goose
Green-winged Teal
Mallard
Northern Pintail
Blue-winged Teal
Cinnamon Teal
Northern Shoveler
Gadwall
American Wigeon
Canvasback
Redhead
Ring-necked Duck
Lesser Scaup
Common Goldeneye
Bufflehead
Common Merganser
Ruddy Duck
Northern Harrier
Red-tailed Hawk
Ferruginous Hawk
Rough-legged Hawk
Golden Eagle
American Kestrel
Prairie Falcon
Ring-necked Pheasant
Lesser Prairie-Chicken
American Coot
Killdeer
American Avocet
Greater Yellowlegs
Common Snipe
Ring-billed Gull
California Gull
Herring Gull
Rock Dove
Mourning Dove
Great Horned Owl
Belted Kingfisher
Downy Woodpecker
Hairy Woodpecker
Northern Flicker
Horned Lark
Gray Jay
Steller's Jay
Blue Jay
Western Scrub-Jay
Black-billed Magpie
American Crow
Common Raven
Black-capped
 Chickadee
Pygmy Nuthatch
American Dipper
Mountain Bluebird
American Robin
American Pipit
Cedar Waxwing
Loggerhead Shrike
European Starling
**American Tree
 Sparrow**
Song Sparrow

that the maps on the previous page update and correct those found in the *Birder's Guide*.

This trip includes Denver, Golden Gate Canyon State Park, Guanella Pass, Hayden, Arapaho National Wildlife Refuge, Cameron Pass, Cache la Poudre River, Fort Collins, Wray, Campo, and Red Rocks Park.

Note: Wray is only a half-day drive from Grand Island, Nebraska (see Chapter 20, Trip B).

Birdfinding Guides

A Birder's Guide to Colorado by James A. Lane and Harold R. Holt (1988) covers most of the areas visited on this trip. (It is currently being updated.)

Rare Bird Alert Number

Statewide 303/424-2144

Special Equipment

Come prepared to dress in layers, some of which include the warmest clothes that you own. Snowshoes are not essential, but could be very helpful at Guanella Pass. At this time of year tire chains or studded tires are advisable and are a must for Guanella Pass. If you are driving your own vehicle to Colorado, bring some cold-weather survival gear, including jumper cables, a shovel, and some sort of traction device or material, such as sand.

Bird tapes will probably be useful in seeking Boreal Owl and possibly for Northern Pygmy-Owl. You will find many places to use a spotting scope if you bring one.

Accommodations

Motels are available throughout the trip area. Prices range from $40 to $60 for two, depending on the area. Camping is not practical in this season.

Key Species — Total of 12 species

1. **White-tailed Ptarmigan**—Guanella Pass is the best spot to see this species in winter plumage, and finding it can be very easy or very time-consuming.

2. **Sage Grouse**—Easy to see at the viewing area 17 miles southwest of Walden. Best at dawn but can also be seen at dusk.

3. **Greater Prairie-Chicken**—Can be located at any one of several leks in the Wray area. See the note in the General section of this chapter concerning access to these leks.

4. **Sharp-tailed Grouse**—Leks for this species are located near Hayden in northwestern Colorado. It wouldn't hurt to check with the Colorado Division of Wildlife staff for the best current location.

5. **Baird's Sandpiper**—Easy to locate around ponds and lakes on the eastern plains in April (less likely in March). Should be found while you are driving between prairie-chicken leks.

6. **Northern Pygmy-Owl**—Can be located in daylight hours along the Cache la Poudre River. Also may be lured out with a tape in several areas, including Golden Gate Canyon State Park. Often found near running water in mountains in winter.

7. **Three-toed Woodpecker**—Best chances on this trip are Guanella Pass and Golden Gate Canyon State Park. Inquire about recent forest-fire sites (one to seven years old) in conifers close to the road. If this method fails, and time permits, you might try going south to the Pueblo area. (See *A Birder's Guide to Colorado* for locations in the "Wet Mountains Loop" section. A snow-covered road and trail may require a rigorous, steep, and intimidating 1-mile or 2-mile hike. It would be wise to check weather, road, and birding conditions beforehand.)

8. **Clark's Nutcracker**—Common; should be seen on the road to Guanella Pass, at Golden Gate Canyon State Park, and on the Cameron Pass route.

9. **Mountain Chickadee**—Look for this relatively common bird at Golden Gate Canyon State Park,

---

Probable Species
(continued)

White-crowned
   Sparrow
Harris's Sparrow
Dark-eyed Junco
Red-winged Blackbird
Western Meadowlark
Common Grackle
Pine Grosbeak
House Finch
Pine Siskin
American Goldfinch
Evening Grosbeak
House Sparrow

Note: The species in **boldface** appear no more than four times in the itineraries as *key* or *probable* species. Watch for them on this trip. As in the other chapters, assume that you will see all of the probable species. You will see only 2 additional species not seen on previous trips.

Possible Species
Total of 46 Species
Horned Grebe
Western Grebe
Clark's Grebe
Black-crowned
   Night-Heron
Red-breasted Merganser
Turkey Vulture
Bald Eagle
Sharp-shinned Hawk
Cooper's Hawk
Swainson's Hawk
Blue Grouse
Wild Turkey
Northern Bobwhite
Scaled Quail
Sandhill Crane
Mountain Plover
Lesser Yellowlegs
Greater Roadrunner
Eastern Screech-Owl
Western Screech-Owl
Long-eared Owl
Short-eared Owl
Lewis's Woodpecker
Red-naped Sapsucker
Ladder-backed
   Woodpecker
Say's Phoebe
Tree Swallow
Violet-green Swallow
Chihuahuan Raven
Bushtit
Red-breasted Nuthatch
White-breasted
   Nuthatch
Brown Creeper
Rock Wren

Possible Species
(continued)

Canyon Wren
Golden-crowned
    Kinglet
Townsend's Solitaire
Spotted Towhee
Canyon Towhee
Swamp Sparrow
White-throated Sparrow
McCown's Longspur
Yellow-headed
    Blackbird
Brewer's Blackbird
Brown-capped
    Rosy-Finch
Red Crossbill

Note: How many of
the possible species
you actually see will
depend to some degree
on whether or not you
go to southeastern
Colorado for Lesser
Prairie-Chicken. Some
of the possible species
are southeastern
Colorado specialties
(e.g., Greater Road-
runner, Ladder-backed
Woodpecker, Chihua-
huan Raven, and
Canyon Towhee). You
will probably see at
least 7 of these listed
possible species.

**Remotely Possible
Species**
Total of 39 Species

Common Loon
Tundra Swan
Greater White-fronted
    Goose
Ross's Goose
Wood Duck
Barrow's Goldeneye
Hooded Merganser
Northern Goshawk
Merlin
Peregrine Falcon
Bonaparte's Gull
Thayer's Gull
Glaucous Gull
Black-legged Kittiwake
Barn Owl
Boreal Owl
Northern Saw-whet
    Owl
Red-bellied
    Woodpecker
Yellow-bellied
    Sapsucker
Eastern Phoebe
Pinyon Jay
Plain Titmouse
Bewick's Wren
Winter Wren

along the Cache la Poudre River, and anywhere in the mountains or among conifers.

10. **Gray-crowned Rosy-Finch**—Look at George-town at feeders, on the road to Guanella Pass, or at Red Rocks Park. Watch for the gray-faced Hep-burn's form, also.

11. **Black Rosy-Finch**—May be seen at feeders at Georgetown or at Red Rocks Park. Much less com-mon than the Gray-crowned.

12. **Cassin's Finch**—Often easy to locate at Gold-en Gate Canyon State Park, or at lower elevations. Usually present at picnic areas and campgrounds between Steamboat Springs and the Highway 14 turn-off to Walden.

Note: If you find Three-toed Woodpecker and Black Rosy-Finch, you should see all of the 12 key species.

Itinerary

Note: Trip begins and ends in Denver.

Day 1 — Denver, Golden Gate Canyon State Park, and Guanella Pass

Get an early start from Denver. Go west on Interstate 70 and take Exit 265 to Golden. Drive north from Golden on Highway 93 to Golden Gate Canyon Road, then turn west to the park entrance. (See Chapter 13 for an inset map of the park.) The distance from Denver to the park is about 30 miles. Birds of special interest that occur in this park in-clude Blue Grouse, Western Screech-Owl, Northern Pygmy-Owl, Three-toed Woodpecker, Gray Jay, Clark's Nutcracker, Black-billed Magpie, Mountain Chickadee, Pygmy Nuthatch, American Dipper, Bo-hemian Waxwing, Northern Shrike, Cassin's Finch, Red Crossbill, and Evening Grosbeak.

A tape of Northern Pygmy-Owl could be tried *sparingly* here; this owl is frequently active in day-light hours and can be fairly easy to locate in the winter and early spring.

Return to I-70 and drive west to Georgetown (Exit 228; 42 miles west of Denver). In this season both

Gray-crowned and Black Rosy-Finches might be located by driving the streets of this small town and watching for swirling flocks among conifers and at bird feeders. Gray-crowned is usually numerous and easy to locate, while Black will be present only in small numbers. Brown-capped Rosy-Finch is sometimes present but should not be expected.

Take Rose Street out the west side of town to Road 381, the route to Guanella Pass. Be aware of the possibility of severe winter weather conditions at this time of year, including snow on the upper parts of this road. Clear Lake Campgroundand Guanella Campgroundare both worth a quick check. The 2 miles between the upper campground and the summit are usually good for Gray Jay, Clark's Nutcracker, and Pine Grosbeak, with both crossbills remotely possible. At Guanella Pass drive up to a quarter-mile past the parking area to scan the hillside on the east side of the road. If you do not see White-tailed Ptarmigans feeding on the low willows here, park at the summit, bundle up, and take the trail up the gentle hill to the southeast. *A Birder's Guide to Colorado* should be consulted for search strategies.

Marsh Wren
Ruby-crowned Kinglet
Curve-billed Thrasher
Bohemian Waxwing
Northern Shrike
Yellow-rumped Warbler
Rufous-crowned Sparrow
Vesper Sparrow
Lapland Longspur
Chestnut-collared Longspur
Rusty Blackbird
Great-tailed Grackle
Brown-headed Cowbird
Purple Finch
Common Redpoll

Note: How many of the remotely possible species you will see will depend, again, on whether or not you go to southeastern Colorado to see Lesser Prairie-Chicken since several of them can be seen only in the southeastern corner of the state. On any trip at this time of year you will probably see only 3 of these species.

After seeing White-tailed Ptarmigan, return to I-70 and drive *east* approximately 5 miles to Exit 223. Get on U.S. Highway 40 for the drive to Hayden (about 160 miles). There are numerous good birding areas along Highway 40; check those you can. Overnight at nearby Craig if you can't find a room in Hayden.

Day 2 — Craig, Hayden, and Sage Grouse viewing area near Coalmont

Start well before daylight. From Hayden drive north on Road 80. Turn left onto Routt County Road 76 after 0.8 mile. Routt CR 76 becomes Moffatt CR 36 in 8.2 miles. After 3.0 miles it reverts to Routt CR 76. At Routt CR 56 (0.8 mile) turn right. At the junction with 74 Road (4.0 miles) you will see a grassy hill just ahead on the left. The Sharp-tailed Grouse lek covers this knoll. *Stay in your vehicle to view and photograph the grouse. This will be a heavily visited lek, and your cooperation is vital to make sure that the birds do not desert it.*

After marveling at the displaying Sharp-tailed Grouse, return to Highway 40 and drive east. Beyond Steamboat Springs you will enter Routt National Forest, where several picnic areas and campgrounds on the approach to Rabbit Ears Pass might give you Pine Grosbeak, Cassin's Finch, Red Crossbill, and Evening Grosbeak, among other species. Turn left onto Highway 14, which winds down into North Park, one of Colorado's vast intermountain valleys so important to migratory waterfowl. In about 20 miles turn left onto County Road 26 and drive 1.6 miles west and 0.3 mile north to a Sage Grouse viewing area managed by the Colorado Division of Wildlife (follow the signs). This is probably the best place in Colorado to see Sage Grouse. The grouse can be observed at sunrise or sunset, but *please do not get out of your car for any reason and do not otherwise disturb the birds.* You should be at the viewing-area by 5 pm; from then until dark the grouse will be coming into the lek in good numbers. *After seeing the grouse leave quietly and make every effort not to disturb the birds.* (If you do not find signs pointing to the lek, you must ask for the location of the current public viewing-area when you arrive in Walden—locations may be changed occasionally.)

Overnight in Walden (17 miles northeast of the lek on Highway 14).

Day 3— Walden, Cameron Pass, Cache la Poudre River, and Fort Collins

If you missed seeing the Sage Grouse, be at the lek before daylight for a second chance. Otherwise, you might want to make the 6-mile loop drive through Arapaho National Wildlife Refuge. The entrance is 3.5 miles south of Walden on Highway 125. You will find an abundance of ducks and geese representing a wide array of species, all of them in snazzy breeding plumage. It's a wonderful show!

There have been recent records of Short-eared Owl in North Park, so keep your eyes open for them as you're driving around.

After making one or both of these side trips, return to Walden and head southeast on Highway 14. Twenty miles from Walden you will enter Colorado State Forest, and from this point to the summit of Cameron Pass you should try all the pull-outs and campgrounds for Boreal Owl. The owls are calling at this season, so the *judicious* use of a tape might produce a response. Boreals are year-round residents here, though they are not common. You might gladly settle for a heard-only Boreal Owl once you see the impossibility of chasing cross-country for a look at one you might hear. (Boreal Owls in the state have been found in mid- to high elevation mature spruce/fir or spruce/fir/Lodgepole Pine forests often near small meadows.)

Beyond Cameron Pass and down to Fort Collins, Highway 14 follows the Cache la Poudre River. You will want to stop at the many campgrounds and picnic areas on this scenic drive, because they are all good birding spots. Species to watch for along the road, other than Boreal Owl, are Northern Goshawk, Northern Pygmy-Owl, Three-toed Woodpecker, Gray Jay, Clark's Nutcracker, Mountain Chickadee, American Dipper, Northern Shrike, Pine Grosbeak, Red Crossbill, Common Redpoll, and Evening Grosbeak. The entire area, particularly along the river, can be reliable in the daytime for Northern Pygmy-Owl.

When you reach Fort Collins, take Highway 287 south to Loveland to pick up Highway 34 east to Brush (about 85 miles).

If you haven't made firm motel reservations for tonight, you need to decide whether you would rather drive the 85 miles to Wray tonight (in the dark) or spend part of the night in Brush and drive to Wray in the middle of the night (in the dark) to either meet your group or to arrive at a lek *before* dawn. Either way, it will be a near-sleepless night.

Day 4 — Wray and the Eastern Colorado Plains

If you arrive in Wray an hour before daylight without a Colorado chicken-tour reservation or without permission to enter private property to reach one of the leks, all may not be lost. Take Highway 385 north about 10 miles to 45 Road. Turn right onto 45 Road and listen for Greater Prairie-Chickens. There are six or seven known leks along this road. At least one of the leks is visible from the road, and with this much chicken action you should be able to see at least one bird even if you have to wait until their morning dance is over and they disperse. *A Birder's Guide to Colorado* gives directions to some of the leks. *All leks are on private property; bird only from the road.*

After you see Greater Prairie-Chicken, a decision must be made as to the next stop. If you didn't go birding in Oklahoma in January (Chapter 2), or missed Lesser Prairie-Chicken there, you will want to drive down to Campo in far southeastern Colorado for a sunrise Lesser Prairie-Chicken display. If you did not miss the chickens, you could return to Brush via Highway 34 and drive on to Denver on I-76. You might see Baird's Sandpiper around the ponds and lakes on this drive, but check *A Birder's Guide to Colorado* to learn about other enjoyable birding locales along the I-76/South Platte Rivercorridor.

If you missed Lesser Prairie-Chicken in Oklahoma, this is your last good opportunity to see it following the itineraries in this book.

To position yourself properly for tomorrow's activities, drive south on Highway 385 (approximately 217 miles) to Springfield. Baird's Sandpiper should be seen easily on this drive through the eastern Colorado prairie. If you have the energy, a birding stop at Bonny State Recreation Area (about 22 miles north of Burlington) is always worth the time.

Depending on where you are, overnight in Denver or in Springfield.

Day 5 — Campo – Lesser Prairie-Chicken Booming Grounds

It will take you at least an hour to drive the 38 miles from your Springfield motel to the Lesser Prairie-Chicken booming grounds. Plan to arrive at the lek-site about an hour before sunrise. Take Highway 385 south from Springfield for 22 miles to Campo. Midway through this tiny town a signpost marks J Road (you will need a flashlight to illuminate this sign). Turn left (east) onto J Road to 36 Road (8.0 miles). Turn right onto 36 Road to G Road (2.0 miles). Turn left onto G Road to a small culvert (4.0 miles). Just short of the culvert turn right through the wire-gate onto a sandy track which leads 1.3 miles to the lek. (Measure this last distance—the lek on the right side of the track is sometimes signed, sometimes not.) Park at the railroad ties and *stay in your car.* The birds are easily seen from the car and will flush if you open your door.

Return to Lamar via Highway 385, go west to Pueblo via Highway 50, and then north on I-25 to Denver. The total drive is about 310 miles. (See *A Birder's Guide to Colorado* for descriptions of many superb birding sites along this route back to Denver.)

If you do not take a side trip to Campo for Lesser Prairie-Chicken, Day 5 is an extra day to try for any key species that you may have missed. The Denver area has many excellent places to investigate. Red Rocks Park is a good location for Gray-crowned and Black Rosy-Finches, which roost in cavities in the rock formations. To reach it take Interstate 70 west to Exit 259; then take Highway 26 south less than 2 miles to the park entrance. If you go to Campo, this area can be checked on the way back to Denver if time and daylight allow.

The trip ends in Denver in the evening.

Bird Numbers This Trip

	Potential	Expected	Actual
Key Species	12	12	
Probable Species	77	77	
Possible Species	46	7	
Remotely Possible Species	39	3	
Totally Unexpected Species . . . . ?		0	
TOTAL	174	99	

Cumulative List

Total key and probable species after 6 trips

Previous trips . . . . 350 species
Spring Colorado Trip . . . . 14 species
TOTAL . . . . 364 species

This Trip's Mileage and Expenses

Approximate miles traveled, Denver to Denver: 1,300

- Fuel: $92; sharing $46 $_____
- Lodging: 6 nights at motels $270; shared $135 $_____
- Food: Using ice-chest/supermarket method
  for most meals, your food will cost less than $60 $_____
  *The total per person cost for the above items with a companion
  to share expenses should be less than $250.*
- Add to this car rental expenses, if any: $_____
- Add to this your expenses to/from Denver: $_____
  This will give you a good idea of the cost of this trip.
- TOTAL $_____

Personal Notes

_____

_____

_____

_____

_____

_____

_____

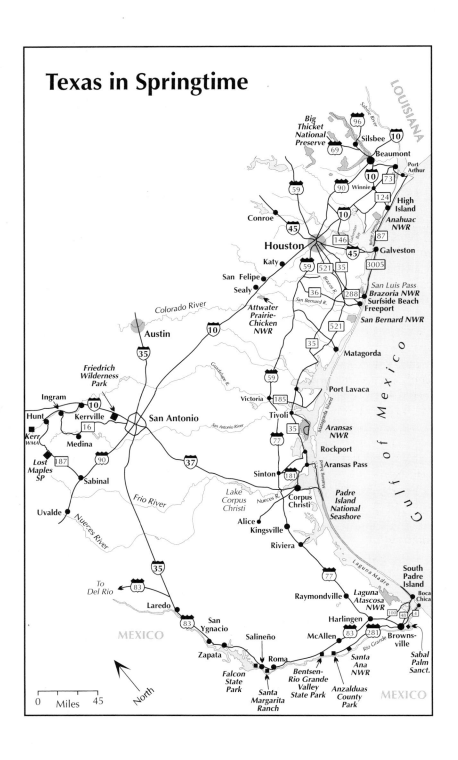

Texas in Springtime

Chapter 7

TEXAS IN SPRINGTIME

April—15 Days

General

Spring migration in Texas can be about as exhilarating as birding gets. Your objectives on this trip are to be in Texas at the statistically right time (dates falling between April 5 and April 28), to keep informed about how the migration is progressing through a network of informants or hotlines, and to find the most important migrants and residents in just over two weeks.

Even if this spring's migration is judged to be routine, this trip will be a highlight of your birding year. A few days at tiny High Island will usually provide you with killer looks at a minimum of 4 species of thrushes, 6 vireos, and 25 warblers, along with a exciting variety of other small landbirds. A day or two at Anahuac National Wildlife Refuge, Bolivar Peninsula, Galveston Island, Corpus Christi, or any number of other coastal locations will give you more waders, geese, ducks, rails, shorebirds, gulls, and terns than you can imagine.

In early April, the summer specialties of the Rio Grande Valley are all present, the Whooping Cranes are still at Aransas National Wildlife Refuge, and it is time for Cave Swallow, Black-capped Vireo, and Golden-cheeked Warbler to be at their most visible on the Edwards Plateau. In the pine forest north and east of Houston the same is true of Red-cockaded Woodpecker, Brown-headed Nuthatch, and Bachman's Sparrow.

This trip is designed to let you explore the best birding areas by following the 'normal' sequence of migration events described below. Hopefully the weather patterns will cooperate, but be flexible enough to alter your plans and be willing to use the 'extra day' on this itinerary to your best birding advantage.

You will visit High Island first for early warblers and then bird the beaches and migrant traps down the coast to Aransas. Arrive there no later than April 10 to assure seeing Whooping Cranes. You can then continue down the coast, bird the Lower Rio Grande Valley, and visit the Edwards Plateau for that area's specialties. Return to High Island at what

Probable Species
Total of 212 Species
Pied-billed Grebe
Eared Grebe
American White
Pelican
Brown Pelican
Double-crested
Cormorant
Neotropic Cormorant
Anhinga
American Bittern
Great Blue Heron
Great Egret
Snowy Egret
Little Blue Heron
Tricolored Heron
Reddish Egret
Cattle Egret
Green Heron
Black-crowned
Night-Heron
Yellow-crowned
Night-Heron
White Ibis
White-faced Ibis
Roseate Spoonbill
Wood Duck
Green-winged Teal
Mottled Duck
Mallard
Northern Pintail
Blue-winged Teal
Northern Shoveler
Gadwall
American Wigeon
Redhead
Lesser Scaup
Red-breasted Merganser
Ruddy Duck
Black Vulture
Turkey Vulture
Osprey
White-tailed Kite
Northern Harrier
Sharp-shinned Hawk
Harris's Hawk
Red-shouldered Hawk
Broad-winged Hawk
Swainson's Hawk
White-tailed Hawk
Red-tailed Hawk
Crested Caracara
American Kestrel
Plain Chachalaca
Wild Turkey
Northern Bobwhite
Scaled Quail
Sora
Purple Gallinule
Common Moorhen
American Coot
Black-bellied Plover
Snowy Plover
Wilson's Plover
Semipalmated Plover
Piping Plover
Killdeer
American
Oystercatcher
Black-necked Stilt

should be the peak of migration and also visit the Big Thicket country north of Beaumont.

When your trip dates are firm, make reservations for the short boat trip out of Rockport to see the Whooping Cranes. These can be made by contacting one of the following: Sea-Gun Resort, 512/729-3292; Ted Appel, 512/729-9589; John Howell, 512/729-7525; Ray Little, 512/749-5760; or the *New Pelican*, 512/729-8448.

This trip includes Houston, High Island, Bolivar Peninsula, Galveston Island, San Luis Pass, Aransas National Wildlife Refuge, Corpus Christi, Mustang Island, Padre Island National Seashore, Highway 77, Laguna Atascosa National Wildlife Refuge, Boca Chica, Sabal Palm Grove Sanctuary, Brownsville, Santa Ana National Wildlife Refuge, Bentsen-Rio Grande Valley State Park, Anzalduas County Park, Santa Margarita Ranch, Salineño, Falcon State Park, Zapata, San Ignacio, San Antonio, Friedrich Wilderness Park, Kerrville, Guadalupe River, Lost Maples State Natural Area, Attwater Prairie-Chicken National Wildlife Refuge, Katy, Anahuac National Wildlife Refuge, and Silsbee.

The value of communicating with other birders while you are on this Texas trip cannot be overstressed. Share your sightings, and you will get good information in return.

Birdfinding Guides

The ABA/Lane Series *A Birder's Guide to the Texas Coast* by Harold R. Holt (1993) covers the entire Texas Coast, the Big Thicket country, and the Houston area. *A Birder's Guide to the Rio Grande Valley of Texas* (1992), also from the ABA/Lane Series and by the same author, covers both the Valley and the Edwards Plateau thoroughly.

Ed Kutac's *Birder's Guide to Texas* (1989) can also be very helpful.

Rare Bird Alert Numbers

Statewide 713/992-2757
Austin 512/483-0952
Corpus Christi 512/265-0377
Rio Grande Valley . . 210/969-2731
San Antonio 210/733-8306

Special Equipment

If you bring a spotting scope, you will find many occasions to use it. Insect repellent is essential in the marshy areas, and you may want to bring along knee-high rubber boots. If you elect to use tapes, be sure that they are tolerated in the area you are in before using them; even then, use discretion. *It is against the law to use tapes to attract birds considered Endangered Species.*

Accommodations

Motels are plentiful and reasonably priced in most places on the route; however, early reservations are a must if you want to stay in or near High Island. Tour groups and the influx of many other birders quickly fill all available rooms. If you strike out, Houston and Beaumont are nearby alternatives. For the economy-minded birder, camping is hard to beat for this entire trip.

Key Species — Total of 61 Species

Note: On the February trip to the Rio Grande Valley, 33 species were targeted (see Chapter 4 for a list). Most of those species are present in the Valley in April.

1. **Least Bittern**—May be seen in suitable habitat almost everywhere you stop on this trip. Easiest to find at Anahuac National Wildlife Refuge.

2. **Fulvous Whistling-Duck**—Can be seen in marshes, wet pastures, and rice fields throughout the coastal area. Also present at Santa Ana National Wildlife Refuge and Bentsen-Rio Grande Valley

Probable Species
(continued)

American Avocet
Greater Yellowlegs
Lesser Yellowlegs
Solitary Sandpiper
Willet
Spotted Sandpiper
Whimbrel
Long-billed Curlew
Marbled Godwit
Ruddy Turnstone
Sanderling
Semipalmated
   Sandpiper
Western Sandpiper
Least Sandpiper
Dunlin
Short-billed Dowitcher
Long-billed Dowitcher
Common Snipe
Wilson's Phalarope
Laughing Gull
Ring-billed Gull
Herring Gull
Gull-billed Tern
Caspian Tern
Royal Tern
Common Tern
Forster's Tern
Black Tern
Black Skimmer
Rock Dove
White-winged Dove
Mourning Dove
Inca Dove
Common Ground-Dove
White-tipped Dove
Yellow-billed Cuckoo
Greater Roadrunner
Eastern Screech-Owl
Great Horned Owl
Barred Owl
Lesser Nighthawk
Common Nighthawk
Whip-poor-will
Chimney Swift
Buff-bellied
   Hummingbird
Ruby-throated
   Hummingbird
Black-chinned
   Hummingbird
Belted Kingfisher
Red-headed
   Woodpecker
Golden-fronted
   Woodpecker
Red-bellied
   Woodpecker
Yellow-bellied
   Sapsucker
Ladder-backed
   Woodpecker
Downy Woodpecker
Red-cockaded
   Woodpecker
Northern Flicker
Pileated Woodpecker
Eastern Wood-Pewee
Eastern Phoebe

Probable Species
(continued)

Ash-throated Flycatcher
Great Crested
   Flycatcher
Great Kiskadee
Eastern Kingbird
Horned Lark
Purple Martin
Tree Swallow
Northern Rough-
   winged Swallow
Bank Swallow
Cliff Swallow
Barn Swallow
Blue Jay
Green Jay
Western Scrub-Jay
American Crow
Fish Crow
Chihuahuan Raven
Carolina Chickadee
Tufted Titmouse
Verdin
Bushtit
Cactus Wren
Carolina Wren
Bewick's Wren
House Wren
Marsh Wren
Ruby-crowned Kinglet
Blue-gray Gnatcatcher
Eastern Bluebird
Swainson's Thrush
Hermit Thrush
American Robin
Gray Catbird
Northern Mockingbird
Brown Thrasher
Long-billed Thrasher
Curve-billed Thrasher
Cedar Waxwing
Loggerhead Shrike
European Starling
White-eyed Vireo
Bell's Vireo
Solitary Vireo
Warbling Vireo
Red-eyed Vireo
Orange-crowned
   Warbler
Nashville Warbler
Northern Parula
Yellow Warbler
Yellow-rumped
   Warbler
Pine Warbler
Blackpoll Warbler
Black-and-white
   Warbler
American Redstart
Ovenbird
Common Yellowthroat
Wilson's Warbler
Yellow-breasted Chat
Summer Tanager
Northern Cardinal
Pyrrhuloxia
Blue Grosbeak
Olive Sparrow
Rufous-sided Towhee

State Park. Best bet is usually the rice fields near Katy or Winnie.

3. **Black-bellied Whistling-Duck**—May show up anywhere in the coastal area but becomes more common the farther south you go. Should be seen at Aransas, Laguna Atascosa, and Santa Ana National Wildlife Refuges, Bentsen-Rio Grande Valley and Falcon State Parks, the resacas in Brownsville, and ponds and marshes along the highways.

4. **Mississippi Kite**—Found throughout; is usually seen flying and is common enough that you should find it easily.

5. **Black Rail**—The most difficult key species to see on this trip. Considered rare in Anahuac and Aransas National Wildlife Refuges and on Galveston Island. Local knowledge is essential. A tape and night birding will probably be necessary to find this difficult-to-locate species.

6. **Clapper Rail**—Most common rail on the upper coast; easy at Anahuac National Wildlife Refuge, in marshy areas on the Bolivar Peninsula, in marshes near South Jetty on Galveston Island, and in rice fields throughout the coastal area.

7. **King Rail**—Common on the lower coast; fairly easy to locate at Laguna Atascosa and Aransas National Wildlife Refuges. Common on Galveston Island and easy to see at Anahuac National Wildlife Refuge.

8. **Whooping Crane**—Normally seen only at Aransas National Wildlife Refuge and is not reliable after April 15. Can usually be spotted at a great distance from the refuge observation tower, but the best look is from a commercial boat out of Rockport (see General section of this chapter).

9. **American Golden-Plover**—Should be seen at Anahuac National Wildlife Refuge, in rice fields around Katy and Winnie, on ranchland of West Galveston Island, and in wet pastures along Highway 77.

10. **Hudsonian Godwit**—Can be seen throughout the entire coastal area but is common only in late

April and early May. Look for it in rice fields at Katy and south of Winnie, also on wet pastures and grassy marshes throughout.

11. **Red Knot**—Occurs on the entire coast, but easiest to find at Bolivar Flats, San Luis Pass, Mustang Island, and Padre Island National Seashore, where it can be common throughout April.

12. **White-rumped Sandpiper**—Present in small numbers after about April 15, but migrates through mainly in May. Should be found in marshes at Bolivar Flats or one of the other coastal areas; also expected on wet pastures and rice fields throughout.

13. **Pectoral Sandpiper**—Common to abundant in this season at Anahuac National Wildlife Refuge and Bolivar Flats. Also seen in marshy areas and around ponds throughout the upper coastal area.

14. **Stilt Sandpiper**—Abundant at Anahuac National Wildlife Refuge and Bolivar Flats. Easy to see thoughout April.

15. **Buff-breasted Sandpiper**—Migrates through coastal area with numbers peaking in late April and early May. Look on wet, but not flooded, rice fields, over-grazed pastures, golf courses, air fields, and in other short-grass areas.

16. **Sandwich Tern**—Easy to see at Bolivar Flats or South Jetty on Galveston Island. You will see it many times on this trip.

17. **Least Tern**—Common at Anahuac National Wildlife Refuge and at Bolivar Flats. You will see it many times on this trip

18. **Groove-billed Ani**—Look from Aransas National Wildlife Refuge south to Laguna Atascosa National Wildlife Refuge and along the Rio Grande Valley to Falcon State Park. Reasonably common at Santa Ana National Wildlife Refuge and at Falcon State Park in the summer. It can be difficult to find until late April or early May.

19. **Chuck-will's-widow**—Even though it is a common summer resident of the Edwards Plateau and can be found most nights by driving the back roads, it is more likely to be seen on this trip in the

---

Probable Species
(continued)

Canyon Towhee
Bachman's Sparrow
Rufous-crowned
  Sparrow
Chipping Sparrow
Field Sparrow
Vesper Sparrow
Lark Sparrow
Savannah Sparrow
Song Sparrow
Lincoln's Sparrow
Swamp Sparrow
White-throated Sparrow
White-crowned
  Sparrow
Red-winged Blackbird
Eastern Meadowlark
Brewer's Blackbird
Great-tailed Grackle
Boat-tailed Grackle
Common Grackle
Brown-headed Cowbird
Orchard Oriole
Altamira Oriole
House Finch
American Goldfinch
House Sparrow

Note: The species in **boldface** appear no more than four times in the itineraries as *key* or *probable* species. Watch for them on this trip. As on previous trips, assume that you will see all of the probable species. You will gain 30 new species not seen on previous trips.

Possible Species
Total of 61 Species
Common Loon
Least Grebe
Horned Grebe
Northern Gannet
Greater White-fronted
  Goose
Snow Goose
Canada Goose
Muscovy Duck
Canvasback
Bald Eagle
Cooper's Hawk
Merlin
Peregrine Falcon
Prairie Falcon
Ring-necked Pheasant
Montezuma Quail
Yellow Rail
Virginia Rail
Upland Sandpiper
Baird's Sandpiper
Franklin's Gull

brushy thickets at High Island or Corpus Christi as it migrates through in large numbers. Can also be found in the area north of Silsbee.

20. **Acadian Flycatcher**—Should easily be seen migrating through the High Island area. Can be found elsewhere on the coast or on its nesting grounds in the Silsbee area.

21. **Brown-crested Flycatcher**—Usually seen in Rio Grande Valley, though sometimes found northward beyond Corpus Christi. Common at Laguna Atascosa and Santa Ana National Wildlife Refuges, Sabal Palm Grove Sanctuary, Bentsen-Rio Grande Valley State Park, Falcon State Park, and other stops in the Valley.

22. **Couch's Kingbird**—You will see it easily and many times from Laguna Atascosa National Wildlife Refuge to Falcon State Park.

23. **Scissor-tailed Flycatcher**—From mid-April it is abundant throughout; you can't miss this one.

24. **Cave Swallow**—Common on Edwards Plateau, especially in Kerrville area. This species has been expanding its range and is now common from Kingsville south (look around road culverts). (A relatively new site on the upper Texas Coast is the airboat shed at Sea Rim Park.)

25. **Brown-headed Nuthatch**—Probably the two best locations are near Silsbee in the Big Thicket and at Jones State Forest 35 miles north of Houston. Common if you get into the correct habitat.

26. **Sedge Wren**—Common; can be located in most marshy areas anywhere in the coastal area. Can be found easily at Anahuac and Aransas National Wildlife Refuges.

27. **Veery**—Should be seen at High Island. The later in April the more common it becomes. Numbers peak in early May, but it should be seen anytime after April 15.

28. **Gray-cheeked Thrush**—Should be seen at High Island anytime from April 15 through May 21.

29. **Wood Thrush**—Common migrant throughout April and May. High Island is the best place.

30. **Black-capped Vireo**—Must be located on the Edwards Plateau, or it will be missed on this trip. Should be seen in San Antonio area or at Lost Maples State Natural Area. Local help can make this endangered vireo easy to locate, but getting a real good look at it is another matter.

31. **Yellow-throated Vireo**—Usually common at High Island throughout April. It is more common on the upper coast than on the lower. Nests in the Silsbee area.

32. **Philadelphia Vireo**—Not as common as Yellow-throated Vireo but can be found at High Island and other migrant traps the length of the coast.

33. **Blue-winged Warbler**—Fairly common at High Island and other coastal migrant traps during first three weeks in April. Much more common on the upper coast than on the lower.

34. **Golden-winged Warbler**—Frequently seen at High Island throughout April. Common only on upper coast, and your chance of seeing it diminishes as you go south down the coast.

35. **Tennessee Warbler**—Common at migrant traps throughout the coastal area. Easy to see during the entire month of April.

36. **Chestnut-sided Warbler**—Regular at High Island during the latter half of April and into May. Frequently seen at Aransas, Laguna Atascosa, and Santa Ana National Wildlife Refuges.

37. **Magnolia Warbler**—Regular at High Island the last two weeks of April and into May. Becomes less common south of Aransas National Wildlife Refuge.

38. **Black-throated Green Warbler**—Commonly seen throughout April from High Island to Padre Island National Seashore. Less common farther down the coast.

39. **Golden-cheeked Warbler**—Fairly common but local in Edwards Plateau area, the only place you can find this bird. Easy at Friedrich Wilderness Park in San Antonio, at Lost Maples State Natural Area, and at Audubon Sanctuary in Austin.

Remotely Possible Species
(continued)

Golden Eagle
Aplomado Falcon
Greater Prairie-Chicken
Mountain Plover
Northern Jacana
Eskimo Curlew
Ruff
*Ferruginous
  Pygmy-Owl*
Burrowing Owl
Short-eared Owl
Acorn Woodpecker
Hairy Woodpecker
*Northern Beardless-
  Tyrannulet*
Olive-sided Flycatcher
*Yellow-bellied
  Flycatcher*
Willow Flycatcher
Tropical Kingbird
Rose-throated Becard
Red-breasted Nuthatch
*White-breasted
  Nuthatch*
Townsend's Solitaire
Sage Thrasher
Sprague's Pipit
Gray Vireo
Tropical Parula
*Black-throated Blue
  Warbler*
*Black-throated Gray
  Warbler*
Townsend's Warbler
Prairie Warbler
Palm Warbler
Mourning Warbler
MacGillivray's Warbler
Green-tailed Towhee
Henslow's Sparrow
Fox Sparrow
Dark-eyed Junco
Bobolink
Purple Finch

Note: You will probably see 4 of the species on the remotely possible list. A further comment may be in order concerning two of these species. There has not been a documented record, in Texas, of Eskimo Curlew since 1962, but birders always search for it at this season. Aplomado Falcon is being reintroduced at Laguna Atascosa, making identification of free-flying, wild birds a problem. Any sighting of these 2 species should be well-documented.

40. **Blackburnian Warbler**—Normally seen throughout April from High Island to Padre Island National Seashore. Not nearly as easy to see farther south.

41. **Yellow-throated Warbler**—Fairly common first three weeks of April at High Island. Less likely the farther south you go. Some nest from Houston to the Big Thicket country, and it is an uncommon nesting species along the cypress-lined rivers of the Edwards Plateau. One of the "early" warblers.

42. **Bay-breasted Warbler**—Not regular until last week of April, but with work, can be found after April 15 at High Island, Galveston Island, and Aransas National Wildlife Refuge.

43. **Cerulean Warbler**—Uncommon at High Island after mid-April. Unlikely farther south than Corpus Christi.

44. **Prothonotary Warbler**—Frequently seen in April at High Island. Less likely farther south. Nests in swamps throughout East Texas.

45. **Worm-eating Warbler**—Regular at High Island and as far south as Aransas National Wildlife Refuge the first two weeks of April. An "early" warbler that is scarce after mid-month.

46. **Swainson's Warbler**—An "early" warbler that is fairly common but may be hard to see. Found at High Island the first two weeks in April but is difficult to find after that. Not likely to be seen farther south. Nests from Houston to Big Thicket country in moist wooded areas.

47. **Northern Waterthrush**—Common at High Island the last two weeks of April. Uncommon farther south than Galveston Island.

48. **Louisiana Waterthrush**—Common at High Island the first two weeks of April, becoming scarce after mid-month. Seldom seen south of Galveston Island. Another "early" warbler, it can be found nesting in the Big Thicket country.

49. **Kentucky Warbler**—Common at High Island throughout April. Less common south of Galveston Island. Can be found on territory in Houston and Silsbee areas.

50. **Hooded Warbler**—Common from Padre Island National Seashore up the coast. Very common throughout April; nests north of Silsbee.

51. **Scarlet Tanager**—Common at High Island in April. Fairly common the length of the coast.

52. **Rose-breasted Grosbeak**—Common at High Island the last three weeks of April. May be seen down the coast but is less common the farther south you go.

53. **Indigo Bunting**—Common throughout the entire trip area and easy to see.

54. **Painted Bunting**—Common along coast and throughout the inland areas after mid-April.

55. **Dickcissel**—Fairly common at High Island the last three weeks of April. Abundant at Anahuac National Wildlife Refuge; can be seen at most of the stops on this trip.

56. **Cassin's Sparrow**—Common at Laguna Atascosa and Santa Ana National Wildlife Refuges and Falcon State Park. Easy to locate at this time of year.

57. **Clay-colored Sparrow**—Can be a fairly common migrant, found in dry grasslands, invaded fields, and brushlands in South Texas. Sometimes found at Laguna Atascosa National Wildlife Refuge but more common to the west, such as at Falcon State Park.

58. **Nelson's Sharp-tailed Sparrow**—Usually fairly easy to locate at Bolivar Flats. May be seen at Anahuac and Aransas National Wildlife Refuges and South Jetty on Galveston Island.

59. **Seaside Sparrow**—Common at Anahuac National Wildlife Refuge and the marshes along entire Bolivar Peninsula; very easy to locate.

60. **Bronzed Cowbird**—May be seen at Aransas National Wildlife Refuge. Common to abundant at Santa Ana and Laguna Atascosa National Wildlife Refuges, Bentsen-Rio Grande Valley State Park, and Falcon State Park.

61. **Baltimore Oriole**—Common migrant on the upper Texas coast in this season. It's hard to miss this brightly colored, conspicuous bird.

> Note: If you have luck at finding Black Rail and Groove-billed Ani, you could see all 61 key species.

Itinerary
Note: Trip begins and ends in Houston.

Day 1 — Houston and High Island
Leave Houston early for the one-and-a-half-hour drive to High Island. The small town of High Island has long been the center of birding activities during migration on the Texas coast. When weather conditions are right (cool front and/or rain), birding can be remarkable at High Island. On days when the weather is warm with southeast winds, birding can be slow. Two wooded areas in particular at High Island serve the migrating birds as feeding-and-rest sites after their long flight across the Gulf of Mexico. The first of these areas is known as Smith Oaks Sanctuary or Smith Woods (at least partially maintained by Houston Audubon Society); the second, Louis Smith Woods Sanctuary (known for many years as Boy Scout Woods), is now wholly maintained by the Houston Audubon

Society. Both of these wooded areas are well covered in *A Birder's Guide to the Texas Coast*.

The purpose of this one-day visit to High Island, early in the trip, is to try to see the "early" warblers as they migrate through the area. These "early" warblers pass through primarily prior to April 15 and after that date are pretty scarce. The "early" warblers are Orange-crowned, Yellow-rumped, Yellow-throated, Worm-eating, Swainson's, and Louisiana Waterthrush. All of these can be seen, as well as a number of other species that migrate through the area in good numbers during the entire month.

Your whole day can be spent at Smith Oaks Sanctuary and Louis Smith Woods. Communicate with the other friendly birders in these areas to keep abreast of what species are being seen, and make every effort to see the 4 "early" key warblers.

Other key species to be alert for at this time are Scissor-tailed Flycatcher, Wood Thrush, Yellow-throated Vireo, Northern Waterthrush, Blue-winged, Golden-winged, Tennessee, Black-throated Green, Blackburnian, Prothonotary, Kentucky, and Hooded Warblers, Scarlet Tanager, Rose-breasted Grosbeak, Indigo and Painted Buntings, Dickcissel, and Baltimore Oriole. Birding can be productive at both wooded areas until it is too dark to see.

Motels are available in Anahuac, High Island, and Winnie, but early reservations are recommended. Camping is allowed on the beach just off Highway 87 between High Island and Gilchrist. There are no facilities provided, but the location is convenient—less than 10 miles from High Island.

Day 2 — High Island, Bolivar Peninsula, and Galveston Island

If you missed Yellow-throated Warbler, Worm-eating Warbler, Swainson's Warbler, or Louisiana Waterthrush on Day 1, another stop at Smith Oaks Sanctuary and Louis Smith Woods should be made prior to traveling down the coast. This is your very best chance on this trip for these 4 species.

If you did not miss any of them, or after your early stops at the two woods, take Highway 87 toward Galveston. Just beyond Gilchrist you will come to the Rollover Pass; just before the canal you can drive west to the bay, a likely spot for gulls, terns, and shorebirds.

Return to Highway 87; at Farm Road 108 turn left drive to the beach, then right to Bolivar Flats, one of the premier birding spots on the Texas Coast for shorebirds and waders. You should see Red Knot, White-rumped Sandpiper, Pectoral Sandpiper, Stilt Sandpiper, Sandwich Tern, and Least Tern, as well as numerous other shorebirds, waders, gulls, and terns. By walking through the salt-marsh, you should flush Nelson's Sharp-tailed Sparrow and possibly Sedge and Marsh Wrens.

When you leave Bolivar Flats, return to Highway 87 and drive to the end of the peninsula. Here you can take the 3-mile ferry ride to Galveston Island. This ferry is an excellent way to see most of the terns that are present in this season. You should watch for Gull-billed, Caspian, Royal, Sandwich, Common, Forster's, Least, and Black Terns during this crossing of the bay. You will also see many Laughing Gulls and both Double-crested and Neotropic Cormorants.

When you exit the ferry, follow Ferry Road to Seawall Boulevard, turn left, and drive to the road's end at the bay. Turn right onto Boddecker Drive to reach the South Jetty. This drive is excellent for viewing waders, shorebirds, gulls, and terns. The marshy areas along the drive are easy places to see Clapper and King Rails. Sedge Wren, Marsh Wren, and Nelson's Sharp-tailed and other sparrows are numerous in this area, also.

Return to Seawall Boulevard, turn left, and follow the road to 27th Street, then turn right to Avenue O. Here you will find Kempner Park, which is a good migrant trap in Galveston. A few minutes spent in this small park will give you another chance at migrants, including Veery and Worm-eating, Kentucky, and Hooded Warblers. (Some birders have had their cars burglarized at Kempner Park. Be careful.)

Return to Seawall Boulevard and turn right to continue out Galveston Island. West Galveston has several good birding sites. *A Birder's Guide to the Texas Coast* covers many of them; visit them as time allows. Seawall Boulevard soon becomes Farm Road 3005. The ranch lands that you pass through can be good for American Golden-Plover, Long-billed Curlew, Whimbrel, Upland Sandpiper, and Buff-breasted Sandpiper. Any area of trees or bushes can produce migrating warblers and other small landbirds. The San Luis Pass toll bridge is at the south end of the island. The flats on the Galveston County side (north side) of this bridge are about as good as Bolivar Flats for shorebirds. Birds to be seen here are similar to those listed for Bolivar Flats on Day 2.

After checking the flats, cross the toll bridge and continue 14.5 miles to Surfside Beach. Take Highway 332 to the Lake Jackson area if you are looking for a motel; they are plentiful there. If you want to camp, continue on Highway 332 past Lake Jackson to the Highway 36 intersection at Brazoria. Turn left onto Highway 36 to Farm Road 521. Follow Farm Road 521 to Wadsworth and turn left onto Highway 60 to Matagorda. At Matagorda take Farm Road 2031 to Matagorda Beach. Camping is permitted here, but it is primitive.

Day 3 — Aransas National Wildlife Refuge

Whether you spend the night at Lake Jackson or at Matagorda Beach, it is a two-hour drive to Aransas National Wildlife Refuge. Use Farm Road 521 and Highway 35 to drive to Tivoli near Aransas. (You might want to call the Corpus Christi hotline before continuing to the refuge.)

Just beyond Tivoli, take Highway 239 left to Austwell, and then Farm Road 2040 to the Aransas entrance. Stop at the visitor center for a bird checklist and area map. From the visitor center it is a 5-mile drive to the observation tower. Here you may see the Whooping Cranes, but not on every visit. To assure that you get to see the Whooping Cranes or at least to get a closer look, it is advisable to make reservations for one of the boat rides as outlined in the General section at the beginning of this chapter. Each boat may have a slightly different schedule, minimum load, embarkation point, and/or price.

The paved Aransas tour road is 16 miles long. From the visitor center to the observation tower is two-way for easy access to the tower. The remainder is one-way and should be traveled more than once if time allows. There are six walking-trails, and all can be good for a large variety of species.

Species to watch for at Aransas include all of the heron family to be expected in the ABA Area, White and White-faced Ibises; Roseate Spoonbill; many duck species including both Fulvous and Black-bellied Whistling-Ducks; Mississippi Kite; Clapper and King Rails; Whooping Crane; Hudsonian Godwit; White-rumped, Baird's, Pectoral, Stilt, and Buff-breasted Sandpipers; Sandwich and Least Terns; Chuck-will's-widow; Scissor-tailed Flycatcher; Sedge and Marsh Wrens; five of the brown-backed thrushes; six species of vireos, including Yellow-throated and Philadelphia; all of the key warblers except Golden-cheeked; Rose-breasted Grosbeak; Indigo and Painted Buntings; Dickcissel; Cassin's and Seaside Sparrows; Bronzed Cowbird; Baltimore Oriole; and numerous other species. In years past Greater Prairie-Chicken (the Attwater race) was found in the area. Today, they have virtually disappeared.

This day should be spent at Aransas, scheduled around your boat trip to see the cranes.

Goose Island State Park is an excellent place to camp (hot showers) and is near enough to allow you to bird Aransas as late in the day as you wish.

Day 4 — Rockport, Corpus Christi, and Mustang and Padre Islands

Get an early start and bird your way down the coast through Rockport and on to Aransas Pass (these areas are well covered in *A Birder's Guide to the Texas Coast).* At Aransas Pass take Highway 361, make the ferry-crossing to Port Aransas, and continue birding down Mustang Island. The birding on this island is mostly for shorebirds; it is a likely place for Red Knot and Sandwich Tern. Continue on Highway 361 until it meets Park Road 22, where you turn left for Padre Island National Seashore. The birds here are about the same as those seen on Mustang Island, but something different may be around.

When leaving Padre Island National Seashore on Park Road 22, watch for Packery Channel Park. Under the right conditions, the trees at this small area can be alive with migrants. Continue across Laguna Madre on the causeway. The residential areas to the left between the causeway and Cayo del Oso may harbor many migrants. Drive the streets in this area and check it thoroughly.

Cayo del Oso is excellent for shorebirds. After crossing it, take Ennis Joslin Road to the right. Watch for Hans Suter Park, which has a boardwalk that overlooks a marshy area on the edge of Cayo del Oso that can be excellent birding. When you leave the park, continue on Ennis Joslin Road until you reach Ocean Drive. Take a right up Ocean Drive; the tree-lined area behind Corpus Christi State University is usually good for migrants. Continue on Ocean Drive; across another bridge over Cayo del Oso to the entrance to the Corpus Christi Naval Air Station. The guard will not let you enter, but birding along the road for shorebirds is usually profitable. The short grass inside the air station can be viewed from the highway; at this season it often has Upland Sandpipers.

Corpus Christi has many good birding sites, several of which are covered in detail in *A Birder's Guide to the Texas Coast*. Check these areas as time allows.

There are plenty of motels in the area, and camping with showers is available at Padre Island National Seashore and at Lake Corpus Christi northeast of town. To reach Lake Corpus Christi take Interstate 37 to Mathis and then go south on Highway 359.

Day 5 — Highway 77 and Laguna Atascosa National Wildlife Refuge

Note: Days 5, 6, 7, and part of Day 8 are spent in areas detailed in Chapter 4. Chapter 4 has general directions, species, and other details. Any species targeted on that trip that you missed should be re-targeted now.

Check the area hotlines (both the Corpus Christi and the Rio Grande Valley numbers) prior to starting out today. At this time of year anything can show up. If nothing else, the tapes will have information on some of the more desirable species to be found in the Valley.

Take Highway 77 south. Beyond Kingsville you should watch all hawks closely; White-tailed Hawk is common here and should be seen easily. Crested Caracara is also common in the fields along the highway, and in this season Mississippi Kites and Broad-winged Hawks should be plentiful. Try the first rest-area south of Sarita for Tropical Parula. This species is an uncommon permanent resident in this area, and you may need information from the hotline or from local birders for current best locations. Wet pastures and ponds along Highway 77 can yield Black-bellied Plover, American Golden-Plover, Hudsonian Godwit, and White-rumped, Pectoral, Stilt, and Buff-breasted Sandpipers, as well as other species.

When you reach Raymondville, turn left (east) onto Highway 186, follow it for about 10 miles, and turn right onto Farm Road 1420. Go south on Farm Road 1420 for 19 miles and turn left onto Farm Road 106; follow it to Laguna Atascosa National Wildlife Refuge.

Laguna Atascosa is covered in *A Birder's Guide to the Texas Coast* and *A Birder's Guide to the Rio Grande Valley of Texas*. (That area is also discussed in Chapter 4 of this book.) It is a large refuge with varied habitat that offers a good opportunity to see several of the key species and another look at a number of species targeted on the February Rio Grande Valley trip. Both Bayside Drive (a 15-mile loop road) and Lakeside Drive (2 miles) should be driven at least once. Try each of the four walking-trails. In addition, the area around the visitor center should be birded thoroughly; it is the location where the Yellow-green Vireos have nested. The birds have not been seen here in the past few years, but the chance of a return certainly rates a look. *Use of tapes is prohibited in the refuge.*

The following key species are usually seen at Laguna Atascosa during April: Least Bittern; Black-bellied Whistling-Duck; Mississippi Kite; Clapper and King Rails; Hudsonian Godwit; Red Knot; White-rumped, Pectoral, Stilt, and Buff-breasted Sandpipers; Sandwich and Least Terns; Groove-billed Ani; Acadian and Brown-crested Flycatchers; Couch's Kingbird; Scissor-tailed Flycatcher; Sedge Wren; Veery; Gray-cheeked and Wood Thrushes; Yellow-throated and Philadelphia Vireos; Blue-winged, Tennessee, Chestnut-sided, Magnolia, Black-throated Green, Blackburnian, Yellow-throated, Bay-breasted, Cerulean, Prothonotary, Worm-eating, Northern Waterthrush, Louisiana Waterthrush, Kentucky, and Hooded Warblers; Scarlet Tanager; Rose-breasted Grosbeak; Indigo and Painted Buntings; Dickcissel; Cassin's and Clay-colored Sparrows; and Bronzed Cowbird. You should be able to locate several of these species but do not expect to see them all in one day.

Be alert to the possibility of seeing an Aplomado Falcon on or near the refuge. These birds are from a release program begun in 1985 and therefore cannot yet be counted on your lifelist. Of course, that does not make them any less beautiful; enjoy the look.

When you have completed your tour of Laguna Atascosa National Wildlife Refuge, there are camping facilities available at Adolph Thomae Jr. County Park. To reach the campground, exit the refuge and go north on Farm Road 1847. If you prefer a bed tonight, take Farm Road 1847 south to Brownsville and Harlingen, where motels are numerous.

Day 6 — Boca Chica, Sabal Palm Grove Sanctuary, Brownsville, and Santa Ana National Wildlife Refuge

If you camped for the night, take Farm Road 1847 south to Brownsville. Boca Chica is 22 miles east on Highway 4. The beach at Boca Chica is undeveloped, and you can drive on it to the north or to the south. You will be able to get close looks at shorebirds and terns. To the south, the beach ends at the mouth of the Rio Grande. Many birds frequent this area, so it is always worth a look.

After exploring Boca Chica, return to Brownsville. Visit the Brownsville City Dump if you have not seen Mexican Crow, the Gladys Porter Zoo if you need Buff-bellied Hummingbird, and the area in Brownsville known for Red-crowned Parrots if you have not seen them previously. See Chapter 4, and especially *A Birder's Guide to the Rio Grande Valley of Texas*, for more specifics on these areas and species.)

Sabal Palm Grove Sanctuary is another reliable place for Buff-bellied Hummingbird. The sanctuary should be visited for Groove-billed Ani and Brown-crested Flycatcher—both key species. This is also a standard place for many of the "Mexican" specialties (see Chapter 4). In the morning and evening hours, during this season, the sanctuary can be very good for migrating warblers. (Remember that it is closed on Tuesdays and Wednesdays.)

Continuing the trip, take Highway 281 west from Brownsville to Santa Ana National Wildlife Refuge (a one-hour drive). Along Highway 281 watch the ponds for Least Grebe, Fulvous and Black-bellied Whistling-Ducks, and White-rumped, Pectoral, and Stilt Sandpipers.

At Santa Ana, look for Least Bittern, Fulvous and Black-bellied Whistling-Ducks, Groove-billed Ani, Brown-crested Flycatcher, Couch's Kingbird, Cassin's Sparrow, and Bronzed Cowbird.

Here at Santa Ana National Wildlife Refuge many of the birds sought in Chapter 4 will be found again. If some species were missed on the February trip, they could be found this time.

The loop road through Santa Ana is open to car traffic during only part of the year. The schedule for this availability seems both complicated and ever-changing. The road is usually opened in mid- to late April for about three months. If it is open when you visit, make the drive at least once. Santa Ana National Wildlife Refuge has recorded more than its share of rare or uncommon species. Watch for Least Grebe, Masked Duck, Hook-billed Kite, Red-billed Pigeon, Pauraque, Buff-bellied Hummingbird, Ringed and Green Kingfishers, Northern Beardless-Tyrannulet, Rose-throated Becard, Clay-colored Robin, Yellow-green Vireo, and Tropical Parula. Also be sure to check the Rio Grande Valley hotline.

From Santa Ana proceed to Bentsen-Rio Grande Valley State Park for camping with hot showers or to the McAllen area for a motel.

If you camp at Bentsen, give the nightbirds a try. Elf Owl can be rather common, and during the spring season Chuck-will's-widow, Whip-poor-will, and Common Poorwill, as well as the resident Pauraque, can sometimes be found.

Day 7 — Bentsen-Rio Grande Valley State Park, Anzalduas County Park, Santa Margarita Ranch, Salineño, and Falcon State Park

Start the day at Bentsen-Rio Grande Valley State Park. The birdlife here is similar to that at Santa Ana, but you will probably see something here that you missed there. At Bentsen, like Santa Ana, you will see many of the Lower Valley specialties. Drive the loop roads, check the resacas (lakes), and try the Singing Chaparral Nature Trail and especially the Rio Grande Hiking Trail. Many key species for this trip—Least Bittern, Black-bellied Whistling-Duck, Mississippi Kite, Pectoral Sandpiper, Groove-billed Ani, Chuck-will's-widow, Acadian and Brown-crested Flycatchers, Tennessee, Magnolia, and Black-throated Green Warblers, Indigo and Painted Buntings, Dickcissel, and Bronzed Cowbird—are regularly seen in this season. A number of the others, especially warblers, are seen occasionally. Other surprises may be encountered (e.g., Northern Beardless-Tyrannulet has been found around the trailer-loop).

Make the short drive to Anzalduas County Park. This park's species are very similar to those of both Bentsen and Santa Ana, but a good number of rarities have been recorded here over the years.

Drive to Santa Margarita Ranch (private property; a small fee must be paid to bird here). The species are pretty much the same but with a better chance of seeing some of the area specialties, such as Muscovy Duck, Red-billed Pigeon, and Brown Jay.

Continue on to Falcon State Park; if you have missed Groove-billed Ani, Couch's Kingbird, Cassin's or Clay-colored Sparrows, or Bronzed Cowbird, they are all possible here.

Spend the night at Falcon State Park (camping with hot showers), or drive to Zapata (27 miles) for a motel.

All of the areas visited today are covered in detail in *A Birder's Guide to the Rio Grande Valley of Texas*. They are also discussed in Chapter 4 of this book.

Day 8 — Zapata, San Ygnacio, San Antonio, and Friedrich Wilderness Park

This day is mainly a travel day. Leave Falcon State Park and take Highway 83 to Zapata (27 miles). Check the culverts on this stretch of road for Cave Swallows; they have nested here the past few years. In Zapata stop at the city park to look for White-collared Seedeaters. If you do not find them there, continue on Highway 83 to San Ygnacio (14 miles), where this species has been regular for many years. Check behind the post office, at the end of Washington Avenue in the canes along the river edge, and behind the cemetery if the area has weeds; call the Rio Grande Valley hotline for current locations. If you are not interested in seedeaters, pass on through these towns and drive 35 miles farther on Highway 83 to Laredo. At Laredo take Interstate 35 north to San Antonio (155 miles).

You should reach San Antonio by early afternoon. Once there, take Interstate Loop 410 west and connect with Interstate 10 west. Approximately 10 miles northwest on Interstate 10, exit onto Camp Bullis Road, pass back under Interstate 10, take the frontage road to the right for about 1 mile, and turn left at the sign to Friedrich Wilderness Park.

This park is one of the more reliable places in the San Antonio area for Golden-cheeked Warbler and Black-capped Vireo. The former can often be found on the cooler, north-facing slopes of the central ravine; the latter can be found on the hotter, southwest-facing rim of the ravine.

Return to Interstate 10 and drive to Kerrville. Just south of Kerrville on Highway 173 is the Kerrville-Schreiner State Park with campsites and hot showers. Motels are easy to find if you do not want to camp.

Day 9 — Kerrville, Guadalupe River, and Lost Maples State Natural Area

You might want to bird the Kerrville-Schreiner State Park before you leave in the morning. Birding here is fair for the area's typical species.

Drive back through Kerrville and take Highway 27 west 7 miles to Ingram, then take Highway 39 west to Hunt. At Hunt, take Farm Road

1340, which follows the North Fork of the Guadalupe River for several miles through an excellent birding area. It is an easy place to locate Yellow-throated and other vireos. Thirteen miles on Farm Road 1340 will bring you to Kerr Wildlife Management Area. Both Golden-cheeked Warbler and Black-capped Vireo can be found here; the personnel are helpful and a 4-mile driving tour will take you to the best areas.

Take Farm Road 1340 back to Hunt and turn right (west) onto Highway 39 to follow the South Fork of the Guadalupe River, just as good for birds as the North Fork. After you leave the river, you will pass through grassland where Cassin's Sparrow is common, and you may see Mississippi Kite, Scissor-tailed Flycatcher, and Painted Bunting, too. At Farm Road 187, turn left and begin watching on wires and at culverts for Cave Swallows. The first 5 or 6 miles of this road have been reliable for Cave Swallows for many years. They are common here and nest in the culvert near the farmhouse that is approximately 1.5 miles from Highway 39.

Our next stop is Lost Maples State Natural Area a few miles farther along Farm Road 187. This area can produce Mississippi Kite, Chuck-will's-widow, Acadian and Scissor-tailed Flycatchers, Black-capped and Yellow-throated Vireos, Golden-cheeked and migrant warblers, Indigo

Golden-cheeked Warbler
Gail Diane Yovanovich

and Painted Buntings, and Cassin's Sparrow. *The use of tapes is not allowed in Lost Maples State Natural Area.*

After leaving Lost Maples, take Farm Road 187 south to Highway 90, then turn left for the 60-mile drive to San Antonio.

This day's route provides you a fine sample of the area's birdlife, and you should easily find the three primary key species: Cave Swallow, Black-capped Vireo, and Golden-cheeked Warbler. If you have missed any of them, check with local birders; there are many other good locations for these species in the San Antonio and Austin areas.

Take Interstate 10 east toward Houston. It is a two-and-a-half-hour, 150-mile drive to the little town of San Felipe. Just north of town on Park Road 38, Stephen F. Austin State Park provides full camping facilities. If you do not want to camp, choose among the motels along Interstate 10.

Day 10 — Attwater Prairie-Chicken National Wildlife Refuge, Katy, and Anahuac National Wildlife Refuge

From Stephen F. Austin State Park, return to Interstate 10, drive the few miles west to the Sealy exit, take Highway 36 south, and then Farm Road 3013 west for 10 miles to Attwater Prairie-Chicken National Wildlife Refuge. In recent years, Attwater's Prairie-Chicken has decreased in numbers at an alarming rate. It has been determined that this decline is in part due to the disturbance caused by people viewing them on their booming-grounds. Most of these areas have been closed to the public and there is very little chance at this time for you to see these birds. Check with refuge personnel, though, because this policy could change.

The refuge is excellent for many other species, so you will want to bird the loop drive and two walking-trails. Of your key species you might find Least Bittern, Fulvous and Black-bellied Whistling-Ducks, King Rail, Hudsonian Godwit, White-rumped, Pectoral, Stilt, and Buff-breasted Sandpipers, Scissor-tailed Flycatcher, Sedge Wren, Yellow-throated and Philadelphia Vireos, Northern Waterthrush, Tennessee, Chestnut-sided, Magnolia, Black-throated Green, Blackburnian, Bay-breasted, Kentucky, and Hooded Warblers, Rose-breasted Grosbeak, Indigo and Painted Buntings, and Dickcissel. In addition, White-tailed Hawk, Crested Caracara, Sprague's Pipit, and Le Conte's Sparrow are all considered common here in the spring.

Return to Interstate 10 and drive east about 20 miles to Katy. The rice farms around Katy provide good birding in the spring. You should find Fulvous Whistling-Duck, American Golden-Plover, Hudsonian Godwit, and White-rumped, Pectoral, Stilt, and Buff-breasted Sandpipers. Katy and vicinity are detailed in *A Birder's Guide to the Texas Coast.*

Return to Interstate 10 east and drive through Houston and on to Winnie (about 95 miles). At Winnie take Highway 124 south to Farm Road 1985, where you turn right for a 13-mile drive to Anahuac National Wildlife Refuge. Watch the rice fields for the key shorebirds (especially Hudsonian Godwit); all of them should be here during this season.

Spend the remainder of the day at Anahuac National Wildlife Refuge. (Wear your insect repellent.) There are 12 miles of graveled roads on the refuge that should be driven at least once. A number of key species can be found here with varying degrees of difficulty. Least Bittern, King and Clapper Rails, American Golden-Plover, Pectoral and Stilt Sandpipers, Least Tern, Chuck-will's-widow, Scissor-tailed Flycatcher, Sedge Wren, Tennessee, Magnolia, and Black-throated Green Warblers, Northern Waterthrush, Rose-breasted Grosbeak, Indigo and Painted Buntings, Dickcissel, and Seaside Sparrows are all common to abundant. Fulvous Whistling-Duck, Mississippi Kite, Hudsonian Godwit, Red Knot, and White-rumped and Buff-breasted Sandpipers are all considered occasional. Nelson's Sharp-tailed Sparrows are scarce but can usually be located if you work at it. Furthermore, this is one of the best places in Texas in which to locate the rare Black Rail.

In addition, Yellow Rail can be found here and is considered to be more common than Black Rail. Without using a tape, however, you will probably not see either rail. Both of these species are active mainly at night, when they will frequently respond to a tape. *Prior to using a tape, be sure that it is allowed in the area you are in; tapes are normally not allowed in refuges.* Both rails are present in nearby marshy areas not on the refuge.

Camping is not encouraged at Anahuac National Wildlife Refuge, but it is allowed along the shore of East Galveston Bay. Camping facilities are available at nearby Fort Anahuac Park and at White Memorial Park north of Anahuac on Interstate 10. You can also drive to the coast and camp on the beach between High Island and Gilchrist. Motels are located at Anahuac, High Island, and Winnie; reservations are recommended if this is your plan.

Day 11 — High Island, Smith Oaks Sanctuary, and Louis Smith Woods

This day should be primarily spent at Smith Oaks Sanctuary and Louis Smith Woods at High Island. The birding can be good in the morning, and classic fallouts are afternoon events, so almost anything can show up at any time. Both the "early" warblers and "late" warblers will be scarce, but you have returned to High Island at the peak of migration.

The following species should now be here in good numbers: Acadian and Scissor-tailed Flycatchers; Veery; Gray-cheeked and Wood Thrushes; Yellow-throated and Philadelphia Vireos; Blue-winged, Golden-winged, Tennessee, Chestnut-sided, Magnolia, Black-throated Green, Blackburnian, Bay-breasted, Cerulean, Prothonotary, Northern Waterthrush, Kentucky, and Hooded Warblers; Scarlet Tanager; Rose-breasted Grosbeak; Indigo and Painted Buntings; Dickcissel; and Baltimore Oriole.

There may also be a few late Yellow-throated, Worm-eating, and Swainson's Warblers and Louisiana Waterthushes straggling through, and you may see an early Mourning or Canada Warbler. There will be many other species migrating through this area; most are common but during migration you should stay alert for the unusual.

Spend the night at your choice of the places listed in Day 10.

Day 12 — High Island

A large part of this day should be a repeat of Day 11. There will still be many other birders at High Island for migration, and the more eyes there are, and the better you communicate, the more successful your trip will be. You should check especially with all area birders whom you encounter to ask about the best place to locate Black Rail. Fit the Black Rail search into your day, or, more appropriately, into your evening. If you have missed any of the shorebirds targeted on this trip, try the rice fields north of High Island in the Winnie area or go back to Bolivar Flats. Anahuac National Wildlife Refuge is always worth another visit, and the marshy area west of High Island can be very good, too.

The main thing is to concentrate on the two wooded areas at High Island, and when the birding there slows down, visit one or more of these other nearby areas.

Spend the night in the area as in Days 10 and 11.

Day 13 — High Island

A repeat of Day 12. Overight in same area as Days 10, 11, and 12.

Day 14 — Silsbee, Upper Coast, and High Island

Leave High Island and drive north on Highway 124 to Interstate 10. Take Interstate 10 east to Beaumont, and then proceed on Highway 96 north to Silsbee (total of about 65 miles). This is the center of the "Big Thicket" country and is a good place to locate Brown-headed Nuthatch. *A Birder's Guide to the Texas Coast* covers Hardin County in general and the Silsbee area in particular. Brown-headed Nuthatch is your primary reason for this visit, but you can also see Red-cockaded Woodpecker and Bachman's Sparrow in this same area. The Smart School Fire-Tower area north of Silsbee is good for these 3 species. Nearby sites described by Holt can give you another chance, if needed, at several of the other key species. Acadian Flycatcher and Yellow-throated, Prothonotary, Swainson's, Louisiana Waterthrush, Kentucky, and Hooded Warblers are all possible.

After finishing here, spend the night at your High Island base or at a site convenient to your next day's plans.

Day 15 — Extra Day

After spending fourteen days on this trip, you should have seen all of the key species except possibly Black Rail and Groove-billed Ani. Day 15 should be used to pursue any key species that you may have missed that can be found on the central or upper Texas coast. There are many other good birding locales that you can visit; in fact, there are several very near to Houston. Check your sources and make a last try for any key species missed to this point.

Trip ends in Houston in the evening.

Bird Numbers This Trip

	Potential	Expected	Actual
Key Species	61	61	
Probable Species	212	212	
Possible Species	61	12	
Remotely Possible Species	47	4	
Totally Unexpected Species	?	2	
TOTAL	381	291	

Cumulative List

Total key and probable species seen after 7 trips.

Previous trips	364 species
Spring Texas Trip	291 species
TOTAL	455 species

This Trip's Mileage and Expenses
Approximate miles traveled, Houston to Houston: 2,500

- Fuel: $180; sharing $90 $_____
- Lodging: camping for 15 nights $70; sharing $35 $_____
- Food: Using the ice-chest/supermarket
  method for most meals $180 $_____
  The total per person cost for the above items with a companion to share fuel and lodging expenses should be less than $305.
- Add to this car rental expenses, if any: $_____
- Add to this your expenses to/from Houston: $_____
  This will give you a good idea of the cost of this trip.
- TOTAL $_____

Personal Notes

_____

_____

_____

_____

_____

_____

_____

_____

_____

_____

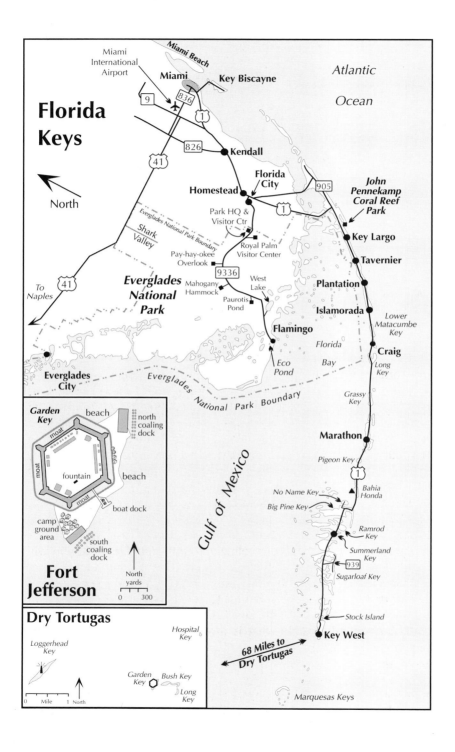

Chapter 8

FLORIDA KEYS AND DRY TORTUGAS

Last week of April or first week of May—
5 Days

General

A trip to the Florida Keys and the Dry Tortugas during the last week of April or the first week of May is perfectly timed for three reasons: the summer specialties of the Keys are on their nesting grounds, spring migration is in progress, and the Dry Tortugas specialties are all present.

This trip's schedule will revolve around the dates you arrange for your Dry Tortugas visit. Independent travel—by charter boat or seaplane—is possible, but your best bet is to join a professionally guided, 3-day boat tour. The annual pelagic trip directory in *Winging It* (see Chapter 1 for details) lists a half-dozen tour operators. Many other bird-tour companies also offer Dry Tortugas trips, in some cases combined with land-birding in South Florida. You can normally join these tours for just the Dry Tortugas portion, and be charged only for those days. The current price is around $425 for a 3-day trip, including meals.

There are a number of reasons to use professionals. The first is easy access to the Dry Tortugas. The second is to take advantage of the pelagic birding on the boat trips to and from the islands. A third, and very important reason, is that by traveling with a tour and by boat you will usually have access to all of the islands and not just Garden Key, where Fort Jefferson is located. The last reason is that you can sleep, eat, and shower on the boat if you so desire. To get the most from your trip, this is the very best way to visit the Dry Tortugas.

Be sure to ask exactly what is included in the price of your Dry Tortugas tour. There is no source of food, water (other than a drinking fountain), or other supplies at Fort Jefferson. If you plan to camp on Garden Key, you must bring all of your own gear. Boat trips leave Key West for the Dry Tortugas in the morning and at night. The former option keeps the sun at your back to aid visibility and increases your pelagic

Probable Species
Total of 82 Species
Brown Pelican
Double-crested
Cormorant
Great Blue Heron
Great Egret
Snowy Egret
Little Blue Heron
Tricolored Heron
Reddish Egret
Cattle Egret
Green Heron
Yellow-crowned
Night-Heron
White Ibis
Turkey Vulture
Osprey
Sharp-shinned Hawk
Red-shouldered Hawk
Broad-winged Hawk
American Kestrel
Merlin
American Coot
Black-bellied Plover
Wilson's Plover
Semipalmated Plover
Piping Plover
Killdeer
Greater Yellowlegs
Lesser Yellowlegs
Willet
Spotted Sandpiper
Whimbrel
Ruddy Turnstone
Sanderling
Semipalmated
Sandpiper
Western Sandpiper
Least Sandpiper
Laughing Gull
Herring Gull
Royal Tern
Sandwich Tern
Least Tern
Rock Dove
Eurasian Collared-Dove
Mourning Dove
Common Ground-Dove
Yellow-billed Cuckoo
Burrowing Owl
Common Nighthawk
Chuck-will's-widow
Ruby-throated
Hummingbird
Belted Kingfisher
Red-bellied
Woodpecker
Northern Flicker
Great Crested
Flycatcher
Eastern Kingbird
Northern Rough-
winged Swallow
Bank Swallow
Barn Swallow
Veery
Gray-cheeked Thrush
Swainson's Thrush
Wood Thrush
Gray Catbird

birding time. A nighttime departure gives you more time at Fort Jefferson, since you arrive at the height of early-morning bird activity. (Both options give you pelagic birding opportunities—usually in the Gulf Stream—on the return trip to Key West.)

This trip includes Miami, the Keys, and the Dry Tortugas.

Birdfinding Guides

A Birder's Guide to Florida by Harold R. Holt (1989) covers the Keys thoroughly. (This book is currently being updated by Bill Pranty for release in 1996.)

Birding in the Florida Keys by the National Audubon Society Research Department is a handy little booklet, most recently revised in early 1995. (For a copy, send $2 for postage and handling to the National Audubon Society, Research Department, 115 Indian Mound Tail, Tavernier, FL 33070)

Rare Bird Alert Numbers

Statewide 941/657-4442
Miami 305/667-7337
Lower Keys 305/294-3438

Special Equipment

A spotting scope is useful on the Dry Tortugas, though some tour companies will try to discourage you from bringing a scope because of space limitations on the boats (leave some clothes at home!). Sunscreen is essential for any Florida trip; a seasickness preventive will help on the boat. Extra gear is essential if you plan to camp on Garden Key. Tapes may help you to locate Mangrove Cuckoo.

Accommodations

Motels are plentiful and ridiculously overpriced while camping facilities are convenient and economical throughout the Keys.

Key Species — Total of 19 Species

1. **Audubon's Shearwater**—Seen on most boat trips to Dry Tortugas. Be ready because you will generally see it only flying by.

2. **Masked Booby**—Best location is Hospital Key in Dry Tortugas. Although there are some birds on Hospital Key all the time, the best time to see them is in evening as they come in to roost. The only way to have access to Hospital Key is to travel with a tour by boat.

3. **Brown Booby**—Usually from 2 to 5 per day are seen at Dry Tortugas. Well known for roosting on navigational markers, park boundary markers, or tall mangroves on Bush Key.

4. **Northern Gannet**—Like Audubon's Shearwater, usually seen on daylight trips to Dry Tortugas.

5. **Magnificent Frigatebird**—Should be easily seen on Dry Tortugas trip. Will definitely be seen floating over Garden Key—up to 100 to 125 per day. Long Key supports a nesting colony that can be visited by boat.

6. **Pomarine Jaeger**—One to 3 are regularly seen on boat trips to Dry Tortugas.

7. **Roseate Tern**—Often found on Stock Island, Key West (check Fort Zachary Taylor and the harbor navigational buoys), and from the boat to Dry Tortugas. It is usually found as a migrant at the Dry Tortugas (e.g., on the buoys).

8. **Bridled Tern**—Often seen on pelagic portion of Dry Tortugas trip. Fairly common at sea.

9. **Sooty Tern**—Nests by the thousands on Bush Key. Can't be missed.

10. **Brown Noddy**—Nests by the thousands on Bush Key. Can't be missed.

11. **White-crowned Pigeon**—Often easy to locate almost anywhere in the Keys. Usually seen flying over the road; watch utility lines and tree tops throughout.

12. **Mangrove Cuckoo**—Toughest of the key species for this trip. Usually found by accident or by

Probable Species
(continued)

Northern Mockingbird
European Starling
White-eyed Vireo
Red-eyed Vireo
Northern Parula
Yellow Warbler=
   Magnolia Warbler
Prairie Warbler
Palm Warbler
Blackpoll Warbler
Black-and-white
   Warbler
American Redstart
Ovenbird
Northern Waterthrush
Common Yellowthroat
Northern Cardinal
Blue Grosbeak
Indigo Bunting
Red-winged Blackbird
House Sparrow

Note: The species in **boldface** appear no more than four times in the itineraries as *key* or *probable* species. Watch for them on this trip. As in all of your trips, assume that you will see all of the probable species. Although you will see a variety of species on this trip, all the species coded "Probable" should have been seen on previous trips outlined in this book.

Possible Species
Total of 59 Species
Wilson's Storm-Petrel
White-tailed Tropicbird
Black-crowned
   Night-Heron
Glossy Ibis
Blue-winged Teal
Red-breasted Merganser
Ruddy Duck
Black Vulture
Northern Harrier
Peregrine Falcon
Clapper Rail
Sora
Purple Gallinule
Black-necked Stilt
American Avocet
Upland Sandpiper
White-rumped
   Sandpiper
Dunlin
Short-billed Dowitcher
Red-necked Phalarope
Ring-billed Gull
Gull-billed Tern

Possible Species
(continued)

Caspian Tern
Common Tern
Forster's Tern
Black Tern
Black Noddy
Black Skimmer
White-winged Dove
Black-billed Cuckoo
Eastern Screech-Owl
Chimney Swift
Eastern Wood-Pewee
Western Kingbird
Scissor-tailed Flycatcher
Purple Martin
Blue-gray Gnatcatcher
Bicknell's Thrush
Brown Thrasher
Blue-winged Warbler
Tennessee Warbler
Chestnut-sided Warbler
Yellow-rumped
   Warbler
Black-throated Green
   Warbler
Blackburnian Warbler
Yellow-throated
   Warbler
Prothonotary Warbler
Worm-eating Warbler
Louisiana Waterthrush
Kentucky Warbler
Hooded Warbler
Summer Tanager
Scarlet Tanager
Rose-breasted Grosbeak
Painted Bunting
Dickcissel
Common Grackle
Orchard Oriole
Baltimore Oriole

Note: You will
probably see 11 of the
birds on the possible
list.

**Remotely Possible
Species**
Total of 43 Species
Common Loon
Horned Grebe
Black-capped Petrel
Band-rumped
   Storm-Petrel
Red-footed Booby
Least Bittern
Roseate Spoonbill
Greater Flamingo
Masked Duck
Common Moorhen
American
   Golden-Plover
American
   Oystercatcher
Solitary Sandpiper
Red Knot
Baird's Sandpiper

using a tape in the correct habitat. See Day 1 of the itinerary for best locations.

13. **Antillean Nighthawk**—Has become a fairly common summer resident in the Keys. The three best locations are the air fields at Marathon and Key West and at the Community College on Stock Island.

14. **Gray Kingbird**—Common throughout the Keys. Perches on utility lines and is easy to see along Highway 1.

15. **Black-whiskered Vireo**—Common species that is easy to find (*listen* for it) in most dense thickets throughout the Keys.

16. **Cape May Warbler**—Easily found on Garden Key and Loggerhead Key in Dry Tortugas. In this season, it is not uncommon to see 15 to 20 per day.

17. **Black-throated Blue Warbler**—Fairly easy to see on all trips during this season to Garden Key in Dry Tortugas.

18. **Bobolink**—Often easy to see on Garden Key at this time of year. May be found in Homestead area.

19. **Shiny Cowbird**—Becoming fairly common both at Dry Tortugas and in South Florida. Seen at Dry Tortugas on almost all late April/early May trips. Sometimes found in Homestead area or at Key West.

Note: You should see all 19 key species.

Itinerary

Note: This trip begins and ends in Miami.

Day 1 — Miami to Key West

Leave Miami early and head south on Highway 1. Although it is only a three-hour drive to Key West, you should use the entire day to bird down the Keys. *A Birder's Guide to Florida* covers most of the good locations. The booklet, *Birding in the Florida Keys* can also be informative. It is possible to pick up all of your target species by looking in appropriate habitat at a few excellent locations. Key species are White-crowned Pigeon, Mangrove Cuckoo, Antillean Nighthawk, Gray Kingbird, Black-whiskered

Vireo, Cape May Warbler, Black-throated Blue Warbler, Bobolink, and Shiny Cowbird.

(Directions for the Keys refer to the posted mileage markers, which start with Mile 0 at Key West.)

The Upper Florida Keys are heavily developed, and the only notable species you are likely to see this morning are White-crowned Pigeon, Eurasian Collared-Dove, and Gray Kingbird. The pigeon is usually just a dark figure zipping over the road, but it will sometimes cooperate by sitting in plain sight. Gray Kingbird and the introduced Eurasian Collared-Dove perch obligingly on utility wires.

At Islamorada you will find the Green Turtle Inn just before Mile 81. Fifty yards northeast of the inn a nature trail is usually good for Black-whiskered Vireo and other migrating landbirds.

As you move down the Keys, any beach area can be good for gulls, terns, and shorebirds, but Roseate Tern is not likely until you are well south of Marathon. This species becomes more likely the farther south you go and is often found on Stock Island and Key West, as well as at the Dry Tortugas.

When you reach Big Pine Key, watch on the left for Long Beach Drive just beyond Mile 33. Turn here; the road curves to the right in about one-quarter mile, and on the south side of the curve you will see a trailhead. Walk along this trail through Cactus Hammock; it can be good for White-crowned Pigeon, Mangrove Cuckoo, Black-whiskered Vireo, Cape May Warbler, and Black-throated Blue Warbler. Unless you are extremely lucky, you will need a tape to find the cuckoo. *A Birder's Guide to Florida* lists several other locations for Mangrove Cuckoo on Big Pine Key and adjacent No Name Key.

Return to Highway 1 and continue south to Sugarloaf Key. Watch for County Road 939 at Mile 17. Turn left and drive approximately 2.5 miles to the point where this road T's into another section of County Road 939. Here you can go left (this road may be closed to vehicles, so walking may be necessary) and check mangrove thickets for about 1.3 miles, or turn right and check them for 3.5 miles. This is prime Mangrove Cuckoo habitat, and you should be able to locate this species by being patient. (Unfortunately, there are too many birders using tapes in this area.)

Remotely Possible Species
(continued)

Pectoral Sandpiper
Stilt Sandpiper
Long-billed Dowitcher
Wilson's Phalarope
Red Phalarope
Parasitic Jaeger
Lesser Black-backed Gull
Sabine's Gull
Olive-sided Flycatcher
Yellow-bellied Flycatcher
Acadian Flycatcher
La Sagra's Flycatcher
Tree Swallow
Cliff Swallow
Cave Swallow
Bahama Mockingbird
Warbling Vireo
Philadelphia Vireo
Golden-winged Warbler
Nashville Warbler
Pine Warbler
Bay-breasted Warbler
Cerulean Warbler
Connecticut Warbler
Wilson's Warbler
Canada Warbler
Yellow-breasted Chat
Brown-headed Cowbird

Note: You will probably be lucky to see more than 2 of the species on the remotely possible list.

Return to Highway 1 and continue south to Stock Island. Turn right and drive about one-quarter mile on the last road before the bridge to Key West. The Botanical Gardens here usually harbor White-Crowned Pigeon, Black-whiskered Vireo, and perhaps some migrating warblers. The nearby Community College parking lot directly across from the hospital has become one of the most reliable places to see Antillean Nighthawk. Look for them near dusk feeding over the school, the hospital, and the adjacent golf course.

Cross the bridge to Key West. On the far end of the island is Fort Zachary Taylor State Park, which is a good place from which to see Roseate Terns offshore (they breed on nearby rooftops). The Key West airport is another of the known places to view Antillean Nighthawk. This species can usually be found in the last hour of daylight feeding over the nearby swamps.

If your trip to the Dry Tortugas is leaving this evening, you will not need a place to spend the night. If it is leaving in the morning you can choose a motel in Key West at extremely high rates or, better yet, drive back north on Highway 1 to Bahia Honda State Park to camp. If you plan to camp, you need to make arrangements earlier in the day because the campground gate is normally locked at sunset.

Days 2, 3, and 4 — Key West to the Dry Tortugas and back

Some Dry Tortugas trips leave Key West in the early morning. On these boats the sun will be at your back throughout the voyage, aiding visibility. This departure time also gives you two chances to see the key pelagic species. Other boat trips leave Key West at night, depositing you at Fort Jefferson in early morning. This option is good for increased landbirding, but you give up some pelagic birding opportunities on the way out.

As you leave Key West, your first key species are usually Magnificent Frigatebird and, with luck, Roseate Tern. Both can be seen very soon after leaving the dock. Other key species normally sighted between Key West and the Dry Tortugas are Audubon's Shearwater, Northern Gannet, Pomarine Jaeger, and Bridled Tern. Stay alert; there are always other pelagic species around, and some might prove to be really exciting finds.

A gradual build-up of Sooty Tern numbers lets you know that you are approaching the Dry Tortugas. The first Brown Noddies for the trip will soon wing past. Both of these species nest by the thousands on Bush Key, but you won't tire of watching them.

A typical Dry Tortugas tour allows you to be as active a birder or as laid-back a tourist as you please. The boat will dock at Fort Jefferson on

Garden Key. Inside the fort you will find a dozen or so trees, various brushy tangles, and a maintained grassy area. A small fountain provides only source of fresh water for migrating birds. You may want to sit here quietly to watch a constantly changing array of species come in to drink. At the minimum you should see Gray Kingbird, Cape May Warbler, Black-throated Blue Warbler, and possibly Bobolink and Shiny Cowbird. Look overhead regularly for swallows, raptors, and White-tailed Tropicbirds. Search all the trees for feeding and perched birds. Climbing to the upper level of the old fort gives you a tree-top view, as well as serving as an excellent vantage point for scoping Bush Key and the surrounding waters.

The area outside of the fort is also good for migrating landbirds, and the small beach areas are stop-overs for migrating waders. The shady grove where campers pitch their tents is attractive to migrating owls and a variety of passerines. If you are lucky enough to be at Fort Jefferson when a weather front with rain passes through, you can be inundated with migrants.

Most tour companies take participants in small boats around Bush Key (no landings allowed) to study the nesting Sooty Terns and Brown Noddies. It will take close scrutiny of the noddies to determine if there are any Black Noddies present (but they may not be visible from the boat). They are not predictable but do occur almost regularly. Sometimes a Black Noddy will be found on the north coaling-docks perched along with the Brown Noddies. Some very lucky folks have scanned Bush Key with a powerful scope from the top of the fort to find a Black Noddy. (Because of the lighting, this last method is feasible only in the afternoon or early evening.) The small boats can also be used for visiting the Magnificent Frigatebird colony on nearby Long Key.

Most tour boats take participants over to Loggerhead Key which is good for migrating landbirds, Hospital Key where Masked Boobies roost, and through the channel-marker areas for Brown Boobies.

All of the key species for this portion of the trip should be easily seen.

The two nights at Fort Jefferson can be spent on the boat or camping at the tent area on Garden Key.

The return trip to Key West is a second chance at any pelagic key species that you may have missed, or if your outbound trip was at night, it is your only chance for these pelagic species.

By the time you return to the dock at Key West, all key species for the trip should have been seen. If you have missed any, it will probably be Mangrove Cuckoo and/or Antillean Nighthawk. These possible omissions will determine your strategy for the remainder of the trip. If

Antillean Nighthawk was missed, you might dock in time to try again at the Key West airfield or at the Community College on Stock Island. The Marathon Airport (49 miles) is another of the better known locations for that species. If Mangrove Cuckoo was missed, return to the areas which you tried on Day 1 or visit the other locations described for that species in *A Birder's Guide to Florida*.

The possible need to find these species will also help to determine where you spend the night. There are campgrounds at Bahia Honda, Long Key, and John Pennekamp State Park, and numerous, and usually over-priced, motels are available throughout the Keys.

Day 5 — Extra Day

This day may be spent locating any missed key species. If there are no misses, you may choose to visit Everglades National Park, the Homestead area, or South Miami. All are good for a number of species and can provide second chances at some species targeted both in this chapter and in Chapter 5.

This trip ends in Miami in the evening.

Bird Numbers This Trip

	Potential	Expected	Actual
Key Species	19	19	
Probable Species	82	82	
Possible Species	59	11	
Remotely Possible Species	43	2	
Totally Unexpected Species	?	1	
TOTAL	203	115	

Cumulative List

Total key and probable species seen after 8 trips.

Previous trips	455	species
Florida Keys and Dry Tortugas Trip	19	species
TOTAL	474	species

This Trip's Mileage and Expenses

Approximate miles traveled, Miami to Miami: 400

- Fuel: $28; sharing $14 $_____
- Lodging: camping every night $20; sharing $10 $_____
- Food: No meals in restaurants $25 $_____
- Three-day tour to Dry Tortugas: $425 $_____
  *The total per person cost for the above items, sharing fuel and lodging
  expenses, should be less than $475.*
- Add to this car rental expenses, if any: $_____
- Add to this your expenses to/from Miami: $_____
  This will give you a good idea of the cost of this trip.
- TOTAL $_____

Personal Notes

_____

_____

_____

_____

_____

_____

_____

_____

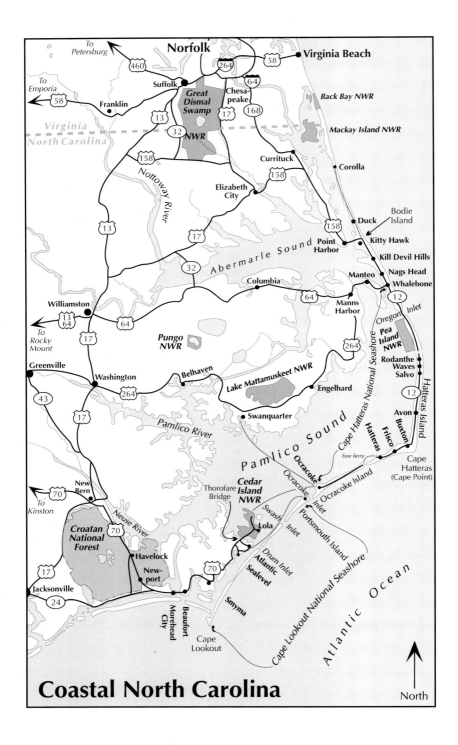

Coastal North Carolina

Chapter 9

COASTAL
NORTH CAROLINA

Mid- to Late May—4 Days

General

An Atlantic Coast pelagic trip out of a central United States port can give a real boost to your seabird list. There are trips almost every month of the year out of ports from New Jersey to North Carolina, organized by qualified individuals and tour companies. Most of these outings are listed in the annual pelagic directory of *Winging It* (see Chapter 1 for details). Trips that are organized too late to be included in the directory are usually advertised in later issues in the newsletter's classified section.

Considering the variety of species that can be expected on the various pelagic trips, and looking for the opportunity to see some specific species such as Band-rumped Storm-Petrel and Black-capped Petrel, a North Carolina trip is best for you overall.

Not only will North Carolina provide you with fine pelagic birding, but it also can yield good landbirding and excellent shorebirding. Though the main object of this visit to North Carolina is pelagic birding, you would do well to spend time on other birding endeavors, too.

Pelagic birding trips out of North Carolina usually leave from Manteo or Hatteras. These two embarkation points are on the Outer Banks, are about an hour apart, and are reached by the same route. In addition, the trips are all similarly priced, ranging from $80 to $100 per day.

The best way to plan this trip is to first check January's *Winging It* pelagic directory. Look for a set of two-day or three-day, mid- to late May trips. If you cannot find anything that will work into your schedule, call the organizers since some trips may not be listed in the pelagic directory.

Birders with time to spare will even extend their visit over two weekends, providing for two sets of pelagic trips over two weekends and furnishing opportunities for plenty of landbirding and shorebirding in

119

Probable Species
Total of 93 Species
Sooty Shearwater
Audubon's Shearwater
Northern Gannet
Brown Pelican
Double-crested Cormorant
Great Blue Heron
Great Egret
Snowy Egret
Little Blue Heron
Tricolored Heron
Cattle Egret
Green Heron
Black-crowned Night-Heron
White Ibis
Glossy Ibis
American Black Duck
Blue-winged Teal
Gadwall
Osprey
Red-shouldered Hawk
Clapper Rail
King Rail
Common Moorhen
Black-bellied Plover
Semipalmated Plover
Piping Plover
American Oystercatcher
Black-necked Stilt
American Avocet
Greater Yellowlegs
Lesser Yellowlegs
Willet
Whimbrel
Ruddy Turnstone
Red Knot
Sanderling
Semipalmated Sandpiper
Least Sandpiper
White-rumped Sandpiper
Dunlin
Short-billed Dowitcher
Pomarine Jaeger
Laughing Gull
Ring-billed Gull
Herring Gull
Gull-billed Tern
Caspian Tern
Royal Tern
Sandwich Tern
Common Tern
Forster's Tern
Least Tern
Black Skimmer
Rock Dove
Mourning Dove
Yellow-billed Cuckoo
Chuck-will's-widow
Chimney Swift
Ruby-throated Hummingbird
Northern Flicker
Great Crested Flycatcher
Eastern Kingbird

between. This means expanding your four-day trip into a nine-day trip, but it also increases the birding opportunities accordingly.

Under either plan, when you locate the pelagic trips that will fit your schedule, make your reservations and go for it!

This four-day-trip itinerary will take you through the Outer Banks and their offshore waters.

Birdfinding Guides

John O. Fussell, III's *A Birder's Guide to Coastal North Carolina* (1994) is a very helpful and detailed book. I would recommend it especially if you plan to do additional landbirding along the coast. Some birders simply taking the pelagic trip may find it unnecessary to bring along a birdfinding guide. Still, you do need your favorite seabird field guide to facilitate seabird identification. It is best to do your homework, studying the species that you may see, prior to making the trip.

Rare Bird Alert Number

Statewide 704/332-2473

Special Equipment

For the pelagic outings, deck shoes are recommended. Temperatures can be extremely warm during the summer; sunscreen and a wide-brim hat are essential. It might be wise to bring along a jacket in case the wind picks up. Remedies or preventives for seasickness are advised for all pelagic outings. If you are doing serious birding ashore, bring a supply of insect repellent.

Accommodations

Lodging most convenient for the tour group is usually recommended by the pelagic trip organizer. In this season, it will cost $40 to $65 per night for two people. Advance reservations are recommended. Most of the tours will have you check in with them on the night prior to the pelagic trip; they will tell you a time and a place to meet the next morning, and you can stay where you like. If you are economy-minded, campgrounds are at Oregon Inlet (about 15 miles from Manteo), at Cape Point, and at Frisco (5 miles from Hatteras). The campgrounds all charge a fee, and all provide showers.

Key Species — Total of 12 Species

1. **Black-capped Petrel**—Seen on the overwhelming majority of the trips in May; in fact, it is common throughout the year. You need to get out 20 to 40 miles; this is a deep-water Gulf Stream species.

2. **Cory's Shearwater**—Open ocean species that is seen on all trips and is considered common May through September. Best bet is 20+ miles offshore.

3. **Greater Shearwater**—Open-ocean bird to be seen 20 to 40 miles offshore. Not as common as Cory's, it is usually seen in smaller numbers and in some years is virtually absent.

4. **Wilson's Storm-Petrel**—Open-ocean species, follows ships, often appears to be suspended in air with feet touching the water. Common; sometimes seen from land.

5. **Leach's Storm-Petrel**—Open-ocean species, but may be seen from land in late May. Not nearly as common as Wilson's and when seen is usually well out to sea.

6. **Band-rumped Storm-Petrel**—Deep-water Gulf Stream species. Uncommon in late May with about an 80 percent chance of being seen on this trip. The later in May, the better your chances.

7. **Red-necked Phalarope**—Uncommon in spring and fall. Sometimes feeds in coastal areas like other shorebirds, but your best bet is the open ocean. Usually seen in small flocks.

8. **Parasitic Jaeger**—Not common but is seen on most pelagic trips in May in this area. Frequently migrates along the coast within 2 miles of land and is the jaeger most often seen from shore.

Probable Species
(continued)

Purple Martin
Barn Swallow
Blue Jay
American Crow
Fish Crow
Carolina Chickadee
Carolina Wren
Marsh Wren
Gray Catbird
Northern Mockingbird
Brown Thrasher
European Starling
White-eyed Vireo
Yellow Warbler
Pine Warbler
Prairie Warbler
Prothonotary Warbler
Common Yellowthroat
Yellow-breasted Chat
Northern Cardinal
Indigo Bunting
Rufous-sided Towhee
Field Sparrow
Seaside Sparrow
Song Sparrow
Red-winged Blackbird
Eastern Meadowlark
Boat-tailed Grackle
Common Grackle
Brown-headed Cowbird
House Sparrow

Note: The species in **boldface** appear no more than four times in the itineraries as *key* or *probable* species. Watch for them on this trip. As usual, assume that you will see all of the probable species. You will only see 1 species not seen on a previous trip.

Possible Species
Total of 49 Species
Common Loon
Least Bittern
Yellow-crowned
  Night-Heron
Wood Duck
Mallard
Red-breasted Merganser
Black Vulture
Turkey Vulture
Northern Harrier
Ring-necked Pheasant
Northern Bobwhite
Black Rail
Virginia Rail
Wilson's Plover
Spotted Sandpiper
Marbled Godwit
Western Sandpiper
Stilt Sandpiper
Red Phalarope

9. **Long-tailed Jaeger**—Seen in small numbers on most late-May trips. May be seen from shore during storms with strong onshore winds.

10. **South Polar Skua**—May be seen anywhere offshore, does not flock, and is usually seen singly. Often found where shearwaters or gulls are feeding.

11. **Great Black-backed Gull**—Commonly seen along the coast throughout the Outer Banks. Easy to see and to identify. Not seen offshore, but should be spotted as you are leaving or returning to port.

12. **Arctic Tern**—Very rarely seen from shore; migrates at least 10 miles offshore. Uncommon in this area in May but should be found on most trips.

Note: If you can find a Band-rumped Storm-Petrel, you have a good chance of seeing all 12 key species.

Itinerary

Note: This trip begins and ends in Norfolk, Virginia

Day 1 — Norfolk and the Outer Banks

The Outer Banks is a barrier-island chain curving out into the Atlantic Ocean and back again, forming a protective shelter for the mainland coast. To reach the Outer Banks, drive south on Interstate 64 to Chesapeake. Take Highway 168 south about 40 miles to Highway 158; continue south on Highway 158 for about 30 additional miles, reaching the Outer Banks near Kitty Hawk, North Carolina (total milage about 75 miles).

If you have the time and the interest, you can take an alternate route in Virginia to go past the Great Dismal Swamp National Wildlife Refuge. In the northwest portion of the refuge along Jerico Lane you can try for Swainson's Warbler. *Do not use tapes here.* (Other species of regional interest here include Acadian Flycatcher, Brown-headed Nuthatch, Yellow-throated Vireo, Yellow-throated, Prothonotary, and Hooded Warblers, and Summer Tanager.) For details see *A Birder's Guide to Coastal North Carolina.*

Bird your way down the Outer Banks to Whalebone Junction (about 15 miles). From Whalebone Junction on Bodie Island south to Ocracoke Inlet the islands constitute Cape Hatteras National Seashore. Highway 12 is the only access, by land, to any of this area. Along Highway 12 there are eight small villages. The villages are not part of the park, but the bulk of the surrounding lands is park land.

The first part of Cape Hatteras National Seashore is on Bodie Island. Bodie Island offers a beach, a visitor center, and a nature trail—all before you reach the lighthouse. Past the lighthouse you will come to a marina. Oregon Inlet Campground is across Highway 12 from the marina.

Continuing on Highway 12, cross Oregon Inlet onto Pea Island National Wildlife Refuge. Be sure

Remotely Possible Species
(continued)

Pectoral Sandpiper
Curlew Sandpiper
Ruff
Long-billed Dowitcher
American Woodcock
Bonaparte's Gull
Black-legged Kittiwake
Sabine's Gull
Roseate Tern
Black Tern
Brown Noddy
Belted Kingfisher
Bank Swallow
House Wren
Cedar Waxwing
Northern Parula
Scarlet Tanager
Rose-breasted Grosbeak
Salt-marsh Sharp-tailed Sparrow
Bobolink
Baltimore Oriole

Note: You'll probably not see any of these species on the Outer Banks, though a few are possible if you visit Great Dismal Swamp or Cedar Island NWRs, or Croatan Nat'l Forest.

Black-capped Petrel
Gail Diane Yovanovich

to walk along the nature trail starting a few miles farther, on your right. The shorebirding can be excellent here, with Black-necked Stilt, American Avocet, both yellowlegs, Whimbrel, Red Knot, numerous peep, and Short-billed Dowitcher in evidence. Watch for herons, egrets, and ibises, and check the reeds for Marsh Wren and Seaside Sparrow.

After leaving Pea Island National Wildlife Refuge, continue south on Highway 12 down Hatteras Island. There are piers at Rodanthe, Avon, and south of Frisco. Campgrounds can be found at Cape Hatteras Point and at Frisco (all have showers). Another nature trail at Cape Hatteras is worth investigating.

During May one of the best places to bird is Cape Point; it is well worth the walk. Some of the following pelagic species may be seen streaming by: Sooty Shearwater and other shearwaters, Wilson's and Leach's Storm-Petrels, all three jaegers, and South Polar Skua. The local tern colonies sometimes have Roseate and Sooty Terns. There may be Piping Plovers in the vicinity, and a variety sandpipers can be at any wet area. The nearby pond is worth checking; it is usually good for several species of waterfowl. Rarities that have occurred at Cape Point include Curlew Sandpiper and Ruff.

At Hatteras, if time permits, you can take a free 40-minute ferry ride to Ocracoke Island, where you will find a campground and a nature trail.

Bird down the Outer Banks as far as your time allows. (If you have scheduled a trip beyond the minimum four days, you'll be able to bird some of these locations later. *John Fussell's book A Birder's Guide to Coastal North Carolina* is packed with birding advice and sites to cover on the Outer Banks.) Then, depending on which port you are using for the pelagic trip, drive to that location and check in with your trip leader.

After checking in, get a motel for the night or drive to the nearest campground.

Days 2 and 3 — Pelagic Birding
Join your tour group at the predetermined location each morning. Pelagic trips normally are eleven to twelve hours in length and make a very full day. All of the key species should be seen during the pelagic outings. Other possibilities are Northern Fulmar, Herald Petrel, Sooty, Manx, and Audubon's Shearwaters, White-tailed Tropicbird, Northern Gannet, Red Phalarope, Pomarine Jaeger, Black-legged Kittiwake, Sabine's Gull, Roseate, Common, Bridled, and Sooty Terns, and Brown Noddy.

Note: Not all of the key species are likely to be seen in one day. In May, the average pelagic outing in this area records approximately 20 species; with two days at sea you do have a reasonable chance at all 12.

Use a motel or a campground on Days 2 and 3. See Accommodations section for campground locations.

Day 4 — The Outer Banks and Options

If you were not able to get on a two-day pelagic trip or opted for the three-day excursion, you will need this day for pelagic birding.

If the two-day pelagic trip was available, use this day to enjoy the various nature trails, Cape Point, and Pea Island National Wildlife Refuge again. If you opted for a longer visit, including the two-weekend alternative, spend some time birding along the coast looking at shorebirds and going inland to pursue some regional specialties.

For some satisfying birding, try Cedar Island National Wildlife Refuge and Croatan National Forest. Combining these two locations, you may find Black Rail, Red-cockaded Woodpecker, Swainson's Warbler, and Bachman's Sparrow. Brown-headed Nuthatch is another southeastern bird which you can find here. Even if you've seen these birds elsewhere (see especially Chapter 7), you may want to enjoy them again.

To get to these locations, take the ferry to Cedar Island from the far south end of Ocracoke Island. Reservations in advance are required (919/225-3841); the fare is currently $10 for car and driver.

For the Cedar Island marshes you are here at about the peak time of year. Try a calm morning at sunrise or a calm night after midnight. Route 12 along the 3.5-mile stretch northeast of the Thorofare Bridge is the place to try for Black Rail. Be patient and use your tape sparingly at a number of likely-looking sites. There is also a chance for Swainson's Warbler at a few locations on Cedar Island.

For additional likely places to see Swainson's Warbler, try the Croatan National Forest—North Section (Neuse River Recreation Area or the Gum Swamp Bottomland Forest site). The South Section of Croatan National Forest is particularly good for Red-cockaded Woodpeckers, Brown-headed Nuthatch, and Bachman's Sparrow. *A Birder's Guide to Coastal North Carolina* has details on each of these species and suggests some likely locations.

Give yourself enough time to drive back to Norfolk, Virginia, to complete this trip.

Bird Numbers This Trip

	Potential	Expected	Actual
Key Species	12	12	
Probable Species	93	93	
Possible Species	49	4	
Remotely Possible Species	39	0	
Totally Unexpected Species . . . . . ?		1	
. . . .	193	110	

Cumulative List

Total key and probable species seen after 9 trips.

Previous trips . . . . 474 species
Coastal North Carolina . . . . 13 species
TOTAL . . . . 487 species

This Trip's Mileage and Expenses

Miles from Norfolk to Norfolk (not including landbirding): 400

- Fuel: $30; sharing $15 $_____
- Lodging: 3 nights at motels $135; sharing $67.50 $_____
-   OR camping $30; sharing $15   or $_____
- Food: Ice-chest/supermarket for all meals $40 $_____
- Fare for 2-day pelagic trip: $200 $_____
  *The total per person cost for the above items with a companion
  to share expenses will be less than $300.*
- Add to this car rental expenses, if any: $_____
- Add to this your expenses to/from Norfolk: $_____
  This will give you a good idea of the cost of this trip.
- TOTAL $_____

Personal Notes

_____

_____

_____

_____

_____

_____

_____

_____

_____

_____

_____

_____

_____

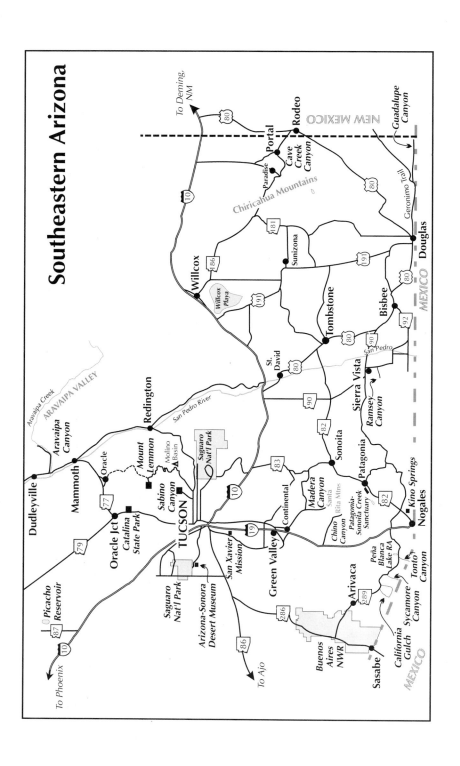

Southeastern Arizona

Chapter 10

LATE SPRING IN SOUTHEASTERN ARIZONA

Late May—9 Days

General

Southeastern Arizona is an area of diverse habitats which supports a large number of bird species that cannot be seen elsewhere north of Mexico. Of the 46 species specifically pursued on this trip, over 30 either do not occur elsewhere in the ABA Area or, if they do, their range is very limited. Because of the nearness of the Mexican border and the topography of the area, numerous rarities can occur, too. The many canyons and small mountain ranges that span the border funnel these species into Arizona and create exciting prospects for the birder.

It is worthwhile to visit Southeastern Arizona at two different seasons—late May before the weather gets extremely hot and in late July or early August after the rains come to cool things down again. An August trip is described in Chapter 16. This itinerary is scheduled for the latter half of May. During that fortnight the summer birds are present and the weather is ordinarily very nice, not usually heating up until June 1.

Many birders visit Arizona specifically for the hummingbirds; 14 species occur, the rarer ones in late summer and fall—but you will see at least 7 species in May. Other birders come for the nightbirding, and there is no better place in the ABA Area for this specialty. With some effort you may see 11 species of owls and 5 species of nightjars. If the hummingbirds, owls, and nightjars are not enough, add the many other specialties of the region and then throw in the real possibility of a Mexican rarity and you have all the ingredients for a near-perfect birding trip.

Locations for camping are plentiful throughout the trip area, both with and without fees. The only real drawback to camping is that in an arid region like this, most campgrounds do not have shower facilities.

Southeastern Arizona is usually defined as the Tucson vicinity and everything south and east of that city to the state's boundaries. This area includes the "Mexican Mountains" which shelter many of the birding

Probable Species
Total of 122 Species
Pied-billed Grebe
Great Egret
Black-bellied
Whistling-Duck
Mallard
Blue-winged Teal
Cinnamon Teal
Turkey Vulture
Cooper's Hawk
Harris's Hawk
Swainson's Hawk
Red-tailed Hawk
Golden Eagle
American Kestrel
Prairie Falcon
Wild Turkey
Scaled Quail
Common Moorhen
American Coot
Killdeer
Black-necked Stilt
American Avocet
Spotted Sandpiper
Wilson's Phalarope
Rock Dove
Band-tailed Pigeon
White-winged Dove
Mourning Dove
Inca Dove
Common Ground-Dove
Greater Roadrunner
Barn Owl
Great Horned Owl
Northern Pygmy-Owl
Burrowing Owl
Lesser Nighthawk
Whip-poor-will
White-throated Swift
Black-chinned
Hummingbird
Broad-tailed
Hummingbird
Acorn Woodpecker
Ladder-backed
Woodpecker
Hairy Woodpecker
Northern Flicker
Western Wood-Pewee
Cordilleran Flycatcher
Black Phoebe
Say's Phoebe
Ash-throated Flycatcher
Brown-crested
Flycatcher
Cassin's Kingbird
Western Kingbird
Horned Lark
Purple Martin
Violet-green Swallow
Northern Rough-
winged Swallow
Cliff Swallow
Barn Swallow
Steller's Jay
Western Scrub-Jay
Chihuahuan Raven
Common Raven
Plain Titmouse
Verdin

hotspots for which Arizona is famous. You will visit the Santa Catalina, Santa Rita, Pajarito, Huachuca, and Chiricahua Mountains as well as arid canyons and the oases created by any dependable water supply. You can make a side trip or two outside the southeast part of the state, but you should not stray far or for long.

This trip includes Tucson, the Arizona-Sonora Desert Museum, Saguaro National Park, Mount Lemmon, Aravaipa Canyon, Chino Canyon, Madera Canyon, Tonto Canyon, Sycamore Canyon, California Gulch, Patagonia-Sonoita Creek Preserve, Scheelite Canyon, Sawmill Canyon, Ramsey Canyon, the San Pedro Riparian National Conservation Area, Guadalupe Canyon, Cave Creek Canyon, Rustler Park, Pinery Canyon, and numerous other stops along the way.

Birdfinding Guides

A Birder's Guide to Southeastern Arizona by Richard Cachor Taylor (1995) is the ABA/Lane birdfinding guide for the area, highly recommended for route planning, information about local facilities, and as a comprehensive source of bird distribution, habitat, and seasonal abundance information.

Davis and Russell's Finding Birds in Southeast Arizona by the Tucson Audubon Society (1995) includes details and expected species lists for over 90 regional sites.

Rare Bird Alert Numbers

Tucson 520/798-1005
Phoenix 602/832-8745

Special Equipment

A portable spotlight and bird tapes, although not absolutely essential, are a great aid to efficient nightbirding. A canteen is a must for hiking in the more arid areas on this trip. Faithful use of sunscreen is essential. This trip will be made much easier if you are willing to do some camping. A high-clearance vehicle is recommended for a few destinations on this trip.

Accommodations

Motels are not plentiful in much of this area. Outside of Tucson, Nogales, Sierra Vista, and Douglas, lodging can be scarce and advance reservations are highly recommended. Both birdfinding guides and this chapter furnish information about most locations where your choices are extremely limited.

The best alternative for the economy-minded birder is camping; there is no shortage of campsites in this area.

Key Species — Total of 47 Species

1. **Common Black-Hawk**—Aravaipa Canyon is the current best location close to Tucson for this species. It should also be watched for in other low-elevation riparian woodlands.

2. **Gray Hawk**—Normally easy to see at Patagonia-Sonoita Creek Preserve; frequently seen from nearby Patagonia Roadside Rest Area on Highway 82. Another excellent spot is the San Pedro Riparian National Conservation Area (especially just north of San Pedro House).

3. **Zone-tailed Hawk**—Can be found at Madera, Guadalupe, and Cave Creek Canyons. There are usually active nest sites in the Patagonia area, but these are not likely to be found without local guidance.

4. **Gambel's Quail**—Common and easily seen in desertscrub. Numerous and unwary at the Desert Museum.

5. **Flammulated Owl**—Sometimes easy to locate in Madera Canyon (e.g., at the start of the Josephine Saddle Trail). Miller Canyon (Huachucas) and Cave Creek Canyon (Chiracahuas) are two other good locations. Hearing this owl is much easier than seeing it.

Probable Species
(continued)

Bushtit
White-br. Nuthatch
Pygmy Nuthatch
Brown Creeper
Cactus Wren
Rock Wren
Canyon Wren
Bewick's Wren
House Wren
Blue-gray Gnatcatcher
Eastern Bluebird
Western Bluebird
Hermit Thrush
American Robin
Northern Mockingbird
Curve-billed Thrasher
Cedar Waxwing
Phainopepla
Loggerhead Shrike
European Starling
Bell's Vireo
Solitary Vireo
Hutton's Vireo
Warbling Vireo
Orange-crowned
    Warbler
Yellow Warbler
Yellow-rumped
    Warbler
Black-throated Gray
    Warbler
Townsend's Warbler
Common Yellowthroat
Wilson's Warbler
Yellow-breasted Chat
Summer Tanager
Western Tanager
Northern Cardinal
Pyrrhuloxia
Black-headed Grosbeak
Blue Grosbeak
Spotted Towhee
Canyon Towhee
Cassin's Sparrow
Rufous-crowned
    Sparrow
Chipping Sparrow
Lark Sparrow
Black-throated Sparrow
Grasshopper Sparrow
Song Sparrow
Red-winged Blackbird
Eastern Meadowlark
Great-tailed Grackle
Bronzed Cowbird
Brown-headed Cowbird
Hooded Oriole
Bullock's Oriole
House Finch
Pine Siskin
Lesser Goldfinch
American Goldfinch
House Sparrow

Note: The species in **boldface** appear no more than four times in the itineraries as key or probable species.

Probable Species
(continued)

Watch for them on this trip. Assume that you will see all of the probables. You gain 13 species not seen on previous trips.

Possible Species
Total of 29 Species
Great Blue Heron
Green Heron
Black-crowned
  Night-Heron
Green-winged Teal
Ruddy Duck
Black Vulture
Mississippi Kite
Northern Goshawk
Montezuma Quail
Yellow-billed Cuckoo
Spotted Owl
Violet-crowned
  Hummingbird
Anna's Hummingbird
Green Kingfisher
Olive-sided Flycatcher
Willow Flycatcher
Dusky Flycatcher
Sulphur-bellied
  Flycatcher
Golden-crowned
  Kinglet
Ruby-crowned Kinglet
American Pipit
Gray Vireo
Hermit Warbler
MacGillivray's Warbler
Green-tailed Towhee
Lark Bunting
Dark-eyed Junco
Western Meadowlark
Red Crossbill

Note: You will probably see 4 of the species on the possible list.

Remotely Possible Species
Total of 25 Species
Double-crested
  Cormorant
Neotropic Cormorant
Snowy Egret
Gadwall
White-tailed Kite
Sharp-shinned Hawk
Peregrine Falcon
Ring-billed Gull
Ruddy Ground-Dove
Ferruginous
  Pygmy-Owl
Long-eared Owl
Common Nighthawk
Calliope Hummingbird

6. **Western Screech-Owl**—Easy to locate in Guadalupe Canyon, using a tape. It is also easy to locate in the lower parts of Cave Creek Canyon and in the mesquite around Portal.

7. **Whiskered Screech-Owl**—Easy to locate in either Madera or Cave Creek Canyons. Will usually be at higher elevation than Western Screech-Owl. The only safe identification is by voice.

8. **Elf Owl**—Usually easy to find near Sabino Canyon visitor center, at the Desert Museum, or near Santa Rita Lodge in Madera Canyon.

9. **Common Poorwill**—Can be found most nights at McCleary Wash (branching off Florida Wash) and Sabino Canyon.

10. **Buff-collared Nightjar**—For the last several years the best location has been McCleary Wash, which branches off Florida Wash near Madera Canyon. It is found at times in Guadalupe Canyon, California Gulch, Chino Canyon, and Aravaipa Canyon. Local birders will know the current hotspot.

11. **Broad-billed Hummingbird**—Common at Patagonia-Sonoita Creek Preserve. Also easy to find at lower elevations in Madera, Ramsey, and Cave Creek Canyons.

12. **Blue-throated Hummingbird**—Easy to see at feeders in Ramsey, Madera, Cave Creek Canyons.

13. **Magnificent Hummingbird**—Another cinch at feeders in Ramsey, Madera, and Cave Creek Canyons.

14. **Costa's Hummingbird**—Lower elevation species. Easy to see at Desert Museum, Chino Canyon, Florida Wash, or Sabino Canyon.

15. **Elegant Trogon**—Easiest to find on the South Fork Trail in Cave Creek Canyon. Can also be found in upper Madera Canyon and many other harder-to-reach areas (e.g., in the Huachucas).

16. **Gila Woodpecker**—Cannot be missed in stands of Saguaro cactus, such as at Desert Museum.

17. **Strickland's Woodpecker**—Fairly common in Madera and Cave Creek Canyons. Can be seen in the oak belt in most canyons that you will visit.

18. **Gilded Flicker**—Common in Saguaro cactus stands. Easiest to locate at Desert Museum and surrounding areas. Also common at Sabino Canyon.

19. **Northern Beardless-Tyrannulet**—Easiest to find in Guadalupe Canyon but may be seen at Patagonia-Sonoita Creek Preserve, the Proctor Road overlook area in Madera Canyon, and other lower-elevation locations with water.

20. **Greater Pewee**—Fairly common. See it at Mount Lemmon, Madera Canyon, Ramsey Canyon, Sawmill Canyon, and many locations in the Chiricahua Mountains.

Remotely Possible Species (continued)
Hammond's Flycatcher
Gray Flycatcher
Black-capped Gnatcatcher
Black-and-white Warbler
Flame-colored Tanager
Yellow Grosbeak
Lazuli Bunting
Indigo Bunting
Brewer's Sparrow
Streak-backed Oriole
Cassin's Finch
Evening Grosbeak
Note: You will be lucky to see 2 of these species on this trip.

21. **Buff-breasted Flycatcher**—Sawmill Canyon in the Huachuca Mountains is the best location. Several pairs nest there in a small area, making them easy to locate.

22. **Vermilion Flycatcher**—Common at lower elevations near water. Easy at Patagonia-Sonoita Creek Preserve and along San Pedro River.

23. **Dusky-capped Flycatcher**—Easy to see at Madera, Ramsey, or Cave Creek Canyons; also at Peña Blanca Lake and Patagonia-Sonoita Creek Preserve.

24. **Tropical Kingbird**—Regularly seen at Kino Springs; sometimes at the pond south of San Pedro House.

25. **Thick-billed Kingbird**—Easiest to find in Guadalupe Canyon, but is also regularly seen across the highway from Patagonia Roadside Rest Area and at nearby Patagonia-Sonoita Creek Preserve.

26. **Rose-throated Becard**—Best locations have been Patagonia-Sonoita Creek Preserve and across the highway from the Patagonia Roadside Rest Area. May be found in Sycamore Canyon, too.

27. **Mexican Jay**—Very common, noisy, and easy to locate at Madera, Cave Creek, and Pinery Canyons. Found at any other locations.

28. **Mexican Chickadee**—Fairly easy to locate on trails at Rustler and Barfoot Parks or at Pinery Canyon Campground, all in the Chiricahua Mountains.

29. **Bridled Titmouse**—Cannot be missed at Madera Canyon, Patagonia-Sonoita Creek Preserve, or South Fork of Cave Creek Canyon.

30. **Black-tailed Gnatcatcher**—Can usually be located easily at Chino Canyon, Sabino Canyon, or Florida Wash.

31. **Bendire's Thrasher**—Best bet may be Silverbell Road along the Santa Cruz River northwest of Tucson. San Xavier Mission south of Tucson has also become a reliable spot.

32. **Crissal Thrasher**—Usually easy to find in Florida Wash, Florida Canyon, or Guadalupe Canyon. Frequents dense mesquite along streams or low-desert chaparral.

33. **Virginia's Warbler**—Best spot is Onion Saddle in the Chiricahua Mountains. Can be hard to locate but is regularly seen along Josephine Saddle Trail, in upper Ramsey Canyon, and in Scheelite Canyon.

34. **Lucy's Warbler**—Common; should be seen at San Xavier Mission, Patagonia-Sonoita Creek Preserve, Florida Wash, and Guadalupe Canyon.

35. **Grace's Warbler**—Easy to find; try Rose, Sawmill, and Cave Creek Canyons as well as Rustler Park.

36. **Red-faced Warbler**—Easiest to locate at Rustler Park, Pinery Canyon, or along Barfoot Lookout Trail in the Chiricahuas. Also can be found at upper Ramsey Canyon and on Mount Lemmon near ski lodge.

37. **Painted Redstart**—Cannot be missed at Madera or Cave Creek Canyons.

38. **Olive Warbler**—Best spot is Barfoot Lookout Trail at Rustler Park. Can also be seen in Rose Canyon on Mount Lemmon or Sawmill Canyon.

39. **Hepatic Tanager**—Can be seen in most of the higher-elevation canyons—Madera and Cave Creek Canyons are among the best bets.

40. **Varied Bunting**—Not abundant this early in the season, but can usually be found in Chino Canyon, Florida Wash, Sycamore Canyon, and Guadalupe Canyon.

41. **Abert's Towhee**—San Xavier Mission, Kino Springs, Patagonia-Sonoita Creek Preserve, and Silverbell Road northwest of Tucson are some good locations.

42. **Botteri's Sparrow**—Can be found in Chino Canyon, lower Garden Canyon, Florida Wash, and lower Ramsey Canyon. Easiest to find in grassland above Florida Wash.

43. **Rufous-winged Sparrow**—Usually found in Florida Wash. With luck can also be located just outside Tucson; you can try along Wilmot Road just a half-mile north of I-10 and at San Xavier Mission across from the cemetery.

44. **Black-chinned Sparrow**—Usually difficult to locate, but try on the road to Paradise north of Portal (Chiricahuas). Usually easier to find at Sabino Canyon and farther north.

45. **Five-striped Sparrow**—Current best locations are California Gulch, Tonto Canyon, and Sycamore Canyon. (Has been seen in Chino Canyon, though not recently.)

46. **Yellow-eyed Junco**—Hard to miss at Rustler Park or above upper parking area in Madera Canyon.

47. **Scott's Oriole**—Common throughout in yucca or agaves. Also seen in most canyons at lower elevations. Not hard to find.

> Note: How many of these species you see will depend on how hard you work. Buff-collared Nightjar, a Code 4 species, can be difficult. The Code 3s can also throw you a curve. You might get all 47 species, and if you have good luck with Code 3 and 4 birds, you will score 100%.

Itinerary

Day 1 — Tucson, San Xavier Mission, Arizona-Sonora Desert Museum, Molino Basin, and Sabino Canyon

The first day of the trip should be spent in the immediate Tucson vicinity. Several of the key species can be found—and in fact the best locations for some of them—are within the city limits or very nearby.

Leave Tucson on Interstate 19 south. Soon, you will see San Xavier Mission on your right. Birding in the vicinity of the mission will produce some common species of this arid, sparsely vegetated area. The main reason for visiting this site, however, is to look for Bendire's Thrasher, which has been fairly reliable here. You might also pick up Abert's Towhee; Rufous-winged Sparrow is found across the road from the cemetery from time to time.

Drive back to Tucson on Interstate 19 to get on Ajo Way (Highway 86) west to Kinney Road. Turn right onto Kinney Road to the Arizona-Sonora Desert Museum. This is a great place to familiarize yourself with the flora, fauna, and common desert birds. Around the grounds and at the several feeding-stations you should see Gambel's Quail, White-winged Dove, Costa's Hummingbird, Gila Woodpecker, Gilded Flicker, Verdin, Cactus Wren, Black-tailed Gnatcatcher, Curve-billed Thrasher, Black-throated Sparrow, Bronzed Cowbird, Hooded Oriole, and Scott's Oriole.

Saguaro National Park's (western unit) Red Hills Information Center is just 2 miles north of the Desert Museum. Take the Bajada Loop Drive through the park and exit on the northeast side toward Interstate 10. You will reach Silverbell Road before you get to Interstate 10. Turn left onto Silverbell Road; this road follows the Santa Cruz River for several miles, and the mesquite thickets along the way may be possible for Bendire's Thrasher and even Abert's Towhee. Turn right at Cortaro Road, where Burrowing Owls have been seen near the river. You should also see Bronzed Cowbirds and Hooded Orioles along Silverbell Road.

Bird your way back toward Tucson through the same areas on Silverbell Road. Approximately 6 miles south of Cortaro Road you will reach Sweetwater Drive. Turn left (east) and cross the river; the Tucson

Sewage Ponds are on your left. This area is another possible location to find Bendire's Thrasher and Abert's Towhee.

Return to Silverbell Road, continue south, and turn left onto Speedway Boulevard. Drive to Wilmot Road, but then continue on east on Speedway approximately 5 miles past this intersection and start checking the vacant lots, especially the brushy ones, for Rufous-winged Sparrows. (Two other good Tucson-area locations for Rufous-winged Sparrow are on the extention of Wilmot below Davis-Monthan Air Force Base, about a half-mile short of I-10, and the junction of Shannon and Broadway (2 miles south and east of the junction of Speedway and Anklam on the west side of town.)

Follow Speedway Boulevard back to Wilmot Road, turn right (north). At Tanque Verde Road turn right and then turn left onto the Catalina Highway. In less than 5 miles you will begin the ascent to Mount Lemmon and Summerhaven. Another 5 miles brings you to Molino Basin Campground (open for camping only from September through April). You will pass through desert areas that can be good for the typical desert species, including Abert's Towhee, and enter the oak zone as you near Molino Basin. Here the birdlife changes and you can expect Strickland's Woodpecker, Western Scrub-Jay, Mexican Jay, Bridled Titmouse, and Black-throated Gray Warbler.

If you are planning to camp tonight, you will find several campgrounds (Rose Canyon, General Hitchcock, and Spencer Canyon) farther up the Catalina Highway. Catalina State Park (see Day 2) is farther away, but has nice facilities and good birding.

Near dusk, take the Catalina Highway back to Tanque Verde Road, turn right to Sabino Canyon Road, and follow that road to the Sabino Canyon visitor center parking area (13 miles). The small trees in the area are great for Elf Owl. The owl is common and noisy, so it is easy to locate here after the crowds have left for the day. This area has also produced the now extremely rare Ferruginous Pygmy-Owl on occasion. Your best bet, if you want to see one, is to contact local birders to see if any locations are known.

Return to your campground for the night or to Tucson for a motel.

Day 2 — Rose Canyon, Mount Lemmon, Aravaipa Creek, and Catalina State Park

In the morning continue birding your way up the Catalina Highway. Rose Canyon is a good place to locate a number of higher-elevation species (7,000 feet), which might include Northern Goshawk, Zone-tailed Hawk, Broad-tailed Hummingbird, Greater Pewee, Steller's Jay,

Virginia's Warbler, Grace's Warbler, Painted Redstart, Olive Warbler, Hepatic Tanager, Western Tanager, Black-headed Grosbeak, Yellow-eyed Junco, and Evening Grosbeak.

Continue up the highway, turn right at Ski Valley Road, drive past the lodge, and on to the top of Mount Lemmon. Here you might find Red-faced Warbler, Olive Warbler, and Red Crossbill (irregular). Cordilleran Flycatchers are fairly easy to find along the road to the top. The feeders back at the Iron Door Restaurant are good for Broad-tailed and, infrequently, White-eared Hummingbirds.

Take the 28-mile dirt road to Oracle. It is a very rough road, but with a high-clearance vehicle you can go slow and bird your way back down the mountain. If you would rather not take this rough road, return to Tucson, take Highway 77 north to Oracle Junction, and then east to near Oracle. From the intersection of Highway 77 and the dirt road from Mount Lemmon, continue on Highway 77 to Mammoth and then another 10.6 miles to Aravaipa Canyon Road. This road follows Aravaipa Creek for roughly 11 miles. Common Black-Hawk and Zone-tailed Hawk are both summer residents here. The Aravaipa Canyon Wilderness Area is at the end of this road; permission to enter the area is restricted and permits must be obtained from the Bureau of Land Management, phone 520/428-4040. (You must make reservations at least *13 weeks* in advance.) (In early 1993 a flash-flood washed out access to the last 3 miles of the road. Repairs are due in late 1995. With patience, however, the hawks can usually be seen before you reach the end of the road and without your having to enter the preserve.)

If you want to see Mississippi Kite, continue north on Highway 77 for about 5 miles to Dudleyville. The kites nest along the San Pedro River and can be seen from the highway. Common Black-Hawk and Zone-tailed Hawk are also possible here. There have been some other interesting species here—Gray Hawk, Tropical and Thick-billed Kingbirds, and the first North American nesting of the rare Streak-backed Oriole, for example.

Return on Highway 77 to Oracle Junction, and then turn left (still on Highway 77) toward Tucson. Between Catalina and Oro Valley watch for Catalina State Park. This park is worth a quick visit since it offers another chance for desert species, such as Crissal Thrasher and Abert's Towhee.

Return to Tucson, if you want a motel; otherwise, camp at Catalina State Park.

Day 3 — Chino Canyon, Florida Wash, and Madera Canyon

Leave early enough to make the approximately one-hour drive to Chino Canyon by near daylight. Take Interstate 19 south from Tucson to Canoa (Exit 56) 5.5 miles south of Green Valley. Specific directions to Chino Canyon from this exit can be found in both of the bird guides recommended earlier in this chapter. Follow the directions to the parking area near the base of Elephant Head, if you have a high-clearance vehicle.

The main reason for a visit to Chino Canyon is the possibility of seeing Black-capped Gnatcatcher. This was once the only reliable place to see this species in the United States, but there have been no recent sightings. It was usually found in the hackberry trees on the south slope of Elephant Head near the big oak tree. Remember that Blue-gray, Black-capped, and Black-tailed Gnatcatchers have all occurred here, so be careful with your identification.

Other species reported from Chino Canyon include Buff-collared Nightjar, Costa's Hummingbird, Canyon Wren, Varied Bunting, and Botteri's Sparrow. Five-striped Sparrow has been seen, but is not regular. *Do not use tapes in Chino Canyon.*

Return to Interstate 19 and turn north toward Green Valley. Take Exit 63 east to Continental, pass through this small community, and follow the surfaced road as it turns right in 7 miles toward Madera Canyon in the Santa Rita Mountains. The third one-lane bridge that you encounter crosses Florida Wash. A walk in either direction is worthwhile, though birding is usually better to the east. Key species to seek along the wash include Costa's Hummingbird, Crissal Thrasher, Lucy's Warbler, Varied Bunting, and Rufous-winged Sparrow. Other species of interest commonly found here are Bell's Vireo and Black-throated Sparrow. Cooper's Hawks have nested in the big trees near the old foundations (an abandoned ranch) that you will find well up the wash to the east.

Continuing up the road to Madera Canyon another 0.7 mile, you will find a road on the right. After another 2.2 miles, Proctor Road is also on the right. Both Botteri's and Cassin's Sparrows are found in the area between these two side roads. You may need to study a tape to safely identify these two very similar-looking species by voice.

Soon you will leave the grassland and enter the woodland. Stop frequently as you drive up to the Madera Picnic Grounds. Bird this area thoroughly, for there are many interesting species to be found here. A partial list of those includes Northern Goshawk, Zone-tailed Hawk, Broad-billed, Blue-throated and Magnificent Hummingbirds, Acorn and Strickland's Woodpeckers, Greater Pewee, Dusky-capped and Sulphur-bellied Flycatchers, Mexican Jay, Bridled Titmouse, Black-throated Gray

Warbler, Painted Redstart, Hepatic Tanager, Yellow-eyed Junco, and Scott's Oriole.

Birding your way up the canyon, you will soon reach Santa Rita Lodge. Be sure to check the hummingbird feeders around the front of the cabins. This is a delightful place to stay, but advance reservations are necessary: 520/625-8746.

At the end of the canyon road there are two parking lots and a picnic area. At the lower of the two parking lots (to the left of the main road), you will find the trailheads for the Vault Mine Trail (and up Hopkins Fork) and the trail to Josephine Saddle. Each of the trails offers good birding for about the first mile; Elegant Trogon has been found on both. Everything else to be seen beyond the first mile can probably be seen more easily elsewhere.

If you have time before dusk, a quick trip to upper Florida Canyon can be worthwhile. Road 488, a short distance below Florida Wash, goes east and joins Road 62A, and then continues 3.2 miles to the Santa Rita Experimental Range Work Center. The Florida Canyon trailhead is at the parking area. This trail is usually good for Crissal Thrasher; Black-chinned Sparrow has been seen here.

In the evening, just before dark, you need to locate the short trail to McCleary Wash, which branches off Florida Wash. This is the area where the Buff-collared Nightjars have been found. The trail is on the east side of Madera Canyon Road just before a cattle-guard 1.3 miles past the Florida Wash bridge (as you are driving upslope). Watch for the trail following along an old fence-line. Walk this trail to the small canyon that has been used as a trash dump. *Please do not use a tape here.* You do not need a tape to locate Buff-collared Nightjar. Common Poorwill can usually be located at this same spot.

Be aware that the vigil to hear or possibly see Buff-collared Nightjar takes place at exactly the same time as the owl-watchers are assembling in the parking lot at Santa Rita Lodge. You cannot do both. If Elf Owls and/or Whiskered Screech-Owls are currently nesting in the utility poles near the lodge, someone in the Santa Rita Lodge crowd will know to the minute when they will leave these cavities to begin the night's hunt. Ask around.

Then drive to the upper parking lot, and walk past the cable across the old road which leads to the Josephine Saddle Trail. You may find a Flammulated Owl within the first few hundred yards past the cable, and Whiskered Screech-Owls are common here.

You can spend the night at Bog Springs Campground in Madera Canyon. Water and toilets are provided, but there are no showers. You might also consider staying at Santa Rita Lodge (prior reservations strongly recommended) or at accommodations in nearby Green Valley.

Day 4 — Sycamore Canyon, California Gulch, Tonto Canyon, and Peña Blanca Lake Recreation Area

Leave Madera Canyon and return to Interstate 19 through Continental. (If you stayed overnight in Green Valley, you'll be right by I-19, and you'll have a head start.) Go south on Interstate 19, bird your way down the interstate to Ruby Road (Highway 289), and turn right (west) toward the Pajarito Mountains.

The schedule for today depends largely on information obtained from local birders and the hotline. Five-striped Sparrow is often found at Sycamore Canyon, California Gulch, and/or Tonto Canyon; all are reached by traveling Ruby Road and then hiking. Based on current information from local birders, decide which location you want to try, and, by all means, if they suggest a better location, try it. All of these locations are hot and difficult to reach but they may be your only chance for Five-striped Sparrow.

The first canyon-access road that you will reach is the one for Tonto Canyon. Drive west on Ruby Road (Highway 289) for 5.3 miles after the pavement ends. The track to the south leads to Tonto Canyon. A high-clearance, four-wheel-drive vehicle is necessary. After 3.4 miles you park and hike the rest of the way to densely grown hillsides near the Mexico border where Five-striped Sparrows nest.

Sycamore Canyon is reached by continuing west on Ruby Road for another 4.2 miles to the sign for Sycamore Canyon. Turn left for 0.5 mile and park by Hank and Yank Spring. A tough 5.0-mile hike along the stream-bed awaits you. After you have hiked downstream for about 2 miles, Peñasco Canyon enters from the left. From this point to the Mexican border, anything is possible. Key species in this area include Elegant Trogon, Rose-throated Becard, Varied Bunting, and, of course, Five-striped Sparrow. (You would be wise to read the section on Syca-more Canyon in *A Birder's Guide to Southeastern Arizona* before con-templeting this hike; it is not a mid-day stroll.)

California Gulch is not too much farther along Ruby Road. A four-wheel-drive vehicle is preferable, but standard vehicles often have no problem reaching the *top* of the short steep hill leading into the canyon. It's best to hike that last distance. Five-striped Sparrows nest on the steep canyon slopes, Buff-collared Nightjars have be found here at dusk, and Montezuma Quail is frequently seen.

Currently, the sparrows are being seen at each of these three locations, but conditions may change. Ask experienced birders who have visited these sites lately. You can get further details on most of these locations from the birdfinding guides mentioned at the beginning of this chapter. *Carefully follow their specific warnings about directions, water, vehicles, heat, maps, general safety, and other conditions.*

Whichever of these places you try, return to Ruby Road and drive east toward Interstate 19 when you are finished. The entry to Peña Blanca Lake Recreation Area is on your left where the gravel ends and the blacktop begins (about 10 miles from Interstate 19). The birding is fair around the lake; the only key species that you are likely to find are Strickland's Woodpecker, Vermilion and Dusky-capped Flycatchers, and Scott's Oriole.

Camp here for the night, or drive to Nogales for a motel.

Day 5 — Kino Springs, Patagonia-Sonoita Creek Preserve, and the Huachuca Mountains

If you stayed overnight in Nogales, take Highway 82 north toward Patagonia. If you camped at Peña Blanca Lake, follow Ruby Road to Interstate 19, take the Interstate to Highway 82 in Nogales and then turn north toward Patagonia.

Drive northeast about 4.5 miles on Highway 82, and you will come to Kino Springs, a golfing community, with a few houses, three ponds, and, of course, the golf course. Visits by courteous birders are tolerated (ask at the pro shop), and a quick tour through the area will often produce Black-bellied Whistling-Ducks and, almost always, Tropical Kingbirds.

Some 10 miles farther north, you will reach the famous Patagonia Roadside Rest Area. The rest-stop, including the narrow band of trees across the highway from it, has been for many years one of the better places to see Gray Hawk, Thick-billed Kingbird, and Rose-throated Becard. Some of the trees along the highway have been cut, but this area is always worth checking. (*Do not trespass beyond the barbed-wire fence across the road onto Circle Z Ranch property.*)

Continue northeast on Highway 82 for over 1 mile into Patagonia. Turn west onto 4th Avenue; turn south onto Pennsylvania Avenue, ford the creek, and go 0.7 mile to the entrance. The Nature Conservancy (which owns and operates the Patagonia-Sonoita Creek Preserve) is in the process of building a visitor center and will have a resident caretaker soon. At present, the sanctuary is open Wednesday to Sunday (7:30 am to 4 pm), and your plans must take this schedule into consideration.

This is one of the most productive birding areas in Arizona. Key species frequently seen in or adjacent to the sanctuary include Gray Hawk, Zone-tailed Hawk, Gambel's Quail, Broad-billed Hummingbird, Gila Woodpecker, Northern Beardless-Tyrannulet, Vermilion Flycatcher, Dusky-capped Flycatcher, Thick-billed Kingbird, Rose-throated Becard, Mexican Jay, Bridled Titmouse, Lucy's Warbler, and Varied Bunting.

When you leave the sanctuary, return to Highway 82 and drive northeast toward Sonoita. Continue on Highway 82 for about 32 miles to the Highway 90 junction. Take Highway 90 south to Sierra Vista. The main gate into Fort Huachuca is at the west end of Fry Boulevard; get in the right lane and stop for an entry pass. After entering the fort, stay in the left lane, and turn hard left at the Garden Canyon sign. This road is paved for about 8 miles; the pavement ends at a picnic area that can be good for Elegant Trogon, Strickland's Woodpecker, and Sulphur-bellied Flycatcher. Continue 0.7 mile to Scheelite Canyon. Park here and hike the steep trail. There are several species to be seen on this trail, but it is primarily known for Spotted Owl. The owls can usually be found about thirty minutes up the trail. (See *A Birder's Guide to Southeastern Arizona* for Spotted Owl-watching etiquette.)

Return to the gravel road and continue about 2 miles to an old cabin. Behind this cabin is the entrance to Sawmill Canyon; it is closed with a cable so you must walk up from this point. This canyon is well known as one of the better places to see Buff-breasted Flycatcher, which nests here and is usually easy to locate. Other key species here include Greater Pewee, Grace's Warbler, and Hepatic Tanager. Try to whistle up a Northern Pygmy-Owl (*no tapes are allowed on the military post*); these little owls can usually be found in this area.

Return to Sierra Vista for the night.

Day 6 — Ramsey Canyon, San Pedro Riparian National Conservation Area, and Guadalupe Canyon

The road to Ramsey Canyon Preserve leads west off Highway 92 exactly 6 miles south of the junction of Highways 90 and 92 in Sierra Vista. Drive 4 miles to the Preserve, operated by The Nature Conservancy and world famous for the variety of hummingbirds seen there. You may visit the preserve from 8 am to 5 pm daily, but reservations are strongly suggested due to very limited parking (520/378-2785). It is best to plan your visit for a weekday. *Use of tape players is absolutely forbidden at the preserve.*

Large numbers of hummingbirds swarm around the feeders in a small area with benches where you can sit and observe the birds. There are six small cabins that are available to rent. Early reservations (at least six months in advance) for the cabins are a must since they are extremely popular.

Obviously, hummingbirds are the main attraction at Ramsey Canyon. July and August visits provide a larger variety by far, but May is still exciting. You should see Black-chinned, Broad-tailed (uncommon), Magnificent, Blue-throated, Broad-billed, and if you are lucky Violet-crowned Hummingbirds in a short visit.

In the large trees around the feeder area, you may also see Greater Pewee, Dusky-capped Flycatcher, and perhaps Sulphur-bellied Flycatcher. In the lower Ramsey Canyon area, look for Botteri's Sparrow.

Several other canyons in the Huachuca Mountains offer good birding. Most of them are covered in *A Birder's Guide to Southeastern Arizona* and *Finding Birds in Southeast Arizona*. Visit them as time allows.

When you leave Ramsey Canyon, go back north on Highway 92 to Fry Boulevard (Highway 90) and turn east. In about 7 miles you will approach the San Pedro River and San Pedro House on the right. Part of the San Pedro Riparian National Conservation Area run by the Bureau of Land Management, this area hosts Green Kingfishers and sometimes Tropical Kingbirds at the pond south of the house. Vermilion Flycatchers are common there; and be sure to try across the river, walking northward for Gray Hawks.

Continuing on Highway 90, turn south when it reaches Highway 80 to Bisbee and beyond to Douglas. Camping is no longer allowed in Guadalupe Canyon, which makes it more difficult to bird this excellent location. Therefore, when you reach Douglas, you will have three options to consider.

Option one: Get a motel in Douglas, get to bed early, and leave for Guadalupe Canyon very early in the morning to have at least some chance at the nightbirds.

Option two: Make the drive to the entrance road of Guadalupe Canyon, but continue beyond it for approximately 16 miles to a picnic area across the Arizona/New Mexico boundary in the Peloncillo Mountains. Camping is allowed there. From here, visit Guadalupe Canyon very early in the morning for the nightbirds.

Option three: Drive to Guadalupe Canyon, bird until after dark, and then drive to your choice of the above two locations to spend the night. This, of course, will mean a short night's rest, in order to return again to the canyon before daylight the next morning.

To reach Guadalupe Canyon from Douglas, take 15th Street east; this becomes the Geronimo Trail. Follow it about 23 miles to Guadalupe

Canyon Road. Turn right onto this road; it is about 9 miles to Guadalupe Canyon. The road to Guadalupe Canyon is very rough, so you have to travel slowly; there are not many birds, but if you check under the bridge you may find Barn Owls nesting.

Guadalupe Canyon is 4 miles long and is really not much of a canyon. There is a stream and trees and in this arid country that combination draws many birds. The canyon is all private property, but the owners do not object to groups of no more than four courteous of birders. *Do not build a fire, do not walk on revegetated areas, and be sure to take all trash out with you.* The owners do not want anyone driving in the canyon; park outside the entrance gate. Conduct yourself in a manner that will enable other birders to be welcome in the future. *Please obey all the 'no trespassing' signs and do not block the gate or the road.*

Key species regularly seen in the canyon include Zone-tailed Hawk, Gambel's Quail, Western Screech-Owl, Common Poorwill, Broad-billed Hummingbird, Gila Woodpecker, Northern Beardless-Tyrannulet, Vermilion Flycatcher, Thick-billed Kingbird, Mexican Jay, Bridled Titmouse, Crissal Thrasher, Lucy's Warbler, and Varied Bunting.

This is the best location on this trip to find Northern Beardless-Tyrannulet, Thick-billed Kingbird, and Varied Bunting.

In addition to the above species, Buff-collared Nightjar, Violet-crowned and Lucifer Hummingbirds, and Rose-throated Becard are found occasionally.

Your options for spending the night were outlined above.

Day 7 — Guadalupe Canyon and the Chiricahua Mountains
Whatever your decision for spending the previous night, you need to be in Guadalupe Canyon before daylight. Spend the early morning birding the canyon. It will be hot by 10 am, when the bird activity almost stops.

When you leave Guadalupe Canyon, return to Douglas and take Highway 80 north to Rodeo, New Mexico (82 miles). Watch the last few miles before you reach Rodeo for Burrowing Owls along the highway. After passing through Rodeo, continue for about 2.5 miles on Highway 80 to the Portal turn-off. Turn left, and go back across the state-line into Arizona. It is about 7 miles to Portal.

Just beyond Portal, turn left into Cave Creek Canyon. About a mile farther stop at the U.S. Forest Service information station for a birdlist and an area map.

Continue on to South Fork; get a campsite at one of the campgrounds you pass on your way. Campsites are not numerous, and they go early. There are no showers, but the creek is clear and cool.

The best birding in Cave Creek Canyon is on the South Fork Trail to Sentinel Peak; this trail starts at South Fork Picnic Ground. Many birders have seen their first Elegant Trogon on this trail, and Flame-colored Tanager has been found here. Spend the rest of the day in Cave Creek Canyon, explore the road to Herb Martyr Lake, or bird the Portal area and along the road to Paradise.

Key species and other species of interest found in these areas include Northern Goshawk, Zone-tailed Hawk, Gambel's Quail, Broad-tailed, Magnificent, Blue-throated, and Broad-billed Hummingbirds, Elegant Trogon, Strickland's Woodpecker, Sulphur-bellied and Dusky-capped Flycatchers, Greater Pewee, Mexican Jay, Bridled Titmouse, Crissal Thrasher, Lucy's Warbler, Painted Redstart, Hooded and Scott's Orioles, Bronzed Cowbird, and Cassin's and Black-chinned Sparrows.

The Chiricahua Mountains also provide ample opportunity for night-birding. *Check first on current regulations regarding tape use.* At this writing, tape use is not allowed in the South Fork area from April 1 to September 1. The night birds can be found as follows:

Western Screech-Owl—In lower areas of Cave Creek Canyon, South Fork, and in mesquite along the Portal-Rodeo Road.

Whiskered Screech-Owl—Near Paradise and in oak/juniper forests at higher elevations than Western Screech-Owl.

Flammulated Owl—Found above 7,000 feet on the Barfoot and Rustler Park roads.

Elf Owl—Found in riparian areas, such as Cave Creek Canyon and South Fork, primarily in sycamore trees.

Spotted Owl—Usually above 7,000 feet and found mostly along trails, such as South Fork Trail.

Northern Pygmy-Owl—Usually found from Ponderosa Pine forests down to the oaks. Best spot is road from Rustler Park to Paradise Road.

Whip-poor-will—Can be found in Cave Creek Canyon, at South Fork, and near Paradise.

Poorwill—Found in desertscrub and pinyon around Portal and Rodeo. Camp for the night.

Day 8 — Chiricahua Mountains

Continue birding in the Chiricahua Mountains with a trip to Rustler Park. The road to Rustler Park from Onion Saddle on can be good for several species which are not found too frequently at the lower elevations.

Look for Mexican Chickadee, Virginia's, Black-throated Gray, Grace's, Red-faced, and Olive Warblers, Hepatic Tanager, Yellow-eyed Junco, and Red Crossbill.

The Barfoot Peak Trail at Rustler Park is one of the better places to see most of the higher elevation species listed above. If you do not find them all, try the Pinery Canyon Campground; it is another good spot for higher-elevation species.

Spend the rest of the day birding the Chiricahuas and spend the night at one of the campgrounds in the area.

Day 9 — Extra Day

Use this day to go for any missed species and for the drive back to Tucson (about three hours from Portal). You might just want to spend a long morning at Cave Creek Canyon or re-visit Ramsey Canyon on the way back to Tucson.

The trip ends in Tucson in the evening.

Bird Numbers This Trip

	Potential	Expected	Actual
Key Species	47	47	
Probable Species	122	122	
Possible Species	29	4	
Remotely Possible Species	25	2	
Totally Unexpected Species	?	1	
TOTAL	223	176	

Cumulative List

Total key and probable species seen after 10 trips.

Previous trips	487	species
Southeastern Arizona trip	60	species
TOTAL	547	species

This Trip's Mileage and Expenses

Approximate miles traveled, Tucson to Tucson: 1,025

- Fuel: $74; sharing $37 $_____
- Lodging: 2 nights at motels; other nights
  camping $90; sharing $45 $_____
- Food: Ice-chest/supermarket for all meals - $90 $_____
  *The total per person cost for the above items with a companion
  to share expenses should be about $172.*
- Add to this car rental expenses, if any: $_____
- Add to this your expenses to/from Tucson: $_____
  This will give you a good idea of the cost of this trip.
- TOTAL $_____

Personal Notes

_____

_____

_____

_____

_____

_____

_____

_____

_____

_____

_____

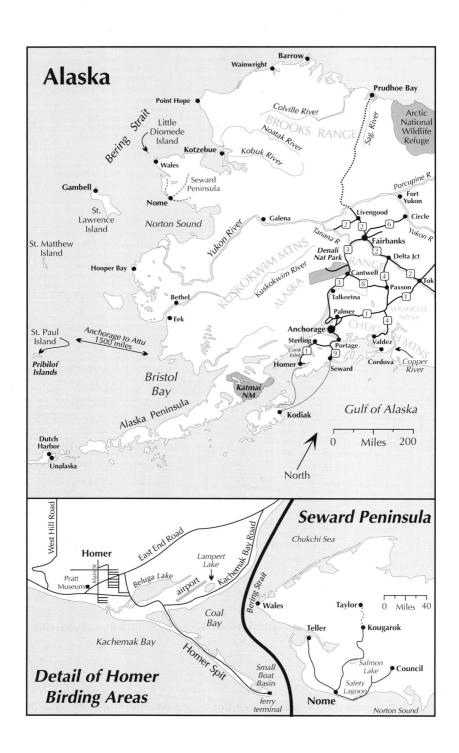

Alaska

Barrow
Wainwright
Prudhoe Bay
Point Hope
Colville River
BROOKS RANGE
Little Diomede Island
Bering Strait
Noatak River
Sag. River
Arctic National Wildlife Refuge
Kotzebue
Kobuk River
Wales
Porcupine R
Seward Peninsula
Fort Yukon
Nome
Livengood
Circle
Galena
2
6
Yukon R
St. Lawrence Island
Gambell
Norton Sound
Yukon River
Tanana R
2
Fairbanks
St. Matthew Island
Denali Nat Park
3
Delta Jct
RANGE
Cantwell
4
2
Tok
Hooper Bay
KUSKOKWIM MTNS
Kuskokwim River
3
8
Paxson
ALASKA
Talkeetna
WRANGELL MTNS
Bethel
Palmer
1
St. Paul Island
Eek
Anchorage
4
Pribilof Islands
Anchorage to Attu 1500 miles
Sterling
Portage
Valdez
CHUGACH MTNS
Cook Inlet
1
9
St. Paul Island
Homer
Seward
Cordova
Copper River
Bristol Bay
Katmai NM
Alaska Peninsula
Gulf of Alaska
Dutch Harbor
Kodiak
0   Miles   200
Unalaska
North

Detail of Homer Birding Areas

West Hill Road
East End Road
Seward Peninsula
Homer
Lampert Lake
Chukchi Sea
Main St
Pratt Museum
Beluga Lake
airport
Kachemak Bay Road
Bering Strait
Coal Bay
Wales
Taylor
0   Miles   40
Kachemak Bay
Teller
Kougarok
Homer Spit
Small Boat Basin
Salmon Lake
Council
Safety Lagoon
ferry terminal
Nome
Norton Sound

Chapter 11

ALASKA

Early June—12 Days

General

A laskan birds, with their combined northern and Asian character, have dazzled many a birder. It is the northern birdlife and especially the nearness to the Asiatic mainland which provide a thrilling list of birds for Alaska—with new species for the state discovered almost every year. An extensive Alaskan visit is a much-desired trip for most birders, but that trip and the bird sightings which it would bring are, and will remain, cost-prohibitive to many.

Alaska is enormous; it covers 586,000 square miles, one-fifth the size of the Lower 48. It is a land of extremes, with the highest mountain peak in North America, over five thousand glaciers, three thousand rivers, and three million lakes. Distances between the prime birding areas can be imposing, as can the expenses to travel from one to the other. The highway system is limited; therefore, sea or air travel is necessary to reach many destinations. This fact also means that supplies are expensive, because costly food and fuel must be transported (often air-lifted) to many parts of the state. An extreme example of this situation is a visit to Attu Island, a trip that many birders dream of, which requires a flight of almost 1,500 miles from Anchorage, and further requires that all food and supplies be flown in.

One of the intentions of this book is to demonstrate to birders that a lifelist, or even a year list of respectable proportions, can be achieved without huge expense. This philosophic basis requires that the Alaska chapter must be a little different from the others. First, you cannot bird all of Alaska, because it is so large and because it would require so many different trips. Secondly, birding it is almost impossible to do economically. Therefore, much of your Alaskan quest must remain a dream until you as an individual can find your own particular way to fulfill it.

The main part of this chapter covers only a small portion of Alaska, the part that can be done at a reasonable cost. Even at that, this trip is expensive. We cover primarily the areas of Alaska serviced by the highway system, with a small sample of the Marine Highway System

Probable Species
Total of 119 Species
Red-throated Loon
Pacific Loon
Common Loon
Horned Grebe
Red-necked Grebe
Northern Fulmar
Short-tailed Shearwater
Double-crested
Cormorant
Pelagic Cormorant
Tundra Swan
Canada Goose
Green-winged Teal
Mallard
Northern Pintail
Northern Shoveler
American Wigeon
Greater Scaup
Harlequin Duck
Oldsquaw
Black Scoter
Surf Scoter
White-winged Scoter
Barrow's Goldeneye
Bufflehead
Common Merganser
Red-breasted Merganser
Bald Eagle
Norther Harrier
Sharp-shinned Hawk
Red-tailed Hawk
Golden Eagle
Merlin
Peregrine Falcon
Sandhill Crane
Black-bellied Plover
Pacific Golden-Plover
American
Golden-Plover
Semipalmated Plover
Black Oystercatcher
Greater Yellowlegs
Lesser Yellowlegs
Wandering Tattler
Spotted Sandpiper
Whimbrel
Ruddy Turnstone
Semipalmated
Sandpiper
Western Sandpiper
Least Sandpiper
Pectoral Sandpiper
Dunlin
Short-billed Dowitcher
Long-billed Dowitcher
Common Snipe
Red-necked Phalarope
Red Phalarope
Pomarine Jaeger
Parasitic Jaeger
Long-tailed Jaeger
Bonaparte's Gull
Mew Gull
Herring Gull
Glaucous-winged Gull
Black-legged Kittiwake
Arctic Tern
Common Murre
Pigeon Guillemot

(ferries) and a little air travel. Some optional additions that can be made if your budget allows them appear at the end of the chapter.

Specifically, this sample of Alaska includes Anchorage, Chugach National Forest, Kenai National Wildlife Refuge, Homer, Kodiak, Seward, Nome, and Denali National Park.

Birdfinding Guides

Guide to the Birds of Alaska by Robert H. Armstrong (1995). This is not a birdfinding guide, but it is helpful to the Alaska birder; it provides photographs and distribution notes for each species.

A Birder's Guide to the Kenai Peninsula by George C. West (1994).

A Bird Finding Guide to Alaska by Nick Lethaby (1994).

Birds of Seward, Alaska by Jon Andrew et al. (1988). A checklist, not a book, which gives occurrence and abundance of area species.

Denali National Park Bird Finding Guide by Kenneth Kertell and Alan Seegert (1984).

Rare Bird Alert Number

Statewide 907/338-2473
Kachemak Bay 907/235-7337

Special Equipment

Bird tapes are worthwhile, especially if you plan to seek Smith's Longspur. A reliable spotting scope is essential at Homer Spit and at Nome's Safety Lagoon. A high-rated sleeping bag is important if you plan to camp. Nights can be cold in Alaska, and the lighter sleeping bags will not do the job.

Accommodations

Hotels, motels, inns, and bed-and-breakfasts are numerous in south-central Alaska. It should not be a problem to locate a place to stay in Anchorage, Homer, or Seward, but reservations are advisable.

Advance reservations are important for Denali National Park, and they are a must for Nome. Prices are high and can run $150 per night, but with prior planning and a reasonable amount of price-checking you can usually locate accommodations for $75 or less per night. The free *Alaska Official State Guide and Vacation Planner*, detailing lodging and prices for the entire state, is available from Alaska Division of Tourism, P.O. Box 110801, Juneau, AK 99811, phone 907/465-2010.

Campgrounds are plentiful, almost all charge a fee, and they are practical to use in some areas. In many places in Alaska you can just camp next to the road. In Nome the temperature factor alone suggests that the only sensible thing to do is rent a room. Camping can save you a lot of money, but you will need heavy-duty equipment.

For Denali National Park campground (and bus) reservations, call one of the following numbers: 800/622-PARK (7275) or 907-272-7275 (a local call from Anchorage).

Key Species — Total of 31 Species

1. **Arctic Loon**—Unlikely to find anywhere other than the Nome area. Try Safety Lagoon, offshore along the beach, or on tundra lakes.

2. **Fork-tailed Storm-Petrel**—May be seen on the ferry trip from Homer to Kodiak, but the best opportunity will be on the ferry from Kodiak to Seward as you cross the more open waters of the Gulf of Alaska. Sometimes seen by lucky birders at the head of Resurrection Bay at Seward or from the end of Homer Spit.

3. **Red-faced Cormorant**—Common on Kachemak and Resurrection Bays. Should be seen in the Homer, Kodiak, and Seward areas. Common nester on Gull Island if all else fails.

4. **Trumpeter Swan**—Surest place is Kenai National Wildlife Refuge. If you don't find it on your own, ask the refuge personnel to recommend a good location. May also be seen in small numbers in the

---

Probable Species
(continued)

Marbled Murrelet
Rock Dove
Great Horned Owl
Northern Hawk Owl
Rufous Hummingbird
Downy Woodpecker
Hairy Woodpecker
Three-toed
 Woodpecker
Say's Phoebe
Horned Lark
Tree Swallow
Violet-green Swallow
Bank Swallow
Cliff Swallow
Gray Jay
Steller's Jay
Black-billed Magpie
Common Raven
Black-capped
 Chickadee
Boreal Chickadee
Chestnut-backed
 Chickadee
Red-breasted Nuthatch
Brown Creeper
American Dipper
Golden-crowned
 Kinglet
Ruby-crowned Kinglet
Gray-cheeked Thrush
Swainson's Thrush
Hermit Thrush
American Robin
Varied Thrush
American Pipit
Bohemian Waxwing
Northern Shrike
Orange-crowned
 Warbler
Yellow Warbler
Yellow-rumped
 Warbler
Townsend's Warbler
Blackpoll Warbler
Northern Waterthrush
Wilson's Warbler
Amer. Tree Sparrow
Savannah Sparrow
Fox Sparrow
Song Sparrow
Lincoln's Sparrow
Golden-crowned
 Sparrow
White-crowned
 Sparrow
Dark-eyed Junco
Lapland Longspur
Snow Bunting
Common Redpoll
Pine Siskin

Note: The species in **boldface** appear no more than four times in the itineraries as key or probable species. Watch for them on this trip.

Probable Species
(continued)

Note: As on all of the trips, assume that you will see all of the probables. You will gain only 1 species not seen on previous trips.

Possible Species
Total of 38 Species
Sooty Shearwater
Greater White-fronted
    Goose
Emperor Goose
Brant
Gadwall
Eurasian Wigeon
Canvasback
Redhead
Ring-necked Duck
Lesser Scaup
Common Goldeneye
Rough-legged Hawk
American Kestrel
White-tailed Ptarmigan
Solitary Sandpiper
Upland Sandpiper
Bristle-thighed Curlew
Hudsonian Godwit
Black Turnstone
Surfbird
Sanderling
Sabine's Gull
Cassin's Auklet
Rhinoceros Auklet
Belted Kingfisher
Northern Flicker
Olive-sided Flycatcher
Western Wood-Pewee
Hammond's Flycatcher
Winter Wren
Bluethroat
Townsend's Solitaire
White Wagtail
Chipping Sparrow
Smith's Longspur
Red-winged Blackbird
Gray-crowned
    Rosy-Finch
Pine Grosbeak

Note: You will probably see 11 of the species on the possible list.

Remotely Possible Species
Total of 24 Species
Yellow-billed Loon
Black-footed Albatross
Great Blue Heron
Blue-winged Teal
King Eider
Spectacled Eider
Osprey

lake area (east of Cantwell) on the Denali Highway, or in Broad Pass (south of Cantwell) on the Parks Highway (Highway 3).

5. **Common Eider**—Best location is Kachemak Bay. You may need a spotting scope, but you should easily locate several from Homer Spit.

6. **Steller's Eider**—Uncommon in early spring at Kodiak; usually some linger and might still be around in spring along Homer Spit. Occurs in small numbers in the Nome area.

7. **Northern Goshawk**—Common species in the spruce forests. Should be found at Kenai National Wildlife Refuge or Chugach National Forest. Also might be seen at Denali National Park.

8. **Gyrfalcon**—Prefers open expanses of alpine tundra and is a cliff-nester. The best locations are along Teller Highway or Kougarok Road in the Nome area and in Denali National Park between Polychrome Pass and Eielson Visitor Center. Local advice is helpful.

9. **Spruce Grouse**—Not usually an easy species to locate but can be found around Anchorage, at Denali National Park, in Chugach National Forest, or almost anywhere on the Kenai Peninsula. At Denali the best locations are the dense spruce forest from Mile 3 to Mile 6 and around Teklanika Campground near Mile 29 on the park road.

10. **Willow Ptarmigan**—Found at much the same places as Rock Ptarmigan at slightly lower elevation. Prefers moist tundra with heavy brush. Easy to see in the vicinity of Wonder Lake at Denali National Park and in proper habitat along the first 30 miles of the park road. Also found on Kougarok Road north of Nome, or the Glen Alps area above Anchorage.

11. **Rock Ptarmigan**—Can be found at Denali National Park, Chugach National Forest, and several other places on this trip. Probably the best place is along Kougarok Road near Nome. Primary habitat is alpine tundra with low vegetation.

12. **Bar-tailed Godwit**—The best places are all in the Nome area—the tundra around Safety Lagoon and along Kougarok and Teller Roads.

13. **Rock Sandpiper**—Usually still around in early June on Homer Spit. Can also be found at Nome in small numbers. It may take some work, but it can be found.

14 **Glaucous Gull**—Should easily be seen on the Nome waterfront. Nome is the only reasonable chance, on this trip, for this species.

15. **Aleutian Tern**—Easy to see at tern colonies near Homer and at Safety Lagoon east of Nome on the Council Road. Also found in Kodiak area.

16. **Thick-billed Murre**—Usually seen in small numbers from the ferry either between Homer and Kodiak or more likely between Kodiak and Seward.

Remotely Possible Species
(continued)
Ruffed Grouse
Sharp-tailed Grouse
Killdeer
Great Knot
Red Knot
Rufous-necked Stint
Baird's Sandpiper
Thayer's Gull
Slaty-backed Gull
Black Guillemot
Snowy Owl
Great Gray Owl
Northern Saw-whet Owl
Black-backed Woodpecker
Red-throated Pipit
European Starling
Red Crossbill
Note: You will probably be lucky to see more than 2 of these species.

17. **Kittlitz's Murrelet**—Commonly seen, usually in good numbers, from the ferry. Also regular but uncommon off Homer Spit.

18. **Ancient Murrelet**—At least a few should be seen from the ferry; sometimes large numbers occur between Kodiak and Seward.

19. **Parakeet Auklet**—Seen in small numbers, alone or in pairs, on both legs of the ferry trip.

20. **Tufted Puffin**—Common on both legs of the ferry trip.

21. **Horned Puffin**—Same as Tufted Puffin. It is very unlikely that you will miss either puffin.

22. **Short-eared Owl**—Look for it on moist tundra around Nome or at Denali National Park.

23. **Boreal Owl**—Considered common in central Alaska. In the Anchorage area it can be found with local help. Sometimes nests near Savage River Campground at Denali National Park. Very difficult without local information and after they are finished calling in early April.

24. **Alder Flycatcher**—Common and easy to find on the Kenai Peninsula, in the Anchorage area, and along the Parks Highway to Denali National Park.

25. **Northwestern Crow**—Common resident at Homer, Seward, and Kodiak; can't be missed along the waterfronts.

26. **Arctic Warbler**—The easiest place to find this species is in the willows scattered along the west end of the Denali Highway. Other reliable locations include the Nome River Valley on Kougarok Road and along Igloo Creek near Igloo Campground at Denali National Park.

27. **Northern Wheatear**—Probably will be easiest along Teller or Kougarok Roads out of Nome. It can also be found in rocky areas at Denali National Park, especially near Eielson Visitor Center and at Polychrome Pass.

28. **Yellow Wagtail**—Usually easy to find near Nome on Kougarok and Teller Roads or right in town. Must be seen on the Nome leg of the trip.

29. **Rusty Blackbird**—Easy to find at Homer and in the Anchorage area in parks, around lakes, and in spruce bogs.

30. **White-winged Crossbill**—Erratic wanderer; can be very common in Anchorage, on the Kenai Peninsula, or at Denali in the first 6 miles of the park road. Often seen on the drive from Anchorage to Denali.

31. **Hoary Redpoll**—Easy to see in the Nome area. Frequently found with Common Redpolls, so check the redpoll flocks closely. Must be seen on the Nome leg of the trip.

> Note: You might expect to see all 31 species with hard work and excellent luck. You may need local help for Boreal Owl and some luck to see Arctic Loon, Steller's Eider, and Rock Sandpiper.

Special Considerations

The toughest part of traveling in Alaska is meshing the schedules of a limited transportation system into a smooth trip. The first thing to consider is the schedule of the ferry that will take you from Homer to Kodiak and then to Seward. This is not a daily scheduled trip, and your plans must be built around the departure date and time from Homer as well as the arrival date and time in Seward. For information and reservations, contact the Alaska Marine Highway System, P.O. Box 25535, Juneau, AK 99802-5535, phone 800/642-0066.

For this trip to stay as economical as possible, you must board the ferry as a foot passenger; leave your car at the ferry terminal in Homer. When you arrive in Seward, you will find that there is no air service back to Homer. However, there is daily bus service, departing Seward at 9 am and arriving in Homer at 3:45 pm. The cost of this trip is $30 per passenger. Contact the Seward Bus Line, P.O. Box 1338, Seward, AK 99664, phone 907/224-3608 for information.

Itinerary

Note: This trip begins and ends in Anchorage.

Day 1 — Anchorage, Chugach National Forest, Kenai National Wildlife Refuge, and Homer

In June, sunrise occurs at about 3:30 am and sunset at about 10:30 pm, giving you approximately nineteen hours of daylight. The only problem that this schedule creates is that you may want to bird all the time, to the point of exhaustion. Good luck!

Take Highway 1 south from Anchorage; it is a 240-mile drive to Homer, and a very long day can be spent birding along the way. The highway follows Cook Inlet's Turnagain Arm for about 50 miles, giving you the opportunity to scope for a variety of ducks and geese. You will also pass through Chugach National Forest, which can be dependable for several key species, including Northern Goshawk, Spruce Grouse, Willow and Rock Ptarmigans, Short-eared and Boreal Owls, Alder Flycatcher, and White-winged Crossbill. Other species of interest include Red-necked Grebe, White-tailed Ptarmigan, Red-necked Phalarope, Northern Hawk Owl, Three-toed Woodpecker, Boreal Chickadee, Varied Thrush, Bohemian Waxwing, Golden-crowned Sparrow, and Common Redpoll. (The route from Anchorage to Portage Glacier is covered in *Field Guide to Birding in Anchorage* by Robert L. Scher.)

Stay on Highway 1 when it turns west toward Sterling. The birding is good all along this highway, and the scenery is great. When you reach Skilak Lake Road, turn left to bird the campgrounds along this side road until it returns you to Highway 1 several miles nearer to Sterling. The birds here are much the same as those previously listed, with the addition of Trumpeter Swan. These swans nest on remote lakes throughout Kenai National Wildlife Refuge. If you can't find a Trumpeter Swan, stop at refuge headquarters just south of Soldotna to ask the refuge personnel to recommend a good location.

South of Soldotna Highway 1 soon reaches the coast and follows along Cook Inlet the rest of the way to the tip of the Kenai Peninsula at Homer.

Homer Spit, a 4.5-mile peninsula jutting out into Kachemak Bay, has many places where you can pull over to scan for ducks and shorebirds. Species of interest include Red-faced Cormorant, Greater Scaup, Common Eider, Harlequin Duck, all three scoters, Wandering Tattler, Glaucous-winged Gull, Black-legged Kittiwake, and Arctic and Aleutian Terns. In addition, check the grassy areas for Lapland Longspur and Snow Bunting. The rocky area near the small boat harbor should produce lingering Rock Sandpipers and other shorebirds. Drive the entire spit, stopping frequently to scan the beaches and Kachemak Bay; many rarities have turned up here over the years.

Beluga Lake, accessed through Ben Walters Park, is another good location. Key species usually found around this lake include Rusty Blackbird and White-winged Crossbill. In addition, Trumpeter Swan is found here on occasion.

A third area deserving of a good look is Kachemak Drive. Take Kachemak Drive east from Homer Spit Road, go past the airport, and about 0.3 mile after the pavement ends look on your left for Lampert Lake. Alder Flycatchers nest here and Rusty Blackbird is common. Continue 0.6 mile to a road on the left that leads to a tern colony, where both Arctic and Aleutian Terns nest and are easy to see. As you continue on Kachemak Drive to its end at East End Road, you will pass through habitat that supports Alder Flycatcher, Northwestern Crow, Rusty Blackbird, and White-winged Crossbill.

A *Birder's Guide to the Kenai Peninsula* by George C. West covers each of the above areas, and many more, in detail.

The departure time for the Homer-Kodiak ferry may vary somewhat, but it usually leaves port at either 11 pm or 1 am. Foot passengers must check in one hour in before departure; reservations are advised. You can park your vehicle in the terminal parking lot and board with carry-on luggage only. Take your sleeping bag with you unless you intend to rent a cabin on the ferry. A heated bay on the top deck is provided for you to sleep, using your sleeping bag. The ferry has a restaurant, a bar, and public showers. The current fare for a foot passenger from Homer to Kodiak to Seward is $98.

Night aboard the M/V *Tustemena*.

Days 2 and 3 — Kodiak, Seward, and return to Homer

The ferry trip from Homer to Kodiak takes about 12 hours, giving you a chance to catch a few hours of sleep before sunrise. Birding from the ferry is very productive, and it may be just fantastic from Kodiak to Seward. Key species you should record are Fork-tailed Storm-Petrel, Red-faced Cormorant, Common and maybe Steller's Eiders, Arctic and Aleutian Terns, Thick-billed Murre, Kittlitz's and Ancient Murrelets, Parakeet Auklet, and Tufted and Horned Puffins. You should also see Northern Fulmar, Short-tailed Shearwater, Red-necked and Red Phalaropes, Pomarine and Long-tailed Jaegers, Black-legged Kittiwake, Common Murre, Pigeon Guillemot, Marbled Murrelet, and possibly Cassin's and Rhinoceros Auklets. This ferry is the only chance that you will have for several of these species, so stay on deck and be alert.

When you reach Kodiak, there will be a wait of up to three hours prior to departure for Seward. Use the time to bird around the harbor and the town. Common Eiders should be here, and both Arctic and Aleutian Terns might be encountered at Women's Bay south of town.

Tufted Puffins
Shawneen E. Finnegan

The thirteen-and-a-half-hour trip from Kodiak to Seward crosses the Gulf of Alaska, which increases your chances of seeing some of the more pelagic species (like Fork-tailed Storm-Petrel). Usual departure time is 3 pm, so you will have approximately eight hours of daylight to bird at sea followed by a few hours of darkness for sleeping prior to your arrival in Seward at about 4:30 am on Day 3.

The Seward Bus Line depot is two blocks to your right on Railway Avenue as you exit the ferry terminal. Once again, there's time to bird before your departure. Northwestern Crow and White-winged Crossbill are two of the key species found around town. Another key species, Kittlitz's Murrelet, is occasionally seen from shore south of town toward Miller's Landing. Your bus to Homer will leave at 9 am; it goes north to Portage, where you change buses and turn south to Homer. This round-about route puts you in Homer at 3:45 pm, but it is currently the most economical way to make this trip. One-way fare is only $30, and you can catch up on your sleep during the ride.

Upon your arrival in Homer, pick up your vehicle and continue birding the area as outlined for Day 1. *A Birder's Guide to the Kenai Peninsula* suggests a number of good locations to investigate.

Night at one of the many inns or at one of the campgrounds at Homer.

Day 4 — Homer, Kenai National Wildlife Refuge, Chugach National Forest, and Anchorage

If you missed any key seabirds, there is one additional possibility. Several boats make half-day trips to Gull Island or other locations in Kachemak Bay, leaving Homer at 8 am and returning at noon. The half-day trip usually costs $50 per person. If you are interested, try Kachemak Bay Adventures, phone 907/235-8206; Alaska Maritime Tours, Inc., phone 907/235-2490; or ask around the waterfront. At Gull Island you will see nesting Red-faced Cormorants and Tufted and Horned Puffins, as well as several other species. Going to and from the island, watch for Kittlitz's and Marbled Murrelets and for Arctic and Aleutian Terns.

Retrace your route back to Anchorage, birding through Kenai National Wildlife Refuge and the Chugach National Forest as time allows. (You might want to detour through the town of Kenai, in order to check the rivermouth for gulls and other waterbirds.)

When you return to Anchorage, pick up a local map. Bird the city parks, particularly Earthquake Park, Westchester Lagoon, Potter Marsh, and the lakes near the airport just off Spenard Road. Several key species can be located in these areas, and with local help Boreal Owl can be found in the Anchorage area. *Field Guide to Birding in Anchorage* covers the area hotspots. We will have more time in Anchorage later in the trip, so it is not necessary to try to do everything today.

Night in Anchorage. It should not be difficult to find lodging or a campsite.

Days 5 and 6 — Anchorage and Nome

Note: At this time of year there are about 22 hours of daylight per day in Nome.

Currently, there are at least two daily departures for Nome via Alaska Airlines (800/468-2248). As on most airlines, you can usually get a break on the price by making reservations at least fourteen days in advance. Current price is about $400, round-trip. Take the earliest flight that you can get, to increase your time in Nome.

Advance reservations for both a room and a car in Nome are an absolute must. The highway system in the Nome area is very limited, and there are no traditional car-rental agencies. However, your hotel can usually help you to locate a vehicle to rent for a day or two. For more information on accommodations and transportation options, call or write the Nome Convention and Visitors Bureau, P.O. Box 240, Nome, AK 99762, phone 907/443-5535.

Nome's three major roads all provide good birding. Teller Road goes west and then north for about 71 miles, Taylor or Kougarok Road allows you to travel about 86 miles north, and Council Road goes about 73 miles to the east. The only birdfinding guide that treats these roads is Nick Lethaby's *A Bird Finding Guide to Alaska.*

Nome's waterfront is usually good for Glaucous Gull (key species), Black-legged Kittiwake, and Arctic Tern, with Slaty-backed Gull seen here on occasion. Any body of water may have loons, and the coast and adjoining low coastal tundra can offer Steller's Eider, Rock Sandpiper, Red-necked Phalarope, and flocks of Snow Buntings. Both Common and Hoary Redpolls favor tundra shrub thickets, while Parasitic and Long-tailed Jaegers can show up anywhere. Yellow Wagtail is regular both around the edges of town and by tundra thickets, and White Wagtail has been seen around old gold dredges, at the harbor, and along the beach between town and the airport.

Head east out of Nome on Council Road for 3 miles to the Nome River mouth, a good area for both ducks and shorebirds. Harlequin Duck, Bar-tailed Godwit, and Long-tailed Jaeger are regular.

Continue east for 15 miles to Safety Lagoon to visit an Aleutian Tern colony that has been active for many years. The terns should be present in large numbers. Both Safety Lagoon and the nearby tundra are good for a number of species, including Arctic and Pacific Loons, Bar-tailed Godwit, Semipalmated and Western Sandpipers, and Parasitic Jaeger. In addition, Rufous-necked Stint has been recorded here a number of times. Council Road is all good birding, but when it turns inland the species are about the same as those which you will see on the other two roads.

Return to Nome and take Teller Road to the west. Watch for White Wagtail, especially from Mile 5 to Mile 10, and Gyrfalcon and Northern Wheatear from Mile 20 to Mile 26. Other tundra species include American and Pacific Golden-Plovers, Whimbrel, Bar-tailed Godwit, and Yellow Wagtail. Some lucky birders have found Bluethroats in willows as close as Mile 14.

The third road, the Taylor Road (or Kougarok Road), leads northward into the interior. If the road is free of snow, bird all the way to its northern end. Look for Gyrfalcon, Willow and Rock Ptarmigans, American and Pacific Golden-Plovers, Bar-tailed Godwit, Parasitic and Long-tailed Jaegers, Arctic Warbler, Northern Wheatear, and Yellow Wagtail. Bluethroats have been seen on territory in willows as close as Mile 20. In addition, Bristle-thighed Curlew and Bluethroat have nested regularly beyond Mile 73 off this road. It is worth the drive for a chance at either of these two species. The better areas to bird for the curlew are at Mile 74 opposite Coffee Dome and from Mile 83 to Mile 86.

Spend nights 5 and 6 in Nome. (See Days 11 and 12 for scheduling extra days.)

Day 7 — Nome and Anchorage
Wind up your Nome area birding and fly back to Anchorage. Having a number of flights to choose from between Nome and Anchorage gives you some flexibility in departure time. If you arrive in Anchorage early enough, continue birding the city parks and lakes that you covered on Day 4.

Your key species in the Anchorage area include Boreal Owl, Rusty Blackbird, and White-winged Crossbill.

Overnight in Anchorage.

Day 8 — Anchorage and Denali National Park
Drive to Denali National Park, about 235 miles north of Anchorage on the Parks Highway (Highway 3). The birding is good, especially beyond Talkeetna. Your birding stops should produce loons, Trumpeter Swan, ducks, all three scoters, eagles, Red-necked Phalarope, Arctic Tern, Northern Hawk Owl, Alder Flycatcher, swallows, Gray Jay, Black-

billed Magpie, Common Raven, Boreal Chickadee, American Dipper, Gray-cheeked Thrush, Swainson's Thrush, Varied Thrush, Bohemian Waxwing, warblers, White-winged Crossbill, and Common Redpoll.

At Cantwell detour east on the Denali Highway (Highway 8). (Mileage markers along the Denali begin with Mile 0 at Paxson and end with Mile 134 at Cantwell.) You might pick up some early Arctic Warblers in almost any willow habitat. Approximately 10 miles east of Cantwell (about Mile 124) you'll find lakes that usually have Trumpeter Swans, as well as Upland Sandpiper, Northern Shrike, and many of the species listed for Highway 3. Nesting Smith's Longspurs have been found at a number of locations between Mile 105 and 100, and near Miles 70, 60, 20, and 16. Try moist meadows on the north side of the highway (especially between Miles 105 and 100); these locations have been reliable in the past.

Return to Highway 3 and continue north to Denali National Park. If you do not already have bus and campground reservations (which can be made by phone up to five days in advance), your first priority is to stop at the Visitor Access Center to secure a campsite and to buy tickets for the shuttle bus. The only campground that is practical unless you are completely equipped is Riley Creek Campground. Bus fares vary by destination: $12 to Toklat, $20 to Eielson, and $26 to Wonder Lake. It is not uncommon for the next day's shuttles to be fully booked, particularly for the first bus to leave in the morning at 5 am, which is the one you want. Without prior reservations, you might need to use one of your extra days on the itinerary to stay over to get access to the park by shuttle bus.

You can drive into the park about 15 miles to Savage River (Mile 12.8 is Savage River Campground); all farther access to the park is by shuttle bus. You can ride the bus to any point on the park road (with the appropriate shuttle ticket), hike wherever you like, and catch the next bus going in either direction—if it has an empty seat. Wonder Lake is at Mile 86, and it takes almost 11 hours (round trip) to visit.

While you are at the Visitor Access Center, pick up a map and a bird checklist. You should also buy a copy of the *Denali National Park Bird Finding Guide* by Kenneth Kertell and Alan Seegert. This small booklet costs about $3 and is a very valuable aid to the first-time Denali birder.

Key bird species found in Denali National Park include Northern Goshawk, Gyrfalcon, Spruce Grouse, Willow and Rock Ptarmigans, Short-eared and Boreal Owls, Alder Flycatcher, Arctic Warbler, Northern Wheatear, and White-winged Crossbill. (Don't be so much of a birder that you miss the impressive mammals and dramatic scenery along the way. For example, you might see Dall Sheep, Moose, Grizzly, Caribou, and Gray Wolf. You might even see the often cloud-covered Mt. McKinley, or 'Denali,' on a good day.)

Other birds to look for include Harlequin Duck, American Golden-Plover, Wandering Tattler, Long-tailed Jaeger, Arctic Tern, Northern Hawk Owl, Three-toed Woodpecker, Boreal Chickadee, Bohemian Waxwing, Northern Shrike, Lapland Longspur, Snow Bunting, Gray-crowned Rosy-Finch, and Common Redpoll.

Many of the key species can be found along the first 14 miles of the park road. A good plan is to finish out Day 8 birding that section of the park road, since you can use your own vehicle to access it.

There are many hotels, motels, bed-and-breakfasts, and campgrounds in the area. Advance reservations are suggested. Night in the area.

Day 9 — Denali National Park

Using the shuttle bus system, spend the day touring Denali. Go at least as far as Eielson Visitor Center at Mile 66. Be sure to bring food, drink, warm clothes, and raingear. Try stopping at some of the following locations for birding: Igloo Creek at Mile 36 for Arctic Warbler; Polychrome Pass at Mile 46 for possible Gyrfalcon; Highway Pass at Mile 58.3 for Rock Ptarmigan and Northern Wheatear; Thorofare Pass at Mile 64.5 for Gyrfalcon, Rock Ptarmigan, and Northern Wheatear, and finally Eielson Visitor Center at Mile 66 and a mile beyond for Gyrfalcon and Northern Wheatear. With time to spare, you might want to extend your trip all the way to Wonder Lake at Mile 86.

Again spend the night in the Denali area.

Day 10 — Denali National Park and Anchorage

Finish up at Denali. Another visit to the lakes and the longspur meadows along the Denali Highway is optional. If any of the area's key species have been missed, spend the time looking for them before leaving for Anchorage.

Make the drive back to Anchorage. Night in the Anchorage area.

Days 11 and 12 — Extra Days

Allow two extra days in Alaska since inclement weather frequently hampers travel; you can lose a day gaining access to Denali, and you may want to schedule an extra day at Nome or even on the Kenai Peninsula to find the species to be located in those areas.

If these extra days have not been used by now and you have seen all the key species, you may elect to sightsee or rest up. If you still have time and want to continue birding, check the hotline and local birders. Also, *Field Guide to Birding in Anchorage* has directions to other fine birding locations in the Anchorage area.

Spend the night of Day 11 in the area; this trip ends in the evening on Day 12 in Anchorage.

ALASKAN OUTPOSTS:
Some Optional Add-on Trips

As promised early in the chapter, here is a list of some worthwhile add-on trips and a little information on each. Some—but not all—of the more interesting birds in each of these locations are listed. These areas are also covered lightly in Nick Lethaby's *A Bird Finding Guide to Alaska*. (The birds from these "Alaskan outposts" *are not included* in the running total of birds from chapter to chapter, but they are included in the Birdfinder Chart as shading in the Alaska column.)

1. The Pribilof Islands

An add-on trip that is popular with many birders is taken via Reeve Aleutian Airways from Anchorage to St. Paul Island in the Pribilofs. This package tour is the only way for the average person to bird the Pribilofs. (The bird-tour companies use this same package as part of their Alaskan trips since there is only one airline servicing St. Paul and only one hotel when you get there.)

Currently the tour, which consists of three days and two nights, departs only from Anchorage; it departs only on Tuesdays and Thursdays, and the current cost is nearly $750. This price includes everything but your meals. Reservations may be made by contacting Reeve Aleutian Airways, Inc., 4700 International Airport Road, Anchorage, AK 99502, phone 800/544-2248. Or you can contact TDX, which is the Native Corporation on the Pribilofs, with an office at 1500 West 33rd Avenue, Suite 220, Anchorage, AK 99503, phone 907/278-1312.

St. Paul Island is 14 miles long and 8 miles wide. Your tour package includes regular bus transportation to the bird rookeries and cliffs where the nesting birds number in the hundred of thousands. There are also hiking-trails on the island, and you are free to venture out on your own and set your own schedule.

Some of the species here include Northern Fulmar, Pelagic and Red-faced Cormorants, Harlequin Duck, Bar-tailed Godwit, Rock Sandpiper, Red-necked Phalarope, Glaucous-winged Gull, Black-legged and Red-legged Kittiwakes, Common and Thick-billed Murres, Parakeet,

Least, and Crested Auklets, Tufted and Horned Puffins, Snow and McKay's Buntings, and Gray-crowned Rosy-Finch. In addition, most trips in this season will turn up at least one or two honest-to-goodness Asian vagrants.

The King Eider Hotel will be your inn for each of the two nights spent on St. Paul. On the third night you will return to Anchorage and will need accommodations there.

2. Gambell

Gambell is a small Eskimo village on St. Lawrence Island, about 40 miles from the Siberian coast. There are no hotels or public accommodations of any kind. It is difficult logistically to visit Gambell on your own, and it is recommended that you go with a group. The tours that go to Gambell use available heated buildings in the village, and the group basically camps indoors. Several tour companies visit Gambell, and you can often sign on with them for just that portion of their Alaska tour if that fits your plans. Temperatures are usually below 40° F, and most days are what any rational Outsider would call inclement. Tours usually are six to eight days long, include airfare (usually from Anchorage), food, and lodging, such as it is. The cost of this 6- to 8-day trip is $2,000 to $2,500 per person.

Birding at Gambell is an incredible experience, with many Asian strays and semi-regular migrants. A typical bird list after a week's visit will include most of the following species: Arctic and Yellow-billed Loons; Northern Fulmar; Brant; Emperor Goose; Steller's, Common, King, and Spectacled Eiders; Mongolian and Common Ringed Plovers; Gray-tailed Tattler; Rufous-necked Stint; Rock Sandpiper; Pomarine, Parasitic and Long-tailed Jaegers; Black-legged Kittiwake; Slaty-backed, Ross's, and Ivory Gulls; Dovekie; Common and Thick-billed Murres; Pigeon Guillemot; Parakeet, Crested, and Least Auklets; Horned and Tufted Puffins; Snowy and Short-eared Owls; Bluethroat; Northern Wheatear; White and Yellow Wagtails; Red-throated Pipit; Brambling; Hoary Redpoll; and Snow and McKay's Buntings. A trip to Gambell can really hike up your lifelist. Of course, you probably won't see all of the species enumerated here, but then, too, this is just a partial list of the possibilities.

3. Barrow

A summer trip to Barrow, where the sun never sets between May 17 and July 26, can be very interesting, but the birdlife is not as varied as that of the other "Alaskan outposts" in this chapter. Still, many birders do visit this far-northern town on the edge of the Arctic Ocean. Airfare from Anchorage, with fourteen-day advance purchase, is about $450 round-trip. Accommodations are limited but a hotel room overlooking the Arctic Ocean can be had for about $75 per person. A stay of three days (two nights) is recommended. Birding is often done by foot in the immediate Barrow area since the road system is limited. However, you can check with your hotel about renting a vehicle.

Far-north species that may be seen include Yellow-billed Loon, Tundra Swan, Brant, all four eiders (especially the otherwise hard-to-find Spectacled Eider), Red-necked and Red Phalaropes, Buff-breasted Sandpiper, all three jaegers, Sabine's Gull, Arctic Tern, Snowy Owl, Bluethroat, Yellow Wagtail, Lapland Longspur, and Snow Bunting. Check the town dump for Slaty-backed Gull and any beached marine mammal carcasses for Ivory Gull. Sift through all the shorebirds for Asian strays.

4. Attu Island

Note: This trip must come earlier than any other Alaska trip. It begins in mid-May.

A trip to Attu is the goal of many birders, but the very thing that makes an Attu trip so fabulous also makes the trip cost-prohibitive for the average birder. Attu Island is so remote that it is a five-hour flight from Anchorage, approximately 1,500 miles by air. It is much closer to Asia than to mainland North America and almost yearly provides one or more new species to the North American list.

The island is served by a small contingent of Coast Guard personnel, maintaining a LORAN navigation station. Lodging on Attu consists of semi-rugged, but still comfortable, accommodations in two abandoned buildings; the food is near-gourmet quality. Transportation around the northeastern end of the island is by foot or bicycle. Each day, bands of organized birders cover the regular birding areas, maintaining contact through CB radios.

Since Attu is so remote and the expense of getting there is so great, the tours are usually three weeks long, although one- and two-week tours are somtimes offered. Springtime tours to Attu are from mid-May to early June. The Coast Guard will abandon their Attu base in 2000, so the last Attu birding tour will probably take place in 1999 or 2000.

Some of the species seen at Attu are Yellow-billed Loon; Red-faced Cormorant; Bean Goose; Falcated Teal; Garganey; Tufted and Harlequin Ducks; Smew; White-tailed Eagle; Rock Ptarmigan; Mongolian Plover; Common Greenshank; Spotted Redshank; Wood and Common Sandpipers; Far Eastern Curlew; Black-tailed and Bar-tailed Godwits; Rufous-necked, Temminck's, and Long-toed Stints; Sharp-tailed and Rock Sand-pipers; Ruff; Slaty-backed Gull; Tufted and Horned Puffins; Eurasian Skylark; Red-breasted and Gray-spotted Flycatchers; Siberian Rubythroat; Eyebrowed and Dusky Thrushes; Yellow, Gray, and Black-backed Wagtails; Olive Tree-, Pechora, and Red-throated Pipits; Rustic Bunting; Common Reed-Bunting; Brambling; Common Rosefinch; Oriental Greenfinch; and Hawfinch.

As you can imagine, a journey to Attu is often the trip of a birder's lifetime; the above is just a partial list of the species possible there. The cost of an Attu trip is currently about $4,900 per person from Anchorage. (There is only one company making birding trips to Attu: Attour Inc., 2027 Partridge Lane, Highland Park, IL 60035.)

To sum up this list of possible additions to your Alaskan trip, it should be recognized that without at least the Gambell and Attu trips, no one sees 700 ABA-Area species in a year, and very few people can see 700 species in North America in a lifetime. Without these trips you can still see 600+ species, and you can become just as skillful a birder as those with larger lists. Expertise does not come with a large lifelist; it comes with time in the field and with the love of your chosen avocation...birding.

Bird Numbers This Trip

(The birds for the four "Alaskan Outpost" trips are *not* included in this summary.)

	Potential	Expected	Actual
Key Species	31	31	
Probable Species	119	119	
Possible Species	38	11	
Remotely Possible Species	24	2	
Totally Unexpected Species	?	1	
TOTAL	212	164	

Cumulative List

Total key and probable species seen after 11 trips.

Previous trips . . . . 547 species
Alaska trip . . . . 32 species
TOTAL . . . . 579 species

This Trip's Mileage and Expenses

Miles driven Anchorage to Anchorage (includes Nome): 1,850 miles

- Fuel: $200; sharing $100 $_____
- Lodging: camping 4 nights, motel 6 nights,
  ferry 2 nights (no room) $434; sharing $235 $_____
- Food: Assuming restaurants for some meals $280 $_____
- Air travel round-trip Nome, each $400 $_____
- Ferry expense per person $98 $_____
- Car rental in Nome $150; sharing $75 $_____
- Bus - Seward to Homer, each $30 $_____
- Boat to Gull Island, each $50 $_____
- Denali shuttle buses, each $36 $_____
  The total per person cost of the above items with a companion to share
  fuel, lodging, and car rental expenses will be about $1,305.
- Add to this car rental expenses, if any: $_____
- Add to this your expenses to/from Anchorage: $_____
  This will give you a good idea of the cost of this trip.
- TOTAL $_____

Personal Notes

_____

_____

_____

_____

_____

_____

_____

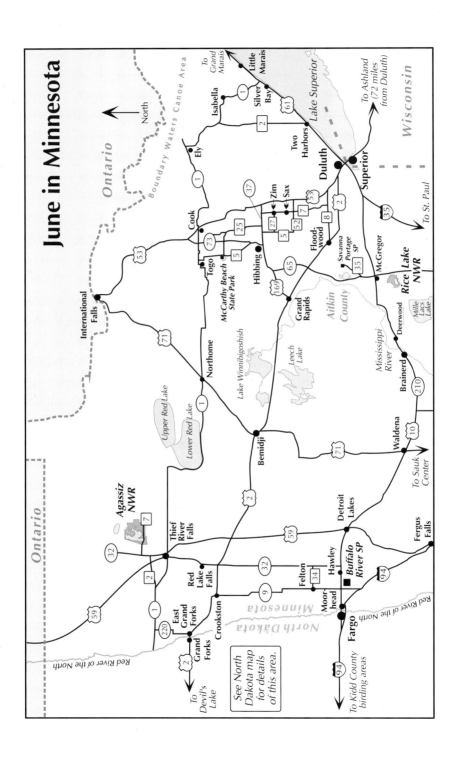

June in Minnesota

Chapter 12

JUNE IN MINNESOTA AND NORTH DAKOTA

Mid-June—8 Days

General

This trip is designed to enable you to see several of the Minnesota and North Dakota specialties. The majority of your trip will be spent in Minnesota, a state with over 400 species on its bird checklist and one with great habitat diversity. A few days will be spent in North Dakota, an under-appreciated and under-birded state. Prairie birds are easier to find in North Dakota than in Minnesota. Concentrate on 14 key species— you should see them all with little difficulty, most in a very small area. This means that you will do a lot of driving to see the remaining few. Another aspect of this trip is that it gives you a second or a third opportunity to see many species that you originally pursued on migration (flycatchers, thrushes, warblers, etc.). Several species of grouse and owls that have been specifically pursued on previous trips can also be found here. For that reason you need to review the probable list closely; if any of those species have been missed, now is the time to find them.

While this trip plan is straightforward and good locations are provided for most species, do not neglect the hotlines or personal contact with local birders. See Chapter 3 for Minnesota network details.

This trip includes Duluth, Lake County, McGregor Marsh, Rice Lake National Wildlife Refuge, Big Sandy Lake, Buffalo River State Park, Felton Prairie, the Fargo area, Chase Lake, Kidder County, Arrowwood National Wildlife Refuge, Devil's Lake, Kelly's Slough, Agassiz National Wildlife Refuge, McCarthy Beach State Park, Superior National Forest, and Sax-Zim Bog.

Note: Two add-on trips, which can be scheduled before or after this itinerary, are possible from Duluth at this season: Churchill, Manitoba (Chapter 20, Trip F) and North-Central Michigan (Chapter 20, Trip D).

Probable Species
Total of 145 Species
Common Loon
Pied-billed Grebe
Horned Grebe
Red-necked Grebe
Eared Grebe
Western Grebe
Am. White Pelican
Double-crested
Cormorant
American Bittern
Great Blue Heron
Green Heron
Black-crowned
Night-Heron
Canada Goose
Wood Duck
Green-winged Teal
American Black Duck
Mallard
Northern Pintail
Blue-winged Teal
Northern Shoveler
Gadwall
American Wigeon
Canvasback
Redhead
Ring-necked Duck
Lesser Scaup
Hooded Merganser
Ruddy Duck
Osprey
Bald Eagle
Northern Harrier
Cooper's Hawk
Broad-winged Hawk
Swainson's Hawk
Red-tailed Hawk
Ferruginous Hawk
American Kestrel
Ring-necked Pheasant
Sharp-tailed Grouse
Virginia Rail
Sora
American Coot
Sandhill Crane
Killdeer
American Avocet
Willet
Spotted Sandpiper
Marbled Godwit
Common Snipe
Wilson's Phalarope
Ring-billed Gull
California Gull
Forster's Tern
Black Tern
Rock Dove
Mourning Dove
Common Nighthawk
Chimney Swift
Ruby-throated
Hummingbird
Belted Kingfisher
Red-headed
Woodpecker
Yellow-bellied
Sapsucker
Downy Woodpecker
Hairy Woodpecker

Birdfinding Guides

The guide for the Minnesota portion of this trip is *A Birder's Guide to Minnesota* by Kim R. Eckert (1994). It covers the entire state with detailed maps and much useful information, including ID tips.

Birds in Minnesota by Robert B. Janssen, is not a birdfinding guide, but has range maps and distribution information on all Minnesota species. Published in 1987, it is currently out of print, but copies can be found with a little effort.

Checklist of North Dakota Birds, with Bar-Graphs Showing Relative Abundances and Seasonal Occurrences, by Gordon Berkey, David Lambeth, and Ron Martin (1994) is currently the best resource for North Dakota briding.

Rare Bird Alert Numbers

Minnesota 612/780-8890
Duluth 218/525-5952

Special Equipment

You will need a powerful flashlight and rubber boots or spare tennis shoes for any marsh wading that you do to locate Yellow Rail. You may also need your bird tapes to help locate that species as well as Baird's and Le Conte's Sparrows. Don't forget insect repellent.

Accommodations

Motels in most of the trip area range from $40 to $60 per night. Once again, the economy-minded birder will find that camping is the best way to go, with good campsites available on most nights.

Key Species — Total of 14 Species

1. **Gray Partridge**—Usually fairly easy to see by driving quiet backroads in the early morning hours in North Dakota or western Minnesota, although it is more common in North Dakota.

2. **Yellow Rail**—It is possible to find this rail in almost any marshy area in north-central Minnesota. Your best bet is McGregor Marsh; it has been for many years the most reliable place in the state. Yellow Rail is often easier to find in North Dakota's Kidder County and near Minnewaukan. (At this season Yellow Rails usually wait until it is quite dark to begin calling, but may often continue to call for an hour or two after sunrise.) This trip provides you multiple opportunities and sites to find Yellow Rail.

3. **Upland Sandpiper**—Look in any open grassy area throughout. Best bet in Minnesota is Felton Prairie. In North Dakota, some suggestions are Chase Lake, Kidder County, and Arrowwood National Wildlife Refuge.

4. **American Woodcock**—Common in the eastern two-thirds of Minnesota. Should be seen at Rice Lake, Lake County, or Sax-Zim Bog. Look for it—primarily at dawn or dusk—in brushy forest openings and heavily vegetated marshy areas.

5. **Franklin's Gull**—Will be seen at Chase Lake, Arrowwood NWR, and Devil's Lake in North Dakota; numerous at Agassiz National Wildlife Refuge in Minnesota.

6. **Black-billed Cuckoo**—Uncommon throughout Minnesota. Should be seen in Lake County and possible in any wooded area, including in North Dakota. (Invasion years in North Dakota seem to be correlated with peak grasshopper populations—rather than caterpillar outbreaks. Even found in shelterbelts and small woods in North Dakota.)

7. **Yellow-bellied Flycatcher**—Should see in Lake County and at Sax-Zim Bog. It is fairly common in the northeastern third of Minnesota in bogs and coniferous forests.

8. **Least Flycatcher**—Common in wooded areas throughout Minnesota. Will see at Rice Lake National Wildlife Refuge and many other locations. Also common in North Dakota in multi-row shelterbelts and natural or planted woods; Turtle River State Park is a typical location.

Probable Species
(continued)
Northern Flicker
Pileated Woodpecker
Eastern Wood-Pewee
Alder Flycatcher
Eastern Phoebe
Great Crested Flycatcher
Western Kingbird
Eastern Kingbird
Horned Lark
Purple Martin
Tree Swallow
Northern Rough-winged Swallow
Bank Swallow
Cliff Swallow
Barn Swallow
Blue Jay
American Crow
Common Raven
Black-capped Chickadee
Red-breasted Nuthatch
White-breasted Nuthatch
House Wren
Sedge Wren
Marsh Wren
Golden-cr. Kinglet
Ruby-crowned Kinglet
Eastern Bluebird
Veery
Hermit Thrush
Wood Thrush
American Robin
Gray Catbird
Brown Thrasher
Sprague's Pipit
Cedar Waxwing
European Starling
Yellow-throated Vireo
Warbling Vireo
Red-eyed Vireo
Golden-winged Warbler
Nashville Warbler
Northern Parula
Yellow Warbler
Chestnut-sided Warbler
Magnolia Warbler
Cape May Warbler
Yellow-rumped Warbler
Black-throated Green Warbler
Blackburnian Warbler
Black-and-white Warbler
American Redstart
Ovenbird
Northern Waterthrush
Common Yellowthroat
Scarlet Tanager
Rose-breasted Grosbeak
Indigo Bunting
Chipping Sparrow
Clay-colored Sparrow
Vesper Sparrow

Probable Species
(continued)

Savannah Sparrow
Grasshopper Sparrow
Nelson's Sharp-tailed
 Sparrow
Song Sparrow
Lincoln's Sparrow
Swamp Sparrow
White-throated Sparrow
Chestnut-collared
 Longspur
Bobolink
Red-winged Blackbird
Western Meadowlark
Brewer's Blackbird
Common Grackle
Brown-headed Cowbird
Orchard Oriole
Baltimore Oriole
Purple Finch
House Finch
Pine Siskin
American Goldfinch
House Sparrow

Note: Species in **boldface** appear infrequently in the itineraries as *key* or *probable*. Watch for them on this trip. Assume that you will see all probable species. This trip offers second chances at some species keyed on earlier trips. There are no new species from the probables for our cumulative and sequential listings.

Possible Species
Total of 36 Species
Clark's Grebe
Great Egret
Snowy Egret
Cattle Egret
Sharp-shinned Hawk
Northern Goshawk
Ruffed Grouse
Semipalmated Plover
Piping Plover
Greater Yellowlegs
Lesser Yellowlegs
Solitary Sandpiper
Semipalmated
 Sandpiper
Least Sandpiper
Pectoral Sandpiper
Eastern Screech-Owl
Great Horned Owl
Barred Owl
Great Gray Owl
Short-eared Owl
Whip-poor-will
Olive-sided Flycatcher
Willow Flycatcher
Say's Phoebe
Black-billed Magpie

9. **Connecticut Warbler**—Can be found in bogs in Lake County and at Sax-Zim Bog. Seems to prefer spruce/tamarack bogs. Hard-to-locate, but can be seen in proper habitat throughout northeastern Minnesota. Fortunately, it has a very loud song for a warbler.

10. **Mourning Warbler**—Common and easy to see at Rice Lake National Wildlife Refuge. Look in brushy areas and wet woodlands throughout northeastern Minnesota.

11. **Canada Warbler**—Uncommon in northern Minnesota. Should see on Day 1 in Lake County. If it is missed in Lake County, you will probably miss it for the trip.

12. **Baird's Sparrow**—Found most easily in North Dakota. See Day 4 and Day 5 itineraries for specific sites. Casual on Felton Prairie in Minnesota.

13. **Le Conte's Sparrow**—Common at McGregor Marsh, Rice Lake and Agassiz National Wildlife Refuges, and Sax-Zim Bog. In North Dakota look at Chase Lake, Arrowwood NWR, Devil's Lake area, and Kelly's Slough. Will be seen many times.

14. **Yellow-headed Blackbird**—Very common at this season in marshes in most of Minnesota, and throughout North Dakota.

Note: You should see all 14 key species. Yellow Rail is the most difficult to see, but you will hear it.

Itinerary

Note: This trip begins and ends in Duluth.

Day 1 — Duluth and Lake County

There are some wonderful Minnesota birds to see on this trip. On Day 1 it is important to see both Yellow-bellied Flycatcher and Canada Warbler; there will be little chance of finding either on the remainder of the trip. This first day also gives you the first opportunity to find Connecticut Warbler; your second—and perhaps better—opportunity is on Day 7. If you want to take your chances, you might want to move the Day 1 route to the end of your trip when you return to the Duluth area. That way you would concentrate on other species—especially prairie species—at the beginning of your trip.

Take Highway 61 northeast from Duluth to Two Harbors (about 23 miles). If you are in a hurry, take new Highway 61; if not, take old 61 (Scenic 61), which begins in Duluth as Congdon Boulevard. Scenic 61 gives you a better look at Lake Superior (possibile waterfowl and gulls). This road is also reliable, especially at dawn and dusk, for Ruffed Grouse in the aspens.

At Two Harbors, look over the harbor before driving north on Lake County Road 2. You will pass through mixed woods, coniferous woods, and open areas, each good for seeking the key species of that particular habitat. American Woodcock favors logged areas and low-lying stands of alder and willow. Black-billed Cuckoo can be found throughout the forested areas, especially in forest edges and in alders and willows. Yellow-bellied Flycatcher is partial to coniferous forests and bogs. Least Flycatcher is common in both coniferous and deciduous woods. Connecticut Warbler is possible in any bog, but it seems to favor spruce/tamarack bogs. Mourning Warbler is abundant in brushy forest openings and edges as well as in alder and willow stands. Canada Warbler prefers brushy forests and swampy areas in coniferous, deciduous, or mixed woods.

Each of these key species can be found along County Road 2 or nearby on forest roads in the state and national forest lands. The following locations are some of the better areas to try. The Langley Riverarea is about 21 miles north of Two Harbors, and the conifers there have boreal species and warblers. One mile farther, County Road 204 to the east is worth checking as far as Jordan. From the Road 204 turn-off, the next 3 to 4 miles north on County Road 2 pass through spruce bogs; a mile later White Pines Picnic Area is worth a look. One mile past the picnic area, try Forest Road 104 to the east, which

Possible Species
(continued)

Boreal Chickadee
Brown Creeper
Winter Wren
Loggerhead Shrike
Tennessee Warbler
Pine Warbler
Dickcissel
Rufous-sided Towhee
Lark Sparrow
Lark Bunting
Eastern Meadowlark

Note: You will probably see 8 of the birds on the possible list.

Remotely Possible Species
Total of 38 Species
Least Bittern
Cinnamon Teal
Common Goldeneye
Bufflehead
Common Merganser
Turkey Vulture
Spruce Grouse
Greater Prairie-Chicken
Black-bellied Plover
Am. Golden-Plover
Ruddy Turnstone
Sanderling
White-rumped Sandpiper
Baird's Sandpiper
Stilt Sandpiper
Short-billed Dowitcher
Long-billed Dowitcher
Red-necked Phalarope
Bonaparte's Gull
Herring Gull
Caspian Tern
Common Tern
Yellow-billed Cuckoo
Long-eared Owl
N. Saw-whet Owl
Black-backed Woodpecker
Gray Jay
Philadephia Vireo
Black-throated Blue Warbler
Palm Warbler
Bay-breasted Warbler
Field Sparrow
Henslow's Sparrow
Dark-eyed Junco
Rusty Blackbird
Red Crossbill
White-winged Crossbill
Evening Grosbeak

Note: You will see at least 3, possibly more depending on the timing of shorebird migration during your trip.

bisects an extensive spruce bog. The last few miles of County Road 2 pass through more spruce bogs, where Spruce Grouse is sometimes found. There are many other sites along County Road 2 as well as several forest roads that can be good, so do a little exploring.

When County Road 2 reaches Highway 1, you can follow it to Highway 61 along Lake Superior, return back down County Road 2, or circle around to the west on various routes to return to Duluth.

Spend the night in Duluth.

Day 2 — McGregor Marsh, Rice Lake National Wildlife Refuge, and Big Sandy Lake

The drive from Duluth to McGregor Marsh takes about one hour, and you need to leave in time to arrive there before sunrise. Drive south from Duluth on Interstate 35 for about 12 miles to the Highway 210 exit. Go west on Highway 210 for about 41 miles to Highway 65. Turn left onto Highway 65; there are grassy marshes on both sides of the road for the first 2 miles. This is McGregor Marsh, and for many years it has been the best place to locate the Yellow Rail in Minnesota. Stop anywhere, pinpoint a calling rail (you may have to use a tape), wade into the marsh with your flashlight, and locate the bird. In *A Birder's Guide to Minnesota*, Kim Eckert describes the best method to see and hear Yellow Rails. If you miss the rail, you will have other chances to see it on this trip. The reason for trying this morning is to use every opportunity you can for this bird since on some nights they do not call at all.

Other marsh species are Sora, Virginia Rail, Sedge Wren, Le Conte's and Nelson's Sharp-tailed Sparrows, and Yellow-headed Blackbird.

When you are ready to leave, continue south on Highway 65 for an additional 2 or 3 miles to the entrance to Rice Lake National Wildlife Refuge. This refuge is a good place to look for the following key species: American Woodcock, Black-billed Cuckoo, Least Flycatcher, Mourning Warbler, Le Conte's Sparrow, and Yellow-headed Blackbird.

You can spend most of the day at Rice Lake and McGregor Marsh; at least 7 of the 14 key species can be found in this area. The refuge has two outlying wildlife management areas, Grayling and Kimberly. Both are nearby and are well worth a visit.

Other species of interest include Ruffed and Sharp-tailed Grouse, Black Tern, Eastern Wood-Pewee, Alder Flycatcher, Sedge Wren, Veery, Wood Thrush, Yellow-throated Vireo, Golden-winged, Chestnut-sided, Black-throated Green, and Blackburnian Warblers, Scarlet Tanager, Rose-breasted Grosbeak, Clay-colored Sparrow, and Bobolink.

A Birder's Guide to Minnesota lists a few specific locations in the refuge that are reliable for certain species. Two hiking trails and a loop road help you explore the refuge's grassland, marsh, deciduous and coniferous woods, bogs, and several lakes; maps are available at the refuge office. There are restrooms and a picnic area, but no camping is allowed on the refuge.

Nearby McGregor has a motel, and campgrounds available in the Big Sandy Lake area thirty minutes north of Rice Lake National Wildlife Refuge. At least one, Savannah Portage State Park, has showers. You should probably make arrangements early in the day for a campsite or a motel room.

The birding is not particularly good in the Big Sandy Lake area, but several of the key species can sometimes be seen there. If you camp there, and if time allows, take a quick look.

Wind up the day at McGregor Marsh. Yellow Rails should start calling at dusk and usually will call all night. Some of the local experts think that it is easier to locate this species around midnight. Don't necessarily insist on *seeing* this bird; hearing its distinctive *tic-tic tic-tic-tic* call should suffice.

Spend the night at McGregor or at Savannah Portage State Park.

Day 3 — Buffalo River State Park and Felton Prairie

Depending on how your luck has been so far, you may want to start the day at McGregor Marsh again.

Then drive west across much of the state to Buffalo River State Park. Take State Route 210 west from McGregor until it joins Highway 10, then follow Highway 10 to the park entrance a few miles past Hawley. This is about a 175-mile drive and will take at least four hours, if you do a little birding along the way.

Buffalo River State Park is mostly grassland with woods along the river. Greater Prairie-Chicken occurs here, as well as Alder and maybe Willow Flycatchers.

Felton Prairie, an area of mostly unplowed and lightly grazed grassland, is north of the state park and is worth at least a drive through. (Most of the birds found on Felton Prairie are more easily found in North Dakota, your destination for the next two days.) To reach the prairie, follow Highway 10 a short distance west from the state park entrance to its intersection with Highway 9. Turn north to Felton, then take Secondary Road 34 east from Felton for 2 miles. From this point, the prairie is roughly 3 miles wide east to west and 5 miles long north to south. All of the roads should be driven at least once. Most of this land is private

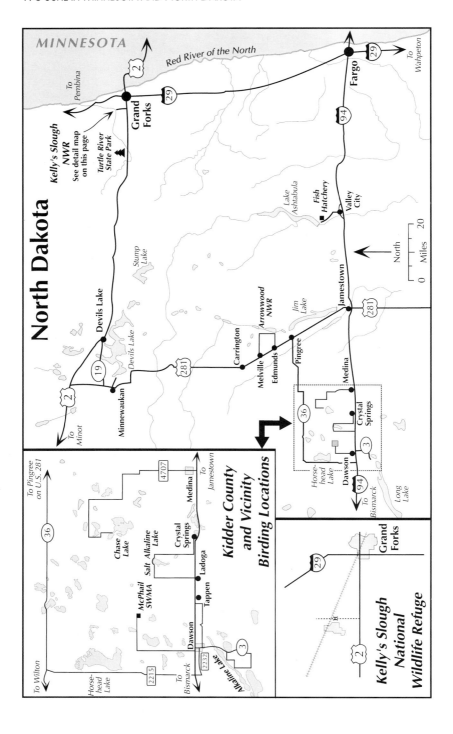

property. *Please obey the no trespassing signs and respect the owners' rights.* Key species in this area include Gray Partridge, Upland Sandpiper, and Baird's (casual) and Le Conte's Sparrows. Other species of interest here are Greater Prairie-Chicken, Sedge Wren, Sprague's Pipit (casual), Clay-colored Sparrow, Henslow's Sparrow (casual), and Chestnut-collared Longspur.

A Birder's Guide to Minnesota details this area under Clay County along with several other nearby areas of grassland.

You can camp at Buffalo River State Park; if not, there are many motels a few miles west in Fargo, North Dakota.

Day 4 — Fargo to Kidder County, North Dakota

On the north end of Fargo, 36-acre Oak Grove Park borders the Red River; it might be worth a peek if you have time to spare. This small park has provided some good sightings, including a number of owls, not the least of which was Long-eared in spring. To get there, take the 12th Avenue North exit to 4th Street North; take 4th southward to 6th Avenue North, then go east to the park gate.

Leaving Fargo on westbound Interstate 94, you will reach Valley City in 60 miles. Again, if you have time to spare, you might take Barnes County Road 17 for 3 miles north to the Valley City National Fish Hatchery/Wetland Management District. The surrounding prairie is a good place to start looking for Baird's Sparrow. Don't spend too much time here, because you'll have better opportunities farther along. You should pick up some other sparrows; the next two days in North Dakota are sparrow-laden.

Some birders get a special kick out of sparrow-watching in North Dakota, with at least Chipping, Clay-colored, Vesper, Savannah, Baird's, Grasshopper, Le Conte's, Nelson's Sharp-tailed, and Song on the potential list.

Back on Interstate 94 continue approximately 59 miles past Valley City to the Medina exit. This is the way to Chase Lake, a Fish and Wildlife property with the largest nesting colony of American White Pelicans in North America (10,000 to 12,000 birds). Key species here include Gray Partridge, Upland Sandpiper, Franklin's Gull, and Yellow-headed Blackbird. Less common key species are Black-billed Cuckoo, Least Flycatcher, and Baird's and Le Conte's Sparrows. You might also find Ferruginous Hawk, Sharp-tailed Grouse, Piping Plover, American Avocet, Marbled Godwit, Black Tern, Sprague's Pipit, Clay-colored Sparrow, and Chestnut-collared Longspur in the vicinity. To get there, travel north from the Medina exit on Stutsman County Road for 9.6 miles, west for 3 miles, north for 4 miles, west for 5 miles, and then south for about 3 miles to the access road.

Your next stops are in Kidder County for some excellent prairie birding. Continue westward on Interstate 94 for 11 miles to the Crystal Springs exit. Drive west from Crystal Springs about 1.5 miles on the frontage road, and then turn north on the gravel road. The next 5 miles to Salt Alkaline Lake is all good Baird's Sparrow habitat. Baird's Sparrow does very little fence-sitting but has a distinctive song; knowing this song is an important aid to locating this species. Continue 3 miles west and then 5 miles south to cover more prairie and marsh habitats. You will end up at Tappen on Interstate 94.

Upland Sandpiper
Shawneen E. Finnegan

So far along this route in Kidder County you should have found 3 other key species: Gray Partridge, Upland Sandpiper, and Yellow-headed Blackbird. If you have not seen Gray Partridge yet, be aware that this is a common species throughout much of North Dakota. The best way to find this bird is to drive the quiet backroads (among farmed lands, not grazed lands), especially in early morning. Their numbers, though, may decline during wet years. (You will have another good chance for the Gray Partridge on Day 5.) Again, it helps to be familiar with the bird's call. Upland Sandpiper should be seen along these roads, especially on fenceposts.

Now take Interstate 94 west for 8.5 miles from Tappen to Dawson. This is where you will have alternate opportunities, depending on how much daylight you have and what birds you seek. Here are your options: For another try at Baird's Sparrow go to McPhail State Wildlife Management Area (7 miles north and 5 miles east). For waterbirds, including guaranteed Yellow-headed Blackbird and possible Clark's Grebe and Least Bittern, try Alkaline Lake (not to be confused with Salt Alkaline Lake), located just 3 miles south and continuing along the shore 4 miles to the southwest. For impending darkness and Yellow Rail, go a mile south and then east on the gravel road for 2.5 miles to the curve. The unfenced and idle area on the south side of the road has been a very good spot. For Ferruginous Hawk with daylight and later multiple chances at hearing (and perhaps seeing) Yellow Rail, try the west side of Horsehead Lake. To get to Horsehead Lake from Dawson, take County Road 2232 west for 3.5 miles and turn right (north) onto the gravel road (2215) toward Horsehead Lake. Try the transmission towers along the power-lines north of the lake for Ferruginous Hawk. With darkness, you can pursue Yellow Rails along the road from the lower end of the lake up to State Route 36, about an 8-mile stretch. *Most of these sites are behind fences.* You should at least be able to *hear* the birds from this route.

When you finish up in Kidder County, retrace your way to Interstate 94 and drive east to Jamestown, about 50 miles.

Spend the night at Jamestown, where there are about a dozen motels, or camp in the Jamestown area or north toward Pipestem Lake, areas which have about eight private campgrounds.

Day 5 — Arrowwood, Devil's Lake, and Grand Forks

This might be a good morning to search for Gray Partridge. Get an early start for Arrowwood National Wildlife Refuge and check likely farmlands along the way. From Jamestown go 26 miles north on U.S. 281 and 6 miles east on County Road 44 from Edmunds. On the refuge (or just outside) you might see Eared and Western Grebes, American White Pelican, Ferruginous Hawk, Piping Plover, Upland Sandpiper, Franklin's Gull, Short-eared Owl, and Yellow-headed Blackbird. Two grouse are found on the refuge: Greater Prairie-Chicken and Sharp-tailed Grouse. Greater Prairie-Chicken is struggling to make a slow comeback here, with a re-introduction effort. To see Sharp-tailed Grouse, visit a lek site (there is a blind available at the refuge). Though there may not be dancing in mid-June, the male birds are usually not far from the grounds. Some prairie passerine specialties occur in the grassland portion of the 5.5-mile self-guided auto-tour, including Sprague's Pipits, Baird's and Le Conte's Sparrows, and Chestnut-collared Longspur (sometimes more common on heavily-grazed pastures off the refuge).

Return to Highway 281 and continue north to the Devil's Lake area. At Minnewaukan turn east toward the western arm of the lake. In 3.5 miles you will reach the Minnewaukan Flats, where Eared and Western Grebes, Black-crowned Night-Heron, Franklin's Gull, Forster's and Black Terns, and Yellow-headed Blackbird nest. You may see egrets and possibly Clark's Grebe. You should also pick up some shorebirds here. Fluctuating water-levels will certainly influence the presence of some of these species.

Continuing past Minnewaukan back on U.S. 281, look for Route 19 in 4 miles. The meadow to the east of 281 and south of Route 19 has Yellow Rails when wet enough. Le Conte's and Nelson's Sharp-tailed Sparrows may be in the same meadow. The nearby haying-areas are also good for Baird's Sparrows, and Sprague's Pipits are sometimes present.

Drive east on Highway 19 for 10 miles and pause at Six Mile Bay for a look at waterbirds. Some 7 miles later you will reach the town of Devil's Lake, where you merge eastbound with U.S. Highway 2.

You can camp at Turtle River State Park on the north side of U.S. 2 (a 63-mile drive). If there is still daylight, you might want to squeeze in some birding here, along the forest and grassland nature trails. This is a typical site for Least Flycatcher, and American Woodcock has been found here. If you want a choice of motels, continue on U.S. 2 for another 22 miles into Grand Forks.

Day 6 — Kelly's Slough and Agassiz National Wildlife Refuges and McCarthy Beach State Park

Kelly's Slough National Wildlife Refuge is just outside of Grand Forks; it is one of the best birding spots in northeastern North Dakota. This is a fine place for Upland Sandpiper, Marbled Godwit, Sedge Wren, Le Conte's and Nelson's Sharp-tailed Sparrows, and Yellow-headed Blackbird. There are also plenty of waterfowl species. Just 7.5 miles west of Grand Forks on U.S. 2, turn north onto the unmarked (except for a refuge sign) road for 3.3 miles to the bridge. A short distance farther is an old railroad bed that crosses the refuge southeast to northwest. Hiking along the gravel road or the railroad bed should provide you with some good sightings. Your last chance for Yellow Rail in North Dakota would be back along the road, driving another 4.7 miles north, and looking to either the east or the northwest.

Leaving North Dakota behind, you will have one more opportunity to get some prairie species in western Minnesota, just in case you haven't had your fill. If you want this option, after crossing the Red River take State Route 220 north to State Route 1 (19 miles). Follow State Route 1 east for approximately 23 miles, then angle onto County Road 2 as State Route 1 bears right. Continue on County Road 2 to State Route 32. Take State Route 32 north to Holt and turn east onto County Road 7 to the entrance of Agassiz National Wildlife Refuge.

Key species at Agassiz include Yellow Rail, American Woodcock, Franklin's Gull, Black-billed Cuckoo, Least Flycatcher, Le Conte's Sparrow, and Yellow-headed Blackbird. Other species of interest include 5 species of grebes, both bitterns, many species of ducks, Ruffed Grouse, Black Tern, Alder Flycatcher, Sedge and Marsh Wrens, Veery, Yellow-throated Vireo, Rose-breasted Grosbeak, Nelson's Sharp-tailed Sparrow, and Bobolink.

Stop at refuge headquarters for a map and a birdlist. There is a 4-mile loop drive, a short hiking trail, and an observation tower. The map will show you alternate area roads with access to other parts of the refuge.

A half-day visit should be sufficient to tour this refuge and locate the key species.

Leave Agassiz National Wildlife Refuge and bird your way back across Minnesota to McCarthy Beach State Park. To do this, take Highway 1 east from Thief River Falls to a few miles past the small town of Togo (about 170 miles), and turn right onto County Road 5 to the state park.

Spend the night at McCarthy Beach State Park, where showers are available.

Day 7 — McCarthy Beach State Park, Superior National Forest, and Sax-Zim Bog

Spend the morning birding McCarthy Beach State Park and the surrounding area. A section of Superior National Forest can be reached by taking County Road 65 east from County Road 5 near the state park entrance. A drive through a small part of Superior National Forest can be made by taking County Road 65 east to County Road 25 and then taking 25 south to Highway 37. You will pass through forest habitat good for several key species. American Woodcock, Black-billed Cuckoo, Yellow-bellied and Least Flycatchers, Connecticut and Mourning Warblers, and Le Conte's Sparrow can all be found in their respective habitats.

When you reach Highway 37, turn left and proceed to County Road 7, then turn south to Zim. The area around this small village and the next one on County Road 7, (Sax), is known as the Sax-Zim Bog. Not all of the area is bog, of course, but there are large tracts of bog. *A Birder's Guide to Minnesota* covers this area well and provides a detailed map showing the bogs. Sax-Zim Bog is good for most of the key species listed above as well as Great Gray Owl and Sharp-tailed Grouse. It is the best place on this trip to find Connecticut Warbler.

When you are through birding Sax-Zim Bog, continue south to Duluth or Savannah Portage State Park for the night.

You might still have time for another visit to McGregor Marsh or Rice Lake National Wildlife Refuge this evening or tomorrow.

Day 8 — Extra Day

If you have missed any key species, it is time to check with local birders for specific locations and make another attempt. There are many good birding locations north and northeast of Duluth where key species can be found. See *A Birder's Guide to Minnesota* for other nearby locations. Another suggestion for the extra day, if you have found all of the key species, is to drive to Ashland, Wisconsin, to see the Mute Swans. This is a short drive east from Duluth and is the only chance in the 19 trip plans to see this species.

The trip ends in Duluth in the afternoon.

Bird Numbers This Trip

	Potential	Expected	Actual
Key Species	14	14	
Probable Species	145	145	
Possible Species	36	8	
Remotely Possible Species	38	3	
Totally Unexpected Species . . . . ?		2	
TOTAL	233	172	

Cumulative List
Total key and probable species seen after 12 trips.

Previous trips . . . . 579 species
Minnesota/North Dakota trip . . . . 14 species
TOTAL . . . . 593 species

This Trip's Mileage and Expenses
Approximate miles traveled, Duluth to Duluth: 1,750

- Fuel: $125; sharing $63 $_____
- Lodging: 3 nights at motels $190; sharing $95 $_____
- Food: Ice-chest/supermarket for all meals $80 $_____
  *The total per person cost for the above items with a companion
  to share expenses should be less than $240.*
- Add to this car rental expenses, if any: $_____
- Add to this your expenses to/from Duluth: $_____
  This will give you a good idea of the cost of this trip.
- TOTAL $_____

Personal Notes

_____

_____

_____

_____

_____

_____

_____

_____

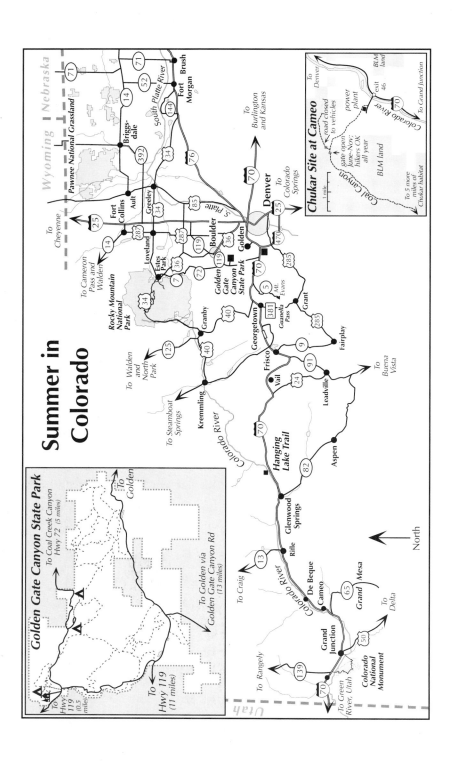

Summer in Colorado

Golden Gate Canyon State Park

To Coal Creek Canyon
Hwy 72 (5 miles)

To Golden

To Golden via
Golden Gate Canyon Rd
(13 miles)

To Golden

Hwy 119
(11 miles)

To Hwy 119
(0.5 miles)

To Hwy 119

Chukar Site at Cameo

To Denver

To Grand Junction

exit 46

BLM land

power plant

road closed to vehicles

gate open June–Nov; hikers OK all year

BLM land

Coal Canyon

Colorado River

To 5 more miles of Chukar habitat

1 mile

Wyoming | Nebraska

Pawnee National Grassland

71

71

52

14

14

Briggs-dale

392

34

South Platte River

Fort Morgan

Brush

76

To Burlington and Kansas

70

To Colorado Springs

Denver

25

470

285

Ault

Fort Collins

25

To Cheyenne

287

Greeley

34

85

Loveland

14

To Cameron Pass and Walden

Estes Park

36

7

Rocky Mountain National Park

34

Granby

40

125

To Walden and North Park

Kremmling

40

To Steamboat Springs

Colorado River

70

Vail

Frisco

24

82

Aspen

Glenwood Springs

Hanging Lake Trail

Rifle

13

To Craig

De Beque

Cameo

Colorado River

Grand Junction

70

To Green River, Utah

To Rangely

139

50

Grand Mesa

65

To Delta

Colorado National Monument

Utah

Boulder

36

119

Golden

72

Golden Gate Canyon State Park

119

70

Mt. Evans

5

Georgetown

381

Guanella Pass

Grant

285

Fairplay

9

91

Leadville

To Buena Vista

287

S. Plate

S Platte

Colorado River

North

Leadville

Chapter 13

SUMMER IN COLORADO

Late June—6 Days

General

A summertime visit to Colorado is a delightful experience in varied altitudes, habitats, and birds. This itinerary takes you from the sweeping prairie of Pawnee National Grassland through the majestic beauty of the Rocky Mountains to the semi-arid western slope of the state. You will sample the birdlife in all five life zones represented in Colorado.

We will focus on 19 species, of which 3 should be found in the grassland, 12 in the mountains (foothills to high elevation), and 4 in the more arid western lands. A few of the key species can be hard to locate, and some of them are hard to identify after you do locate them, but you will have enough time in the field to do both.

This trip, like the previous several trips, will afford second and third chances at a number of species targeted on earlier trips. Be sure to check the probable list closely for any species that you missed previously. These can be seen on this trip and can be added to your personal key list.

You will visit Pawnee National Grassland, Rocky Mountain National Park, Golden Gate Canyon State Park, Hanging Lake, Cameo, the Grand Junction area, Colorado National Monument, Red Rocks Park, and Mount Evans.

Note: Two add-on trips are possible from Grand Junction at this season:
North-Central Utah (see Chapter 20, Trip I)
and Northwestern Wyoming (see Chapter 20, Trip G).

Birdfinding Guides

A Birder's Guide to Colorado by Harold R. Holt and James A. Lane (1988) covers all of the areas to visit. (A revision of this currently out-of-print guide is expected in 1996.)

Rare Bird Alert Number

Statewide 303/424-2144

Special Equipment

Bird tapes are important—some of the species that you are after cannot always be seen well without the use of tapes, and some of them are difficult to identify except by voice. *The use of tapes to attract wildlife is prohibited in some areas; be sure that they are allowed before you use them.*

Accommodations

Motels are plentiful throughout the trip area, but remember that you are visiting a tourist state at the busiest season. Motels can be expensive in certain areas, but can usually be found for $30 to $80 per night, depending on location and your personal standards.

Campgrounds are also numerous. Most charge a fee, yet because of the heavy tourist load at this time of year they fill up early. The best course of action is to plan well, secure campsites early in the day, and camp most nights.

Key Species — Total of 18 Species

1. **Chukar**—Can be difficult to locate. Your best bet is Cameo on Day 4. If your luck is bad there, try the Mack area on Day 5. Local information can be a big help.

2. **Blue Grouse**—Although a common resident of the foothills and mountains, this grouse is almost always hard to find. Try the hiking trails in the Bear Lake region of Rocky Mountain National Park or at Golden Gate Canyon State Park.

3. **Mountain Plover**—Fairly common but widely dispersed at Pawnee National Grassland and not usually difficult to locate.

4. **Black Swift**—Should be seen at Loch Vale in Rocky Mountain National Park or at Hanging Lake near Glenwood Springs. Either place will require hiking, but if you see this species without hiking on this itinerary, you are just plain lucky.

5. **Red-naped Sapsucker**—Fairly easy to locate at Rocky Mountain National Park and at Golden Gate Canyon State Park.

6. **Williamson's Sapsucker**—Can be more difficult to find than Red-naped Sapsucker but should be found in the same two parks.

7. **Olive-sided Flycatcher**—Fairly common in the Canadian Life Zone. You should see it in Rocky Mountain National Park above Glacier Basin Campground and at Golden Gate Canyon State Park.

8. **Hammond's Flycatcher**—Common at Rocky Mountain National Park and Golden Gate Canyon State Park, usually in mature conifers with dense canopy. Easy to locate; harder to identify.

9. **Dusky Flycatcher**—Like Hammond's Flycatcher, it is easy to find but hard to identify. Will be seen at the same two parks. It seems to prefer conifers with shrubs or willow thickets in the mountains.

10. **Gray Flycatcher**—Can be found at Colorado National Monument in pinyon/juniper habitat.

11. **Pinyon Jay**—Another species that should be found at Colorado National Monument in pinyon/juniper habitat.

12. **Townsend's Solitaire**—Common resident in coniferous forests of foothills and lower mountains. Should be easily found at Rocky Mountain National Park and Golden Gate Canyon State Park.

13. **Sage Thrasher**—Common in sagebrush shrublands in low foothills, mesas, and plateaus. Your best bet is in the Grand Junction area.

14. **MacGillivray's Warbler**—Easy to locate around water-courses with shrubs or in aspens with shrubby understory in Rocky Mountain National Park and many other places.

15. **Lazuli Bunting**—May be seen at Pawnee National Grassland, Colorado National Monument, or anywhere in between in proper habitat. Look in oak hillside shrubland and lowland riparian habitat with shrubs. The likely spots are Golden Gate Canyon State Park or Red Rocks Park.

Probable Species
(continued)

Say's Phoebe
Ash-throated Flycatcher
Western Kingbird
Eastern Kingbird
Horned Lark
Tree Swallow
Violet-green Swallow
Cliff Swallow
Barn Swallow
Gray Jay
Steller's Jay
Blue Jay
Western Scrub-Jay
Clark's Nutcracker
Black-billed Magpie
American Crow
Common Raven
Black-capped
 Chickadee
Mountain Chickadee
Plain Titmouse
Bushtit
Red-breasted Nuthatch
White-breasted
 Nuthatch
Pygmy Nuthatch
Brown Creeper
Rock Wren
Canyon Wren
House Wren
American Dipper
Ruby-crowned Kinglet
Western Bluebird
Mountain Bluebird
Hermit Thrush
American Robin
Gray Catbird
Northern Mockingbird
Brown Thrasher
American Pipit
Loggerhead Shrike
European Starling
Solitary Vireo
Warbling Vireo
Virginia's Warbler
Yellow Warbler
Yellow-rumped
 Warbler
Black-throated Gray
 Warbler
Common Yellowthroat
Wilson's Warbler
Yellow-breasted Chat
Western Tanager
Black-headed Grosbeak
Blue Grosbeak
Spotted Towhee
Chipping Sparrow
Vesper Sparrow
Lark Sparrow
Black-throated Sparrow
Savannah Sparrow
Grasshopper Sparrow
Song Sparrow
Lincoln's Sparrow
White-crowned
 Sparrow
Dark-eye Junco
McCown's Longspur

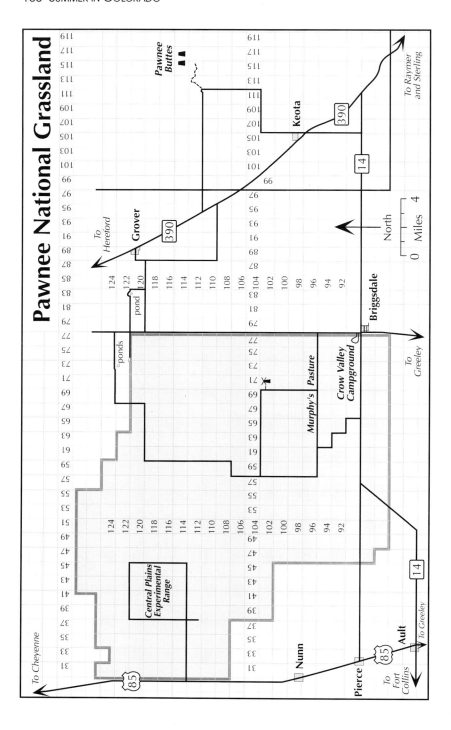

16. **Green-tailed Towhee**—Should be seen in Rocky Mountain National Park at lower elevations in dry hillside shrubs, sometimes with oak. Easy to see at Golden Gate Canyon State Park and may be seen even at Colorado National Monument.

17. **Brewer's Sparrow**—Will be easily seen at Pawnee National Grassland and at Colorado National Monument. Listen for its unmistakable song.

18. **Lark Bunting**—This bird of the dry grassland should be seen at a number of locations; it is a common roadside bird. Can't miss at Pawnee National Grassland.

19. **Brown-capped Rosy-Finch**—Should be seen at one of the stops on Trail Ridge Road on Day 3. If not, you can look for it on Mount Evans at Summit Lake on Day 6.

> Note: You should see all 19 key species. Chukar and Blue Grouse are the only difficult-to-locate species, and they should be found, given adequate field time.

Itinerary

Note: This trip begins and ends in Denver.

Day 1 — Pawnee National Grassland and Rocky Mountain National Park

Leave early and go north from Denver on Highway 85 to Greeley (about 50 miles). At Greeley stop at the U.S. Forest Service Office at 660 O Street; the U.S. Forest Service administers Pawnee National Grassland. Here you can obtain a bird checklist, a map of the grassland ($3), and a pamphlet outlining a 36-mile self-guided tour. If you would like to write for these items prior to the trip, the ZIP code is 80631 and the phone is 970/353-5004.

Continue north from Greeley on Highway 85 to Ault and turn right onto Highway 14. (Look for Yellow-headed Blackbirds in a small marshy area just past Ault.) Continue east to Briggsdale. Turn left (north) onto Road 77 for a short distance to Crow Valley Park and Campground, where the self-guided tour begins.

Probable Species
(continued)

Chestnut-collared Longspur
Red-winged Blackbird
Western Meadowlark
Yellow-headed Blackbird
Brewer's Blackbird
Common Grackle
Brown-headed Cowbird
Orchard Oriole
Bullock's Oriole
Pine Grosbeak
Cassin's Finch
House Finch
Pine Siskin
Lesser Goldfinch
American Goldfinch
Evening Grosbeak
House Sparrow

Note: The species in **boldface** appear no more than four times in the itineraries as *key* or *probable* species. Watch for them on this trip. Assume that you will see all probable species. You will gain only 1 species not seen on a previous trip but will have good second chances at previously keyed species.

Possible Species
Total of 31 Species
Clark's Grebe
American Bittern
Cattle Egret
Northern Shoveler
Gadwall
American Wigeon
Lesser Scaup
Turkey Vulture
Northern Bobwhite
Virginia Rail
Franklin's Gull
Barn Owl
Eastern Screech-Owl
Northern Pygmy-Owl
Long-eared Owl
Short-eared Owl
Northern Rough-winged Swallow
Bank Swallow
Bewick's Wren
Marsh Wren
Golden-crowned Kinglet
Blue-gray Gnatcatcher
Swainson's Thrush
Gray Vireo
Red-eyed Vireo
Orange-crowned Warbler
Indigo Bunting
Cassin's Sparrow

Possible Species
(continued)

Sage Sparrow
Fox Sparrow
Red Crossbill

Note: You will probably see 6 of these species.

Remotely Possible Species
Total of 28 Species
Eared Grebe
Green Heron
Wood Duck
Canvasback
Ring-necked Duck
Bald Eagle
Northern Goshawk
Peregrine Falcon
Black-necked Stilt
Upland Sandpiper
Long-billed Dowitcher
Caspian Tern
Least Tern
Yellow-billed Cuckoo
Northern Saw-whet Owl
Three-toed Woodpecker
Least Flycatcher
Eastern Phoebe
Cassin's Kingbird
Purple Martin
Chihuahuan Raven
Eastern Bluebird
Cedar Waxwing
American Redstart
Dickcissel
Bobolink
Great-tailed Grackle
Scott's Oriole

The tour brochure provides locations for most of the species of interest. Key species that can be seen here are Mountain Plover, Brewer's Sparrow, and Lark Bunting. Mountain Plover must be seen here, because the grassland will be your only opportunity to find it. Other species of interest include Swainson's and Ferruginous Hawks, Long-billed Curlew, Black Tern, Burrowing Owl, and McCown's and Chestnut-collared Longspurs (in breeding plumage).

The tour will take about three hours, but you may be intrigued enough by this huge grassland to do some exploring on your own. *A Birder's Guide to Colorado,* suggests a productive route.

When you are ready to leave the grassland, return to Greeley and turn west onto Highway 34. The road enters the foothills, twisting up through scenic Big Thompson Canyon before leveling out temporarily at Estes Park. Turn left onto Highway 36 to enter Rocky Mountain National Park at the Beaver Meadows entrance station. Be sure to stop at the visitor center for a map and a birdlist.

You should secure a campsite soon after you arrive at the park. Moraine Park and Glacier Basin campgroundsare convenient to this entrance, but Moraine Park Campgroundis better situated for your needs if you can obtain a campsite there.

Moraine Park should be explored from the campground to the Fern Lake trailhead. Key species here include Red-naped and Williamson's Sapsuckers, Hammond's and Dusky Flycatchers, Townsend's Solitaire, and MacGillivray's Warbler. Other species of interest are Willow and Cordilleran Flycatchers, Cassin's Finch, Red Crossbill, and Evening Grosbeak.

Spend the night at one of the campgrounds listed above, or return to Estes Park for a motel.

Day 2 — Rocky Mountain National Park

Start the day with a trip to Loch Vale to try for Black Swift. To reach Loch Vale take Bear Lake Road to the shuttle bus parking area across the road from Glacier Basin Campground. Board the next free shuttle bus and ride to Glacier Gorge Junction. Here you will find the trailhead for the 2.7-mile hike to Loch Vale, where Black Swifts nest.

While hiking to and from the loch, stay alert for Blue Grouse. The only way to see Blue Grouse is to hike trails through the right habitat. You should also see Olive-sided Flycatcher in this area. Other species at this elevation include Three-toed Woodpecker, Clark's Nutcracker, Pine Grosbeak, and Cassin's Finch.

Several other trails in the area might produce Blue Grouse. At Bear Lake the trails to Dream Lake (1.1 miles) and Lake Haiyaha (2.2 miles) are known to be good for it.

The entire area along Bear Lake Road offers good birding. The area below Glacier Basin Campground near the Mill Creek and Big Thompson River bridges are especially good for MacGillivray's Warbler and Green-tailed Towhee.

When you are through birding this area, drive to the park's Fall River Entrance. Bird this area all the way to Endovalley Campground. The birds are basically the same as those seen at the Beaver Meadows Entrance, but you may find something new.

Spend the night again camping in Rocky Mountain National Park or make use of an Estes Park motel.

Clark's Nutcracker
Dan Kilby

Day 3 — Rocky Mountain National Park and Golden Gate Canyon State Park

Start the day with an early morning drive up Trail Ridge Road to search for White-tailed Ptarmigan and Brown-capped Rosy-Finch. As you make this drive, there are numerous good spots along the way to bird. Your only problem here is being distracted by the spectacular scenery. The best location to find the ptarmigan is the trail leading out across the tundra at Rock Cut. The ptarmigan is common here but hard to see because of its protective coloration. *Stay on the trail. Tapes are forbidden in the park.* The trail at Rock Cut is a likely spot for Brown-capped Rosy-Finch. The ptarmigan can also be found both above and below the parking area at Medicine Bow Curve beyond the Alpine Visitor Center while rosy-finches are frequently seen at the Lava Cliffs between Rock Cut and Fall River Pass, or even from the visitor center's picture windows.

Other species of interest on Trail Ridge Road are Clark's Nutcracker, American Pipit, and the Gray-headed form of Dark-eyed Junco. Watch for Northern Goshawk and Golden Eagle from the overlooks.

When you are ready to tear yourself away from Rocky Mountain National Park, take Highway 7 south from Estes Park. This is a scenic drive with many places that can provide good birding. Highway 7 becomes Highway 72 and then later Highway 119 as it continues south toward Interstate 70. After it becomes Highway 119, watch on the left for the entrance to Golden Gate Canyon State Park, an excellent place to camp for the night.

Because this park is at a somewhat lower elevation, it's a likely place to find Lazuli Bunting and Green-tailed Towhee as well as Blue Grouse, Red-naped and Williamson's Sapsuckers, Olive-sided, Hammond's, and Dusky Flycatchers, Townsend's Solitaire, and MacGillivray's Warbler.

The park has many miles of trails where there are enough species present or possible to keep you entertained for the evening—Northern Pygmy-Owl, Three-toed Woodpecker, Cordilleran Flycatcher, Clark's Nutcracker, Virginia's Warbler, Cassin's Finch, Red Crossbill, and Evening Grosbeak.

Spend the night at Golden Gate Canyon State Park or continue south on Highway 119 to Interstate 70 for a motel.

Day 4 — Hanging Lake, Cameo, and Colorado National Monument

Leaving Golden Gate Canyon State Park, take Highway 119 south to Interstate 70, and turn west for the long drive to the Grand Junction area (approximately 240 miles). There are many good birding spots along the way, but in particular you should plan two stops for specific species.

The first planned stop is at Hanging Lake, a location known for its nesting Black Swifts. Take Exit 125, follow the frontage road west to the Exit 121 interchange, cross under the freeway, and return to Exit 125, where you can follow signs to the Hanging Lake trailhead. The 1.25-mile trail isn't easy, but your reward will be really close views of Black and the more numerous White-throated Swifts and a well-deserved rest in a stunningly beautiful hanging valley. If you missed Black Swift at Loch Vale in Rocky Mountain National Park, and if you are up to making the climb, this stop is a must.

Our second planned stop is to look for Chukar about 15 miles prior to reaching Grand Junction. Take the Cameo exit (Exit 46), cross the bridge over the Colorado River, and follow the dirt road that skirts the power plant. Stay off of the roads marked *private property* and try either north or south of the power plant; Chukar can be found in both directions. If you go left around the power plant, it is about 2 miles to a gate; if you go to the right, it is about 1.5 miles to a gate. In both cases, park and walk into the area. Chukar may be hard to locate, but it is present on the cheatgrass hillsides, and patience will usually be rewarded.

Return to Interstate 70 and continue west, bypass Grand Junction, and exit at Colorado National Monument. There is a campground at the monument and another at Highline Lake State Recreation Area a few miles farther west near Fruita.

Colorado National Monument can be good for the following key species: Chukar, Gray Flycatcher, Pinyon Jay, Sage Thrasher, Lazuli Bunting, Green-tailed Towhee, and Brewer's Sparrow. Other species include Gray Vireo (possible) and Black-throated Sparrow.

Camp at one of the campgrounds mentioned above or return to the Grand Junction area for a motel.

Day 5 — Colorado National Monument, Grand Junction area, and return to Denver

Colorado National Monument is well covered in *A Birder's Guide to Colorado*. That book also lists a good spot near Mack, west of the monument on Interstate 70, for Chukar. It details several loop trips in the Grand Junction area that are productive for many different birds, including several of the key species.

Spend the morning and early afternoon birding the above areas. Before leaving to return to Denver, you should take stock to see which, if any, of the key species have been missed. By this point in the trip, you should have developed a contact or two in the trip area. Call your contact and ask about specific locations that might be good for the missed species.

Then decide whether to spend the night in the Grand Junction area or return to Denver.

Day 6 — Extra Day
This day should be used to seek any missed key species and to soak up the environment. A good way to spend the day, especially if you missed Brown-capped Rosy-Finch on Trail Ridge Road, is to bird Red Rocks Park in Denver and Mount Evans just west of Denver. Red Rocks Park is also a good place for Lazuli Bunting, Green-tailed Towhee, and Brewer's Sparrow, as well as numerous other species. Mount Evans features the highest paved road in the United States. Summit Lake, on the tundra about 9 miles along the drive up Mount Evans, is your likeliest spot in Colorado for Brown-capped Rosy-Finch.

The trip ends in Denver in the evening.

Bird Numbers This Trip

	Potential	Expected	Actual
Key Species	19	19	
Probable Species	144	144	
Possible Species	31	6	
Remotely Possible Species	28	3	
Totally Unexpected Species	?	2	
TOTAL	222	174	

Cumulative List

Total key and probable species seen after 13 trips

Previous trips	594 species
Colorado summer trip	20 species
TOTAL	614 species

This Trip's Mileage and Expenses

Approximate miles traveled, Denver to Denver: 1,050

- Fuel: $75; sharing $37.50 $_____
- Lodging: 1 night at a motel, the rest of the
  nights camping $80; sharing $40 $_____
- Food: Ice-chest/supermarket for all meals - $60 $_____
  *The total per person cost for the above items with a companion
  to share expenses should be less than $140 each.*
- Add to this car rental expenses, if any: $_____
- Add to this your expenses to/from Denver: $_____
  This will give you a good idea of the cost of this trip.
- TOTAL $_____

Personal Notes

_____

_____

_____

_____

_____

_____

_____

_____

_____

_____

_____

_____

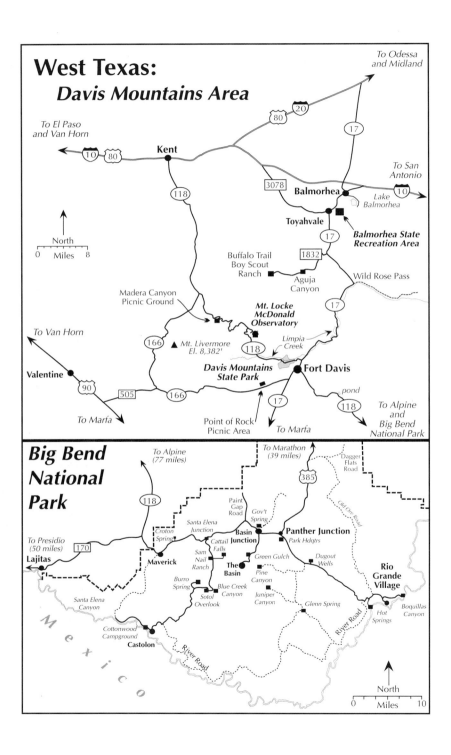

Chapter 14

WEST TEXAS

Early July—4 Days

General

Two areas in West Texas must be visited, sooner or later, by any serious traveling birder. Big Bend National Park is well known to birders as the only place north of Mexico to see Colima Warbler and also the only place for a realistic chance at Lucifer Hummingbird. The Davis Mountains may not be the only location for Montezuma Quail, but it is by far the surest.

These two areas are about 125 miles apart and make a nice three- to five-day trip. Our route takes you first to the Davis Mountains and winds up in Big Bend National Park. Most tourists visit Big Bend in the spring or fall when the temperatures are mild, but a birder needs to visit in June, July, or August when the weather can only be described as hot. Although Big Bend is huge (it covers nearly 1,200 square miles) all of the species you are targeting can be found in The Basin, and you will visit only a small part of the park as part of this four-day trip.

To see all 3 key species in The Basin will require extensive hiking. The trail to see Colima Warbler is 11 miles long, and there is virtually no possibility of hiking less than 7 miles of it to see the bird. In addition, the best location for Lucifer Hummingbird and Gray Vireo is a 5.2-mile hike.

After seeing the key species, you can bird other parts of Big Bend National Park as time allows.

This trip will include Midland-Odessa, Davis Mountains State Park, Big Bend National Park, and the intervening areas.

Birdfinding Guide

A Birder's Guide to the Rio Grande Valley of Texas by Harold R. Holt (1992) covers the entire trip area in detail.

Birder's Guide to Texas by Ed Kutac (1989) is not as detailed, but is still helpful.

Probable Species
Total of 90 Species
Pied-billed Grebe
Mallard
Turkey Vulture
Common Black-Hawk
Swainson's Hawk
Zone-tailed Hawk
Red-tailed Hawk
American Kestrel
Scaled Quail
American Coot
Killdeer
Rock Dove
Band-tailed Pigeon
White-winged Dove
Mourning Dove
Inca Dove
Yellow-billed Cuckoo
Greater Roadrunner
Western Screech-Owl
Great Horned Owl
Elf Owl
Lesser Nighthawk
Common Nighthawk
Common Poorwill
White-throated Swift
Blue-throated
Hummingbird
Black-chinned
Hummingbird
Broad-tailed
Hummingbird
Acorn Woodpecker
Golden-fronted
Woodpecker
Ladder-backed
Woodpecker
Northern Flicker
Western Wood-Pewee
Cordilleran Flycatcher
Black Phoebe
Say's Phoebe
Vermilion Flycatcher
Ash-throated Flycatcher
Cassin's Kingbird
Western Kingbird
Horned Lark
Violet-green Swallow
Northern Rough-
winged Swallow
Cliff Swallow
Barn Swallow
Western Scrub-Jay
Mexican Jay
Common Raven
Tufted Titmouse
Verdin
Bushtit
White-breasted
Nuthatch
Cactus Wren
Rock Wren
Canyon Wren
Bewick's Wren
Blue-gray Gnatcatcher
Black-tailed
Gnatcatcher
Northern Mockingbird
Curve-billed Thrasher
Phainopepla

Field Guide to the Birds of the Big Bend by Ro Wauer (1984) is not a birdfinding guide, but an annotated treatment of the park's birds, with all kinds of details on species that you will be looking for.

Rare Bird Alert Number

Statewide 713/992-2757

Special Equipment

Good hiking shoes or boots and a canteen are absolute necessities. Bird tapes can be helpful with at least two of the key species.

Accommodations

Both of the areas that you will visit have nice lodges for those who do not desire to camp. Advance reservations are required for both lodges. For reservations or information concerning Indian Lodge at Davis Mountains State Park, phone 915/426-3254. For the Chisos Mountain Lodge at Big Bend National Park, call 915/477-2291. Both parks also have fine camping facilities, with showers available, and small fees.

Key Species — Total of 4 Species

1. **Montezuma Quail**—Usually an easy bird to find at the campgrounds at Davis Mountains State Park in the early morning or late evening (check with the park staff for current best locations). Look along Highway 118 near the road to McDonald Observatory and along Highway 166 in the grassland southwest of Fort Davis.

2. **Lucifer Hummingbird**—Best spots are along the lower part of the Window Trail and at Laguna Meadows in Big Bend. It frequents flowering agaves or sage.

3. **Gray Vireo**—Best found in pinyon/juniper habitat along the Window Trail.

4. **Colima Warbler**—The only reliable way to find this very local bird is by taking the trail to Boot Spring. If you are lucky, you can locate it at Laguna Meadows or Boulder Meadows, thus shortening the hike. If you are unable to make this hike, give Pine Canyon a try; Colima Warbler is seen there occasionally. To reach Pine Canyon, leave The Basin and turn right. At Glenn Spring Road turn right again. Pine Canyon is about 2.5 miles in. Park at the trailhead and walk about a mile on fairly level ground to reach the canyon.

Note: You should see all of the 4 key species.

Itinerary

Note: This trip begins and ends in Midland-Odessa.

Day 1 — Odessa and the Davis Mountains

Drive west from Odessa (the closest airport to the Davis Mountains) on Interstate 20; after approximately 80 miles, exit south onto Highway 17 to Balmorhea, and continue south to Fort Davis (71 miles). Twenty miles from Fort Davis the highway swings west to follow Limpia Creek. One or two pairs of Common Black-Hawks reside in the vicinity; one pair nests regularly along this creek. (This is your second opportunity to see this hawk on these trip itineraries. The first site from Chapter 10—in Southeast Arizona—is currently a difficult location to access.) Just prior to reaching Fort Davis, turn right onto Highway 118; after about 2 miles, watch on your left for the entrance to Davis Mountains State Park.

Davis Mountains State Park is a clean, well-maintained park with camping sites and showers. Indian Lodge, with its good restaurant, is a pleasant alternative for non-campers.

Montezuma Quail, found throughout the park, is regularly seen in the camping areas, around Indian Lodge, and along most of the park roads. Montezuma Quails are currently coming to feed and bathe at the park host trailer site. Other species of

---

Probable Species
(continued)

Loggerhead Shrike
Bell's Vireo
Hutton's Vireo
Yellow-breasted Chat
Hepatic Tanager
Summer Tanager
Western Tanager
Northern Cardinal
Pyrrhuloxia
Black-headed Grosbeak
Blue Grosbeak
Varied Bunting
Spotted Towhee
Canyon Towhee
Cassin's Sparrow
Rufous-crowned
     Sparrow
Lark Sparrow
Black-throated Sparrow
Red-winged Blackbird
Eastern Meadowlark
Great-tailed Grackle
Bronzed Cowbird
Brown-headed Cowbird
Orchard Oriole
Hooded Oriole
Scott's Oriole
House Finch
Lesser Goldfinch
House Sparrow

Note: The species in **boldface** appear no more than four times in the itineraries as *key* or *probable* species. Watch for them on this trip. Assume that you will see all species on the probable list. You will gain no new species from the probable list, but you will have some excellent second chances at a number of species sought only once before.

Possible Species
Total of 35 Species
Great Blue Heron
Cattle Egret
Green Heron
Black Vulture
Sharp-shinned Hawk
Harris's Hawk
Gray Hawk
Red-shouldered Hawk
Golden Eagle
Prairie Falcon
Sora
Common Moorhen
Common Ground-Dove
Barn Owl
Whip-poor-will
Magnificent
     Hummingbird

Possible Species
(continued)

Belted Kingfisher
Scissor-tailed Flycatcher
Bank Swallow
Cave Swallow
Chihuahuan Raven
Western Bluebird
American Robin
Crissal Thrasher
European Starling
Black-capped Vireo
Solitary Vireo
Lucy's Warbler
Common Yellowthroat
Painted Redstart
Painted Bunting
Chipping Sparrow
Black-chinned Sparrow
Yellow-headed
    Blackbird
Bullock's Oriole

Note: You will
probably see 6 of these
species.

**Remotely Possible
Species**
Total of 14 Species
Snowy Egret
Peregrine Falcon
Mountain Plover
Flammulated Owl
Eastern Screech-Owl
Burrowing Owl
Broad-billed
    Hummingbird
Thick-billed Kingbird
Tree Swallow
Eastern Bluebird
Hermit Thrush
Warbling Vireo
Rufous-capped Warbler
Green-tailed Towhee

Note: You will
probably be lucky to
see more than 1 of
these species.

interest include Acorn Woodpecker, Western Wood-Pewee, Black Phoebe, Cassin's Kingbird, Bell's Vireo, Black-headed Grosbeak, Cassin's Sparrow, Orchard Oriole, and Scott's Oriole.

A 75-mile scenic loop around the Davis Mountains takes you through the various habitats—woodland, grassland, and the higher elevations—to find most of the area's specialties. To drive this loop, turn left onto Highway 118 as you exit the park, follow it to Highway 166, turn left again, and loop back to Fort Davis. Highway 118 returns you to the park entrance in 3 miles.

The lower part of the McDonald Observatory access road and the grassland along Highway 166 are two of the most likely spots on the loop for Montezuma Quail. The best higher-elevation birding is at Madera Canyon Picnic Grounds, on the left about 23 miles west of the park entrance.

Species you should find are Zone-tailed Hawk, Band-tailed Pigeon, Acorn Woodpecker, Western Bluebird, Hepatic Tanager, Black-headed Grosbeak, and Cassin's Sparrow.

Return to Davis Mountains State Park to spend the night.

Day 2 — Davis Mountains State Park and Big Bend National Park

Take Highway 118 south from Davis Mountains State Park to the west entrance of Big Bend National Park. The birding is interesting along the way, so allow at least three hours for the 110-mile trip.

From the park entrance continue 24 miles to the park headquarters and visitor center at Panther Junction to pick up a bird checklist and map. Drive back 3 miles to Basin Junction, turn left, and follow this road through the pass to The Basin.

If you stop to check the flowering agaves along this road, you might be lucky enough to see Lucifer Hummingbird. Scaled Quail, Black-tailed Gnatcatcher, Bell's Vireo, Varied Bunting, and Scott's Oriole are more likely, however.

When you arrive in The Basin, secure a campsite or check in at the Chisos Mountain Lodge.

A good place to start birding is the Window Trail, a 5.2-mile round-trip hike for which you will find the trailhead directly across the parking lot from the lodge. The Window Trail is known as one of the best places in the park to see both Lucifer Hummingbird and Gray Vireo. This habitat also holds Varied Bunting, Black-chinned Sparrow, and Scott's Oriole.

Spend the night in The Basin, perhaps venturing out after dark to listen and look for Elf Owls.

Day 3 — Big Bend National Park

Get an early start up the trail to Boot Spring before the day becomes hot. There are several ways to reach Boot Spring, but the easiest is to hike up through Laguna Meadow and then return to The Basin through Boulder Meadow. This is an 11-mile hike, but it is not as steep or as rough as the shorter routes.

Bird your way up to Laguna Meadow (3.5 miles) and spend some time there; Colima Warbler can sometimes be found, and the meadow is often good for finding Lucifer Hummingbird. (If you've seen the warbler and are still missing the hummer, you might try a detour on the Blue Creek Trail. It's not an easy walk and will increase your 11-mile hike considerably. However, Upper Blue Creek Canyon is an excellent place to find Lucifer Hummingbird. A burn in 1988 has resulted in a fabulous floral display in later summers.)

After you leave Laguna Meadow, it is 2 more miles to the spring, all through Colima Warbler habitat. After spending some time in the spring area, start back to The Basin via the Boulder Meadow route. Although this trail is much steeper than the one coming up, at least you will be going downhill.

Linger awhile at Pinnacle Pass; the view from up there is delightful, and there are usually hawks and vultures soaring over The Basin. Check them all and you may find a Zone-tailed Hawk. At Boulder Meadow, you will have another chance to look for Lucifer Hummingbird.

Other species encountered along trail might include Band-tailed Pigeon, Blue-throated, Broad-tailed, and possibly Magnificent Hummingbirds, Acorn Woodpecker, Cordilleran Flycatcher, Mexican Jay, Hutton's Vireo, Hepatic Tanager, Black-Chinned Sparrow, and Scott's Oriole.

The hike to Boot Spring and back will consume most of the day if you bird the area well. Unless you are terribly unlucky, you will have seen the 3 key species found at Big Bend National Park. If you have not, and if you have the energy, you may want to try the Window Trail again that evening. Another option is to check *A Birder's Guide to the Rio Grande*

Valley of Texas for other possible locations for the missed species. This guide covers all the areas you have visited and many more throughout the park.

Spend the night in The Basin.

Day 4 — Extra Day

If you have not seen all of the key species, your day's itinerary is obvious: spend the time to find them. If you have seen them all, a fine place to spend the day is at Rio Grande Village; the birding is probably better there than at any alternate location in the park. Get an early start. It is best to bird the cottonwood groves, grassy area, mesquite thickets, and nature trail at Rio Grande Village in the morning; it gets very hot by noon. To get there, leave The Basin, turn right at Basin Junction, and drive 28 miles to the village. You will not see any key species there, but you may bag Gray and Zone-tailed Hawks, Elf Owl, Golden-fronted Woodpecker, Black Phoebe, Vermilion Flycatcher, Bell's Vireo, Bronzed Cowbird, and Orchard and Hooded Orioles.

When you leave Rio Grande Village, drive 25 miles back to Panther Junction; turn right for 29 additional miles and exit the park at Persimmon Gap. From Persimmon Gap it is approximately 185 miles to Odessa following Highway 385 to Fort Stockton, then Highway 18 to Interstate 20, and using the interstate the rest of the way.

The trip ends in the Midland-Odessa area in the evening.

Bird Numbers This Trip

	Potential	Expected	Actual
Key Species	4	4	
Probable Species	90	90	
Possible Species	35	6	
Remotely Possible Species	14	1	
Totally Unexpected Species	?	1	
TOTAL	143	102	

Cumulative List

Total key and probable species seen after 14 trips

Previous trips	613	species
West Texas trip	4	species
TOTAL	617	species

This Trip's Mileage and Expenses
Approximate miles traveled, Odessa to Odessa: 685

- Fuel: $49; sharing $24.50 $_____
- Lodging: camping every night $14; sharing $7 $_____
- Food: No meals in restaurants - $40 $_____
  The total per person cost for the above items with a companion to share expenses should be less than $75 each.
- Add to this car rental expenses, if any: $_____
- Add to this your expenses to/from Odessa: $_____
  This will give you a good idea of the cost of this trip.
- TOTAL $_____

Personal Notes

_____

_____

_____

_____

_____

_____

_____

_____

_____

_____

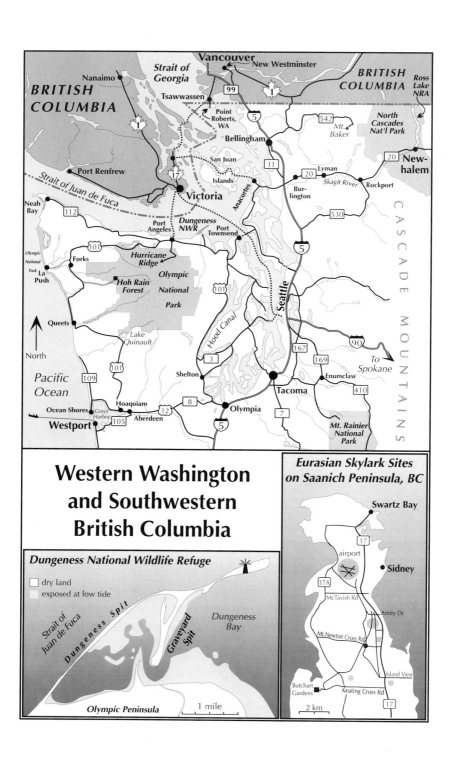

Western Washington and Southwestern British Columbia

Dungeness National Wildlife Refuge

- ☐ dry land
- ☐ exposed at low tide

Strait of Juan de Fuca

Dungeness Spit

Graveyard Spit

Dungeness Bay

Olympic Peninsula

1 mile

Eurasian Skylark Sites on Saanich Peninsula, BC

Swartz Bay

17

airport

Sidney

17A

McTavish Rd

Amity Dr

Mt. Newton Cross Rd

Island View

Butchart Gardens

Keating Cross Rd

17

2 km

Map labels:

Strait of Georgia

Vancouver

New Westminster

BRITISH COLUMBIA

Ross Lake NRA

Nanaimo

Tsawwassen

99

1

Point Roberts, WA

North Cascades Nat'l Park

BRITISH COLUMBIA

1

Bellingham

542

Mt. Baker

San Juan

5

11

20

New-halem

Port Renfrew

Strait of Juan de Fuca

17

Islands

Lyman

20

Skagit River

Rockport

Burlington

Victoria

Neah Bay

112

Port Angeles

Dungeness NWR

Port Townsend

Anacortes

530

5

CASCADE MOUNTAINS

Olympic National Park

101

Forks

Hurricane Ridge

Olympic

Seattle

La Push

Hoh Rain Forest

National

101

Queets

Park

Lake Quinault

Hood Canal

90

To Spokane

North

Pacific Ocean

109

101

Shelton

3

167

169

Enumclaw

410

Ocean Shores

Hoquiam

Grays Harbor

8

12

Olympia

Tacoma

7

Westport

105

Aberdeen

5

Mt. Rainier National Park

Chapter 15

WESTERN WASHINGTON AND SOUTHWESTERN BRITISH COLUMBIA

Late July or Early August—6 Days

General

O ur visit to Washington will cover only a small portion of this beautiful state with a side trip to fascinating British Columbia. All 9 of the key species for this trip can normally be seen without traveling east of the Cascade Mountains. The species lists in this chapter refer only to the trip area. If you have the time to travel east of the mountains, many of the species listed as only possible become easier to see.

The exact timing of this trip must be built around the availability of a pelagic outing. For your purposes, early August is probably best, but you may have to settle for a late July trip. For pelagic trip schedules see the *Winging It* pelagic directory for the current year or contact Terry Wahl, 3041 Eldridge, Bellingham, WA 98225, phone 360/733-8255. Terry Wahl is the top pelagic trip organizer in the Pacific Northwest and will know what is available.

The side trip into British Columbia is specifically designed to see Crested Myna in the Vancouver area and Eurasian Skylark on the Saanich Peninsula of Vancouver Island. Both of these species were introduced and have long been established; both should not be too difficult to locate.

It should be understood that a trip to Washington and British Columbia is certainly another destination in this book worthy of a more extended visit if your time allows it. What is outlined is a short, concise trip to see 9 key species and does not do true justice to the birding potential of Washington and British Columbia.

This trip includes the Seattle-Tacoma area, Skagit River Valley, Ross Lake National Recreation Area, Larrabee State Park, Vancouver, the Saanich Peninsula, Victoria, Olympic National Park, Dungeness National Wildlife Refuge, Westport, and several other stops.

205

Probable Species
Total of 147 Species
Pied-billed Grebe
Sooty Shearwater
Fork-tailed
Storm-Petrel
Brown Pelican
Double-crested
Cormorant
Brandt's Cormorant
Pelagic Cormorant
Great Blue Heron
Green Heron
Canada Goose
Wood Duck
Mallard
Blue-winged Teal
Cinnamon Teal
Gadwall
Harlequin Duck
Surf Scoter
White-winged Scoter
Common Merganser
Turkey Vulture
Osprey
Bald Eagle
Northern Harrier
Cooper's Hawk
Red-tailed Hawk
American Kestrel
Ring-necked Pheasant
Blue Grouse
California Quail
Virginia Rail
Sora
American Coot
Black-bellied Plover
Semipalmated Plover
Killdeer
Black Oystercatcher
Greater Yellowlegs
Wandering Tattler
Spotted Sandpiper
Whimbrel
Ruddy Turnstone
Black Turnstone
Surfbird
Sanderling
Western Sandpiper
Least Sandpiper
Short-billed Dowitcher
Long-billed Dowitcher
Common Snipe
Red-necked Phalarope
Red Phalarope
Pomarine Jaeger
Parasitic Jaeger
South Polar Skua
Bonaparte's Gull
Heermann's Gull
Ring-billed Gull
California Gull
Western Gull
Glaucous-winged Gull
Caspian Tern
Common Murre
Pigeon Guillemot
Marbled Murrelet
Cassin's Auklet
Rhinoceros Auklet
Tufted Puffin

Birdfinding Guides

A Birder's Guide to Ocean Shores, Washington by Bob Morse (1994).

A Bird Watching Guide to the Vancouver Area by the Vancouver Natural History Society (1993).

A Guide to Bird-finding in Washington by Terence R. Wahl and Dennis R. Paulson (1991).

Birder's Guide to Vancouver Island by Keith Taylor (1990).

Rare Bird Alert Numbers

Washington 206/933-1831
Vancouver, BC 604/737-3074
Victoria, BC 604/592-3381

Special Equipment

You would do well to include raingear and waterproof footwear when you pack for this trip. Also, bringing along layers (including jacket, sweater, gloves, and hat) will make the pelagic outing and even the ferries much more enjoyable. As on all pelagic trips, seasickness preventives are recommended.

Accommodations

Motels and campgrounds are available throughout the trip area. As usual, camping is vastly more economical.

Key Species — Total of 9 Species

1. **Black-footed Albatross**—This albatross has rarely, if ever, been missed on a Washington pelagic trip.

2. **Pink-footed Shearwater**—Very rarely missed between May and October on pelagic trips.

3. **Sabine's Gull**—Easily seen most pelagic trips scheduled from late July to early October.

4. **Vaux's Swift**—Fairly common in the proper habitats. Should be seen in the Skagit River Valley and on the Olympic Peninsula.

5. **Calliope Hummingbird**—Probably the hardest bird to see on this trip, but only because of the limits of its range and the length of your trip. You should find it at the camping-area across the river from Newhalem. If you do not, you may have to use an extra day for a trip east of the mountains.

6. **Pacific-slope Flycatcher**—Common in the Skagit River Valley, at Heart o' the Hills Campground in Olympic National Park, and on the west side of the Olympic Peninsula.

7. **Eurasian Skylark**—Should be found on the Saanich Peninsula near Victoria, British Columbia. The population is declining, but the species is still present in most of its traditional places (see map).

8. **Crested Myna**—This established exotic must be seen in the Vancouver, Richmond, or New Westminster, British Columbia, areas. The population has declined in recent years, and it has sometimes become harder to locate.

9. **Red Crossbill**—Often easy to see along the mountain road to Hurricane Ridge in Olympic National Park. It occurs irregularly in coniferous habitat throughout.

Note: All 9 key species should be seen without too much difficulty.

Itinerary

Note: This trip begins and ends in Seattle-Tacoma.

Day 1 — Seattle-Tacoma, Skagit River Valley, and Ross Lake National Recreation Area

Proceed north on Interstate 5 from Seattle to Burlington (approximately 62 miles north) and exit onto Highway 20 east.

From Burlington Newhalem is about 67 miles east on Highway 20. You will pass through some productive birding areas where you should easily see two of the key species—Vaux's Swift and Pacific-slope Flycatcher.

Highway 20 roughly parallels the Skagit River for the entire drive. From near Lyman to Newhalem, the

Probable Species
(continued)

Rock Dove
Band-tailed Pigeon
Mourning Dove
Barn Owl
Great Horned Owl
Black Swift
Rufous Hummingbird
Belted Kingfisher
Red-breasted
  Sapsucker
Downy Woodpecker
Hairy Woodpecker
Northern Flicker
Pileated Woodpecker
Olive-sided Flycatcher
Western Wood-Pewee
Willow Flycatcher
Hammond's Flycatcher
Horned Lark
Tree Swallow
Violet-green Swallow
Northern Rough-
  winged Swallow
Cliff Swallow
Barn Swallow
Gray Jay
Steller's Jay
Clark's Nutcracker
American Crow
Northwestern Crow
Common Raven
Black-capped
  Chickadee
Chestnut-backed
  Chickadee
Bushtit
Red-breasted Nuthatch
Brown Creeper
Bewick's Wren
House Wren
Winter Wren
Marsh Wren
American Dipper
Golden-crowned
  Kinglet
Ruby-crowned Kinglet
Swainson's Thrush
Hermit Thrush
American Robin
Varied Thrush
American Pipit
Cedar Waxwing
European Starling
Solitary Vireo
Warbling Vireo
Red-eyed Vireo
Orange-crowned
  Warbler
Yellow Warbler
Yellow-rumped
  Warbler
Black-throated Gray
  Warbler
Townsend's Warbler
MacGillivray's Warbler
Common Yellowthroat
Wilson's Warbler
Western Tanager
Black-headed Grosbeak

Probable Species
(continued)

Lazuli Bunting
Spotted Towhee
Chipping Sparrow
Savannah Sparrow
Fox Sparrow
Song Sparrow
Lincoln's Sparrow
White-crowned
*   Sparrow*
Dark-eyed Junco
Red-winged Blackbird
Western Meadowlark
Brewer's Blackbird
Brown-headed Cowbird
Purple Finch
House Finch
Pine Siskin
American Goldfinch
Evening Grosbeak
House Sparrow

Note: The species in **boldface** appear no more than four times in the itineraries as *key* or *probable* species. Watch for them on this trip. Assume that you will see all of the probable species. You will not gain any new species from the probable list, but you will have a second opportunity to find some key species.

Possible Species
Total of 105 Species
Red-throated Loon
Pacific Loon
Common Loon
Horned Grebe
Red-necked Grebe
Eared Grebe
Western Grebe
Northern Fulmar
Flesh-footed Shearwater
Buller's Shearwater
Leach's Storm-Petrel
American Bittern
Black-crowned
*   Night-Heron*
Green-winged Teal
Northern Pintail
Northern Shoveler
American Wigeon
Canvasback
Redhead
Ring-necked Duck
Lesser Scaup
Barrow's Goldeneye
Hooded Merganser
Ruddy Duck
Sharp-shinned Hawk
Northern Goshawk
Swainson's Hawk

highway is never far from the river. There are numerous places where you can view the river, and every few miles you will be able to access the river on public property (boat-launches, etc.). You are almost certain to see Vaux's Swift and are likely to see Black Swift flying over the river. One mile before Rockport, you can make a quick visit to Rockport State Recreation Area. At one or more of these locations, you should find Pacific-slope Flycatcher, a common species here.

After you pass Rockport, the terrain changes as you continue to Newhalem. In the Newhalem area, there are three campgrounds that are part of the Ross Lake National Recreation Area which in turn is part of the North Cascades National Park. The first campground is Goodell Creek about 1 mile prior to reaching Newhalem; the second is across the Skagit River from the town and is appropriately named Newhalem; the third is 2.5 miles past town at Gorge Creek. If you bird these three recreation areas, you should locate Calliope Hummingbird. The hummer is often found in this area, especially in the Newhalem Campground.

Other species of interest that you may see along Highway 20 or in the campgrounds are Blue Grouse, Willow and Hammond's Flycatchers, Hermit and Varied Thrushes, MacGillivray's Warbler, and Lazuli Bunting.

After you have seen the 3 key species, retrace your route on Highway 20 to Burlington. Turn north onto Interstate 5 for about 1 mile, then exit onto Highway 11. Continue north for about 20 miles to Larrabee State Park. The park is a good place to camp for the night (with showers), or you can continue to Bellingham for a motel. If you are camping at Larrabee, you might want to look for loons, grebes, and ducks off the state park beach.

Day 2 — Vancouver, the Saanich Peninsula, Victoria, and Olympic National Park

Leave early, since this will be a very long day. It may be particularly difficult to find the key birds as well as to catch two ferries all in this single day.

It is approximately a one-and-a-half-hour drive from Larrabee State Park to Vancouver, British Columbia. Take Interstate 5 north from Bellingham to the Canadian border. The highway signs change there, and the good highway (Highway 99) continues on to Vancouver.

There are several locations in the Vancouver and New Westminster areas to see Crested Myna. Wahl and Paulson list several sites in *A Guide to Bird Finding in Washington,* and the Vancouver Natural History Society's guide is also helpful. One area to try is at the intersection of Marine Drive and Hudson Street at the north end of Arthur Laing Bridge linking Sea Island (site of the Vancouver Airport) to Vancouver proper. Mynas nest in the eves of lowrise apartments in the area. Check under the bridge itself and in the neighborhood's quiet back alleys. (A nice thing about this area is its nearness to Iona Island. You are only ten minutes away from that fabulous location for shorebirds. Another optional trip is within a half-hour north of town. Cypress Provincial Park is good for Vaux's Swift, Red-breasted Sapsucker, Blue Grouse, and possible Northern Pygmy-Owl. If you have the time to take an extra day—see Days 5 and 6—both of these alternate locations are well worth your time.) Another Crested Myna location is the Cambie Street Bridge near downtown Vancouver. This bridge has had an active Crested Myna roost beneath it for a number of years. The problem here is traffic and congestion.

After seeing Crested Myna, drive back south to Tsawwassen to catch the ferry across the Strait of Georgia to Swartz Bay. There may be a long wait, especially in summer. (Some birders have actually parked their cars in line on the ferry-landing and taken taxis to and from Vancouver to see the Crested

Possible Species
(continued)
Golden Eagle
Peregrine Falcon
Prairie Falcon
Spruce Grouse
White-tailed Ptarmigan
Ruffed Grouse
Mountain Quail
Snowy Plover
Black-necked Stilt
American Avocet
Lesser Yellowlegs
Willet
Long-billed Curlew
Marbled Godwit
Red Knot
Semipalmated
Sandpiper
Baird's Sandpiper
Wilson's Phalarope
Long-tailed Jaeger
Mew Gull
Black-legged Kittiwake
Common Tern
Arctic Tern
Forster's Tern
Western Screech-Owl
Northern Pygmy-Owl
Burrowing Owl
Spotted Owl
Barred Owl
Short-eared Owl
Northern Saw-whet
Owl
Common Nighthawk
White-throated Swift
Black-chinned
Hummingbird
Anna's Hummingbird
Lewis's Woodpecker
Red-naped Sapsucker
Williamson's Sapsucker
White-headed
Woodpecker
Three-toed
Woodpecker
Black-backed
Woodpecker
Dusky Flycatcher
Gray Flycatcher
Say's Phoebe
Western Kingbird
Eastern Kingbird
Purple Martin
Bank Swallow
Western Scrub-Jay
Black-billed Magpie
Mountain Chickadee
White-breasted
Nuthatch
Pygmy Nuthatch
Rock Wren
Canyon Wren
Western Bluebird
Mountain Bluebird
Townsend's Solitaire
Veery
Gray Catbird
Sage Thrasher
Loggerhead Shrike

Possible Species
(continued)

Hutton's Vireo
Nashville Warbler
Hermit Warbler
American Redstart
Yellow-breasted Chat
Brewer's Sparrow
Vesper Sparrow
Lark Sparrow
Sage Sparrow
Grasshopper Sparrow
Bobolink
Yellow-headed
   Blackbird
Bullock's Oriole
Gray-crowned
   Rosy-Finch
Pine Grosbeak
Cassin's Finch

Note: Unless you travel to the east side of the Cascades, you will miss most of these species. You should see only about 15 of them on the west side of the mountains.

Remotely Possible Species
Total of 23 Species
Clark's Grebe
American White
   Pelican
Great Egret
Brant
Greater Scaup
Bufflehead
White-tailed Kite
Ferruginous Hawk
Merlin
Pacific Golden-Plover
Solitary Sandpiper
Dunlin
Black Tern
Xantus's Murrelet
Flammulated Owl
Long-eared Owl
Common Poorwill
Ash-throated Flycatcher
Boreal Chickadee
Northern Waterthrush
Green-tailed Towhee
Black-throated Sparrow
White-winged Crossbill

Note: Without extensive travel in the eastern part of the state, you would be lucky to see over 2 of these species.

Mynas.) The ferry leaves the Tsawwassen terminal every hour on the hour from 7 am to 10 pm. The trip is about one hour and forty minutes long and can provide interesting birding. You might find North-western Crows at the ferry dock. During the ferry trip, look for Brandt's Cormorant, Pigeon Guillemot, Rhinoceros Auklet, and other birds, including, possibly, Marbled Murrelet. The current price is $28.50 Canadian (or $21.38 US) for a car and driver with a $6.00 Canadian (or $4.50 US) charge for each additional person. For information and/or reservations call British Columbia Ferries at 604/386-3431.

When you exit the terminal at Swartz Bay, follow Highway 17 or 17A south to the Victoria International Airport; it is one of the better locations to find Eurasian Skylark. (One proven site is at the end of Canoa Street at the south edge of the airport.) Check Keith Taylor's book, *Birder's Guide to Vancouver Island*, for details on this and other sites. You can also usually get a good current location by calling the Victoria Rare Bird Alert. (Sometimes trying to find the Eurasian Skylark can be maddening; you may have to spend an extra day in Victoria. See Days 5 and 6 for getting more time out of your itinerary.)

After seeing Eurasian Skylark, continue south to Victoria to board the ferry to Port Angeles, Washington. Again, there may be a long wait in the ferry-line. (Some birders have made arrangements to park their cars in line while birding at nearby Clover Point. Here you might find Marbled Murrelet, summering Harlequin Duck, Rhinoceros Auklet, and even a Tufted Puffin.) The ferry boat *MV Coho* crosses the Strait of Juan de Fuca four times a day during the summer season. Currently, the ferry leaves at 6:20 am, 10:30 am, 3 pm, and 7:30 pm. The cost for a car and driver is $26 and $6.50 for each additional person (U.S. funds). The trip takes about one hour and thirty-five minutes, and you might pick up Sooty Shearwater or Parasitic or Pomarine Jaeger on the crossing. Contact Black Ball Transport, Inc., at

604/386-2202 (in Victoria) or 360/457-4491 (in Port Angeles) for information and/or reservations.

When you arrive in Port Angeles, check the harbor for summering Harlequin Duck, Black Oystercatcher, and Marbled Murrelet. Make a stop at the Port Angeles visitor center just south of town on State Road 111. After leaving the visitor center continue south for about 5 miles to Heart o' the Hills Campground in Olympic National Park or locate lodging in Port Angeles.

Day 3 — Olympic National Park, Dungeness National Wildlife Refuge, and Westport

From Heart o' the Hills campground, take steep Hurricane Ridge Road 12 miles to Hurricane Ridge. Red Crossbills can be seen along this mountain road by stopping at a few of the turn-outs, but (depending upon the cone crop) they can be totally absent some years.

At Hurricane Ridge, the Hurricane Hill Nature Trail is usually good for Blue Grouse and Vaux's Swift. Other species to be seen in this area include Gray Jay, Chestnut-backed Chickadee, and Varied Thrush.

When you leave Olympic National Park, return to Highway 101 at Port Angeles, turn right (east), and drive to the Dungeness National Wildlife Refuge access road just west of Sequim. Vaux's Swift, Pacific-slope Flycatcher, and sometimes Red Crossbill can all be found in the woods at the base of Dungeness Spit. Other species that can be seen in the Dungeness area include Brandt's Cormorant, California Quail, Marbled Murrelet, Rhinoceros Auklet, Tufted Puffin, Rufous Hummingbird, Olive-sided Flycatcher, Willow Flycatcher, and Chestnut-backed Chickadee. Northwestern Crow can be found here, but it should be noted that the identification criteria for this species remain unclear for the south end of its range.

When you leave Dungeness National Wildlife Refuge, take Highway 101 west and then south for about 185 miles to just past Aberdeen. Allow yourself plenty of time for this segment; it can be a very slow drive. (*If you have the time*, do not resist the temptation to stop at some of the Olympic National Park beaches or Hoh Rain Forest.) Turn right onto Highway 105 and continue to Westport. This entire drive is good birding in varied habitat, so you should bird as time allows.

Twin Harbors State Recreation Area about 4 miles south of Westport is a good place to camp (with showers), or motels are available in Westport. Red Crossbills are sometimes present at the recreation area.

Day 4 — Westport Pelagic

Pelagic trips out of Westport leave early and vary in length from ten to sixteen hours. Cost also varies by the length of the trip, but July and August trips are usually $70 per person. A trip in late July or early August will produce Black-footed Albatross, Pink-footed Shearwater, and Sabine's Gull.

Other birds that may be seen in this season include Northern Fulmar, Flesh-footed and Sooty Shearwaters, Fork-tailed and Leach's Storm-Petrels (July), Red-necked and Red Phalaropes, Pomarine, Parasitic, and Long-tailed Jaegers (August), South Polar Skua (August), Black-legged Kittiwake, Arctic Tern (August), Common Murre, Xantus's Murrelet (casual), Cassin's and Rhinoceros Auklets, and Tufted Puffin.

When you return from the pelagic trip, spend the night again at Twin Harbors State Recreation Area or at an area motel.

Days 5 and 6 — Extra Days

On this trip there are two extra days scheduled—for three good reasons: First, all of this trip's key species should have been seen by this point in the trip. If you missed any of them, it is most likely the Calliope Hummingbird. Your chances of finding this hummingbird are better east of the Cascades. Secondly, a trip east of the mountains can give you another chance at many species that you possibly missed on earlier trips. Finally, you might wish to schedule an extra day at the beginning of the trip in the Vancouver area or Victoria area, or at Ocean Shores at the end of the trip. At Vancouver, try nearby Iona Island, famous for shorebirds. The Vancouver area has good spots for such interesting species as Red-breasted Sapsucker and Vaux's Swift. Your visit to Victoria may necessitate a longer stay, with two ferry rides and potentially uncooperative Eurasian Skylarks involved on busy Day 2. At Ocean Shores, an hour north of Westport on the coast, try the game refuge, jetty, and Catala Spit, offering a variety of shorebirds. Consult *A Guide to Bird Finding in Washington* by Wahl and Paulson or other guides listed at the beginning of this chapter for good birding options and for locations for Calliope Hummingbird or other previously missed species.

The trip can be ended in the Seattle-Tacoma area at the end of Day 5 or Day 6.

Bird Numbers This Trip

	Potential	Expected	Actual
Key Species	9	9	
Probable Species	147	147	
Possible Species	105	15	
Remotely Possible Species	23	2	
Totally Unexpected Species	?	1	
TOTAL	284	174	

Cumulative List

Total key and probable species seen after 15 trips

Previous trips . . . . 617 species
Washington/British Columbia trip . . . . . 9 species
TOTAL . . . . 626 species

This Trip's Mileage and Expenses

Approximate miles traveled, Seattle to Seattle: 800

- Fuel: $60; sharing $30 $_____
- Lodging: camping every night $25; sharing $12.50 $_____
- Food: No meals in restaurants - $60 $_____
- Ferry fares: about $66; sharing $33 $_____
      *The total per person cost for the above items with a companion
      to share expenses should be less than $210.*
- Cost of pelagic boat trip - $70 $_____
- Add to this car rental expenses, if any: $_____
- Add to this your expenses to/from Seattle: $_____
      This will give you a good idea of the cost of this trip.
- TOTAL $_____

Personal Notes

_____

_____

_____

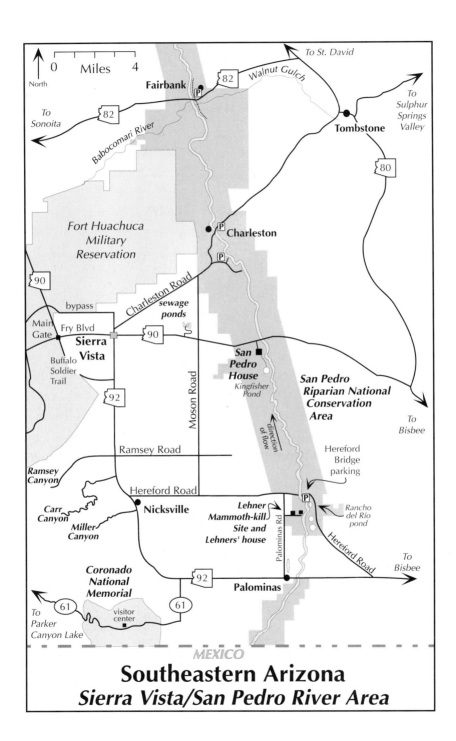

Southeastern Arizona
Sierra Vista/San Pedro River Area

Chapter 16

LATE SUMMER IN SOUTHEASTERN ARIZONA

Early August—4 Days

General

There are some excellent reasons to visit Southeastern Arizona at this season, whether or not you were here in late spring (see Chapter 10). Onset of the "summer monsoons"—regular afternoon rainstorms generally beginning at the end of July—has initiated a second breeding season for some birds. For example, three sparrows—Botteri's, Cassin's, and Rufous-winged—are vocal and very visible at this season. Numerous species begin their second clutches. This is also an opportunity to pursue species which you might have missed during your last trip (e.g., Common Black-Hawk and Five-striped Sparrow). Though owls are quiet in August, the hummingbird activity increases significantly, making this the best time to find up to 14 species of hummers in Southeastern Arizona. In addition to the hummingbirds, other rare species usually occur in this season, and the semi-rare species that regularly occur are all still present.

Unlike previous trips in this book, your main focus for this trip is not on key species but on the rarities that you may be fortunate enough to see at this season. Many other birders will be flocking to Southeastern Arizona in August. Here is another opportunity to mingle and share information. Keep tabs on the RBA, also. Other than making reservations to visit Ramsey Canyon for two key species, keep your schedule flexible so that you're free to chase newly reported rarities.

The Nature Conservancy's Ramsey Canyon Preserve, open from 8 am to 5 pm, has limited parking. Advance reservations are strongly recommended anytime; these can be arranged by calling 520/378-2785. Inquire about a permit for access to the upper canyon when you make reservations.

This trip includes Tucson, Ramsey Canyon Preserve, and other locations in Southeastern Arizona as determined by the individual birder's needs and the rare bird alert.

Probable Species
Total of 156 Species
Black-bellied
Whistling-Duck
Turkey Vulture
Cooper's Hawk
Northern Goshawk
Common Black-Hawk
Harris's Hawk
Gray Hawk
Swainson's Hawk
Zone-tailed Hawk
Red-tailed Hawk
Golden Eagle
American Kestrel
Prairie Falcon
Scaled Quail
Gambel's Quail
Sora
Common Moorhen
American Coot
Killdeer
American Avocet
Spotted Sandpiper
Wilson's Phalarope
Rock Dove
Band-tailed Pigeon
White-winged Dove
Mourning Dove
Inca Dove
Common Ground-Dove
Yellow-billed Cuckoo
Greater Roadrunner
Barn Owl
Flammulated Owl
Western Screech-Owl
Whiskered
Screech-Owl
Great Horned Owl
Northern Pygmy-Owl
Elf Owl
Lesser Nighthawk
Common Poorwill
Whip-poor-will
White-throated Swift
Broad-billed
Hummingbird
Blue-throated
Hummingbird
Magnificent
Hummingbird
Black-chinned
Hummingbird
Broad-tailed
Hummingbird
Rufous Hummingbird
Elegant Trogon
Acorn Woodpecker
Gila Woodpecker
Ladder-backed
Woodpecker
Hairy Woodpecker
Strickland's
Woodpecker
Northern Flicker
Northern Beardless-
Tyrannulet
Greater Pewee
Western Wood-Pewee
Cordilleran Flycatcher

Birdfinding Guides

A Birder's Guide to Southeastern Arizona by Richard Cachor Taylor (1995) is the ABA/Lane bird-finding guide for the area.

Davis and Russell's Finding Birds in Southeast Arizona by the Tucson Audubon Society (1995).

Rare Bird Alert Numbers

Tucson 520/798-1005
Phoenix 602/832-8745

Special Equipment

If you plan to do any night birding, tapes and a portable spotlight are a real help. Don't forget sunscreen and a hat; you are visiting the skin cancer capital of the U.S.

Accommodations

Motels are available throughout the area; there are also plenty of camping areas both with and without fees. Both of the birdfinding guides above furnish information about accommodations throughout the region.

Violet-crowned Hummingbird
Gail Diane Yovanovich

Key Species

1. **Violet-crowned Hummingbird**—Can usually be found at the Ramsey Canyon Preserve feeders. If not, it will probably be at feeders at Patagonia, Madera Canyon, or the Cave Creek Canyon area.

2. **Sulphur-bellied Flycatcher**—Easy to locate. Should be seen at Ramsey Canyon or any of the other wooded sycamore canyons.

Note: These 2 species should be seen without too much difficulty; if you were lucky you may have seen both of them on the late May trip to this same area.

Probable Species
(continued)

Buff-breasted
Flycatcher
Black Phoebe
Say's Phoebe
Vermilion Flycatcher
Dusky-capped
Flycatcher
Ash-throated Flycatcher
Brown-crested
Flycatcher
Tropical Kingbird
Cassin's Kingbird
Thick-billed Kingbird
Western Kingbird
Rose-throated Becard
Horned Lark
Tree Swallow
Violet-green Swallow
Northern Rough-
winged Swallow
Cliff Swallow
Barn Swallow
Steller's Jay
Western Scrub-Jay
Mexican Jay
Chihuahuan Raven
Common Raven
Mexican Chickadee
Bridled Titmouse
Plain Titmouse
Verdin
Bushtit
White-breasted
Nuthatch
Pygmy Nuthatch
Brown Creeper
Cactus Wren
Rock Wren
Canyon Wren
Bewick's Wren
House Wren
Blue-gray Gnatcatcher
Eastern Bluebird
Western Bluebird
Hermit Thrush
American Robin
Northern Mockingbird

Probable Species
(continued)

Bendire's Thrasher
Curve-billed Thrasher
Crissal Thrasher
Phainopepla
Loggerhead Shrike
European Starling
Bell's Vireo
Solitary Vireo
Hutton's Vireo
Warbling Vireo
Virginia's Warbler
Lucy's Warbler
Yellow Warbler
Yellow-rumped
Warbler
Black-throated Gray
Warbler
Townsend's Warbler
Hermit Warbler
Grace's Warbler
Common Yellowthroat
Wilson's Warbler
Red-faced Warbler
Painted Redstart
Yellow-breasted Chat
Olive Warbler
Hepatic Tanager
Summer Tanager
Western Tanager
Northern Cardinal
Pyrrhuloxia
Black-headed Grosbeak
Blue Grosbeak
Lazuli Bunting
Varied Bunting
Spotted Towhee
Canyon Towhee
Abert's Towhee
Botteri's Sparrow
Cassin's Sparrow
Rufous-winged
Sparrow
Rufous-crowned
Sparrow
Lark Sparrow
Black-throated Sparrow
Grasshopper Sparrow

Probable Species
(continued)

Song Sparrow
Yellow-eyed Junco
Red-winged Blackbird
Eastern Meadowlark
Great-tailed Grackle
Bronzed Cowbird
Brown-headed Cowbird
Hooded Oriole
Bullock's Oriole
Scott's Oriole
House Finch
Lesser Goldfinch
House Sparrow

Note: The species in **boldface** appear no more than four times in the itineraries as *key* or *probable* species. Watch for them on this trip. Assume you will see all species on probable list. Realistically, many of them will be seen only if you visit specific areas. Review list prior to your trip; if any species were missed on previous trips add them to your key list. Information to help you locate any of these species is found in Chapter 10 and in the birdfinding guides listed in this chapter. Though you will not add new species to your totals from this list, you will have important second chances at a number of species.

Possible Species
Total of 43 Species
Pied-billed Grebe
Double-crested
Cormorant
Neotropic Cormorant
Great Blue Heron
Green Heron
Black-crowned
Night-Heron
Mallard
Cinnamon Teal
Ruddy Duck
Mississippi Kite
Peregrine Falcon
Wild Turkey
Montezuma Quail
Black-necked Stilt
Greater Yellowlegs
Lesser Yellowlegs
Solitary Sandpiper
Willet
Western Sandpiper
Burrowing Owl
Spotted Owl

Possible Species
(continued)

Spotted Owl
Buff-collared Nightjar
White-eared
  Hummingbird
Berylline Hummingbird
Anna's Hummingbird
Costa's Hummingbird
Calliope Hummingbird
Allen's Hummingbird
Eared Trogon
Green Kingfisher
Gilded Flicker
Willow Flycatcher
Purple Martin
Golden-crowned
  Kinglet
Ruby-crowned Kinglet
Black-tailed
  Gnatcatcher
Gray Vireo
Flame-colored Tanager
Chipping Sparrow
Black-chinned Sparrow
Five-striped Sparrow
Lark Bunting
Red Crossbill

Note: This list includes several Code 4 and Code 5 birds that would not normally make the possible list. However, they are almost dependable in this season, although they do not occur every year. It is impractical to concentrate on them. These species are a major justification for this trip. By using the rare bird alert and contacting local birders, you should see at least 3 of them. Several other species have been targeted on other trips. If they were missed, most of them can be found on this trip by using Chapter 10 for directions or by using the birdfinding guides listed in this chapter. Overall, you will probably see 5 of the species on this list.

Remotely Possible Species
Total of 31 Species
Snowy Egret
Northern Pintail
Northern Shoveler
Black Vulture
White-tailed Kite
Sharp-shinned Hawk

Itinerary

Note: This trip begins and ends in Tucson.

Days 1 through 4 — Tucson, Ramsey Canyon Preserve; various Southeastern Arizona sites

The itinerary for this four-day trip, as stated in the General section of this chapter, must be dictated by the rare bird alert and by the species the individual birder may have missed on the earlier trip to this area.

Ordinarily, the 2 key species can be seen at Ramsey Canyon Preserve. Look for Violet-crowned Hummingbird at the feeders; Sulphur-bellied Flycatcher should be found easily in the tall trees in the feeder area or by taking a short walk up the canyon.

Which day or days you visit Ramsey Canyon Preserve will depend on the results of your call for reservations (see General section of this chapter). Consult Chapter 10 of this book or one of the local birdfinding guides for directions to Ramsey Canyon and other sites in Southeastern Arizona.

A number of species are real possibilities at this season but are too rare to pursue specifically. Call the rare bird alert every day or connect with the local birder grapevine to maximize you chances of seeing any of the following.

White-eared Hummingbird—For the past several years, this Code 4 species has been a regular visitor to Ramsey Canyon feeders in July and August. Might also be at feeders at Cave Creek or Madera Canyons. You should be able to find this one.

Berylline Hummingbird—Another Code 4 hummer that is sometimes seen during this season at Cave Creek, Madera, or Ramsey Canyons. This species has even nested a couple of times. Your chances are about 50-50.

Eared Trogon—Reported more often each year. Has been found in the past few years at Ramsey, Miller, and other Huachuca Mountain canyons, and Cave Creek Canyon. Your chances of seeing this Code 5 species may be increasing.

Flame-colored Tanager—Here is another Code 5 species that has become somewhat regular at Cave Creek, Madera, and Ramsey Canyons over the last few years.

There are recent somewhat regular records for Plain-capped Starthroat, Lucifer Hummingbird, Aztec Thrush, Rufous-capped Warbler, and Streak-backed Oriole. Although most birders are successful only when following directions to staked-out birds, you are about as likely as the next birder to find your own rarity during this season.

This chapter's species lists will help you to decide if you have a good chance of locating any birds missed on the earlier trip. The Southeastern Arizona birdfinding guides recommended at the beginning of this chapter have extensive information about the seasonal status, distribution, and habitat preference of all species recorded for the region. These guides also suggest a number of birding areas not covered in this chapter or in Chapter 10 where you might look for each of the region's specialties or regularly occurring vagrants.

Refer to Chapter 10 for information on camping sites and other accommodations.

Trip ends in Tucson in the evening on Day 4.

Remotely Possible Species *(continued)*
Least Sandpiper
Ruddy Ground-Dove
Ferruginous Pygmy-Owl
Common Nighthawk
Chimney Swift
Plain-capped Starthroat
Lucifer Hummingbird
Bank Swallow
Black-capped Gnatcatcher
Rufous-backed Robin
Aztec Thrush
Le Conte's Thrasher
Orange-crowned Warbler
Black-and-white Warbler
Rufous-capped Warbler
Yellow Grosbeak
Indigo Bunting
Painted Bunting
Green-tailed Towhee
Western Meadowlark
Yellow-headed Blackbird
Streak-backed Oriole
Pine Siskin
Evening Grosbeak
Note: All remotely possible species are either common in other parts of the ABA Area and should have been seen easily on earlier trips, or are so rare that you would be lucky to see more than 1 on this trip.

Montezuma Quail - Georges Dremeaux

Bird Numbers This Trip

	Potential	Expected	Actual
Key Species	2	2	
Probable Species	156	156	
Possible Species	43	5	
Remotely Possible Species	31	1	
Totally Unexpected Species	?	1	
TOTAL	232	165	

Cumulative List

Total key and probable species seen after 16 trips

Previous trips . . . . 626 species
Southeastern Arizona . . . . 2 species
TOTAL . . . . 628 species

This Trip's Mileage and Expenses

Approximate miles traveled from Tucson to Tucson: 400 (estimate)

- Fuel: $30; sharing expenses $15 $_____
- Lodging: 1 night in motel; 3 nights
  camping $65; sharing $32.50 $_____
- Food: No meals in restaurants - $40 $_____
    *The total per person cost of the above items with a companion
    to share expenses should be less than $90 each.*
- Add to this car rental expenses, if any: $_____
- Add to this your expenses to/from Tucson: $_____
    This will give you a good idea of the cost of this trip.
- TOTAL $_____

Personal Notes

_____

_____

_____

_____

_____

_____

_____

_____

_____

_____

_____

_____

_____

_____

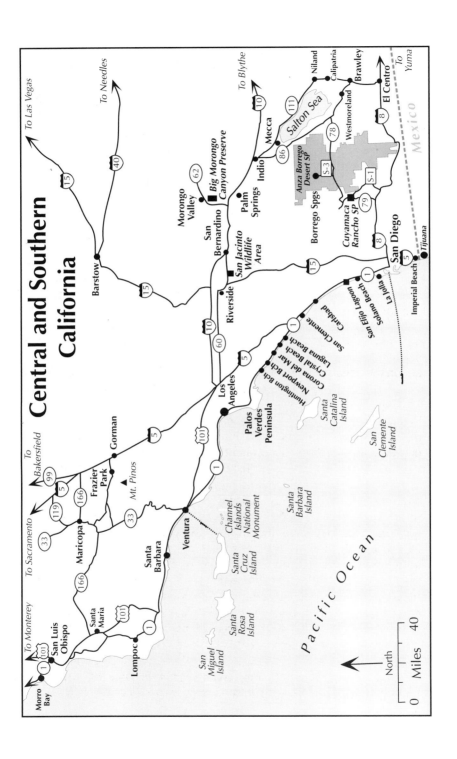

Central and Southern California

Chapter 17

CENTRAL AND SOUTHERN CALIFORNIA

Late August to Early September—11 Days

General

On this trip you will combine some of the best pelagic birding available in North America with landbirding in areas that are extremely varied in both birdlife and terrain. You can concentrate on 17 species, 11 of which will be seen either on the pelagic outings or in the Los Angeles area. This distribution will leave you with what appears to be an excessive amount of time to see the other 6 species. These extra days are necessary because 7 of the species can be seen only by getting out on the ocean, and, for a realistic chance at all 7, you must get offshore from both San Diego and Monterey. You need to accomplish this goal with outings from the two ports on consecutive weekends and use the five intervening days to locate those 6 species mentioned earlier. This may or may not be "overkill" because 3 of the 6 species are either unpredictable or are very difficult to locate. Whichever way it goes, California offers excellent birding which should certainly not be boring.

The key to success is getting on the right pelagic trips. Pelagic trips are not numerous out of San Diego, but with early reservations you can secure a place on an early September trip. You can expect to pay from $65 to $85 for the twelve-hour trip. (In case you do not get on a San Diego pelagic trip, there are sometimes a few trips out of Los Angeles or Ventura at this time of year. The birding is not as productive on those trips, but they are an alternative.) Monterey is a different story, with many trips at this time of year. Shearwater Journeys schedules trips out of Monterey every weekend (and some weekdays) in late summer and fall as well as most of the rest of the year. Reservations well in advance are highly recommended, since trips at this time of year fill early (Shearwater Journeys, P.O. Box 1445, Soquel, CA 95073, 408/688-1990). The best single source of information for other trips is the most current pelagic birding directory of *Winging It* (see Chapter 1 for information).

223

Probable Species
Total of 216 Species
Common Loon
Pied-billed Grebe
Eared Grebe
Western Grebe
Clark's Grebe
Northern Fulmar
Pink-footed Shearwater
Sooty Shearwater
**Black-vented
    Shearwater**
Leach's Storm-Petrel
American White
    Pelican
Brown Pelican
Double-crested
    Cormorant
Brandt's Cormorant
Pelagic Cormorant
Least Bittern
Great Blue Heron
Great Egret
Snowy Egret
Cattle Egret
Green Heron
Black-crowned
    Night-Heron
White-faced Ibis
Green-winged Teal
Mallard
Northern Pintail
Cinnamon Teal
Northern Shoveler
Gadwall
American Wigeon
Surf Scoter
Ruddy Duck
Turkey Vulture
Osprey
White-tailed Kite
Northern Harrier
Sharp-shinned Hawk
Cooper's Hawk
Red-shouldered Hawk
Red-tailed Hawk
Golden Eagle
American Kestrel
Prairie Falcon
Chukar
Gambel's Quail
California Quail
Mountain Quail
Clapper Rail
Virginia Rail
Sora
Common Moorhen
American Coot
Black-bellied Plover
Snowy Plover
Semipalmated Plover
Killdeer
Black Oystercatcher
Black-necked Stilt
American Avocet
Greater Yellowlegs
Lesser Yellowlegs
Solitary Sandpiper
Willet
Wandering Tattler
Spotted Sandpiper

Another boat trip that will have to mesh into your plans is the one to Santa Cruz Island, your destination for Santa Cruz Island Scrub-Jay. Island Packers Company (1867 Spinaker Drive, Ventura Harbor, Ventura, CA 93001, 805/642-1393) runs day-trips to Santa Cruz Island on Fridays, Saturdays, Sundays, and sometimes other days in August and September. The cost is about $47. Plan ahead and make reservations. You'll get a final peek at some pelagic birds from this boat, too.

Once the boat trips are set, the rest of the plan is simple: cover a lot of the better birding spots and use the birding hotlines extensively. At this season there is a good chance of seeing one or two real rarities.

This trip includes Los Angeles, Palos Verdes Peninsula, San Diego, Cuyamaca Rancho State Park, Anza-Borrego Desert State Park, Salton Sea, Indio, Big Morongo Canyon Preserve, San Jacinto Wildlife Area, Mount Pinos, Maricopa, Monterey, and Santa Cruz Island, as well as other stops along the way.

Birdfinding Guides

While not a birdfinding guide, *California Birds: Their Status and Distribution* by Arnold Small (1994), can be very helpful.

Where Birders Go in Southern California by Henry E. Childs (1993).

A Birder's Guide to Southern California by Harold R. Holt (1990) is the ABA/Lane Guide.

Ocean Birds of the Nearshore Pacific by Rich Stallcup (1990) is very helpful in understanding the identification and occurrence of pelagic birds.

Monterey Birds by Don Roberson (1985). This out-of-print book covered birds and birding sites in Monterey County. Ask a friend to loan it to you.

Birding Northern California by Jean Richmond (1985).

Pelagic Birds of Monterey Bay, California, by Rich Stallcup (1981). This now out-of-print booklet is actually a reprint of a very helpful article from *Western Birds* (Volume 7, Number 4, 1976).

Rare Bird Alert Numbers

Los Angeles 213/874-1318
Monterey 408/375-9122
Morro Bay 805/528-7182
Orange County 714/563-6516
San Bernardino 909/793-5599
San Diego 619/479-3400
Santa Barbara 805/964-8240

During this trip, you will be in all of the above areas or nearby, so try them all.

Special Equipment

Suitable clothing and footwear (seasonal) are essential, while seasickness preventives and raingear are recommended for any pelagic trip. Sunscreen and a wide-brim hat are recommended. A spotting scope is useful along the coast and at the Salton Sea.

Accommodations

Motels are usually available through the trip. (In the Monterey area there are fewer available rooms, and they are more expensive than elsewhere on this trip.) The climate is pleasant, and campgrounds are located in most areas, providing an economical alternative. The best plan is a mix of the two.

Key Species — Total of 17 Species

1. **Flesh-footed Shearwater**—May be seen on one of the Monterey pelagic trips. It usually associates with other shearwaters but is not numerous and is in fact the primary reason for scheduling two days out of Monterey.

2. **Buller's Shearwater**—Sometimes common on pelagic trips out of Monterey in this season, but numbers vary from year to year. Should be seen with two days spent at sea.

3. **Ashy Storm-Petrel**—Very common, though some observers think that the population is declining. Still, may be seen in the hundreds or thousands on any fall outing from Monterey.

Probable Species
(continued)

Whimbrel
Long-billed Curlew
Marbled Godwit
Ruddy Turnstone
Black Turnstone
Surfbird
Red Knot
Sanderling
Western Sandpiper
Least Sandpiper
Pectoral Sandpiper
Stilt Sandpiper
Short-billed Dowitcher
Long-billed Dowitcher
Common Snipe
Wilson's Phalarope
Red-necked Phalarope
Red Phalarope
Pomarine Jaeger
Parasitic Jaeger
Laughing Gull
Heermann's Gull
Ring-billed Gull
California Gull
Western Gull
Sabine's Gull
Caspian Tern
Common Tern
Arctic Tern
Forster's Tern
Black Tern
Black Skimmer
Common Murre
Pigeon Guillemot
Marbled Murrelet
Cassin's Auklet
Rhinoceros Auklet
Rock Dove
Band-tailed Pigeon
White-winged Dove
Mourning Dove
Common Ground-Dove
Greater Roadrunner
Barn Owl
Western Screech-Owl
Great Horned Owl
Burrowing Owl
Lesser Nighthawk
Vaux's Swift
White-throated Swift
Anna's Hummingbird
Rufous Hummingbird
Belted Kingfisher
Acorn Woodpecker
Ladder-backed
   Woodpecker
Nuttall's Woodpecker
Downy Woodpecker
Hairy Woodpecker
Northern Flicker
Western Wood-Pewee
Willow Flycatcher
Pacific-slope Flycatcher
Black Phoebe
Say's Phoebe
Cassin's Kingbird
Western Kingbird
Horned Lark
Tree Swallow

Probable Species
(continued)
Violet-green Swallow
Northern Rough-
winged Swallow
Bank Swallow
Cliff Swallow
Barn Swallow
Steller's Jay
Western Scrub-Jay
Clark's Nutcracker
Yellow-billed Magpie
American Crow
Common Raven
Mountain Chickadee
Chestnut-backed
Chickadee
Plain Titmouse
Verdin
Bushtit
Red-breasted Nuthatch
White-breasted
Nuthatch
Pygmy Nuthatch
Brown Creeper
Cactus Wren
Rock Wren
Canyon Wren
Bewick's Wren
House Wren
Marsh Wren
Blue-gray Gnatcatcher
Black-tailed
Gnatcatcher
Western Bluebird
Townsend's Solitaire
Swainson's Thrush
American Robin
Wrentit
Northern Mockingbird
California Thrasher
Crissal Thrasher
Phainopepla
Loggerhead Shrike
European Starling
Solitary Vireo
Hutton's Vireo
Warbling Vireo
Orange-crowned
Warbler
Nashville Warbler
Yellow Warbler
Yellow-rumped
Warbler
Black-throated Gray
Warbler
Townsend's Warbler
Hermit Warbler
MacGillivray's Warbler
Common Yellowthroat
Wilson's Warbler
Western Tanager
Black-headed Grosbeak
Lazuli Bunting
Spotted Towhee
California Towhee
Abert's Towhee
Rufous-crowned
Sparrow
Chipping Sparrow
Lark Sparrow

4. **Black Storm-Petrel**—Will be seen in good numbers on Monterey and San Diego pelagic trips.

5. **Least Storm-Petrel**—Should be seen on the San Diego pelagic trip, with numbers varying from year to year. Not as likely on the Monterey boat, but possible.

6. **Yellow-footed Gull**—You will see this species only at the Salton Sea.

7. **Elegant Tern**—Common all along the coast during fall; will be seen frequently.

8. **Xantus's Murrelet**—Could be seen on one or more of the pelagic outings. Never numerous, usually seen in pairs, it is more likely to be missed than any of the other key species.

9. **Craveri's Murrelet**—Like other murrelets, usually seen in pairs. An uncommon alcid, it is still possible from any of the pelagic trips.

10. **Spotted Dove**—An established, introduced species that is best found in residential areas of Los Angeles. Has spread extensively.

11. **Long-eared Owl**—One of the more difficult ABA Area birds to give a specific location for. It is possible in several places, but your best bet may be Tamarisk Grove Campground at Anza-Borrego Desert State Park.

12. **Allen's Hummingbird**—Easily seen year-round on the Palos Verdes Peninsula. Can always be found at Averill Park. Resident on Santa Cruz Island. (Elsewhere, most adult males have departed by September.)

13. **White-headed Woodpecker**—Primary habitat is pine/fir forest at 5,000 to 7,000 feet elevation. Most likely at Mount Pinos, with sites visited in the Laguna Mountains a possibility.

14. **Santa Cruz Island Scrub-Jay**—The species can be located fairly easily on Santa Cruz Island, where it is endemic. A special trip must be made to the island.

15. **California Gnatcatcher**—Can be seen on Day 1 at Palos Verdes Peninsula. Other good locations are Upper Newport Bay and Crystal Cove State

Park in Orange County. There are also several very productive sites in the San Diego area.

16. **Le Conte's Thrasher**—A difficult-to-locate desert species, but likely spots are the Maricopa area and Anza-Borrego Desert State Park.

17. **Lawrence's Goldfinch**—An erratic species that is hard to pin down. You will pass through several areas where it might be seen; probable spots areMount Pinos and Big Morongo Canyon.

Note: You should find the owl and the thrasher. If you see Xantus's Murrelet, you'll get all 17 key species.

Itinerary

Note: This trip begins and ends in Los Angeles.

Day 1 — Los Angeles, Palos Verdes Peninsula, and down the coast to San Diego

Call each rare bird alert number either prior to or soon after reaching the region it covers. During the fall thousands of California birders are out beating the bushes to see if they can discover the rarest rarity of the season. The rare bird alerts keep score, and you will benefit from their frequently updated reports. You will be in regions covered by three hotlines on Day 1—Los Angeles, Orange County, and San Diego—call them all!

Start the day at Palos Verdes Peninsula. This area is the northernmost coastal location where you can reliably expect California Gnatcatcher. It is also one of the easiest places to see Allen's Hummingbird. To reach the peninsula, take Interstate 405 south from the Los Angeles International Airport to southbound Crenshaw Boulevard (approximately 13 miles). Turn right onto Palos Verdes Drive North, which circles the peninsula counterclockwise, becoming Palos Verdes Drive West, South, and East as it makes the loop. There are many spots along this drive to view the ocean and the birds, but you do not reach California Gnatcatcher habitat until Palos Verdes Drive South. Their shrinking habitat is located primarily between Point Vicente and Western Avenue

Probable Species
(continued)

Sage Sparrow
Savannah Sparrow
Fox Sparrow
Song Sparrow
Lincoln's Sparrow
White-crowned
  Sparrow
Dark-eyed Junco
Red-winged Blackbird
Tricolored Blackbird
Western Meadowlark
**Yellow-headed
  Blackbird**
Brewer's Blackbird
Great-tailed Grackle
Brown-headed Cowbird
Hooded Oriole
Bullock's Oriole
Purple Finch
Cassin's Finch
House Finch
Lesser Goldfinch
American Goldfinch
House Sparrow

Note: The species in **boldface** appear no more than four times in the itineraries as *key* or *probable* species. Watch for them on this trip. Assume that you will see all of the probable species. You will not gain any new species from this list, but the opportunity to see a number of key species a second time should not be discounted.

Possible Species
Total of 78 Species
Red-throated Loon
Pacific Loon
Black-footed Albatross
Short-tailed Shearwater
Wilson's Storm-Petrel
Fork-tailed Storm-Petrel
Red-billed Tropicbird
American Bittern
Little Blue Heron
Wood Stork
Fulvous Whistling-Duck
Brant
Canada Goose
Wood Duck
Blue-winged Teal
Redhead
White-winged Scoter
Red-breasted Merganser
Northern Goshawk
Swainson's Hawk
Merlin
Peregrine Falcon
Wild Turkey

Possible Species
(continued)

Pacific Golden-Plover
Semipalmated
    Sandpiper
Baird's Sandpiper
Dunlin
Long-tailed Jaeger
South Polar Skua
Bonaparte's Gull
Herring Gull
Glaucous-winged Gull
Black-legged Kittiwake
Gull-billed Tern
Royal Tern
Least Tern
Tufted Puffin
Northern Pygmy-Owl
Spotted Owl
Short-eared Owl
Northern Saw-whet
    Owl
Common Poorwill
Black-chinned
    Hummingbird
Costa's Hummingbird
Lewis's Woodpecker
Gila Woodpecker
Red-breasted Sapsucker
Williamson's Sapsucker
Olive-sided Flycatcher
Hammond's Flycatcher
Dusky Flycatcher
Gray Flycatcher
Vermilion Flycatcher
Ash-throated Flycatcher
Pinyon Jay
American Dipper
Golden-crowned
    Kinglet
Ruby-crowned Kinglet
Mountain Bluebird
Hermit Thrush
Sage Thrasher
Cedar Waxwing
Bell's Vireo
Virginia's Warbler
Lucy's Warbler
Blackpoll Warbler
Black-and-white
    Warbler
American Redstart
Yellow-breasted Chat
Blue Grosbeak
Indigo Bunting
Green-tailed Towhee
Brewer's Sparrow
Vesper Sparrow
Black-throated Sparrow
Golden-crowned
    Sparrow
Red Crossbill
Pine Siskin

Note: Most of these species on this list should have been seen on earlier trips. You should see at least 8 species from this list.

with the best area at the end of Forrestal Drive, a left turn from Palos Verdes Drive South. This area can hold Allen's Hummingbird and Rufous-crowned Sparrow, too.

If you do not find Allen's Hummingbird there, return to Palos Verdes Drive South and continue east until the road bears left to become Palos Verdes Drive East. Do not take the left, but go right instead onto 25th Street and continue to Western Avenue. Turn left onto Western Avenue and then right onto Dodson Avenue. After a few blocks, you will reach Averill Park, a sure place for Allen's Hummingbird. See *A Birder's Guide to Southern California* for directions to other good locations on the peninsula.

When you leave Palos Verdes Peninsula, work your way to Interstate 405 and turn south. Spend the remainder of the day birding down the coast to San Diego. Most of the good birding sites on this route are well covered in *A Birder's Guide to Southern California*. Several good locations for key species are mentioned below.

Huntington Central Park (take the Brookhurst Street exit off I-405) in Huntington Beach is dependable for Allen's Hummingbird if you somehow missed it earlier. Spotted Dove is easy in several of the city parks and residential areas. Moving south along the Pacific Coast Highway (Highway 1), check out several locations for California Gnatcatcher, starting with the northeast corner of Upper Newport Bay. At the Big Canyon area you may be diverted by nearby shorebirds and some Elegant Terns, but this is a good spot for the gnatcatcher. Another is Crystal Cove State Park between Corona del Mar and Laguna Beach. The gnatcatcher can be found from the Pelican Point parking area by walking the trails through the coastal scrub. Elegant Tern should also be seen along the coast in several more locations with a minimal amount of searching.

Farther south, in San Diego County, another regular lcoation for California Gnatcatcher is San Elijo Lagoon Sanctuary. To go there, turn west off

Interstate 5 at Lomas Santa Fe Drive in Solana Beach, and then right again onto Rios Avenue, which ends at the sanctuary. Take the trail east along the lagoon.

Locate a motel in San Diego for the night.

Day 2 — San Diego Pelagic Trip

Join the group (usually at Quivira Basin by Mission Bay) for the pelagic trip. The primary reason for making the San Diego pelagic trip is to try to see Black and Least Storm-Petrels and Craveri's and Xantus's Murrelets. Other possible pelagic species include Pink-footed, Sooty, and Black-vented Shearwaters, Leach's Storm-Petrel, Pomarine and Parasitic Jaegers, Sabine's Gull, and Arctic Tern.

Unless you are an expert birder, Rich Stallcup's *Pelagic Birds of Monterey Bay, California,* though a bit out of date and now out of print, is indispensable on any California pelagic trip. Although the book is written for Monterey Bay, all of the species likely to be encountered on a San Diego trip are covered. This book was written to help birders learn to identify West Coast pelagic species, and it does the job well. *Ocean Birds of the Nearshore Pacific,* by the same author, and Arnold Small's *California Birds: Their Status and Distribution,* though not as succinct as the Monterey book, are also helpful.

After the trip you may want to visit the nearby San Diego River Floodway to check out any shorebirds, gulls (e.g., Heermann's), and terns (e.g., Elegant). A few Brant hang out year round, usually at the mouth of the San Diego River.

Leave San Diego on eastbound Interstate 8. After traveling about 40 miles, exit onto Highway 79 and drive north a few miles to Cuyamaca Rancho State Park to camp for the night.

Remotely Possible Species
Total of 42 Species

Streaked Shearwater
Wedge-tailed Shearwater
Wedge-rumped Storm-Petrel
Blue-footed Booby
Brown Booby
Magnificent Frigatebird
Tricolored Heron
Reddish Egret
Roseate Spoonbill
Greater White-fronted Goose
Canvasback
Ring-necked Duck
Lesser Scaup
Oldsquaw
Black Scoter
Common Goldeneye
Bufflehead
Hooded Merganser
Common Merganser
Ferruginous Hawk
Black Rail
American Golden-Plover
Mountain Plover
Ruff
Franklin's Gull
Thick-billed Murre
Inca Dove
Ruddy Ground-Dove
Black Swift
Red-naped Sapsucker
Brown-crested Flycatcher
Tropical Kingbird
Purple Martin
Bendire's Thrasher
Gray Vireo
Red-eyed Vireo
Northern Waterthrush
Summer Tanager
Rose-breasted Grosbeak
Clay-colored Sparrow
Grasshopper Sparrow
Scott's Oriole

Note: Many species on this list are rare and difficult to see. They are worth the chase even if seen previously. You will be lucky to see more than 2 species from this list.

Day 3 — Cuyamaca Rancho State Park, Anza-Borrego Desert State Park, and Salton Sea National Wildlife Refuge

Start the day at Paso Picacho Campground in Cuyamaca Rancho State Park, good for White-headed Woodpecker and several other species of interest including Mountain Quail, Band-tailed Pigeon, and perhaps Green-tailed Towhee.

When you leave the campground, continue north on Highway 79 to Route S-1. Turn right onto Route S-1 and bird this road at least as far as the Pioneer Mail Campground(about 7.5 miles). You might find Lawrence's Goldfinch here; Golden Eagle, Black-headed Grosbeak, and Lazuli Bunting are other possibilities. Don't linger here too long, though; there's a long day ahead.

Retrace your route to Highway 79, turn north to Julian (5.8 miles), and turn east onto Highway 78 toward Anza-Borrego Desert State Park. In about 18 miles, turn left onto Route S-3 (Yaqui Pass Road) and go north to Christmas Circle in Borrego Springs. Continue north from Christmas Circle on Borrego Springs Road; after about 3.5 miles the road makes a right turn and becomes Henderson Canyon Road, passing through Le Conte's Thrasher habitat for the next 2 to 3 miles. This area is also a likely spot for other arid-country birds— Gambel's Quail, Verdin, and Black-throated Sparrow. Finding the secretive Le Conte's Thrasher will take some searching, but it can usually be encountered here. Early morning is best, if you can make it. (You will have another very good chance for this species in Maricopa on Day 6.)

Return to Highway 78 via Route S-3. Both the Yaqui Well Campground and the Tamarisk Grove Campground are worth visits along the way, the latter providing the best chance on this trip for Long-eared Owl. The spring at Yaqui Well attracts most of the local species.

Take Highway 78 east to the Salton Sea, the only place that Yellow-footed Gull occurs in the ABA Area. At Highway 86 turn right toward Westmoreland and watch for Vendel Road on your left; this road leads to Unit 1 of the Salton Sea National Wildlife Refuge. You probably will not find the gull here, but this area is usually worth checking for Least Bittern, Cinnamon Teal, and several other species of ducks. Watch along Vendel Road for Burrowing Owl.

Return to Highway 86 and continue to Westmoreland (5.0 miles) and on to Brawley (7.0 miles). At Brawley, take Highway 111 north through Calipatria to Sinclair Road; turn left to the Salton Sea National Wildlife Refuge headquarters. Most of the best birding locations at Salton Sea are nearby. From headquarters, you can take Gentry Road South to McKendry Road and turn right for a short drive to Obsidian Bay, or go east on Sinclair Road and turn left onto Garst Road to reach Red Hill and the Alamo River mouth. Both locations should produce Yellow-footed Gull.

The Wister Unit of the State Imperial Wildlife Area is another place to check for the gull. It is located north of Niland about 0.3 mile south of Highway 111 on Davis Road. (*Getting close to the shore at the Wister Unit is not always obvious; also, the road can be narrow and gooey.*)

Other species possible around the Salton Sea, often present in large numbers, include Eared Grebe, American White Pelican, White-faced Ibis, Ruddy Duck, Wilson's and Red-necked Phalaropes, California Gull, Caspian, Forster's, and Black Terns, Burrowing Owl, Verdin, Cactus and Marsh Wrens, Abert's Towhee, Yellow-headed Blackbird, and House Finch.

You should also be aware that Blue-footed Booby, Brown Booby, Magnificent Frigatebird, and other rarities are sometimes found at Salton Sea during this season.

Continue north on Highway 111 to the Salton Sea State Recreation Area to camp for the night, or drive north to Indio for a motel.

All of the areas visited today are covered in detail in *A Birder's Guide to Southern California*.

Day 4 — Indio, Big Morongo Canyon Preserve, San Jacinto Wildlife Area, and the drive to Mount Pinos

Indio is notable only for the fact that you might find Spotted Doves by driving those streets lined with trees and power-lines.

From Indio take Interstate 10 west to Highway 62 and turn north to Morongo Valley. Turn right onto East Drive to reach Big Morongo Canyon Preserve. This sanctuary's claims to fame are its Vermilion and Brown-crested Flycatchers, and it is also a good place to look for Long-eared Owl and Lawrence's Goldfinch. A reliable place for migrants, it should provide excellent birding during this season.

Return to Interstate 10 and continue west for about 20 miles. A short distance past the Highway 79 exit, Interstate 10 and Highway 60 diverge. Stay with Highway 60 for approximately 8 additional miles; watch for Theodore Street and turn left for the 5-mile drive to San Jacinto Wildlife Area (Theodore Street becomes Davis Road along the way). This small wildlife area is an excellent place to see migrating shorebirds (depending on the water-levels) and to find Long-eared Owls. Here is one of your best chances for Long-eared Owl, so don't hesitate to ask the park naturalist to recommend current locations. Use this stop to phone the San Bernardino rare bird alert.

Return to Highway 60 and continue west into Los Angeles and to Interstate 5. Take Interstate 5 north to about 2 miles past Gorman (with luck, no more than a 3-hour drive) and turn left onto Frazier Mountain Park Road. Drive west through Frazier Park and then turn right onto Cuddy Valley Road. When you reach Mount Pinos Road, turn left and proceed to McGill Campground for the night (Northern Pygmy-Owl is possible, but rare), or stay in a motel back at Gorman.

Day 5 — Mount Pinos Area

At McGill Campground you should nail White-headed Woodpecker and have yet another good chance for Lawrence's Goldfinch. (The goldfinches might also be higher up the mountain at this time of year.)

Spend the day in the Mount Pinos area, for there are a number of good birding spots nearby. From McGill Campground, continue up the mountain, birding the side roads as well as the main road. When you reach the parking lot at the end of the paved road, park and hike the rest of the way up to the summit. The birding on the trail and around the old California Condor Lookout on the summit can be rewarding; both areas might yield Lawrence's Goldfinch, Clark's Nutcracker, and Mountain Bluebird.

When you return to the parking lot, walk over to Iris Meadow on its north side to look for Mountain Quail, Rufous Hummingbird, Steller's Jay, Mountain Chickadee, Pygmy Nuthatch, Green-tailed Towhee, Fox Sparrow, Purple and Cassin's Finches, and Red Crossbill, among other species.

A Birder's Guide to Southern California, *Where Birders Go in Southern California*, and *Birding Northern California* suggest additional locations.

Overnight again at McGill Campground or in Gorman.

Day 6 — Maricopa

Leave the campground and return to the intersection of Cuddy Valley Road and Mil Portrero Road. Turn left onto Mil Portrero Road; after a few miles this becomes Cerro Noroeste Road. Continue to Highway 33/166 and turn right toward Maricopa. One species that you might add along this route is Mountain Quail.

The Maricopa area is one of the best places in California to locate resident Le Conte's Thrashers. A good location seems to be 1 mile north of Maricopa on Highway 33, then right onto Kerto Road to Petroleum Club Road. Park and search the area to the northeast, especially the wash that runs from Petroleum Club Road to the railroad tracks. Another spot worth trying is north to the next crossroad, Cadet Road. A number of the dry washes in and around Maricopa (even south) can be good for the thrasher, and with patience you will find this species. *A Birder's Guide to Southern California*, *Where Birders Go in Southern California*, and *Birding Northern California* provide further details.

After seeing Le Conte's Thrasher, the remainder of Day 6 and all of Day 7 may be treated as extra days. If everything has gone well, you will have seen all of the key species for this trip with the exception of the

Le Conte's Thrasher
Louise Zemaitis

pelagic species and the Santa Cruz Island Scrub-Jay that you will attempt to see on Days 8, 9, and 10. If you have missed important birds, then the itinerary is obvious—the remainder of Day 6 and Day 7 should be used to try again for those missed species.

If the key species have all been seen, your best plan would be to try all of the rare bird alert numbers in hopes of a rarity. Other possibilities are to use the time to pursue any species that can be seen in the region which may have been missed on earlier trips (Example: Chukar at Mojave or Great Gray Owl at Yosemite National Park). Review the birdfinding guides listed at the beginning of this chapter for alternate sites. You could drive down to Ventura and take the Santa Cruz Island trip on Day 7, instead of Day 10, especially if the boat schedule is convenient. You could also spend the remainder of Day 6 driving up the coast to Monterey. Day 7 can then be spent birding in the Monterey area.

If you elect to go on to Monterey, take Highway 166 west from Maricopa to Highway 101 and turn right to San Luis Obispo. At San Luis Obispo, take Highway 1 north along the coast for an extremely scenic drive to Monterey. The drive from Maricopa to Monterey is about 260 miles and will take the rest of Day 6. Not only is the drive thrilling, but also the coastal birding can be good, and in September any clump of trees can be full of migrants.

Monterey area motels are usually crowded on weekends and are relatively expensive. Campsites are scarce in the immediate area but are numerous south of Monterey in the Big Sur area.

Day 7 — Extra Day

See Day 6 for various options. If you bird in the Monterey area, *Monterey Birds* by Don Roberson describes many good locations.

Stay the night in the Monterey area again.

Days 8 and 9 — Monterey Pelagic Trip

The average pelagic trip out of Monterey will vary from seven to ten hours in length, will travel offshore from 10 to 50 miles, and will cost from $60 to $85 per person. There are even a few twenty-four-hour trips that get 80 to 100 miles offshore and in turn cost about twice as much as a regular day-trip. Try to spend Days 8 and 9 on two separate day-trips. As stated earlier, Shearwater Journeys schedules trips out of Monterey every Saturday and Sunday throughout the fall season, and sometimes even on weekdays.

Rich Stallcup's two publications are a must for any birder going to sea out of Monterey. They will help you hone your identification skills and make your trips much more enjoyable. Shearwater's boats always carry leaders, who will patiently help you learn to identify the birds you see.

Key pelagic species on these trips are Flesh-footed and Buller's Shearwaters and Ashy and Black Storm-Petrels. In addition, during warm-water years, there is at least a fair chance of seeing 3 more key pelagic species: Least Storm-Petrel and Xantus's and Craveri's Murrelets.

Other more or less regular Monterey pelagic species are Black-footed Albatross, Northern Fulmar, Pink-footed, Sooty, and Black-vented Shearwaters, Wilson's Storm-Petrel, Brandt's and Pelagic Cormorants, Red-necked and Red Phalaropes, Pomarine, Parasitic, and Long-tailed Jaegers, South Polar Skua, Sabine's Gull, Arctic Tern, Common Murre, Pigeon Guillemot, and Cassin's and Rhinoceros Auklets.

Spend the night of Day 8 in an area motel; good camping areas are scarce near Monterey. On Day 9 head south immediately after the pelagic trip and camp near San Luis Obispo, Oceano, or farther down the coast. It is approximately 150 miles to San Luis Obispo.

Day 10 — Santa Cruz Island

It's another 135 miles to Ventura from San Luis Obispo, so get a very early start to be at the Ventura Marina for an 8 am boat-departure. The Island Packers Company (805/642-1393) runs day-trips to Santa Cruz Island ($47 per person) at least on Fridays, Saturdays, and Sundays. (Because of the current weekend departures, you may have to shift your trip to either Day 7 or Day 11.) There are sometimes other trips to the island scheduled through Island Packers for The Nature Conservancy (which owns 90 percent of the island), including overnight trips. This is your one-and-only opportunity for Santa Cruz Island Scrub-Jay. Pack a lunch. You may be able to spot some pelagic birds (e.g., Pink-footed, Sooty, and Black-vented Shearwaters, Black Storm-Petrel, jaegers) on the two-hour trip to the east side of Santa Cruz Island (Scorpion Anchorage). Check around the ranch; Santa Cruz Island Scrub-Jay should be about the second-most conspicuous land-bird on the island (after Common Raven). Allen's Hummingbird is also resident on Santa Cruz Island. Your boat will drop you back at Ventura at 5 pm, where you will find a motel.

Day 11 — Extra Day

Use your extra day to catch up on birding in the Los Angeles area (or going to Santa Cruz Island if the boat schedule conflicted with your own). In the afternoon drive the 55 miles to Los Angeles, where the trip will end.

Black-footed Albatross
Georges Dremeaux

Bird Numbers This Trip

	Potential	Expected	Actual
Key Species	17	17	
Probable Species	216	216	
Possible Species	78	8	
Remotely Possible Species	42	2	
Totally Unexpected Species	?	2	
TOTAL	353	245	

Cumulative List

Total key and probable species seen after 17 trips

Previous trips	628 species
Central/Southern California	17 species
TOTAL	645 species

This Trip's Mileage and Expenses

Approximate miles traveled, Los Angeles to Los Angeles: 1,400

- Fuel: $100; sharing $50 $_____
- Lodging: 4 nights at motels; other nights
  camping $250; sharing $125 $_____
- Food: No meals at restaurants - $132 $_____
  *The total per person cost for the above items with a companion
  to share expenses should be less than $585 each.*
- Three pelagic trips will be about $225 $_____
- Santa Cruz Island trip - $47 $_____
- Add to this car rental expenses, if any: $_____
- Add to this your expenses to/from Los Angeles: $_____
  This will give you a good idea of the cost of this trip.
- TOTAL $_____

Personal Notes

_____

_____

_____

_____

_____

_____

_____

_____

_____

_____

_____

_____

_____

_____

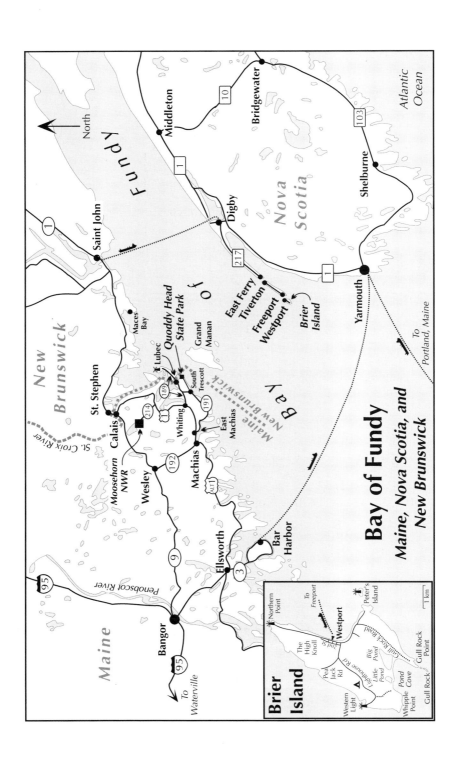

Bay of Fundy
Maine, Nova Scotia, and New Brunswick

North

Atlantic Ocean

Fundy

Nova Scotia

Bay of

Maine

New Brunswick

Middleton

10

Bridgewater

103

Shelburne

Saint John

1

Digby

217

East Ferry
Tiverton

Freeport
Westport

Brier
Island

Yarmouth

1

To Portland, Maine

Maces Bay

Quoddy Head State Park

Grand Manan

Lubec

South Trescott

189

191

Whiting

11

East Machias

St. Stephen

214

Calais

Moosehorn NWR

192

Wesley

Machias

Bar Harbor

A11

9

Ellsworth

3

Bangor

95

95

Penobscot River

To Waterville

St. Croix River

Maine
New Brunswick

Brier Island

Northern Point

To Freeport

Westport

Peter's Island

The High Knoll

Peat Jack Rd

2nd St

Lighthouse Rd

Big Pond

Little Pond

Gull Rock Road

Pond Cove

Gull Rock Point

Western Light

Whipple Point

Gull Rock

1 km

Chapter 18

MAINE, NOVA SCOTIA, AND NEW BRUNSWICK

Early to Mid-September—6 Days

General

Maine and the Canadian Maritimes are splendid places for birds, and this particular visit will allow you to sample some real avian treats. On this six-day adventure, you will concentrate on 5 species, 3 of which are found on the open ocean and 2 along the coast. The route, essentially around major parts of the Bay of Fundy, is designed to give you a maximal amount of time on the open ocean. It also visits some beautiful coastal areas in Maine, Nova Scotia, and New Brunswick.

Although the 5 key species are the primary reason for scheduling a September trip, the timing puts you in the right place at the right time to witness fall migration. Take advantage of this lovely location and productive season to make the most of your birding. Besides, this will give you another chance at a number of species, especially some lingering warblers, that you might have missed on previous trips elsewhere. Check the birdlists in this chapter closely and add any of these earlier misses to your personal key list. It should be noted that migration can be spotty. If the winds are from the north or northwest, some of the species on the possible list might be present in good numbers on Brier Island, Nova Scotia. During the slow periods, however, even migrants on the probable list can be scarce.

It is very important to make advance reservations for both the Bar Harbor, Maine, to Yarmouth, Nova Scotia, ferry and the Digby, Nova Scotia, to Saint John, New Brunswick, ferry. This chapter was written using the 1995 schedules and rates. For current up-to-date information and reservations, call 800/341-7981 from the continental United States or write Marine Atlantic Reservations Bureau, P.O. Box 250, North Sydney, Nova Scotia, B2A 3M3.

You will also need to make advance reservations for the Long Island and/or Brier Island whale-watching and seabird tours. The pelagic

Probable Species
Total of 112 Species
Common Loon
Pied-billed Grebe
Greater Shearwater
Sooty Shearwater
Wilson's Storm-Petrel
Leach's Storm-Petrel
Northern Gannet
Double-crested
Cormorant
American Bittern
Great Blue Heron
Black-crowned
Night-Heron
Canada Goose
Wood Duck
Green-winged Teal
American Black Duck
Mallard
Blue-winged Teal
American Wigeon
Ring-necked Duck
Common Eider
Common Merganser
Red-breasted Merganser
Osprey
Bald Eagle
Northern Harrier
Sharp-shinned Hawk
Broad-winged Hawk
Red-tailed Hawk
American Kestrel
Merlin
Peregrine Falcon
Ring-necked Pheasant
Ruffed Grouse
Black-bellied Plover
American
Golden-Plover
Semipalmated Plover
Killdeer
Greater Yellowlegs
Lesser Yellowlegs
Spotted Sandpiper
Ruddy Turnstone
Sanderling
Semipalmated
Sandpiper
Least Sandpiper
White-rumped
Sandpiper
Pectoral Sandpiper
Short-billed Dowitcher
Common Snipe
Red-necked Phalarope
Red Phalarope
Bonaparte's Gull
Ring-billed Gull
Herring Gull
Great Black-backed
Gull
Black-legged Kittiwake
Common Tern
Rock Dove
Mourning Dove
Great Horned Owl
Barred Owl
Belted Kingfisher
Downy Woodpecker
Hairy Woodpecker

operator on Long Island is Ocean Explorations Whale/Seabird Adventures, Box 719 Tiverton, Nova Scotia, B0V 1G0, telephone 902/839-2417. The other local pelagic operator is Brier Island Whale and Seabird Cruises, Ltd., Westport, Nova Scotia, B0V 1H0, telephone 902/839-2995. Both of these operators travel to the same waters; the primary difference is the size and speed of the crafts used. The Long Island Operator uses Zodiacs that are capable of much greater speed than the larger boats used by the Brier Island operator. This also means fewer passengers on the Long Island tours, making it more economical to use their craft if you are interested in arranging a charter. It should be stressed that both of these operations are primarily whale-watching tours and that the seabirds are secondary.

Both Nova Scotia and New Brunswick provide toll-free tourist-information and reservations phone numbers. Nova Scotia's is 800/565- 0000, and New Brunswick's is 800/561-0123.

This trip includes Bangor, Bar Harbor, the ferry from Bar Harbor to Yarmouth, coastal Nova Scotia to Digby, Long Island, Brier Island, a Brier Island or Long Island pelagic trip, Digby Neck, the ferry from Digby to Saint John, Saint John, Maces Bay, Moose-horn National Wildlife Refuge, West Quoddy Head, and coastal Maine.

Birdfinding Guides

Birding in Atlantic Canada: Acadia by Roger Burrows (1992).

Birding Nova Scotia by the Nova Scotia Bird Society; J. Shirley Cohrs, ed. (1991)

Birding in Atlantic Canada: Nova Scotia by Roger Burrows (1988).

A Birder's Guide to the Coast of Maine by Elizabeth Cary Pierson and Jan Erik Pierson (1981) is helpful for the Maine portion of the trip. A revised edition is planned for 1996.

Rare Bird Alert Numbers

Maine 207/781-2332
5 pm to 8 am weekdays; 24 hours on weekends
Maine Downeast/Cent. 207/244-4116
New Brunswick 506/382-3825
Nova Scotia 902/852-2428

Special Equipment

Daytime temperatures usually reach 60° to 75° Fahrenheit (16° to 24° C), but mornings and evenings can be very cool. Water temperatures on the ocean will be no more than 52° Fahrenheit (11° C). Take clothing that allows you to dress in layers and handle the temperature variations on land and sea. Wool hat and gloves, as well as raingear and waterproof footwear, are recommended for the pelagic trips.

Accommodations

Motels in all price ranges are readily available in most of the areas visited. The exceptions are on Long Island and Brier Island. At this time, there are at least two bed-and-breakfasts on Brier Island, a variety of bed-and-breakfasts on Long Island, and a nice inn at nearby Sandy Cove. Your best bet is to inquire about accommodations when you make pelagic trip reservations. It is advisable to follow up by making firm reservations since your choices are limited. Camping (no facilities) is allowed on Brier Island.

Key Species — Total of 5 Species

1. **Manx Shearwater**—This species is not usually numerous. It will probably be seen on the ferry crossing from Yarmouth to Bar Harbor, and should be seen on the Brier Island or Long Island whale-watching tours.

2. **Great Cormorant**—Fairly common along the coast throughout the trip area. You will have to sort them out from the more numerous Double-crested Cormorants.

Probable Species
(continued)

Northern Flicker
Pileated Woodpecker
Eastern Kingbird
Gray Jay
Blue Jay
American Crow
Common Raven
Black-capped Chickadee
Boreal Chickadee
Red-breasted Nuthatch
Winter Wren
Golden-crowned Kinglet
Ruby-crowned Kinglet
Eastern Bluebird
Hermit Thrush
American Robin
Gray Catbird
American Pipit
Cedar Waxwing
European Starling
Solitary Vireo
Red-eyed Vireo
Nashville Warbler
Northern Parula
Magnolia Warbler
Yellow-rumped Warbler
Black-throated Green Warbler
Palm Warbler
Blackpoll Warbler
Black-and-white Warbler
American Redstart
Common Yellowthroat
Chipping Sparrow
Savannah Sparrow
Nelson's Sharp-tailed Sparrow
Song Sparrow
Lincoln's Sparrow
Swamp Sparrow
White-throated Sparrow
Dark-eyed Junco
Bobolink
Red-winged Blackbird
Common Grackle
Brown-headed Cowbird
Purple Finch
Pine Siskin
American Goldfinch
Evening Grosbeak
House Sparrow

Note: The species in **boldface** appear no more than four times in the itineraries as *key* or *probable* species. Watch for them on this trip. All of these species should have been seen on previous trips, though the second chance factor is important for a number of species.

Possible Species
Total of 94 Species
Red-throated Loon
Horned Grebe
Red-necked Grebe
Northern Fulmar
Cory's Shearwater
Snowy Egret
Green Heron
Northern Pintail
Northern Shoveler
Gadwall
Greater Scaup
Black Scoter
Surf Scoter
White-winged Scoter
Bufflehead
Hooded Merganser
Turkey Vulture
Cooper's Hawk
Northern Goshawk
Spruce Grouse
Virginia Rail
Sora
Solitary Sandpiper
Whimbrel
Red Knot
Dunlin
Stilt Sandpiper
Buff-breasted Sandpiper
American Woodcock
Pomarine Jaeger
Parasitic Jaeger
South Polar Skua
Laughing Gull
Arctic Tern
Common Murre
Black-billed Cuckoo
Yellow-billed Cuckoo
Northern Saw-whet
    Owl
Common Nighthawk
Chimney Swift
Ruby-throated
    Hummingbird
Yellow-bellied
    Sapsucker
Black-backed
    Woodpecker
Olive-sided Flycatcher
Eastern Wood-Pewee
Yellow-bellied
    Flycatcher
Alder Flycatcher
Least Flycatcher
Eastern Phoebe
Horned Lark
Tree Swallow
Bank Swallow
Cliff Swallow
Barn Swallow
White-breasted
    Nuthatch
Brown Creeper
Marsh Wren
Veery
Gray-cheeked Thrush
Bicknell's Thrush
Swainson's Thrush
Wood Thrush
Northern Mockingbird

3. **Razorbill**—Your odds are very good on the Brier Island or Long Island whale-watching trips, but this species may also occur on either of the major ferry crossings.

4. **Black Guillemot**—Common throughout along rocky coastlines, especially on Brier Island. Will be seen easily on the two short ferry crossings in Nova Scotia.

5. **Atlantic Puffin**—Should be seen on the Brier Island or Long Island whale-watching trip(s), but may also be seen on either of the major ferry crossings.

Note: You should see all 5 of the key species.

Itinerary

Day 1 — Bangor and Bar Harbor to Yarmouth, Nova Scotia, via the Bluenose Ferry

You must leave Bangor early enough to allow yourself time to check in at least one hour before scheduled departure at the ferry terminal at Bar Harbor. Ferry departure time is 8 am; your reservations will not be held if you do not check in by 7 am.

From Bangor, take Highway Alt. 1 southeast to Ellsworth, and then Highway 3 to Bar Harbor, allowing at least one hour for this drive.

The one-way fare is $41.25 (U.S.) for each adult and $49.75 (U.S.) for a vehicle under 20 feet in length. Inquire about rates for longer vehicles.

The crossing from Bar Harbor to Yarmouth normally takes seven hours. At this time of year the entire trip is made in daylight. You should see Manx Shearwater fairly easily, but Razorbill and Atlantic Puffin will require luck and perseverance. In addition to the key species, you should see Greater and Sooty Shearwaters, Wilson's and Leach's Storm-Petrels, Northern Gannet, Red-necked and Red Phalaropes, and Common Tern. Less frequently seen species include Northern Fulmar, jaegers, and skuas.

Spend the night in Yarmouth.

Day 2 — Yarmouth, Digby, Digby Neck, Long Island, and Brier Island

Take Highway 1 from Yarmouth to Digby, no more than a 115-mile (185 kilometer) drive with many interesting places (e.g., Cape Saint Mary and Port Maitland) along the way for birding. Enjoy the scenery and the birding; take up to four hours to finish the drive.

When you reach Digby, take Highway 217 south toward Brier Island. As you travel down Digby Neck, any likely-looking place is worth a stop since migrant landbirds can be numerous in this season. Just prior to East Ferry (25.0 miles, 40.2 kilometers) Tiddville Marsh is on your left; it merits at least a quick look for grebes and ducks. The East Ferry across Petite Passage to Long Island runs hourly on the half-hour and charges a small toll. Two key species—Great Cormorant and Black Guillemot—are almost always seen on this short crossing; Common Eider and Black-legged Kittiwake are frequently observed.

After the ferry crossing, drive through Tiverton and continue south on Highway 217 to Freeport (11 miles, 17.7 kilometers). Freeport Harbor is always worth a look prior to boarding the ferry across Grande Passage to Brier Island. This ferry departs every hour on the hour, and the same species will usually be seen as on the previous ferry.

If you plan to camp on Brier Island, the best place is at Northern Point (camping is also allowed at Pond Cove). To reach Northern Point, turn right upon leaving the ferry wharf for a 1.3-mile (2.1-kilometer) drive. If you opt to stay at a local bed-and-breakfast, one should be easy to find in Westport.

Day 3 — Brier Island and Pelagic Outing

On Brier Island all-weather roads link most of the preferred birding locations. The best place to start the day is Northern Point, which is frequently loaded with migrants in early morning, especially if the wind is from the north or northwest.

Possible Species
(continued)

Brown Thrasher
Warbling Vireo
Philadelphia Vireo
Tennessee Warbler
Yellow Warbler
Chestnut-sided Warbler
Cape May Warbler
Black-throated Blue Warbler
Blackburnian Warbler
Pine Warbler
Prairie Warbler
Bay-breasted Warbler
Ovenbird
Northern Waterthrush
Mourning Warbler
Wilson's Warbler
Canada Warbler
Yellow-breasted Chat
Scarlet Tanager
Northern Cardinal
Rose-breasted Grosbeak
Indigo Bunting
Field Sparrow
Vesper Sparrow
Fox Sparrow
White-crowned Sparrow
Eastern Meadowlark
Rusty Blackbird
Baltimore Oriole
Red Crossbill
White-winged Crossbill

Note: You will probably see 15 of the species on the possible list—more if you are lucky and catch a migrant fallout.

Remotely Possible Species
Total of 42 Species
Yellow-nosed Albatross
Little Blue Heron
Yellow-crowned Night-Heron
Glossy Ibis
Snow Goose
Brant
Eurasian Wigeon
Redhead
Lesser Scaup
King Eider
Oldsquaw
Common Goldeneye
Ruddy Duck
Red-shouldered Hawk
Common Moorhen
American Coot
Hudsonian Godwit
Western Sandpiper
Baird's Sandpiper
Purple Sandpiper
Ruff
Wilson's Phalarope

Most of the other good locations on Brier Island can be briefly visited while still leaving time for an afternoon pelagic trip out of Westport or Tiverton. You should visit, in approximate order of importance: the village of Westport, Gull Rock Road to Pond Cove, the Westport Cemetery, the cross-island road to Western Light, Pea Jack Cove, and the Joshua Slocum Memorial at Southern Point. There are few resident species, but many different migrants and vagrants are possible, depending on wind direction and the weather.

The whale-watching tours out of Westport or Tiverton usually travel to Moore's Ledge, are three to five hours in length, and cost about $35 Canadian (or $25.55 U.S.) per person. It is usually more productive to bird on the island in the morning when migrants are more numerous and get out on the Bay of Fundy in the afternoon.

All 5 of the key species are likely on this outing. In addition, you should see Greater and Sooty Shearwaters, Wilson's Storm-Petrel, Northern Gannet, Red-necked and Red Phalaropes, Pomarine and Parasitic Jaegers, and Common Tern.

Use the same accommodations tonight as on Day 2.

Day 4 — Brier Island, Digby, and the ferry from Digby to Saint John, New Brunswick

The itinerary for the fourth day depends on your reservations for the Digby-to-Saint John ferry. Two departure times are currently available: 1 pm and 8:15 pm. Fares for the three-hour crossing are $21.50 Canadian ($15.70 U.S.) for each adult passenger, and $47.00 Canadian ($34.30 U.S.) for a vehicle under 20 feet in length. If you are driving a larger vehicle, be sure to check on rates when you make your reservations. The primary considerations when selecting which departure time to reserve is whether you would prefer more time at Brier Island and a possible second pelagic outing, or if you think a ferry-crossing in daylight might be of more benefit to your birding endeavors. (You might also extend your visit to use your extra day—Day 6—here.)

Whichever departure time you select, Day 4 should begin at Northern Point, birding for migrants. If you have reservations for the early departure, bird the same locations on Brier Island as on Day 3 and then drive to Digby, being sure to allow time to arrive at the ferry an hour early to guarantee your reservations.

If you are making the late departure, after birding early for migrants get back out on the ocean for a second pelagic trip. Here again, be sure to allow time for the drive to Digby, and be sure to arrive at least one hour early for check-in.

The Bay of Fundy crossing to Saint John on the *Princess of Acadia* takes approximately three hours. If you make the crossing in daylight, all 5 of the key species should be sought. Great Cormorant is likely in both harbors. Black Guillemot may be seen almost anywhere on the crossing. Manx Shearwater, Razorbill, and Atlantic Puffin are more likely on the open ocean. Other possibilities are Greater and Sooty Shearwaters, Wilson's Storm-Petrel, Northern Gannet, Red-necked and Red Phalaropes, jaegers, Black-legged Kittiwake, and Common Murre.

Spend the night in Saint John.

Day 5 — Saint John, Maces Bay, Moosehorn National Wildlife Refuge, West Quoddy Head, Coastal Maine, and Bangor

Leave Saint John early in the morning. Take New Brunswick Highway 1 west to St. Stephen, stopping along the way at likely-looking birding spots (e.g., Maces Bay). This is a 66-mile (106-kilometer) drive. At St. Stephen, cross the St. Croix River to Calais, Maine. From Calais, take Highway 1 south about 3 miles to Moosehorn National Wildlife Refuge. Enter on Charlotte Road to reach the refuge headquarters to pick up a map.

Moosehorn should provide you with satisfying looks at several species you may not have seen well on previous trips. Species of interest that may be seen by driving and hiking in the refuge include American Bittern, American Black Duck, Northern Goshawk, Spruce and Ruffed Grouse, American Woodcock, Great Black-backed Gull, Black-backed Woodpecker, Winter Wren, Magnolia, Black-throated Green, American Redstart, and other warblers, Bobolink, and Evening Grosbeak.

When you leave the refuge, go south on Charlotte Road to Highway 214, turn left, and go about 5 miles to Highway 1. Turn right onto Highway 1 and proceed approximately 15 miles to Whiting. Then take Highway 189 east for 10 miles and turn right onto the road to Quoddy Head State Park (about 3 miles).

West Quoddy Head is a 2-mile-long peninsula that juts into Grand Manan Channel, productive for seabirds, shorebirds, and boreal species. As you drive Quoddy Head Road out the peninsula, Lubec Flats is on your left at about the one-half-mile point. The flats are excellent at mid-tide for shorebirds, including Black-bellied Plover, American Golden-Plover, Red Knot, and Semipalmated, Least, and White-rumped Sandpipers.

Continue birding to the lighthouse, where you can bird from the lighthouse itself or take the trail from the parking lot through the woods and along the shore. Two key species may be seen here—watch for Black Guillemots along the rocky shoreline, while Great Cormorants are likely anywhere near the water (check especially the small rocks just offshore from the parking lot). Black-legged Kittiwakes are usually seen offshore. Check the spruce/fir forest for Spruce Grouse, Black-backed Woodpecker, Gray Jay, Boreal Chickadee, Magnolia and Blackpoll Warblers, as well as other species.

When you leave Quoddy Head, drive 5 miles to South Trescott, where you pick up Highway 191 to East Machias (25 miles). The only key species that you are likely to encounter on this stretch is Great Cormorant, but you will probably find American Black Duck, Common Eider, Black-bellied Plover, Boreal Chickadee, and Palm and possibly other warblers. Gray Jays are present but scarce. Nelson's Sharp-tailed Sparrows can usually be found at Holmes Creek, about 18 miles after leaving South Trescott (7 miles before reaching East Machias).

At East Machias turn left onto Highway 1 and continue 4 miles to Machias. At Machias take Highway 192 north 20 miles to Wesley, where you can turn left onto Highway 9 for the final 80 miles to Bangor.

The trip ends in Bangor in the evening.

Day 6 — Extra Day

Here's a day that can be used if bad weather has interfered with your birding plans. The extra day can also be used simply to prolong a visit (e.g., extending your Brier Island visit on Day 4), or to enjoy a location that you wish to savor.

Bird Numbers This Trip

	Potential	Expected	Actual
Key Species	5	5	
Probable Species	112	112	
Possible Species	94	15	
Remotely Possible Species	42	2	
Totally Unexpected Species	?	1	
TOTAL	253	135	

Cumulative List

Total key and probable species seen after 18 trips

Previous trips . . . . 644 species
Nova Scotia trip   . . . .   6 species
TOTAL . . . . 650 species

This Trip's Mileage and Expenses

Approximate miles traveled, Bangor to Bangor: 550

- Fuel: $40; sharing $20 $_____
- Lodging: 6 nights in motels $300, sharing $150 $_____
- Food: Ice-chest/supermarket for most meals - $60 $_____
- Ferry expense - sharing vehicle fees - $100 $_____
- Pelagic trip expense - $26 $_____
    *The per person cost of the above items with a companion
    to share expenses should be less than $360 each.*
- Add to this car rental expenses, if any: $_____
- Add to this your expenses to/from Bangor: $_____
    This will give you a good idea of the cost of this trip.
- TOTAL $_____

Personal Notes

_____

_____

_____

_____

_____

_____

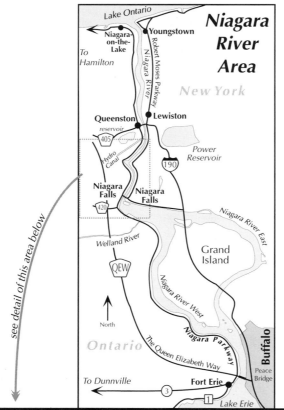

Niagara River Area

Lake Ontario

Youngstown

Niagara-on-the-Lake

To Hamilton

Robert Moses Parkway

Niagara River

New York

Queenston   Lewiston

reservoir

405

Hydro Canal

Power Reservoir

190

Niagara Falls   Niagara Falls

420

Welland River

Grand Island

QEW

North

Niagara River East

Niagara River West

Ontario

The Queen Elizabeth Way

Niagara Parkway

Buffalo

To Dunnville

Fort Erie

3

1

Lake Erie

Peace Bridge

see detail of this area below

Niagara Falls Area Birding Sites

← North

Lewiston Queenston Bridge

Sir Adam Beck Generating Stations

NEW YORK

Niagara River

Queenston Dock

190

Lookout

384

International Control Structure

405

Rainbow Bridge

American Falls

Goat Island

Hydro Gate

Niagara Parkway

Hydro Reservoir

Whirlpool

420

Three Sisters

ONTARIO

To QEW

The Gorge

Horseshoe Falls

Dufferin Island

Murray St.

Old Toronto Hydro Bldg

● = Prime Birding Sites

Chapter 19
NIAGARA RIVER AREA

Early December—3 Days

General

The Niagara River area in winter can be beautiful, with frost-covered rocks and frozen ice-formations decorating the awesome falls, and a layer of snow coating the surrounding landscape along the river. The area is well known to birders for the large number and variety of gulls that occur there, primarily from mid-November to mid-January. Nine species of gulls regularly occur and a total of 18 species have been recorded. Only 35 to 40 miles long, the Niagara River is largely ice-free in winter, resulting in one of the largest concentrations of gulls in North America. In addition, the entire river is accessible, making this a superb place to study an impressive assortment of gulls in a variety of plumages.

The Niagara River flows north from Lake Erie to empty into Lake Ontario. Midway, the river plunges over Niagara Falls. Divided by Goat Island, it is known as the American Falls on the United States side of the border and as Horseshoe Falls on the Canadian side. This short river is mostly smooth, but in places there is turbulence ideal for the gulls. With its combination of partially wooded shores, gorge, and Great Lake terminus, the river hosts many species of waterbirds and landbirds.

Access to the river is better on the Canadian side. The only areas on the American side that should not be missed are the American Falls and Goat Island; both can be easily reached from the Canadian side via Rainbow Bridge.

Unless you spend time away from the river, you are not likely to see much else besides gulls and waterfowl—which are, after all, the emphasis of this short trip. If the key species cooperate, you will have time to visit some of the nearby birding areas. Your list of species might not turn out to be very long, but the quality of that list should definitely be high.

Your time will be spent along the Niagara River unless you break away for a side trip or two.

Probable Species
Total of 47 Species
Common Loon
Horned Grebe
Canada Goose
American Black Duck
Mallard
Northern Pintail
Gadwall
American Wigeon
Canvasback
Redhead
Ring-necked Duck
Greater Scaup
Lesser Scaup
Oldsquaw
White-winged Scoter
Common Goldeneye
Bufflehead
Hooded Merganser
Common Merganser
Red-breasted Merganser
Red-tailed Hawk
American Kestrel
Bonaparte's Gull
Ring-billed Gull
Herring Gull
Thayer's Gull
Glaucous Gull
Great Black-backed Gull
Rock Dove
Mourning Dove
Belted Kingfisher
Downy Woodpecker
Northern Flicker
Blue Jay
American Crow
Black-capped Chickadee
White-breasted Nuthatch
American Robin
Northern Mockingbird
Cedar Waxwing
European Starling
Northern Cardinal
Dark-eyed Junco
Brown-headed Cowbird
House Finch
American Goldfinch
House Sparrow

Note: The species in **boldface** appear no more than four times in the itineraries as *key* or *probable* species. Watch for them on this trip. As usual, assume that you will see all of the probable species. You will not gain a single new species, but the opportunity for a couple of second chances at key species from previous trips certainly exists.

Birdfinding Guides

The only book needed for this trip is your favorite field guide or gull-identification guide.

Rare Bird Alert Numbers

Buffalo, NY 716/896-1271
Hamilton, ON 905/648-9537
Toronto, ON . 416/350-3000 (ext 2293)

Special Equipment

Typical temperatures in this season range from the mid-thirties to the forties; however, it can be much colder, and wind, rain, and snow are possible. You should be prepared to dress in layers. Wet-weather gear is highly recommended, too.

A spotting scope is essential, and a thermos for hot drinks is a great idea.

Accommodations

Motels in all price ranges are abundant throughout the area, and prices are usually very reasonable during this season. Your best choice is a motel in centrally located Niagara Falls, Ontario.

Key Species — Total of 5 Species

1. **Purple Sandpiper**—Might be found in any rocky area upstream from Horseshoe Falls, especially above the old, grounded barge on the Canadian side or opposite the Hydro-Gatehouse Building and in the rocky, shallow areas around Three Sisters Islands. These small islands are on the south side of Goat Island (USA) and can be reached by footbridges that connect the four islands. This sandpiper is never numerous here but can almost always be located in this season.

2. **Little Gull**—Usually occurs with the hordes of Bonaparte's Gulls, primarily from below the falls to Lake Ontario. Best locations are north of the Queenston-Lewiston Bridge and the boat-ramp area.

Also try the late afternoon fly-by at Niagara-on-the-Lake.

3. **Common Black-headed Gull**—Usually present in this season but can be very scarce—no more than one or two individuals in some years. The two best locations are the Queenston boat-ramp and the trail upstream toward the power plants that originates at the parking lot above the boat-ramp. May also be seen at Niagara-on-the-Lake in the late afternoon fly-by. This is probably the most difficult-to-find key species on this trip.

4. **Iceland Gull**—Usually found in small numbers from the water control structure above Horseshoe Falls to just below the falls. The best spot is the overlook at the Sir Adam Beck Hydro-electric Power Station just upstream from the Queenston-Lewiston Bridge. Should be seen without too much difficulty.

5. **Lesser Black-backed Gull**—Observed annually, becoming almost regular. Usually found in the gull concentrations just above and below the falls or from the Sir Adam Beck Hydro-electric Power Station overlook.

Note: You will probably see at least 4 of the key species. You would be lucky to see them all, but that is possible on this itinerary.

Itinerary

Note: This trip begins and ends in Buffalo.

Day 1 — The Niagara River

Prior to leaving Buffalo, call the local rare bird alert. Information obtained from the RBA may determine to some degree your first day's itinerary.

From Buffalo, cross the Peace Bridge (toll) into Ontario. You may want to turn left (south) toward Old Fort Erie and Erie Beach. This is where the Niagara River originates; it can be a good area for ducks.

Retrace your route to the Peace Bridge area and proceed north on the Niagara Parkway. The parkway parallels the Niagara River for its entire length, and you will spend at least two days exploring the

---

Possible Species
Total of 45 Species
Pied-billed Grebe
Double-crested
  Cormorant
Great Blue Heron
King Eider
Black Scoter
Surf Scoter
Bald Eagle
Northern Harrier
Sharp-shinned Hawk
Cooper's Hawk
Northern Goshawk
Rough-legged Hawk
Ring-necked Pheasant
Killdeer
Franklin's Gull
Black-legged Kittiwake
Eastern Screech-Owl
Great Horned Owl
Snowy Owl
Long-eared Owl
Short-eared Owl
N. Saw-whet Owl
Red-bellied
  Woodpecker
Hairy Woodpecker
Horned Lark
Tufted Titmouse
Red-breasted Nuthatch
Brown Creeper
Winter Wren
Golden-crowned
  Kinglet
Eastern Bluebird
Northern Shrike
American Tree Sparrow
Song Sparrow
White-throated Sparrow
White-crowned
  Sparrow
Snow Bunting
Red-winged Blackbird
Rusty Blackbird
Purple Finch
Red Crossbill
White-winged Crossbill
Common Redpoll
Pine Siskin
Evening Grosbeak

Note: Most of these should have been seen on earlier trips. It is unlikely that you will see many of them unless you bird outside immediate river area. (e.g., you can locate some harder-to-find waterfowl in the Hamilton/Burlington area and Tufted Titmouse at Niagara-on-the-Lake.) You will probably see only 4 of these species unless some special efforts or side trips are made.

Remotely Possible Species
Total of 20 Species
Eared Grebe
Black-crowned Night-Heron
Tundra Swan
Snow Goose
Brant
Eurasian Wigeon
Tufted Duck
Harlequin Duck
Barrow's Goldeneye
Merlin
Gray Partridge
American Coot
Common Snipe
Laughing Gull
Mew Gull
California Gull
Sabine's Gull
Ivory Gull
Hermit Thrush
Bohemian Waxwing
Note: It is not likely that you will see more than 1 of these species on this trip.

river from this road. As you travel north, there are numerous pull-outs where you can park and safely view the river to study the ducks and gulls. Each of these stops should be tried at least briefly. There are over a dozen good places to stop in the 21 miles between Fort Erie and Horseshoe Falls. Parking lots on both sides of the International Control Structure afford good views of loafing gulls. As you get nearer to the falls, Purple Sandpiper can often be located along the rocky rapids between the Hydro-Gate-house and the Old Toronto Hydro Building, and gulls will become more plentiful. Above the falls is usually reliable for Bonaparte's, Ring-billed, Herring, Great Black-backed, and sometimes Little, Iceland, Lesser Black-backed, and Glaucous Gulls. The latter 4 gulls will be in small numbers, if present; be patient and study the flocks closely, using a spotting scope at all lookouts.

The gorge from just below the falls to the Rainbow Bridge area is usually good for the same species listed for above the falls with the possible addition of one or more of the following: Franklin's Gull, Little Gull, Thayer's Gull, and, with great luck, Black-legged Kittiwake.

When you reach Rainbow Bridge (toll), cross to the American side of the river to check the area around American Falls. Footbridges connect Goat Island with the islets known as the Three Sisters Islands. Try them all and scan the rocks in the shallow waters; this is probably the best place on the trip to locate Purple Sandpiper.

Return to the Canadian side via Rainbow Bridge (toll) and turn right (north) onto Niagara Parkway. After passing the Whirlpool Rapids Bridge (Bridge Street), you will see two river overlooks, one on each side of the Whirlpool. Both are good for viewing the gulls, and from the Whirlpool to the end of the river the small gulls become more common.

A short distance past the Whirlpool you will reach the Sir Adam Beck Hydro-electric Power Station. The overlook just upstream from the station is one of the finest locations on the river for studying gulls, especially the larger species. Here you should locate Iceland and Lesser Black-backed Gulls, and, with luck, Thayer's and Glaucous Gulls. To find the key species will require that you search through the myriad of Bonaparte's, Ring-billed, and Herring Gulls that are always present. Study the gulls closely; almost any gull species on the river will sooner or later be found here.

Continuing north, you will cross Highway 405 and, soon after that, Portage Road. Then, after descending the Niagara Escarpment past the General Brock Monument, turn sharply right onto York Street (Highway 81) toward the river and then take the first left (Front-Princess Street) downhill to a road to the right which leads to the Queenston boat-ramp lookout. The Queenston dock area and just upriver is well known to local birders as the best location on the Niagara to see and study the smaller gull species, especially Little and Common Black-headed Gulls.

The last major stop is just before the mouth where the river empties into Lake Ontario. At this site at Niagara-on-the-Lake you can view the afternoon fly-by. To be in place to see the fly-by, you should arrive by about 3:30 pm. From then until dark (about 5:15 pm) the small gulls will fly by, traveling downriver to Lake Ontario to spend the night. Bonaparte's Gulls may number in the tens of thousands with small numbers of Little and Common Black-headed, and possibly Franklin's and Sabine's, mixed in. This is an excellent place to see any of the small gulls missed earlier in the day. It should also be noted that for a number of years the rivermouth has harbored King Eider and other duck species.

> Note: It is important to realize that almost any of the gulls may occur at any location. Some spots are better for large species; others are better for small species, but there are no hard boundary lines. In addition to the key species and other gulls mentioned above, several other species have been recorded, varying from the rare to semi-regular—Laughing Gull, Mew Gull, California Gull, Slaty-backed Gull, and Ivory Gull.

Lodging may be found in Niagara-on-the-Lake, but probably a better plan is to return to Niagara Falls, Ontario, to spend the night.

Day 2 — The Niagara River

This day should be a repeat of Day 1, visiting the various locations along the river. In addition to the gulls and Purple Sandpiper, there should be 18 to 20 species of ducks on the river. The better locations for ducks are at the two ends of the river, but there are other good places both above and below the falls. The more interesting ducks include American Black Duck, Greater Scaup, Oldsquaw, all three scoters, and, with luck, King Eider, Harlequin Duck, and Barrow's Goldeneye. See the trip species-lists for a more complete list and a better idea of the chances of seeing each species.

When you have seen the key species, it would be a good idea to call each of the nearby rare bird alert numbers. The information obtained from the rare bird alerts may help you decide where to spend the night.

It should be fairly easy to obtain lodging at either end of the river (Buffalo or Niagara-on-the-Lake); or return to Niagara Falls for the night.

Day 3 — Extra Day

Used this day to try for missed species, to re-visit a productive location, or to pursue good species cited on the various rare bird alerts.

If you are still at a loss as to where to spend this day, various ducks and gulls may be found in the Hamilton/Burlington, Ontario, area. Due to the huge numbers of Zebra Mussels in Lake Ontario, large concentrations of diving waterfowl can easily be observed. Flocks of 20,000 White-winged Scoters are becoming common, accompanied by small numbers of Surf and Black Scoters. Over the past few years up to 10,000 scaup and Common Goldeneyes have been present. Finding a Barrow's Goldeneye or a Harlequin Duck with them is not out of the question. The best area to observe King Eider, as well as Common Eider, is along the Burlington shoreline of Lake Ontario; try between Brant Street and the Appleby line in Burlington. The Windermere Basin in Hamilton at the east end of the Skyway Bridge should not be overlooked. Large numbers of ducks are present all winter, so the site can easily harbor something rare like an Eared Grebe or a Tufted Duck. Also check Van Wagner's Beach and Fifty Point.

Between the Niagara River and Burlington you might find Long-eared, Short-eared, Northern Saw-whet, and Snowy Owls, Bohemian Waxwing, Northern Shrike, Snow Bunting, Red and White-winged Crossbills, Common Redpoll, and Evening Grosbeak.

Trip ends this evening in Buffalo, New York.

Little Gull
Shawneen E. Finnegan

Bird Numbers This Trip

	Potential	Expected	Actual
Key Species	5	5	
Probable Species	47	47	
Possible Species	45	4	
Remotely Possible Species	20	1	
Totally Unexpected Species	?	1	
TOTAL	11	758	

Cumulative List

Total key and probable species seen after 19 trips

Previous trips . . . . 650 species
Niagara area trip . . . .   5 species
TOTAL . . . . 655 species

This Trip's Mileage and Expenses

Approximate miles traveled, Buffalo to Buffalo: 400

- Fuel: $28; sharing $14 $_____
- Lodging: 3 nights at motels $180; sharing $90 $_____
- Food: Assuming restaurants for some meals - $45 $_____
  *The total per person cost of the above items with a companion
  to share expenses should be less than $150.*
- Add to this car rental expenses, if any: $_____
- Add to this your expenses to/from Buffalo: $_____
  This will give you a good idea of the cost of this trip.
- TOTAL $_____

Personal Notes

_____

_____

_____

_____

Chapter 20

THE BAKER'S DOZEN

The preceding nineteen chapters outline birding travel to key locations at choice times of year to enable you to have an excellent chance of seeing 650-odd species of birds. These trips visit some well-known places, but they were also chosen to allow a chronological tour of all nineteen sites in a calendar year if you desire.

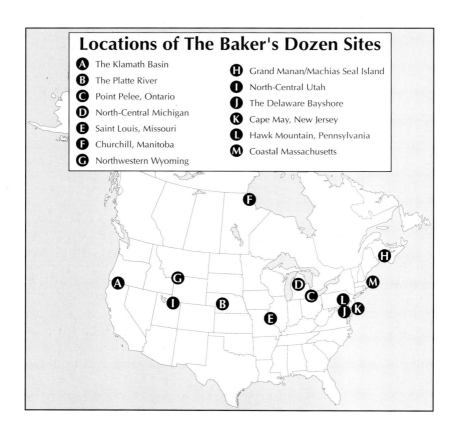

Locations of The Baker's Dozen Sites

- **A** The Klamath Basin
- **B** The Platte River
- **C** Point Pelee, Ontario
- **D** North-Central Michigan
- **E** Saint Louis, Missouri
- **F** Churchill, Manitoba
- **G** Northwestern Wyoming
- **H** Grand Manan/Machias Seal Island
- **I** North-Central Utah
- **J** The Delaware Bayshore
- **K** Cape May, New Jersey
- **L** Hawk Mountain, Pennsylvania
- **M** Coastal Massachusetts

Sage Grouse
David A. Sibley

Many fine birding locations were left out of the chronology simply because they did not fit the premise of seeing over 650 species of birds in one year or because they offered little chance of seeing many new species. If you miss some of the locations neglected in the first nineteen chapters, however, you will also miss a number of exciting trips that add immeasurably to the whole North American birding experience.

In an effort to correct this omission to some degree, Chapter 20 will describe, in less detail, another 13 locations. Taking this "baker's dozen" trips will also allow you the opportunity to see some species not covered in the previous chapters, and you will have additional chances to see some of the species that may have been covered too lightly earlier.

It may be desirable—considering time and finance factors—for many birders to combine trips in this chapter with those trips described in the previous nineteen chapters, and do these baker's dozen over a number of years. Still, the baker's dozen are presented in chronological order for any ambitious birder who may want to visit the sites all in one year.

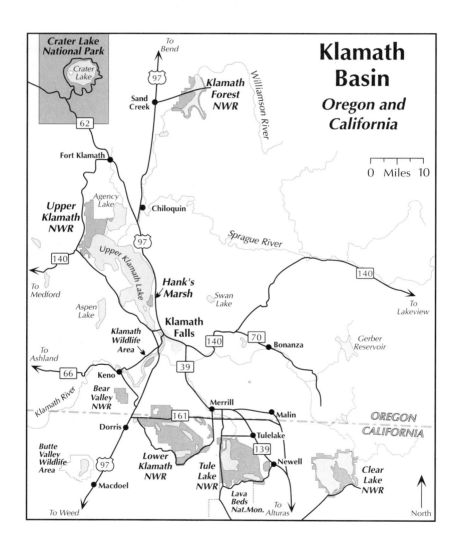

Klamath Basin

Oregon and California

Crater Lake National Park

Crater Lake

To Bend

97

Klamath Forest NWR

Sand Creek

Williamson River

62

Fort Klamath

0 Miles 10

Upper Klamath NWR

Agency Lake

Chiloquin

97

Sprague River

140

Upper Klamath Lake

To Medford

Hank's Marsh

Swan Lake

140

To Lakeview

Aspen Lake

Klamath Wildlife Area

Klamath Falls

140

70

Bonanza

Gerber Reservoir

To Ashland

66

Keno

39

Bear Valley NWR

Klamath River

Merrill

161

Malin

OREGON

Dorris

CALIFORNIA

Butte Valley Wildlife Area

97

Tulelake

139

Lower Klamath NWR

Tule Lake NWR

Newell

Clear Lake NWR

Macdoel

Lava Beds Nat.Mon.

To Alturas

To Weed

North

Trip A

THE KLAMATH BASIN

February—4 Days

General

The Klamath Basin Refuges are a complex of six national wildlife refuges spread over south-central Oregon and northeastern California. Five of the areas (Clear Lake, Tule Lake, Lower Klamath, Upper Klamath, and Klamath Forest) were established as waterfowl refuges. The sixth area, Bear Valley, is a Bald Eagle wintering ground. The six sites encompass 151,375 acres and include approximately 36,000 acres of marsh and open water.

During the winter months, these areas support several hundred thousand waterfowl and large populations of birds of prey. The Klamath Basin's prize attraction is the largest concentration of Bald Eagles in the Lower 48 states. During January and February, the Bald Eagle population reaches a peak of from 600 to 1000 birds. The vast majority of these eagles are on Tule Lake and Lower Klamath Refuges, where it is not uncommon to log 200 to 400 eagles in a day of birding.

Any winter trip to this area should concentrate on Tule Lake and Lower Klamath Refuges. These two areas not only have the largest concentration of eagles, but they also have impressive winter populations of waterfowl. (However, during some winters a freeze may force waterfowl farther south, into California's Central Valley.) The other refuges should be visited as time allows; each of them offers species that cannot be seen at Tule Lake or Lower Klamath Refuges.

Winters in this region are cold and relatively dry with morning temperatures in the teens to low 30s and daytime highs normally ranging from the 20s to 40s. There are numerous motels in Klamath Falls, and several of the nearby small towns in both Oregon and California have at least one motel. If you are well-equipped for cold-weather camping, the campground at Lava Beds National Monument is open year round.

If you are traveling to Lower Klamath and Tule Lake Refuges from the north, use Interstate 5 to Medford, Oregon, and then take Highway 140 to Klamath Falls. If you are coming from the south, use Interstate 5 to Weed and then take Highway 97 to the refuge area.

Birdfinding Guides

A Birder's Guide to the Klamath Basin by Steve Summers (1994) has the most details.

The Birder's Guide to Oregon by Joseph E. Evanich, Jr. (1990).

Birding Northern California by Jean Richmond (1985).

Rare Bird Alert Numbers

Oregon 503/292-0661
Northern California . . 510/524-5592

Species

There is much more to see at Tule Lake and Lower Klamath than the eagles. Tundra Swan, Greater White-fronted Goose, Snow Goose, Ross's Goose, and Canada Goose are all common and can be seen by driving the tour roads through each of the two areas. Emperor Goose has also been seen here but is very rare.

By driving the tour roads, you should see over 15 species of ducks with Eurasian Wigeon usually being the highlight.

Other species include Sharp-shinned, Cooper's, Red-tailed, and Rough-legged Hawks, Golden Eagle, Chukar, Ring-necked Pheasant, California Quail, Barn, Great Horned, and Short-eared Owls, and, some-times, Northern Shrike.

Spending time birding the other refuges can result in some good sightings. Bear Valley is closed to the public during this season to protect the primary roost for the eagles; the other three areas can be toured and birded. A few of the interesting species that may be seen include Northern Goshawk and Blue Grouse at Klamath Forest, Sage Grouse at Clear Lake, Mountain Quail and Spotted Owl at Upper Klamath, and Northern Pygmy-Owl at both Upper Klamath and Klamath Forest. You can see that the Klamath Basin has a lot to offer to the birder.

Personal Notes

_____

_____

_____

Trip B

THE PLATTE RIVER

Late March—3 Days

General

In late February the first Sandhill Cranes of the season arrive on the Platte River. Over the next few weeks the crane population continues to soar, so that by mid-March approximately 500,000 birds can crowd a 150-mile stretch of the river. This busy span of the Platte River lies between Grand Island, Nebraska, on the east and Sutherland, Nebraska, on the west. A large portion of the river between these two towns is not suitable for roosting, so the bulk of this temporary population is concentrated in two areas. One such area runs from Grand Island west to near Lexington, while the other is in the Sutherland/Hershey vicinity on the North Platte branch of the river. In each of these areas the river is wider, more open, and shallower—allowing the cranes to overnight in comparative safety.

After spending the night on the river, the cranes move away from it (although usually remaining within 5 miles of it) to spend the day foraging in wet meadows and fields. The cranes are omnivorous, taking both plant and animal foods with no apparent preference. Waste corn, however,

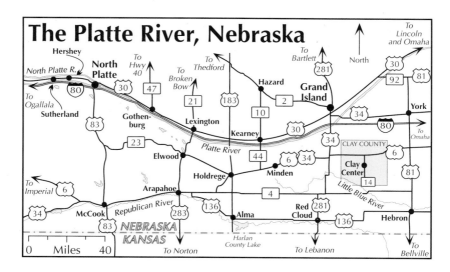

makes up most of their diet. Drive the country roads through these areas; this technique will give you many opportunities to see the cranes as they feed and display.

The best areas for waterfowl are to the southeast of Grand Island, mostly in Clay County. Here lies an area of wetlands known as the Rainwater Basin. It is estimated that nearly ten million ducks and geese visit these wetlands and the Platte River. Huge numbers of Greater White-fronted Geese, Snow Geese (both color morphs), and Canada Geese will be seen. With diligent searching of the Snow Geese flocks you will find a few Ross's Geese. At the peak of migration over a million and a half geese will be present with over twice that many ducks.

This annual occurrence—the gathering of waterfowl and cranes— creates one of the truly great spectacles in birding. Being present to see these huge flocks of cranes either leaving their river roost at dawn or returning at dusk is one of the most wondrous sights that a birder will ever have the good fortune to witness.

Golden Eagle
Dan Kilby

At least two organizations sponsor visits to riverside blinds to view the cranes at dawn or dusk. Reservations for these tours should be made no later than early January. For information and reservations contact The Platte River Whooping Crane Maintenance Trust, 2550 North Diers Avenue, Suite H, Grand Island, NE 68803, phone 308/384-4633 or the National Audubon Society's Rowe Sanctuary, Route 2, Box 146, Gibbon, NE 68840, phone 308/468-5282.

Birdfinding Guide

Birding Crane River: Nebraska's Platte by Gary Lingle (1994) has detailed information on crane sites and other birding locations along the Platte and in the Rainwater Basin.

Rare Bird Alert Number

Nebraska 402/292-5325

Species

In addition to the Sandhill Cranes, geese, and the numerous species of ducks, there are several other species of interest. Driving the roads to and from the Rainwater Basin, you should see birds of prey, including Bald Eagle, Northern Harrier, Red-tailed, Ferruginous, and Rough-legged Hawks, Golden Eagle, American Kestrel, and Prairie Falcon.

American Woodcock can be found in the wooded areas, Harris's and American Tree Sparrows along the brushy roadsides, and Lapland Longspurs and Snow Buntings in the grassland. Both Greater Prairie-Chicken and Sharp-tailed Grouse can be seen strutting on their respective leks. The Taylor Ranch (private) near Grand Island in northern Hall County has a few locations where both these species are visible from public roads. You can also contact the Nebraska Game and Parks Commission (402/464-0641) for information on location and availability of blinds placed near area leks if you are interested in seeing the two grouse species.

Personal Notes

_____

_____

_____

_____

_____

_____

Trip C

POINT PELEE, ONTARIO

Mid-May—3 Days

General

Point Pelee National Park, at 6,002 acres, is one of the smallest parks in Canada's National Park System. For birders, though, it is one of the most important. The park comprises the southern half of a 20-kilometer (12.4-mile)-long peninsula that reaches from the Ontario shore approximately one-quarter of the 80-kilometer (50-mile) distance across Lake Erie. For migrants winging north, the point acts as a natural land funnel that is their first opportunity to rest and forage after making the lake crossing. The park is roughly two-thirds marshland and one-third forest and fields. It is bordered by a sand-and-pebble beach. With north winds and/or rains the park can come alive with birds.

Most birders reach the park by taking Route 3 southeast from the Detroit/Windsor area for approximately 58 kilometers (36 miles) to Leamington, Ontario. The park entrance is 10 kilometers (6.2 miles) south of Leamington. The park opens at 6 am.

The park road parallels the western shore for 7 kilometers (4.4 miles) to the visitor center and parking area. There are four main trails in the park; each provides excellent birding in late April and May, peaking in mid-May.

The experienced Point Pelee birder arrives before dawn and drives to the parking area near the visitor center (after daylight the parking lot is usually full). The Tip Trail, a 0.8-kilometer (0.5-mile) boardwalk, leads to the point. The reason for starting the day at the point is to examine the latest wave of migrants. The rest of the day is usually spent working northward through the park, trying all the trails.

When you have returned to the visitor center, take the Woodland Trail, a 2.8-kilometer (1.75-mile) trail that passes through three habitats: dry forest, swamp forest, and abandoned orchard.

The next trail, as you work your way north, is the DeLaurier Trail, a 1.4-kilometer (0.9-mile) trail across the old DeLaurier homestead to the marsh.

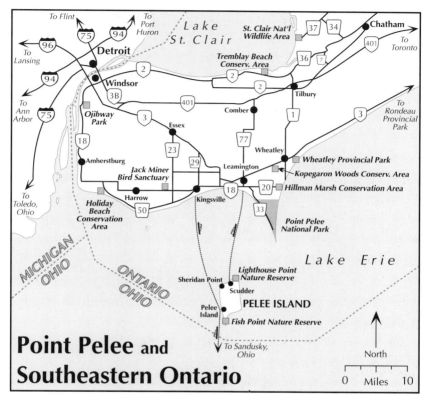

Point Pelee and Southeastern Ontario

The fourth trail is the Marsh Boardwalk, a 1.6-kilometer (1.0-mile) loop boardwalk through the marsh. This trail also has an observation tower which gives you a bird's-eye view of the marsh.

Point Pelee is one of the truly great places to experience spring migration in North America. For information and publications write to: Friends of Point Pelee, RR1, Leamington, Ontario N8H 3V4 or the Superintendent, Point Pelee National Park at the same address.

Note: The park staff monitors the birding in all of the area hotspots and keeps the information posted at the visitor center. Several of these spots are very near to Point Pelee. This information and directions to these locations can make a real difference in how successful your birding is on this trip. The park personnel are very helpful and will go out of their way to direct you to nearby locations and provide any information that you may request.

Birdfinding Guide

A birdfinding guide is not really needed in this small park, though *A Birder's Guide to Point Pelee and Vicinity* by Tom Hince (expected in 1996) will probably be helpful.

Rare Bird Alert Numbers

Windsor/Detroit . . . 810/477-1360
Windsor/Point Pelee . 519/252-2473

With three days spent at Point Pelee and some of the neighboring birding spots such as Hillman Marsh, Kopegaron Woods, Tremblay Beach, Wheatley and Rondeau Provincial Parks, and several nearby sewage ponds, a birder will easily see in excess of 120 species. This list will include over 20 species of warblers, including Blue-winged, Golden-winged, Chestnut-sided, Magnolia, Cape May, Black-throated Blue, Blackburnian, Bay-breasted, and Mourning. White-rumped Sandpipers are regular, and displaying American Woodcock is usually seen. Connecticut Warbler and Henslow's Sparrow should be sought, but they are hard to find.

Your list for this trip will depend on your own identification skills and on how well you communicate with the other birders. The park is small, so with the hordes of birders present, very few species can get through without being located by someone. With good communications you shouldn't miss many species.

Personal Notes

_____

_____

_____

_____

_____

Trip D

NORTH-CENTRAL MICHIGAN

Mid-May to Late June—2 Days

General

In order to see Kirtland's Warbler in the ABA Area, you must eventually make the trek to north-central Michigan. The warbler is an endangered species, so the known areas in which it nests are protected. Access to the nesting areas has been restricted with the exception of free guided tours conducted by the U.S. Fish and Wildlife Service and the U.S. Forest Service. The warbler nests only in young Jack Pines; the proper habitat is controlled by selective plantings and burnings by these two agencies. *Any use of tape recordings in or near these areas is strictly prohibited.*

There are two different areas where tours are offered, one at Grayling and the other at Mio. The free tours are offered annually from mid-May to early July. Reservations are normally not required for groups of four or fewer birders, but larger groups must make advance reservations. Schedules for the tours vary from year to year, so it is best to call ahead for information on dates, times, and departure points. For the Grayling tours, phone the U.S. Fish and Wildlife Service, 517/337-6650. The Mio tours are conducted by the U.S. Forest Service, phone 517/826-3252.

(A 48-mile Jack Pine Wildlife Viewing auto tour was initiated in 1994. Running south and east of Mio, the route goes through some Kirtland's Warbler habitat, and you may spot some warblers *from the road*. Details on the self-guided auto tour route are available from the Forest Service office in Mio.)

Prime viewing time is from late May until late June; however, many birders combine the trip to Point Pelee (Trip C) and time it so that they can drive to north-central Michigan (approximately a 5-hour drive) when they leave. This is by far the most economical plan for the average birder. Even though it is a bit early in the season for the Kirtland's Warbler, most birders who combine trips succeed in seeing it.

Birdfinding Guides

Although a birdfinding guide is not necessary for finding Kirtland's Warbler, *Bird Finding Guide to Michigan* by C. Ted Banks and C. Roy Smith (1994) and *Enjoying Birds in Michigan* by Michigan Audubon Society (1989) will help you to find other birding sites to explore throughout the state.

Birds and Bird Finding in the Saginaw Bay Area by Ron J. Weeks (1995) covers sites you might pass through on your way to Mio or Grayling.

Rare Bird Alert Number

Statewide 616/471-4919

Species

Other than Kirtland's Warbler there are not too many species to be seen on either of the tours that you will not see at Point Pelee, but you might watch for Upland Sandpiper, Pine Warbler, and Clay-colored Sparrow.

Of course, there are other possibilities for birding in Michigan, depending on the amount of time you have and possibly on your direction of travel to and from the Kirtland's Warbler breeding areas. There is a long-established wild population of Mute Swans at Traverse City (approximately 50 miles west of Grayling) and at least as far north as Little Traverse Bay.

Note: One or two small colonies of Henslow's Sparrows have been located in the Fort Gratiot (Port Huron) area of Michigan. (Fortunately, anyone driving from Point Pelee to the Kirtland's Warbler sites could easily go through Fort Gratiot.) Colonies of this hard-to-find species may move every few years, so pinning down a reliable site is hard. Local help is advisable.

Personal Notes

_____

_____

_____

_____

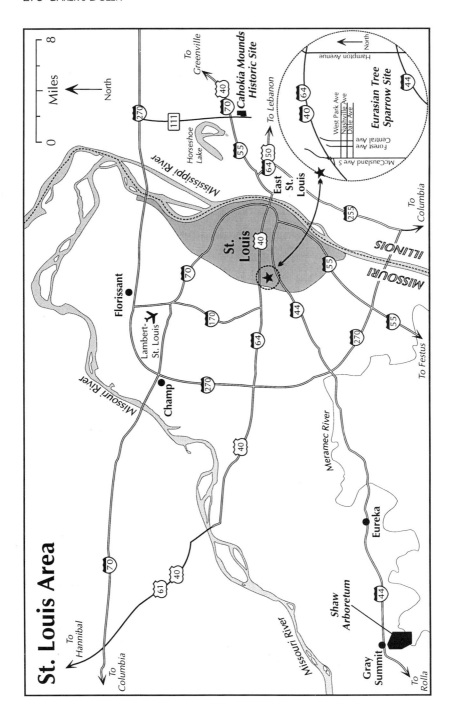

St. Louis Area

Trip E

ST. LOUIS, MISSOURI

June, July, or August—1 Day

General

This is a short trip; it can also be considered a layover. By this I mean that a one-day stopover in the St. Louis area could be made on the way to or from some other destination. This one-day visit to St. Louis can be anytime during the summer months and seeing the 2 key species can be made fairly easy by making a local contact prior to your arrival.

Birdfinding Guide

Birds of the St. Louis Area: When and Where to Find Them by the Webster Groves Nature Study Society will provide thorough coverage of Missouri and Illinois birding areas within a 50-mile radius of St. Louis. Publication is expected by spring 1996.

Rare Bird Alert Number

St. Louis 314/935-8432

Species

The one species that makes a stop in St. Louis necessary for the traveling birder is Eurasian Tree Sparrow. This is a permanent resident (introduced the 1870s) that is found in parts of St. Louis and in a small part of Illinois across the Mississippi River. A local contact can usually give you directions to a sure spot to see this species. If not, the sparrow is fairly common in parks, suburbs, and farmlands near the river and across it on the Illinois side.

An excellent site to see this species in St. Louis that is fairly near to the airport is detailed on the accompanying map. From Interstate 64, take the McCausland Avenue exit south; proceed to Nashville Avenue. Turn left (east) and park at the first intersection (Forest Avenue). One-half block north, past the alley, you should spot a number of active nest boxes. (This is the yard of 6900 West Park Avenue.)

Two other places usually good for Eurasian Tree Sparrow on the Illinois side of the river are Horseshoe Lake State Recreation Area and Cahokia Mounds State Historical Site. Both locations are a few miles east of St. Louis, just off Interstate 55. At Horseshoe Lake, try the picnic areas on both ends of the causeway leading to the camping areas. At Cahokia Mounds, try the edge of the park toward the residential area. (The origin of these impressive mounds should be of interest to anyone with an interest in archeology, too.)

A second interesting species which you should try to see while in the area is Henslow's Sparrow. The Shaw Arboretum of Missouri Botanical Garden has been reliable in the St. Louis area. The arboretum is 23 miles beyond Interstate 270 on Interstate 44. Take the exit at Gray Summit (Exit 253), turn west onto Highway 100, and then drive less than a quarter-mile to the entrance. There is a nominal entrance fee. Look in the Experimental Prairie section of the arboretum for the Henslow's Sparrows.

There is much more to the St. Louis area than these two passerines. (For example, Sedge Wrens are often found near the Henslow's Sparrow site at Shaw Aboretum.) However, if the rare bird alert doesn't give you enough of a reason to linger, resume your trip after seeing Eurasian Tree Sparrow and Henslow's Sparrow.

Personal Notes

_____

_____

_____

_____

_____

Trip F

CHURCHILL, MANITOBA

Mid-to-Late June—5 Days

General

In 1929 the railroad was completed to Churchill, built primarily to haul grain from the prairie provinces for storage and subsequent shipment by sea. From the early 1930s, there has been a steady stream of naturalists traveling to Churchill because the railroad made that area the most accessible tundra in North America. Churchill is a small seaport (population about 1,200) located at the mouth of the Churchill River on the west shore of Hudson Bay, the largest bay in the world. Churchill's location gives the birder the advantage of access to both the tundra and the boreal forest. The mouth of the Churchill River and the coastal areas of Hudson Bay add even more diverse habitat to explore.

Even today, the only access to Churchill is by rail or by air. Many birders travel from Winnipeg to Churchill by rail and make the return trip by air. The train ride is 1,620 kilometers (1,000 miles) long—a 38-hour trip with beautiful scenery along the way. The train makes only three trips weekly, and this limitation must be worked into your plans. For information on the railway service, schedules and rates, phone Canadian National Railroad at 204/675-2241. Canadian Airlines International makes trips to Churchill five days a week in the summer months; for more information call them at 204/675-8851.

Reservations for train, airplane, motel, and car rental must be made well in advance. For information on accommodations and car rental, call the Churchill Chamber of Commerce (tourist information center) at 204/675-2022.

Upon arrival at Churchill you will find it to be a small and somewhat drab town, but it boasts several adequate hotels and motels, restaurants, grocery stores, a taxi company, and very friendly people. There are at least two companies that rent cars, and boat charters are also available. All these factors combine to make Churchill a birder-friendly place.

The area accessible to birders is not large, so with three to five days in Churchill you can cover all of the better sites several times. There is a good variety of species to be seen, with the added pleasure of seeing

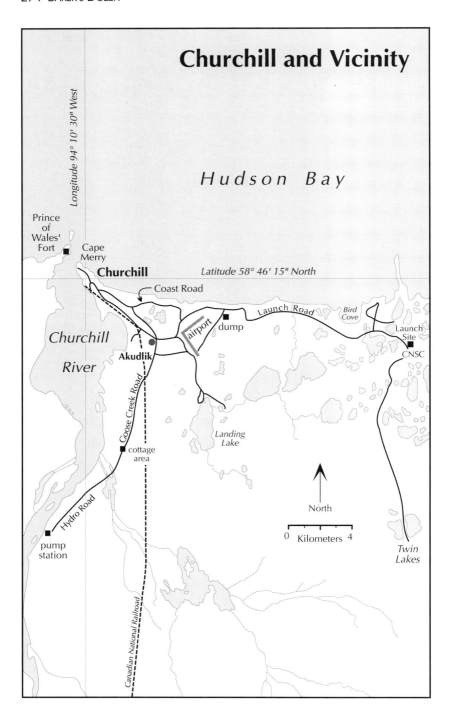

Churchill and Vicinity

Hudson Bay

Longitude 94° 10' 30" West

Prince of Wales' Fort

Cape Merry

Churchill

Latitude 58° 46' 15" North

Coast Road

Launch Road

Bird Cove

Churchill

River

airport

dump

Launch Site

CNSC

Akudlik

Goose Creek Road

Landing Lake

cottage area

North

Hydro Road

0   Kilometers   4

pump station

Twin Lakes

Canadian National Railroad

many familiar species in unfamiliar full breeding plumage, or engaging in unfamiliar behavior. (Imagine, shorebirds sitting in trees!)

For your first trip to Churchill it would probably be best to go in mid-to-late June. At this time the river ice will have broken up, and the weather will be improving with daytime temperatures averaging 12°C (54°F). Daylight at this time of year stretches from 3:30 am to 10:30 pm giving you a lot of birding time. Along with the higher temperatures comes hordes of mosquitoes and black flies—weather dependent, but usually not a problem before June 20. Be well prepared with both repellents and protective clothing. Also be aware that temperatures can be frigid at times, and even with warmer temperatures the wind off the ice-covered bay can be quite cold. Bring clothing that will allow you to dress in layers.

With a little planning, you can have a very pleasant trip to a birding hotspot that is unique in North America.

Birdfinding Guide

A Birder's Guide to Churchill by Bonnie Chartier (1994) is part of the ABA/Lane Series. This guide covers the entire birding area at Churchill with excellent maps and directions.

Species

The high point of a trip to Churchill for most birders is seeing Ross's Gull. The gull has been trying to establish a foothold for several years and is usually seen without too much difficulty.

Other sought-after species include Hudsonian Godwit, White-rumped and Baird's Sandpipers, Red Phalarope, all three jaegers, Thayer's, Glaucous, and Sabine's Gulls, Spruce Grouse, Willow Ptarmigan, Short-eared Owl, Harris's Sparrow, Smith's Long-

Ross's Gull
Dan Kilby

spur, and Hoary Redpoll. A Northern Hawk Owl might be found on the train ride to Churchill; one is sometimes found around Churchill itself.

In addition to the above list of birds a trip to Churchill will also result in most of the following: 3 loons, 1 grebe, American Bittern, Tundra Swan, 3 geese, 15 ducks including Oldsquaw and all 3 scoters, 4 birds of prey, Sora, Sandhill Crane, 18 species of shorebirds, 4 gulls, Arctic Tern, and approximately 30 species of small landbirds.

You would have to admit that this is a high-quality list. Be prepared for a high-quality experience, too.

Personal Notes

_____

_____

_____

_____

_____

_____

_____

_____

_____

_____

Trip G

NORTHWESTERN WYOMING

Late June or Early July—7 Days

General

The northwestern corner of Wyoming boasts two of our nation's most beautiful national parks; the parks in turn are surrounded by national forest land. This area contains some of the most scenic and rugged country in the Lower 48. The birdlife is varied, and it must compete for the birder's attention with the scenery and the great diversity of other easily seen wildlife. Birders visiting this area can see most of the specialties by visiting the two national parks, with a few side trips barely outside their borders.

Yellowstone National Park consists of 3,400 square miles of forest, lakes, streams, mountains, meadows, and the world-famous geysers and hot springs. The vast majority of the park is inaccessible to all but the hardiest of backcountry hikers, but the 142-mile figure-8 loop-road gives visitors access to more attractions than can possibly be seen thoroughly in anything short of a very long visit.

There are five entrances to the park; all of these routes are extremely scenic, following natural paths through the mountains to connect to the figure-8 park road. Campgrounds are located in various spots throughout the park. Camping is by far the most economical way to see this country, but campgrounds in the summer season do fill up daily before noon. Taking the time to make careful plans and to secure campsite reservations prior to your arrival will increase your enjoyment of the park.

Specific information concerning Yellowstone can be obtained by writing to the Park Superintendent, P.O. Box 168, Yellowstone National Park, WY 82190, phone 307/344-7381. *Please note that use of bird tapes is forbidden in the park.*

Grand Teton National Park, in comparison to Yellowstone, is small; it consists of only 425 square miles. The majestic beauty of the Teton Mountains, however, more than compensates for the size difference. The

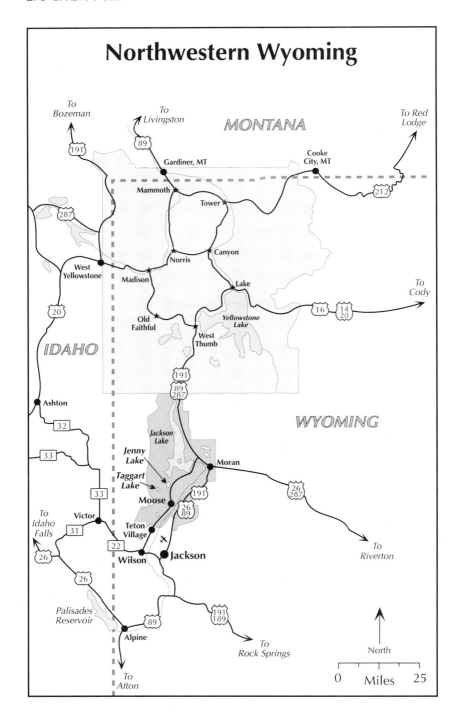

Northwestern Wyoming

To
Bozeman

To
Livingston

MONTANA

To Red
Lodge

191

89

Gardiner, MT

Cooke
City, MT

287

Mammoth

212

Tower

Norris

Canyon

West
Yellowstone

Madison

Lake

To
Cody

20

Old
Faithful

Yellowstone
Lake

16

14
20

West
Thumb

IDAHO

191
89
287

Ashton

WYOMING

32

Jackson
Lake

33

Jenny
Lake

Moran

33

Taggart
Lake

26
287

To
Idaho
Falls

Victor

Moose

191

26
89

31

22

Teton
Village

Jackson

26

Wilson

To
Riverton

26

Palisades
Reservoir

89

191
189

Alpine

To
Rock Springs

North

0   Miles   25

To
Afton

park includes most of Jackson Hole, Jackson Lake, and the eastern side of the Teton Range.

There are two main roads through the park. U.S. Highway 89 comes from the south through Jackson and the park, then continues to the south entrance of Yellowstone. The other main road is the Teton Park Road that begins at Moose and then runs past Jenny Lake and part of Jackson Lake to a junction with U.S. Highway 89.

The camping situation is the same as in Yellowstone, with camp-grounds filling by noon. For information contact Grand Teton National Park, P.O. Drawer 170, Moose, WY 83012, phone 307/739-3300.

Both of the national parks as well as the other surrounding national lands provide excellent birdwatching opportunities. Of the two parks, Grand Teton provides better access to many of the areas where sought-after species can be seen. As you would expect, some species can be seen at one park and not at the other, so it is important to be sure to allow enough time to bird both parks. The sheer grandeur of this scenic area requires that you spend at least a week even to scratch the surface of the natural wonders to be experienced in the two parks.

Birdfinding Guides

Finding the Birds of Jackson Hole by Bert Raynes and Darwin Wile (1994).

A Birder's Guide to Wyoming by Oliver Scott (1993) is an ABA Birdfinding Guide.

Birds of Yellowstone (1988) by Terry McEneaney.

Rare Bird Alert Number

Statewide 307/265-2473

Barrow's Goldeneye
Dan Kilby

Species

The 4 species that are probably the most sought by birders who visit this area are Trumpeter Swan, Great Gray Owl, Three-toed Woodpecker, and Black Rosy-Finch. Here are some of the better locations for each.

Trumpeter Swan—In Yellowstone two of the better locations are Mary Bay on Lake Yellowstone on the east entrance road and Seven Mile Bridge on the west entrance road. Flat Creek just north of Jackson on Highway 89 is probably the surest location in the Teton area.

Great Gray Owl—In Yellowstone scan the meadows along the road between Canyon Junction and Norris Junction at dusk. In the Teton area try the Moose-Wilson Road. It is helpful to ask park personnel, since they sometimes will tell you the location of Great Grays.

Three-toed Woodpecker—Any area of recent burns in either park. Try the Beaver Creek burn-site at Taggart Lake about 3 miles northwest of Moose at Grand Teton National Park.

Black Rosy-Finch—The surest strategy is to take the aerial tramway from Teton Village to the top of the mountain, where you can see the rosy-finch in summer.

Boreal Owl—Another much sought-after species; not often seen and extremely hard to find. However, it is present through much of the area, particularly in the subalpine zone.

By using the suggested birdfinding guides, you should see all of these species: Cinnamon Teal, Barrow's Goldeneye, Harlequin Duck, Northern Goshawk, Blue, Ruffed, and Sage Grouse, Calliope Hummingbird, Red-naped and Williamson's Sapsuckers, Olive-sided Flycatcher, American Dipper, Lazuli Bunting, Green-tailed Towhee, Brewer's Sparrow, Cassin's Finch, and Red Crossbill.

Personal Notes

_____

_____

_____

_____

_____

Trip H

GRAND MANAN AND MACHIAS SEAL ISLAND

July—4 Days

General

Grand Manan is an island of small picturesque fishing villages, beautiful beaches, imposing cliffs, spruce/fir and mixed-wood forests, marshlands, and panoramic views. The island is 24.6 kilometers (15.3 miles) north to south and 10.8 (6.7 miles) east to west. There are approximately 2,500 tourist-friendly permanent residents here.

To reach Grand Manan, you must travel to Black's Harbour, New Brunswick, where you board the daily ferry (toll) for the two-hour crossing. From the ferry docks at North Head local Highway 776 runs the length of the island to well south of Seal Cove. After the paved highway ends, you can continue on a good gravel road to Southwest Head. The total length of this highway is about 29 kilometers (18 miles). It connects all of the fishing villages, making it very easy to find a place of lodging. Grand Manan is a very popular destination, so reservations should be made well in advance. Information concerning accommodations and ferries can be obtained by contacting Tourism New Brunswick, P.O. Box 12345, Fredericton, New Brunswick E3B 5C3. Or you can phone them at 800/561-0123.

If you prefer camping, Anchorage Provincial Park located between Grand Harbour and Seal Cove is a nice park with good facilities.

Birdwatching opportunities on Grand Manan range from boreal species in the extensive areas of forest to shorebirds at Castilia Marsh to the more obvious marine birds to be seen from the many points and ocean overlooks. At least two days should be spent on Grand Manan to explore the many good sites. Some of the locations that should not be missed include Swallow Tail Light at North Head, Pettes Cove, Whale Cove, Ashburton Head, The Whistle (the most northerly point on the island), Castilia Marsh, Dark Harbour, Ingall's Head, Seal Cove, Deep Cove, Pat's Cove, Bradford's Cove, and Southwest Head.

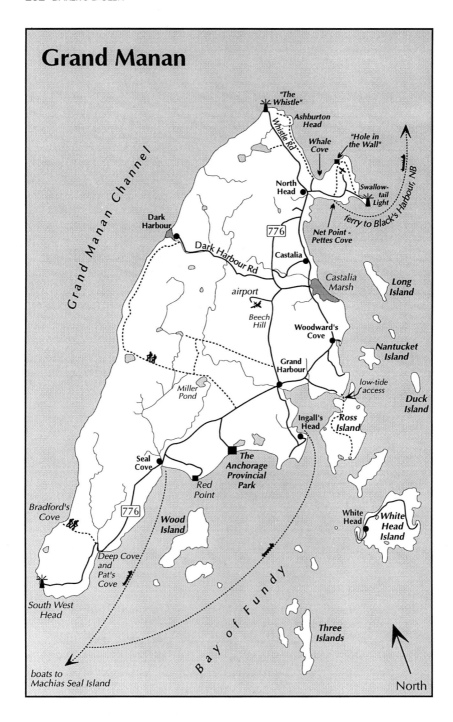

Grand Manan

From Seal Cove, or sometimes from Ingall's Head you can join one of the daily boat tours to Machias Seal Island (approximately $38 U.S.). These tours are popular with the tourists, and it might be advisable to make arrangements long before arriving at Grand Manan to secure your place. (The Grand Manan Tourism Office will have a list of current operators at 506/662-3442.) The water never gets warm here, and air temperatures on the boat trips will seem frosty. Heavy sweaters, wool hats and gloves, raingear, and waterproof boots will all be welcome.

Machias Seal Island is a small, 15-acre, treeless island. Other than the lighthouse, the keeper's houses, boardwalks and trails to the seabird colonies, and blinds to view the nesting species, there is virtually nothing here but grass, rocks, and birds. On this island you can see the nesting species and photograph them from only a few feet away. It is a fantastic experience to get this close to species which you have seen only at a distance and maybe then only bobbing on a wave in and out of view.

Landing at Machias Seal Island can be accomplished only on a calm day. If your group does not land on the island, the boat captain will still maneuver the vessel for a fairly close look at all of the nesting species.

Birdfinding Guides

A guide is not necessary for this trip, but *Grand Manan Birds* by Brian Dalzell (1991) can be useful. It includes a good map and information on 24 birding areas.

Rare Bird Alert Number

New Brunswick 506/382-3825

Species

The primary reason for this trip is to experience the sights and sounds of a large seabird colony. The species that you will see at Machias Seal Island include large numbers of Common Terns, Arctic Terns, Razorbills, and Atlantic Puffins. Small numbers of Common Murres are usually seen, although they probably do not nest on the island. A few Great Cormorants might be seen on the rocks off Machias Seal Island or on nearby Gull Rocks.

Pelagic species often seen on the boat ride to and from the island include Greater, Sooty, and Manx Shearwaters, Wilson's Storm-Petrel, Northern Gannet, Red-necked Phalarope, Pomarine and Parasitic Jaegers, and Black-legged Kittiwake. These species may also be seen from points and ocean overlooks while exploring Grand Manan.

Species on Grand Manan include Common Loon, Common Eider, Red-breasted Merganser, Northern Goshawk, Peregrine Falcon, Ruffed Grouse, White-rumped Sandpiper (after July), Great Black-backed Gull, Black Guillemot, Black-backed Woodpecker, Olive-sided, Yellow-bellied, Alder, and Least Flycatchers, Boreal Chickadee, Magnolia, Black-throated Green, Blackburnian, Bay-breasted, Ovenbird, Mourning, and Canada Warblers, Nelson's Sharp-tailed Sparrow, Purple Finch, and White-winged Crossbill.

A Further Comment—If the trip to Grand Manan does not interest you or if you are short on time or money, there is a more economical, less time-consuming way to visit Machias Seal Island. From late May through August there are almost daily trips to Machias Seal Island departing from Jonesport, Maine, or Cutler, Maine. The trips are five to six hours in length with a typical stay on the island of two hours. The 1995 charge for this trip was $50 per person. For information or reservations contact: Captains John or Barna Norton, RR #1, Box 990, Jonesport, ME 04649 or call 207/497-5933, or Captain Andrew Patterson, Bold Coast Charters, P.O. Box 364, Cutler, ME 04626 or call 207/259-4484.

Personal Notes

Razorbill Georges Dremeaux

Trip I

NORTH-CENTRAL UTAH

June, July, or August—3 Days

General

B ear River Migratory Bird Refuge west of Brigham City is well known both for its breeding species and the huge numbers of waterfowl and shorebirds present in late summer and fall. The fine birding areas east of Salt Lake City in the Wasatch-Cache National Forest are not so well known but provide excellent opportunities to see a number of species that are hard to find elsewhere. Combining visits to these two locales during the summer season is a good way to see the best that each has to offer. (There is a trade-off involved, however, with timing. From June to mid-July the mountain passerine breeders are easier to find; after mid-July it's the waterfowl and shorebirds that are more obvious.)

To reach Bear River Migratory Bird Refuge, take Interstate 15 north from Salt Lake City 50 miles to Exit 364 at Brigham City. Exit and continue 1.9 miles to Main Street, turn left and drive 1.6 miles to Forest Street, and turn left again. Follow the road and the signs for about 15 miles to the refuge, all excellent birding—some local birders feel it is better than the refuge itself. When you reach the refuge, take the 12-mile loop-road. The road passes beside impoundments ranging from shallow marsh to deep water, allowing you an opportunity to see a large variety of species.

Time your visit to this refuge depending on your own areas of interest. June and early July are good for seeing the nesting species and their young, while early August has concentrations of waterfowl and shore-birds moving into the refuge. By late August the waterfowl and shorebird numbers can be nothing short of spectacular. The Wasatch-Cache National Forest leg of the trip should be productive all summer.

Wasatch-Cache National Forest consists of 1,219,748 acres with many good birding areas. One of the best day-trips is the Trial Lake/Bald Mountain/Mirror Lakeroute. From Salt Lake City go east on Interstate 80 for approximately 23 miles and turn right (south) onto Highway 40/189, continue south for 11 miles, and then turn left (east) onto Highway 248 for a 9-mile drive to Kamas. From Kamas take Highway 150 east and then north to Trial Lake (26 miles). Bird in and around the campground;

then return to Highway 150 and continue north another 4.5 miles to Bald Mountain Pass. Watch for the Bald Mountain picnic area sign; turn left into the parking lot. This is a good birding area, and there is a trail from the parking lot to the top of Bald Mountain. It is a strenuous two-mile hike but the view is magnificent.

When you leave Bald Mountain, continue on Highway 150 for another 2.5 miles to Mirror Lake. After birding the campground and the surrounding woods, you might want to try the High Line Trail, which starts at the parking area; it is easy walking and provides excellent birding.

Birdfinding Guide

Utah Birds by William H. Behle and Michael L. Perry, although a bit out of date (1975), is still generally accurate for the area.

The Wasatch-Cache National Forest part of this trip is well covered in *Birdfinding in Forty National Forests and Grasslands* (1994). This work

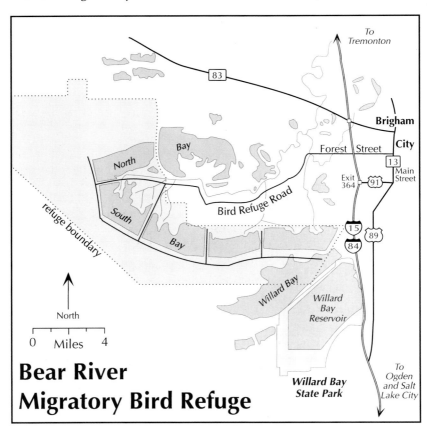

To Tremonton

83

Brigham

Bay

North

Forest Street City

13

Main Street

Exit 364 91

Bird Refuge Road

refuge boundary

South

Bay

15 89

84

North

Willard Bay

0 Miles 4

Willard Bay Reservoir

To Ogden and Salt Lake City

Bear River Migratory Bird Refuge

Willard Bay State Park

was a cooperative effort of the U.S. Department of Agriculture Forest Service and the American Birding Association.

Rare Bird Alert Number

Statewide 801/538-4730

Calliope Hummingbird
Dan Kilby

Species

The species found at Bear River Migratory Bird Refuge and along the 15-mile access road will depend to some degree on water-levels and whether you visit in early or late summer. Some of the nesting species present all summer are Eared, Western, and Clark's Grebes, American White Pelican, Black-crowned Night-Heron, White-faced Ibis, Cinnamon Teal and other waterfowl, Snowy Plover, American Avocet, Black-necked Stilt, Wilson's Phalarope, Franklin's and California Gulls, Caspian, Forster's, and Black Terns, Marsh Wren, and Yellow-headed and Brewer's Blackbirds.

In late summer when migrating waterfowl move into the refuge, in addition to the waterfowl already present the most numerous species are Canada Goose, Green-winged Teal, Northern Pintail, and Canvasback. As the shorebirds move in, the most common peep are Western, Least, and Baird's Sandpiper's. Long-billed Dowitchers are usually present in

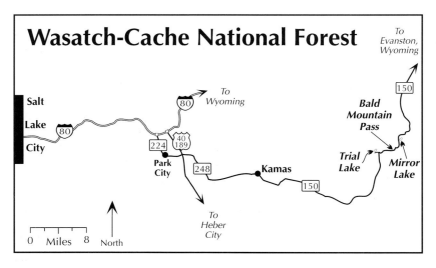

good numbers, and both yellowlegs are seen. There should be plenty of Red-necked Phalaropes, too.

The Wasatch-Cache National Forest tour is excellent for some normally hard-to-locate species. At Trial Lake the trails around the campground and the lake will have Williamson's Sapsucker, Three-toed Woodpecker, Gray Jay, Pine Grosbeak, Cassin's Finch, and Red Crossbill.

At Bald Mountain picnic area you can park in the lot at the Bald Mountain trailhead. Throughout the summer look for Rock Wren, Mountain Bluebird, Townsend's Solitaire, Hermit Thrush, American Pipit, Chipping and White-crowned Sparrows, and Cassin's Finch. Timing is particularly important for Black Rosy-Finch. If you visit in early summer before the snow patches have melted, they can usually be found quite easily. Walk toward the restrooms near the trailhead, up the small rise to your right, down toward the basin, and along the slope that forms the side-face of Bald Mountain. The rosy-finches are usually found among the rocks near the snow banks. If you visit later in the summer, it may be necessary to hike the 2-mile trail to the top of the mountain to see them.

At Mirror Lake both the campground and the surrounding forest offer good birding. Three-toed Woodpecker is possible. The area is suitable for most of the same species as are found at Trial Lake plus Clark's Nutcracker, Mountain Chickadee, Red-breasted Nuthatch, Golden-crowned and Ruby-crowned Kinglets, Lincoln's Sparrow, and Dark-eyed Junco.

The High Line Trail which starts at the parking area and leads into the High Uintas Wilderness Area as well as to trails around the lake provides very good birding. It is an easy walking trail through forest and meadows. Many of the same species can be seen on this trail with the addition of Northern Goshawk, Golden Eagle, Blue Grouse, Calliope Hummingbird, Olive-sided Flycatcher, MacGillivray's Warbler, and Vesper Sparrow.

There are many other good areas to bird in Utah, some fairly near to the locations mentioned. For starters, there are sites for Chukar, Black Swift, Flammulated Owl, and Northern Pygmy-Owl. Utah surely has varied birdlife and warrants a longer stay if you can manage it.

You might consider the following side trip: a five-hour drive west of Salt Lake City lie the Ruby and East Humboldt Ranges of Elko County, Nevada. After June 30, once the snow has melted, birders can attempt to find Himalayan Snowcock, an introduced but established gamebird, in alpine habitat above 9,300 feet. Most snowcock sites are in "wilderness" designated areas, and require strenuous hikes. The shortest hike (about 2 miles) is toward Thomas Peak (El. 11,316 ft). From Lamoille follow the Forest Road 660 into Lower Lamoille Canyon to where it ends 12 miles later. Follow the Island Lake Trail to Island Lake and then hike upward to the southeast cirque of Thomas Peak. An alternative route from the end of Forest Road 660 is to hike to Favre Lake or North Furlong Lake toward Wines Peak (El. 10,893 ft). This is a more difficult, but usually more profitable, hike. Black Rosy-Finches can also be found in Himalayan Snowcock habitat. For more information on conditions, trails, etc., contact the Ruby Mountains Ranger District, P.O. Box 246, Wells, Nevada 89835.

Personal Notes

_____

_____

_____

_____

_____

_____

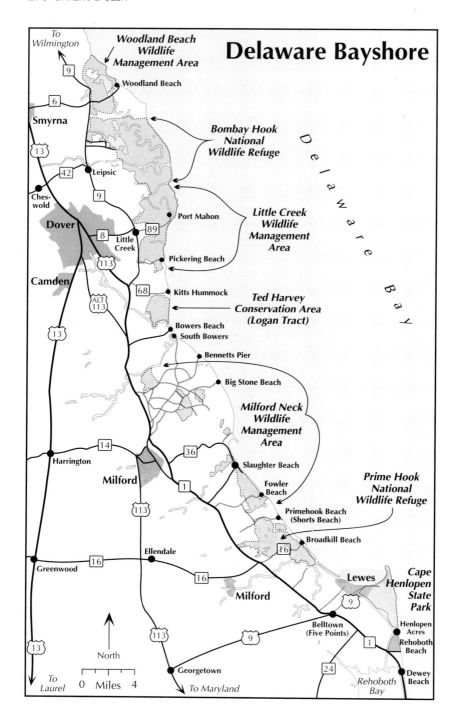

Delaware Bayshore

To Wilmington

Woodland Beach Wildlife Management Area

Woodland Beach

9

6

Smyrna

13

42 Leipsic

9

Ches-wold

Bombay Hook National Wildlife Refuge

Port Mahon

Little Creek Wildlife Management Area

Dover

8 Little Creek

89

113 Pickering Beach

Camden

ALT 113

68 Kitts Hummock

Ted Harvey Conservation Area (Logan Tract)

13

Bowers Beach
South Bowers

Bennetts Pier

Big Stone Beach

Milford Neck Wildlife Management Area

14

36

Harrington

Slaughter Beach

Milford

1

Fowler Beach

Prime Hook National Wildlife Refuge

113

Primehook Beach (Shorts Beach)

16 Ellendale

Broadkill Beach

16

Greenwood

16

Milford

Lewes

Cape Henlopen State Park

9

Henlopen Acres

13

113

Belltown (Five Points)

9

1

Rehoboth Beach

North

0 Miles 4

Georgetown

24

Dewey Beach

To Laurel

To Maryland

Rehoboth Bay

Delaware Bay

Trip J

THE DELAWARE BAYSHORE

Mid-July to Mid-August—3 Days

General

The waters of the Delaware River flow into Delaware Bay on their way to the Atlantic Ocean. This bay lies between portions of New Jersey and Delaware, thus separating two of the finest birding areas on the East Coast. On the New Jersey side of the bay is world-famous Cape May; on the Delaware side is unparalleled shorebirding along 50 miles of bayshore. This southwest shore of the bay is almost entirely lined with easily accessible wildlife management areas, wildlife refuges, beaches, conservation areas, and a state park. The birding is so good during the peak periods of shorebird migration (May and mid-July through September) that this area is challenging the reputation of its across-the-water neighbor. It is likely that there are more rarities recorded annually in this region—encompassing both sides of the Bay to include Cape May Point—than in any other area of similar size short of Attu.

The 50-mile stretch of Delaware Bayshore is the most significant shorebird staging area on the East Coast and is compact enough to enable you to cover it thoroughly from north to south in two or three busy days of birding. May is a good time to bird here, but late July and early August tend to produce the most rarities. If you must travel a long distance to the Delaware Bayshore, late summer is the time to make your first visit.

Some of the rarer species are reported with such regularity and stay in the area so long, that they are almost predictable in occurrence. By communicating with local birders, RBAs, and the staffs at the refuges, you will have a good chance of seeing any rarities present when you visit the bayshore.

A good plan is to start in early morning at Woodland Beach Wildlife Management Area a few miles east of Smyrna, Delaware. After a short visit, continue south on Highway 9 to Bombay Hook National Wildlife Refuge, almost 16,000 acres, three-quarters of which is tidal salt-marsh.

The refuge also has 1,100 acres of fresh-water impoundments. The auto tour route gives good viewing access to the fresh-water impoundments, with observation towers at three locations. All of the areas are viewed from the east and south making this refuge a good place to spend the morning. Curlew Sandpiper and Ruff are both almost regular at Bombay Hook.

When you leave Bombay Hook, continue south to Little Creek and turn left onto Road 89 to Port Mahon. After 1 mile turn right onto a dirt track to view a large impoundment which is part of Little Creek Wildlife Management Area. This location has produced a good number of rarities over the years and is a place where Rufous-necked Stint has been found in late July and early August. Return to Road 89 and turn right to continue to Port Mahon and the bay; birding is good both along the road and at the bay, but the town itself was destroyed in a recent storm.

Return to Highway 9, turn south through Little Creek, and drive about 1.5 miles to the left turn into Little Creek Wildlife Management Area. You will need a scope; views from the observation tower are distant. This location is a prime spot for rarities, and the shorebirds and terns should be studied closely. Curlew Sandpiper, Ruff, and White-winged Tern are among the rarities that have been found here. You can also walk to areas where you can get better views of the birds.

Return again to Highway 9 and turn left (south) for about a mile to the next road on the left. This is Pickering Beach Road; 1.6 miles along it will bring you to the south entrance of Little Creek Wildlife Management Area. Access to this area is by foot; a 0.5-mile damp walk is necessary to reach the ponds where the Whiskered Tern was seen in the summer of 1993.

After returning to Highway 9, turn south for 2 miles and take Road 68 east toward Kitts Hummock. After 2 miles you will reach the entrance (on the right) to the Ted Harvey Conservation Area, Logan Tract. Drive the road to its end. Curlew Sandpiper is a regular here, and the Whiskered Tern also visited here in the summer of 1993.

All of these areas can usually be covered in one day unless you find something really good on which you want to spend extra time.

A second day can be spent driving south on Highway 113 to Milford and then continuing south on Highway 1 to Prime Hook National Wildlife Refuge. During this drive, most of the roads to the bay provide good birding.

At Highway 16 (Broadkill Beach Road) turn left to reach the entrance to Prime Hook National Wildlife Refuge. Prime Hook is not as developed as Bombay Hook; it contains 6,800 acres of fresh marsh, tidal marsh, and water, and another 2,000 acres of timber, brush, and cropland. Most of the access is by foot, and most of the area is under-birded when compared to other places visited earlier in the trip.

After visiting Prime Hook, continue south on Highway 1 to Belltown, turn left to Lewes, and pass through Lewes to Cape Henlopen State Park. This park is good for gulls and terns and is home to nesting Piping Plovers, but a scope may be necessary to see them well.

A third day may be spent taking another look at all of the previously visited areas from Bombay Hook National Wildlife Refuge to the Ted Harvey Conservation Area. This is the best 15 to 20 miles of the Delaware Bayshore.

When planning this trip, an understanding of the tides is helpful. Shorebirding is best in most of these areas at, or near, high tide. You should also visit on weekdays if possible, because the nearby beaches are very popular at this time of year, with non-birders and traffic slowing you down on weekends. Take your scope; insect repellent is a must. Accommodations are plentiful in nearby Dover, and campsites are found at Cape Henlopen State Park.

Birdfinding Guide

Finding Birds in the National Capital Area by Claudia Wilds (1992) covers Bombay Hook National Wildlife Refuge and the Little Creek Wildlife Area.

Birding the Delaware Valley Region by John J. Harding and Justin J. Harding (1980) is somewhat dated, but still useful.

Rare Bird Alert Number

Delaware 610/567-2473

Species

There are other species you might see in the trip area, but the primary targets are shorebirds, gulls, and terns. An average trip should produce over 20 species of shorebirds, 4 species of gulls, and 3 or 4 terns.

Two species that should be seen that fall outside of these families are the recently split Salt-marsh Sharp-tailed Sparrow and Seaside Sparrow. Both should be found without traveling outside the planned itinerary.

Of course, the real excitement is produced by the very real possibility of bagging Curlew Sandpiper or Ruff or some even-rarer bird. A few of the rarities seen in this season over the past few years have been: Rufous-necked Stint, Sharp-tailed Sandpiper, Whiskered Tern, and

White-winged Tern. Delaware birders are patiently awaiting their next shocking discovery; maybe it will come during your visit!

Personal Notes

_____

_____

_____

_____

_____

_____

_____

_____

_____

_____

_____

_____

Trip K

CAPE MAY, NEW JERSEY

September—3 Days

General

The Cape May Peninsula is a standard route and natural migrant trap for birds flying south. The peninsula is bordered on the west by Delaware Bay and on the east and south by the Atlantic Ocean. This geography creates a natural land funnel, catching and channeling southbound birds to the end of the peninsula at Cape May Point. The hesitation of some birds to cross the water causes a stack-up, with some of the hawks actually moving back north and resuming their trip south down the Delaware side of the bay. The different species migrating through Cape May peak at different times in the fall season. Shorebirds are at their largest numbers in late July and August, warblers from late August to early October, and raptors in late September, October, and early November. A trip in September is best for overall species diversity; you will still have the later shorebirds and the early raptors (hawks start through Cape May in late August even though they do not peak until October). Some birders prefer to visit Cape May in October, combining the trip with a visit to Hawk Mountain, Pennsylvania (Trip L), and a visit to the Brigantine Division of the Edwin B. Forsythe National Wildlife Refuge just north of Atlantic City. For the overall feel of Cape May, late September is the best time for a first visit.

Cape May Point State Park is located at the southern tip of the Cape May Peninsula about 2 miles west of the city of Cape May. The park, containing 190 acres, is a shoreline region of dunes, fresh-water marsh, ponds, and woods. It may be reached via the Garden State Parkway or Highway 9. This park is a favorite of birders, partly because the official hawk-monitoring site is there, but it should be realized that all of the Cape May peninsula offers great birding during both migrations.

An excellent place for early morning passerine migration—vireos, warblers, grosbeaks, and sparrows—is Higbee Beach Wildlife Management Area, at the west end of New England Road. Unfortunately, it is usually closed until after Labor Day in an attempt to control illegal activities there. **?**

Birdfinding Guide

The Birds of Cape May by David A. Sibley (1993) is an extensively annotated list of the birds of Cape May with additional details on birdfinding.

Bird-finding Guide to New Jersey by William J. Boyle, Jr. (1986) covers this area well and has a separate section on hawk-watching.

Rare Bird Alert Numbers

Cape May 609/884-2626
Statewide 908/766-2661

Species

With over 400 species recorded on the peninsula, the species you might see at the peak of fall migration are literally too numerous to mention. All of the eastern warblers that range as far north as Cape May are seen each fall with the exception of Cerulean, and even it is recorded in some years. This means that there are 35 species of warblers which will be seen on the peninsula sometime during fall migration. These

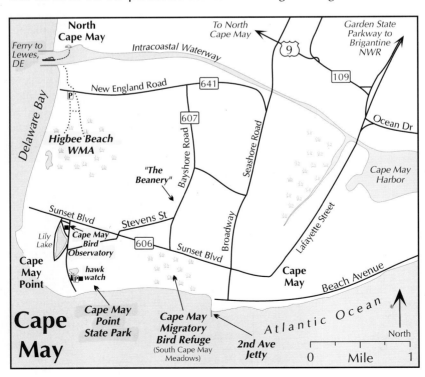

warblers, wearing their fall colors, are more confusing than in spring and require more study to identify; this opportunity to see the warblers' fall plumage is one of the most compelling reasons to bird Cape May between late August and early October.

At dawn be at Higbee Beach for a great migrant show. Then, after a few hours, move to other sites on the peninsula. Be aware of the weather; you will need a westerly component to the wind, especially after a cold front. Otherwise, it can be slow birding, but the butterflying can tide you over.

A second, equally important reason to bird Cape May is the opportunity to see 16 diurnal raptors. The best place is the hawk-watch platform at Bunker Pond in the state park.

Beyond these two groups, and not counting strictly pelagic species, there are over 225 more species that are seen each fall, ranging from abundant to occasional. A birder who spends three full birding days at Cape May should see over 150 species, and with luck and perseverance could exceed 200. A fall trip to Cape May is pure enjoyment.

Personal Notes

_____

_____

_____

_____

_____

_____

_____

_____

Trip L

HAWK MOUNTAIN, PENNSYLVANIA

October—3 Days

General

Hawk Mountain Sanctuary in eastern Pennsylvania was established in 1934 with the primary objective of promoting the conservation of birds of prey. The sanctuary consists of 2,200 acres straddling the Kittatinny Ridge of the Appalachian Mountains and abutting the Appalachian Trail. Hawk Mountain Sanctuary has become world famous as a hawk-observation point and is popular with birders and non-birders alike. The sanctuary is not government-funded; it is privately operated by the Hawk Mountain Sanctuary Association, Rt. 2, Kempton, PA 19529, phone 610/756-6961. Write to the above address for membership information; you will have the satisfaction of helping to support this worthwhile sanctuary.)

To reach the sanctuary from Interstate 78 west from Allentown, take the Lenhartsville exit (Route 143), go north 4 miles, turn left (west) onto Hawk Mountain Road, and drive a bit over 6 miles to the entrance.

When you reach the sanctuary, you will pay a small entrance fee if you are not an association member. The trail to North Lookout is less than a mile long. North Lookout is a large sandstone outcropping, and from mid-August to early December each year an average of 24,000 birds of prey pass by this point. A day spent at North Lookout when air temperatures are cool and there are brisk west or northwesterly winds can be a fantastic experience.

There are restrooms along the trail; water and fruit juice are available at the visitor center, but bring your own food. There are lots of nice places to eat a sack lunch, but there is absolutely no food available in the immediate vicinity.

It is best to spend three days in the area if you have reasonable flight weather. There is no way to predict the weather and no assurance that there will be a good flight on the day when you visit. Some birders try to hedge their bets by visiting two days at Hawk Mountain and then travel to nearby Bake Oven Knob for one day. Personnel at Hawk Mountain can direct you to Bake Oven Knob; it is only 16 miles as the hawk flies, but for birders it's a little farther.

Birdfinding Guides

A birdfinding guide is not a necessary for this area. However, a good hawk identification guide can certainly help.

Rare Bird Alert Numbers

Hawk Mountain . . .   610/756-6961
*This is an important daily taped update
(operating from late afternoon to 9 am the next morning)
on local weather and significant migration events.*

Allentown 610/252-3455
Philadelphia 610/567-2473

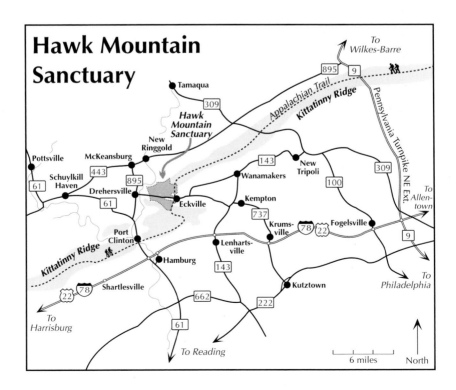

Species

The greatest variety of raptors can be seen in October. Species that should be seen include Black and Turkey Vultures, Osprey, Northern Harrier, Sharp-shinned, and Cooper's Hawks, Northern Goshawk, Red-shouldered, Broad-winged and Red-tailed Hawks, American Kestrel, and Merlin.

With a couple of good flight days you may also see Bald Eagle, Rough-legged Hawk, Golden Eagle, and Peregrine Falcon. The average birder with three days in the field will see 14 species of raptors.

Personal Notes

Trip M

COASTAL MASSACHUSETTS

Early December—5 Days

General

E ach winter coastal Massachusetts plays host to at least a dozen species (mostly "northern" species) that many birders either have not seen, have seldom seen, or have seen all too briefly. This is an excellent excuse for any birder to travel to Massachusetts. Add to this the useful facts that the area is small enough so that distances between locations are short and that you are never far from gas, food, and lodging. The only difficulty to be experienced on this trip is cold temperatures, and by dressing for the cold you can enjoy a pleasant winter outing.

The best itinerary to follow is to spend two-and-a-half days north of Boston, birding the following areas: Salisbury Beach State Park, the mouth of the Merrimack River at Newburyport, North Plum Island Jetty, Parker River National Wildlife Refuge, and, on Cape Ann: Andrews Point, Halibut Point, Folly Cove, Rockport Harbor, Bass Rocks, Eastern Point and Dog Bar Breakwater, Gloucester Harbor, and the Hammond Castle area. A good map of the area will show all of these locations. Then bird your way down the coast to Cape Cod for half a day. Some of the better places to try along the coast are the Marblehead, Nahant, and Plymouth areas. Your final two days should be spent on Cape Cod.

It is best to locate lodging somewhere near the elbow of Cape Cod. Most of the best birding spots are on the arm of the Cape (where the Cape goes back north and then curls to the west), but it is more economical to stay in the Harwich or Chatham areas than farther out on the Cape.

Any of the beach areas can be good for sea ducks and alcids, but some places that you should not miss include: Nauset Beach in Orleans; Fort Hill Marsh, First Encounter Beach, and Coast Guard Beach in Eastham; Wellfleet Harbor; Coast Guard Beach at North Truro; and Race Point, Herring Cove Beach, and Provincetown Harbor at Provincetown. The

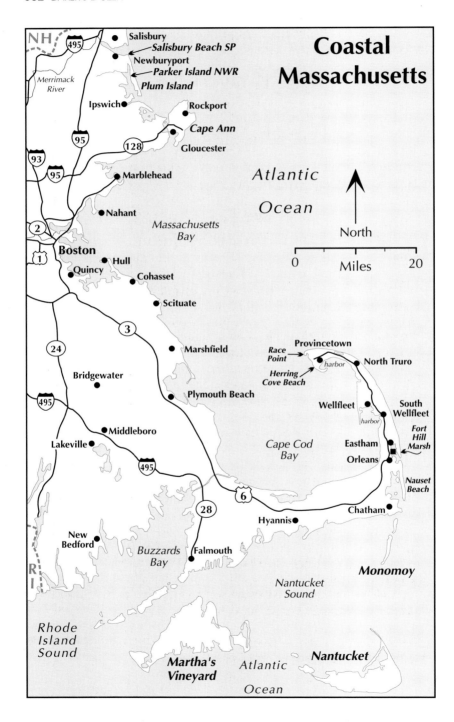

Coastal Massachusetts

NH

495

Merrimack River

Salisbury
Salisbury Beach SP
Newburyport
Parker Island NWR
Plum Island

95

Ipswich

Rockport

Cape Ann

128

Gloucester

95

93

95

Marblehead

Nahant

Massachusetts Bay

Atlantic

Ocean

North

0   Miles   20

2

1

Boston

Hull

Quincy

Cohasset

Scituate

3

Marshfield

24

Bridgewater

495

Plymouth Beach

Race Point
Provincetown
harbor
North Truro

Herring Cove Beach

Wellfleet
South Wellfleet
harbor

Middleboro

Lakeville

495

6

Cape Cod Bay

Eastham
Orleans

Fort Hill Marsh

Nauset Beach

28

Hyannis

Chatham

New Bedford

Buzzards Bay

Falmouth

Monomoy

RI

Nantucket Sound

Rhode Island Sound

Martha's Vineyard

Atlantic Ocean

Nantucket

entire upper arm of the Cape is good birding, so explore it thoroughly. Any detailed map of the Cape will identify all of the above locations.

Birdfinding Guides

A Birder's Guide to Eastern Massachusetts, an ABA Birdfinding Guide (1994), is a compilation of revised articles from the magazine *Bird Observer*. This guide covers the coastal (and many inland) birding sites in great detail.

Birding Cape Cod is a co-effort of the Cape Cod Bird Club and the Massachusetts Audubon Society (1990).

Rare Bird Alert Number

Boston 617/259-8805

Species

This area is a good place to see a representative sample of northern and northeastern species. The following list covers most of these species and gives an idea of where they might be found.

Red-necked Grebe—Uncommon; should be at Cape Ann or on the drive south at Marblehead or Nahant.

Northern Gannet—Should see from Cape Ann (e.g., Andrews Point) and off Cape Cod.

Mute Swan—Very common; may show up anywhere but usually around Plymouth or on Cape Cod.

Brant—Common at Newburyport, or on Cape Cod in the Brewster and Eastham areas.

King Eider—Very uncommon winter visitor, but may turn up at Cape Ann, Nahant, or outer Cape Cod.

Harlequin Duck—Uncommon winter visitor; most likely places are Cape Ann, Nahant, and Orleans on Cape Cod.

Barrow's Goldeneye—An uncommon winter visitor, but possible anywhere on the coast, especially Newburyport and Cape Ann areas.

Rough-legged Hawk—Salisbury Beach State Park and Plum Island are the best locations.

Purple Sandpiper—Locally common; less likely south of Boston. Best locations are Merrimack River mouth, Cape Ann, Marblehead, and Nahant.

Little Gull—Scarce in winter, but can be found with patience. Try Newburyport Harbor in flocks of Bonaparte's Gulls.

Snowy Owl
Louise Zemaitis

Common Black-headed Gull—Uncommon, but can usually be found in the gull flock on Lewis Lake in Winthrop. Sometimes at other locations, such as Newburyport Harbor or Revere.

Iceland Gull—Locally common; look for it especially at Newburyport Harbor, North Plum Island, Cape Ann, and Provincetown Harbor on Cape Cod.

Glaucous Gull—Uncommon, but sometimes found at Plum Island jetties, Gloucester Harbor on Cape Ann, and Provincetown Harbor on Cape Cod.

Dovekie—Rare most years, but should be watched for especially after any coastal storm, and especially from Cape Ann.

Thick-billed Murre—Another alcid that regularly shows up after coastal storms or with onshore winds. May be found at Cape Ann in small numbers.

Razorbill—Regular; should be seen at Cape Ann and Provincetown Harbor. Most common alcid on this trip.

Black Guillemot—Should be seen easily at Cape Ann.

Snowy Owl—Annually present at Salisbury Beach State Park and on Plum Island; ask park staff about this one. Sometimes visible at Boston's Logan Airport from Winthrop.

Northern Shrike—Rare, but possible at Plum Island.

Salt-marsh Sharp-tailed Sparrow—In winter, best found at Fort Hill Marsh in Eastham on Cape Cod.

Lapland Longspur—Usually seen by searching carefully at Salisbury Beach State Park or Parker River National Wildlife Refuge.

In addition, Red-throated Loon, Great Cormorant, Common Eider, Oldsquaw, Black, Surf, and White-winged Scoters, and Snow Bunting are all common and each should be seen several times in the trip area.

Personal Notes

_____

_____

_____

_____

THE BIRDFINDER CHART

GENERAL

Using this book as a trip planning guide, you can either make the nineteen separate trips over a period of years or spend a very exciting year doing them all consecutively. The nineteen trips outlined in this book visit some (though not nearly all) of the best birding hotspots in the ABA Area. The trips provide the traveling birder with more than the chance to see the 650-odd listed species, or build multiple state lists. He or she will see much of North America's beauty, make friends that will last a lifetime, have experiences that will become priceless memories, and vastly improve the quality time in his or her life. Using the hints in the previous chapter, the birder can visit another thirteen major sites for birds, another source for great birding experiences.

SPECIES

The trips and species outlined in this book are realistic goals, but there are no guarantees. If you put a reasonable amount of effort into seeing the birds, use the rare bird alerts, read the essential birdfinding guides, and allow the local birders to impart some of their knowledge to you, no more than 5 percent of the 650-odd species should be missed. This 5 percent can be offset to some degree by staying tuned to the birders' grapevine, by subscribing to the North American Rare Bird Alert, and simply by spending more time in the field.

Additionally, if you are able to include Attu, Gambell, Barrow, and the Pribilofs in your travels, you will approach 700 species and might, with a little luck, surpass that number. The "Baker's Dozen" locations in the last chapter will be added insurance for a large list and an all-round wonderful birding experience.

THE BIRDFINDER CHART

The following chart lets you determine quickly the likelihood of seeing any species on each of the birding trips outlined in the first nineteen chapters of this book. (All the birds of North America are included, regardless of whether or not they appear in the chapterss of this book.) **The chart also serves as an operational species index for the book.**

There is room along the right side of the Birdfinder chart to add the date and place of your individual species sightings.

Understanding the ABA Codes in the Chart:

Code 1 and 2 are species which occur routinely in North America and are easily found. (Code 2 birds are simply a bit more difficult to find than are Code 1 birds because of their localized distribution or habitat.)

Code 3 birds occur annually in the ABA area but are extremely local, are difficult to see, or have a very short season when they may be readily observed.

Code 4 birds probably occur more-or-less regularly, but either there is no place in our area where they can be expected or their regular North American range is so remote that reaching it is very difficult.

Code 5—a code used rarely in this book—indicates that the species are true accidentals, with little predictability of occurrence again.

Understanding the Symbols in the Chart:

Key ● : These species are the primary targets for a particular trip. They are species that can be seen only in that specific area or that are more likely to be seen on that trip as opposed to a later trip. The classification of "key" has nothing to do with the rarity of the species.

Probable ◉ : These species will probably be seen without any special effort. If they are not seen on that trip, they will easily be seen on a subsequent trip.

Possible ◎ : This group includes species that take extra effort or luck to locate, but which are realistically possible.

Remotely Possible ○ : These species are remotely possible and are not to be expected. The birder should, however, be aware of their possible presence in the trip area.

Most of the birds which are mentioned in the "outposts" portion of the Alaska chapter—Chapter 11—are very uncommon. Therefore, they are not included in the running total of birds seen through the nineteen trips. However, to assist the reader in appreciating their occurrence, these species are shaded in the following chart under the Alaska column.

Chapter 20, "The Baker's Dozen," is coded differently from the other chapters. This chapter lightly covers thirteen additional quality birding locations which are lettered "A" through "M." Each of these letters assigned to a species means that that species is mentioned in that lettered segment of Chapter 20.

Legend

●	Key Species
●	Probable Species
⊙	Possible Species
○	Remotely Possible Species

Location	chapter	date	Red-throated Loon (1)	Arctic Loon (4)	Pacific Loon (1)	Common Loon (1)	Yellow-billed Loon (2)	Least Grebe (2)	Pied-billed Grebe (1)	Horned Grebe (1)	Red-necked Grebe (1)	Eared Grebe (1)	Western Grebe (1)	Clark's Grebe (1)	Wandering Albatross (5)	Short-tailed Albatross (4)	Black-footed Albatross (3)	Laysan Albatross (4)
The Baker's Dozen	20		M			H					M	−	−	−				
Niagara River Area	19	Dec				●			⊙	●		○						
Maine to Nova Scotia	18		⊙			●			●	⊙	⊙							
Central & Southern California	17	Sep	⊙		⊙	●			●			●	●	●			⊙	
Southeastern Arizona	16	Aug							⊙									
W. Wash. & SW British Columbia	15	Jul	⊙		⊙	⊙			●	⊙	⊙	⊙	⊙	○			●	
West Texas	14								●									
Colorado	13								●		○		●	⊙				
Minnesota & North Dakota	12	Jun				●			●	●	●	●	●	⊙				
Alaska	11		●	●	●	●	◌			●	●						○	
Southeastern Arizona	10	May							●									
Coastal North Carolina	9		○			⊙			○									
Florida Keys & Dry Tortugas	8	Apr				○					○							
Texas	7					⊙		⊙	●	⊙		●						
Colorado	6	Mar				○			●	⊙		●	⊙	⊙				
South Florida	5					●			●	●								
Lower Rio Grande Valley	4	Feb				○		●	●			●	⊙					
Northeastern Minnesota	3																	
Oklahoma	2	Jan							●	○		○						
Northern & Central California	1		●		●	●	○		●	●	●	●	●	●			⊙	○

Species Seen — place / date

ABA Code

Legend (Species Seen — date / place)

- ● Key Species
- ◉ Probable Species
- ⊙ Possible Species
- ○ Remotely Possible Species

chapter	month	Species	Black-browed Albatross	Shy Albatross	Yellow-nosed Albatross	Northern Fulmar	Black-capped Petrel	Mottled Petrel	Murphy's Petrel	Herald Petrel	Cook's Petrel	Steineger's Petrel	Streaked Shearwater	Cory's Shearwater	Pink-footed Shearwater	Flesh-footed Shearwater	Greater Shearwater	Wedge-tailed Shearwater
20		The Baker's Dozen															H	
19	Dec	Niagara River Area																
18		Maine to Nova Scotia				○	◉									⊙	●	
17	Sep	Central & Southern California					●							○	●	●		○
16		Southeastern Arizona																
15	Aug	W. Wash. & SW British Columbia				⊙									●	⊙		
14		West Texas																
13	Jul	Colorado																
12		Minnesota & North Dakota																
11	Jun	Alaska				●												
10		Southeastern Arizona																
9	May	Coastal North Carolina				○	●			○				●		●		
8		Florida Keys & Dry Tortugas					○											
7	Apr	Texas																
6		Colorado																
5	Mar	South Florida																
4		Lower Rio Grande Valley																
3	Feb	Northeastern Minnesota																
2		Oklahoma																
1	Jan	Northern & Central California				●									⊙	○		
		ABA Code	5	5	4	2	3	4	4	5	4	5	5	2	2	3	2	5

Legend

- ● Key Species
- ◉ Probable Species
- ◎ Possible Species
- ○ Remotely Possible Species

Columns for user notes: Species Seen / place / date

chapter	Location	Month	Buller's Shearwater	Sooty Shearwater	Short-tailed Shearwater	Manx Shearwater	Black-vented Shearwater	Little Shearwater	Audubon's Shearwater	Wilson's Storm-Petrel	White-faced Storm-Petrel	British Storm-Petrel	Fork-tailed Storm-Petrel	Leach's Storm-Petrel	Ashy Storm-Petrel	Band-rumped Storm-Petrel	Wedge-rumped Storm-Petrel	Black Storm-Petrel
20	The Baker's Dozen					H		H			H							
19	Niagara River Area	Dec																
18	Maine to Nova Scotia	Sep		●		●				●				●				
17	Central & Southern California		●	◉	◎		●			◎			◎	◉	●		○	●
16	Southeastern Arizona	Aug																
15	W. Wash. & SW British Columbia	Jul	◎	●									●	◎				
14	West Texas																	
13	Colorado																	
12	Minnesota & North Dakota	Jun																
11	Alaska			◎	●								●					
10	Southeastern Arizona	May																
9	Coastal North Carolina			●		○			●	●				●		●		
8	Florida Keys & Dry Tortugas	Apr							●	◎				○				
7	Texas																	
6	Colorado	Mar																
5	South Florida																	
4	Lower Rio Grande Valley	Feb																
3	Northeastern Minnesota																	
2	Oklahoma	Jan																
1	Northern & Central California			●	●		●						○		○			
ABA Code			3	1	2	2	2	5	2	2	4	5	2	2	2	4	5	2

Legend (Species Seen — date / place):
- ● Key Species
- ◑ Probable Species
- ◉ Possible Species
- ○ Remotely Possible Species

Chapter	Month	Location	Least Storm-Petrel	White-tailed Tropicbird	Red-billed Tropicbird	Red-tailed Tropicbird	Masked Booby	Blue-footed Booby	Brown Booby	Red-footed Booby	Northern Gannet	American White Pelican	Brown Pelican	Great Cormorant	Double-crested Cormorant	Neotropic Cormorant	Brandt's Cormorant	Pelagic Cormorant
20		The Baker's Dozen									H-M		I		H-M			
19	Dec	Niagara River Area													◉			
18		Maine to Nova Scotia									●			●	◉			
17	Sep	Central & Southern California	●		◉			○	○			●	●		●		●	●
16	Aug	Southeastern Arizona													◉	◉		
15	Jul	W. Wash. & SW British Columbia										○	●		●		●	●
14		West Texas																
13		Colorado										●			●			
12	Jun	Minnesota & North Dakota										●			●			
11		Alaska													●			◉
10	May	Southeastern Arizona													○	○		
9		Coastal North Carolina		○			○				●	●	○		●			
8	Apr	Florida Keys & Dry Tortugas			◉		●		●	○	●	●	●		●			
7		Texas									◉	●	●		●	●		
6	Mar	Colorado													●			
5		South Florida										●	●		●			
4	Feb	Lower Rio Grande Valley										●			●	●		
3		Northeastern Minnesota																
2	Jan	Oklahoma													◉			
1		Northern & Central California										●			●		●	●
ABA Code			4	4	4	5	3	4	3	4	1	1	1	1	1	1	1	1

Key: ● Key Species ● Probable Species ⊙ Possible Species ○ Remotely Possible Species

Species Seen: place / date	chapter	date	Red-faced Cormorant	Anhinga	Magnificent Frigatebird	Great Frigatebird	Lesser Frigatebird	American Bittern	Least Bittern	Yellow Bittern	Great Blue Heron	Great Egret	Chinese Egret	Little Egret	Western Reef-Heron	Snowy Egret	Little Blue Heron	Tricolored Heron
The Baker's Dozen	20							F										
Niagara River Area	19	Dec									⊙							
Maine to Nova Scotia	18	Sep						●			●					⊙	○	
Central & Southern California	17	Sep			○			⊙	●		●	●				●	⊙	○
Southeastern Arizona	16	Aug									⊙					○		
W. Wash. & SW British Columbia	15	Jul						⊙			●	○						
West Texas	14	Jul									⊙					○		
Colorado	13	Jun						⊙			●					●		
Minnesota & North Dakota	12	Jun						●	○		●	⊙				⊙		
Alaska	11	Jun	●								○							
Southeastern Arizona	10	May									⊙	●				○		
Coastal North Carolina	9	May							⊙		●	●				●	●	●
Florida Keys & Dry Tortugas	8	Apr			●				○		●	●				●	●	●
Texas	7	Apr		●				●	●		●	●				●	●	●
Colorado	6	Mar									●							
South Florida	5	Mar		●				●	⊙		●	●				●	●	●
Lower Rio Grande Valley	4	Feb		⊙				⊙			●	●				●	⊙	●
Northeastern Minnesota	3	Feb																
Oklahoma	2	Jan						●			●							
Northern & Central California	1	Jan						●			●	●				●		
ABA Code			2	1	1	5	5	1	1	5	1	1	5	5	5	1	1	1

Legend:

- ● Key Species
- ● Probable Species
- ⊙ Possible Species
- ○ Remotely Possible Species

Chapter	No.	Month / place	Reddish Egret	Cattle Egret	Green Heron	Black-crowned Night-Heron	Yellow-crowned Night-Heron	White Ibis	Scarlet Ibis	Glossy Ibis	White-faced Ibis	Roseate Spoonbill	Jabiru	Wood Stork	Greater Flamingo	Fulvous Whistling-Duck	Black-bellied Whistling-Duck	Tundra Swan
ABA Code			1	1	1	1	1	1	5	1	1	1	5	1	4	1	1	1
The Baker's Dozen	20	A-F				—					—							A-F
Niagara River Area	19	Dec				○												○
Maine to Nova Scotia	18	Sep			⊙	●	○			○								
Central & Southern California	17	Sep	○	●	●	●	●				●	○		⊙		⊙		
Southeastern Arizona	16	Aug				⊙	⊙										●	
W. Wash. & SW British Columbia	15	Jul				●	⊙											
West Texas	14					⊙	⊙											
Colorado	13					⊙	○	●										
Minnesota & North Dakota	12	Jun				⊙	●	●										
Alaska	11																	◉
Southeastern Arizona	10	May				⊙	⊙									●		
Coastal North Carolina	9	May		●	●	●	●	⊙	●	●								○
Florida Keys & Dry Tortugas	8	Apr	●	●	●	⊙	●	●		⊙	○		○					
Texas	7	Apr	●	●	●	●	●	●			●	●				●	●	
Colorado	6	Mar				⊙												○
South Florida	5	Mar	●	●	●	●	●	●			●		●	○		⊙		
Lower Rio Grande Valley	4	Feb	●	●	⊙	●	○	○			●	⊙				○	⊙	
Northeastern Minnesota	3	Feb																
Oklahoma	2	Jan																
Northern & Central California	1	Jan		⊙	⊙	●				⊙								●

Legend:
- ● Key Species
- ◉ Probable Species
- ⊙ Possible Species
- ○ Remotely Possible Species

Location	Chapter	Month	Species Seen (date / place)	Whooper Swan	Trumpeter Swan	Mute Swan	Bean Goose	Pink-footed Goose	Greater White-fronted Goose	Snow Goose	Ross's Goose	Emperor Goose	Brant	Barnacle Goose	Canada Goose	Muscovy Duck	Wood Duck	Green-winged Teal	Baikal Teal
The Baker's Dozen	20					G	D-M		A-B	A-B	A-B	A	M		A-B-I			—	
Niagara River Area	19	Dec								○			○		●				
Maine to Nova Scotia	18	Sep								○			○		●		●	●	
Central & Southern California	17								○			⊙			⊙		⊙	●	
Southeastern Arizona	16	Aug																	
W. Wash. & SW British Columbia	15	Jul											○		●		●	⊙	
West Texas	14																		
Colorado	13														●		○	●	
Minnesota & North Dakota	12	Jun													●		●	●	
Alaska	11				●		▨		⊙		⊙	⊙			●			●	
Southeastern Arizona	10	May																⊙	
Coastal North Carolina	9									○		○	○		⊙				
Florida Keys & Dry Tortugas	8	Apr																	
Texas	7								⊙	⊙					⊙	⊙	●	●	
Colorado	6	Mar							○	●	○				●		○	●	
South Florida	5																●	●	
Lower Rio Grande Valley	4	Feb							●	●	○				●	●	○	●	
Northeastern Minnesota	3																		
Oklahoma	2	Jan							●	⊙	⊙				●		●	●	
Northern & Central California	1								⊙	●	●	○	●		●		●	●	
ABA Code				4	1	1	4	5	1	1	1	2	1	4	1	4	1	1	5

Legend:
- ● Key Species
- ◉ Probable Species
- ⊙ Possible Species
- ○ Remotely Possible Species

Species Seen: date / place

ABA Codes by species: Falcated Teal 5, American Black Duck 1, Mottled Duck 1, Mallard 1, Spot-billed Duck 5, White-cheeked Pintail 4, Northern Pintail 1, Garganey 4, Blue-winged Teal 1, Cinnamon Teal 1, Northern Shoveler 1, Gadwall 1, Eurasian Wigeon 3, American Wigeon 1, Common Pochard 4, Canvasback 1

#	Chapter	Month	Falcated Teal	Am. Black Duck	Mottled Duck	Mallard	Spot-billed Duck	White-cheeked Pintail	Northern Pintail	Garganey	Blue-winged Teal	Cinnamon Teal	Northern Shoveler	Gadwall	Eurasian Wigeon	American Wigeon	Common Pochard	Canvasback
20	The Baker's Dozen								—		G-I					A		—
19	Niagara River Area	Dec		●		●			●					●	○	●		●
18	Maine to Nova Scotia	Sep		●		●			⊙		●		⊙	⊙	○	◉		
17	Central & Southern California	Sep				●			●			⊙	●	●		●		○
16	Southeastern Arizona	Aug				⊙			○			⊙	○					
15	W. Wash. & SW British Columbia	Jul				●			⊙		●	●	⊙	●		⊙		⊙
14	West Texas	Jul				●												
13	Colorado					●			●		●	●	⊙	⊙		⊙		○
12	Minnesota & North Dakota	Jun		●		●			●		●	○	●	●		●		●
11	Alaska		░			●			●	░	○		●	⊙	⊙	●		⊙
10	Southeastern Arizona	May				●					●	●	○					
9	Coastal North Carolina	May			●	⊙					●		●					
8	Florida Keys & Dry Tortugas	Apr							⊙									
7	Texas	Apr			●	●			●		●	○	●	●		●		⊙
6	Colorado	Mar				●			●		●	●	●	●		●		●
5	South Florida	Mar	○	●	●	●		○	⊙		●	●	●	●		●		●
4	Lower Rio Grande Valley	Feb		●	⊙				●		●	●	●	●		●		●
3	Northeastern Minnesota					●												
2	Oklahoma	Jan			●	●			●		○	⊙	●			●		⊙
1	Northern & Central California	Jan				●			●		●	●	●	●	●	●		●

Key: ● Key Species ◉ Probable Species ◎ Possible Species ○ Remotely Possible Species

Species Seen / place / date	chapter	Month	Redhead	Ring-necked Duck	Tufted Duck	Greater Scaup	Lesser Scaup	Common Eider	King Eider	Spectacled Eider	Steller's Eider	Harlequin Duck	Oldsquaw	Black Scoter	Surf Scoter	White-winged Scoter	Common Goldeneye	Barrow's Goldeneye
The Baker's Dozen	20							H-M	M			G-M	F-M	F-M	F-M	F-M		G-M
Niagara River Area	19	Dec	◉	◉	○	◉	◉		◎			○	◉	◎	◎	◉	◉	○
Maine to Nova Scotia	18		○	◉		◎	○	●	○			○	◎	◎	◎	○		
Central & Southern California	17	Sep	◎	○			○					○	○	●	◎	○		
Southeastern Arizona	16	Aug																
W. Wash. & SW British Columbia	15		◎	◎		○	◎					●		●	●			◎
West Texas	14	Jul																
Colorado	13		◉	○			◎											
Minnesota & North Dakota	12	Jun	◉	◉			◉										○	
Alaska	11		◎	◎		●	◎	●	○	○	●	●	●	●	●	●	◎	●
Southeastern Arizona	10	May																
Coastal North Carolina	9																	
Florida Keys & Dry Tortugas	8	Apr																
Texas	7		●				●									○		
Colorado	6	Mar	◉	◉			◉										●	○
South Florida	5			◉			●											
Lower Rio Grande Valley	4	Feb	◉	◉			●										○	
Northeastern Minnesota	3											○	◎				●	
Oklahoma	2	Jan	◉	◉	○		◉										●	
Northern & Central California	1		●	●	●	●	◉		○			●	●	●	●	●	◉	●
ABA Code			1	1	3	1	1	1	1	3	2	1	1	1	1	1	1	1

Key

- ● Key Species
- ◉ Probable Species
- ⊙ Possible Species
- ○ Remotely Possible Species

Region	chapter	month	Bufflehead	Smew	Hooded Merganser	Common Merganser	Red-breasted Merganser	Ruddy Duck	Masked Duck	Black Vulture	Turkey Vulture	Osprey	Hook-billed Kite	American Swallow-tailed Kite	White-tailed Kite	Snail Kite	Mississippi Kite	Bald Eagle
The Baker's Dozen	20						H			L	L	L						A-B-L
Niagara River Area	19	Dec	●		●	●	●											⊙
Maine to Nova Scotia	18	Sep	⊙		⊙	●	●	○			⊙	●						●
Central & Southern California	17		○			○	○	⊙	●		●	●			●			
Southeastern Arizona	16	Aug						⊙		○	●				○		⊙	
W. Wash. & SW British Columbia	15	Jul	○			⊙	●		⊙		●	●			○			●
West Texas	14									⊙	●							
Colorado	13						●		●		⊙	●						○
Minnesota & North Dakota	12	Jun	○			●	○		●			○						●
Alaska	11		●	▓		●	●					○						●
Southeastern Arizona	10	May						⊙		⊙	●				○		⊙	
Coastal North Carolina	9							⊙		⊙	⊙	●						
Florida Keys & Dry Tortugas	8	Apr					⊙	⊙	○	⊙	●	●						
Texas	7		○				●	●	○	●	●	●	○	○	●		●	⊙
Colorado	6	Mar	●			○	●	⊙			⊙							⊙
South Florida	5					○	●	●	○	●	●	●		●	○	●		●
Lower Rio Grande Valley	4	Feb	●		●	○	●	●	○	●	●	⊙	●		●			⊙
Northeastern Minnesota	3					●												
Oklahoma	2	Jan	●		●	●		⊙										●
Northern & Central California	1		●		●	●	●	●			●	●			⊙			⊙
ABA Code			1	4	1	1	1	1	4	1	1	1	3	1	1	2	1	1

Species Seen: place / date

● Key Species
◉ Probable Species
◎ Possible Species
○ Remotely Possible Species

chapter	month	Location	White-tailed Eagle	Steller's Sea-Eagle	Northern Harrier	Sharp-shinned Hawk	Cooper's Hawk	Northern Goshawk	Crane Hawk	Common Black-Hawk	Harris's Hawk	Gray Hawk	Roadside Hawk	Red-shouldered Hawk	Broad-winged Hawk	Short-tailed Hawk	Swainson's Hawk	White-tailed Hawk
		ABA Code	4	5	1	1	1	1	5	2	1	2	5	1	1	2	1	2
		✓																
		Species Seen: date																
		Species Seen: place																
20		The Baker's Dozen			B-L	A-L	A-L	A-G-H-I-L						L	L			
19	Dec	Niagara River Area			◎	◎	◎	◎										
18	Sep	Maine to Nova Scotia			◉	◉	◎	◎						○	◉			
17	Sep	Central & Southern California			◉	◉	◉	◎						◉			◎	
16	Aug	Southeastern Arizona				○	◉	◉		◉	◉	◉					◉	
15	Jul	W. Wash. & SW British Columbia			◉	◎	◉	◎									◎	
14	Jul	West Texas				◎				◉	◎	◎		◎			◉	
13	Jun	Colorado			◉	◉	◉	○									◉	
12	Jun	Minnesota & North Dakota			◉	◎	◉	◎							◉		◉	
11	Jun	Alaska			◉	◉		●										
10	May	Southeastern Arizona				○	◉	◎		●	◉	●					◉	
9	May	Coastal North Carolina			◎		○							◉	○			
8	Apr	Florida Keys & Dry Tortugas			◎	◉								◉	◉			
7	Apr	Texas			◉	◉	◎			○	◉	○		◉	◉		◉	◉
6	Mar	Colorado			◉	◎	◎	○									◎	
5	Mar	South Florida			◉	◉	◎							◉	◎	●	○	
4	Feb	Lower Rio Grande Valley			◉	◉	◉			○	●	◎	○	◉				●
3	Feb	Northeastern Minnesota						◎										
2	Jan	Oklahoma			◉	◉	◎				○							
1	Jan	Northern & Central California			◉	◉	◉							◉	○			

Legend:
- ● Key Species
- ● Probable Species
- ◉ Possible Species
- ○ Remotely Possible Species

Species Seen: date / place

chapter	Location	month	Zone-tailed Hawk (2)	Red-tailed Hawk (1)	Ferruginous Hawk (1)	Rough-legged Hawk (1)	Golden Eagle (1)	Crested Caracara (2)	Eurasian Kestrel (5)	American Kestrel (1)	Merlin (2)	Aplomado Falcon (5)	Northern Hobby (5)	Peregrine Falcon (2)	Gyrfalcon (3)	Prairie Falcon (1)	Plain Chachalaca (2)	Himalayan Snowcock (3)
20	The Baker's Dozen			A-B-L	B	A-B-L-M	A-B-I-L			B-L	L			H-L		B		I
19	Niagara River Area	Dec		●			◉			●	○							
18	Maine to Nova Scotia	Sep		●						●	●			●				
17	Central & Southern California			●	○		●			●	◉			◉		●		
16	Southeastern Arizona	Aug	●	●			●			●				◉		●		
15	W. Wash. & SW British Columbia	Jul		●	○		◉			●	○			◉		◉		
14	West Texas		●	●			◉			●				○		◉		
13	Colorado			●	●		●			●				○		●		
12	Minnesota & North Dakota	Jun		●	●					●								
11	Alaska			●		◉	●			◉	●			●	●			
10	Southeastern Arizona	May	●	●			●			●				○		●		
9	Coastal North Carolina																	
8	Florida Keys & Dry Tortugas	Apr								●	●			◉				
7	Texas		○	●			○	●		●	◉	○		◉		◉	●	
6	Colorado	Mar		●	●	●	●			●	○			○		●		
5	South Florida			●				●		●	◉			●				
4	Lower Rio Grande Valley	Feb	○	●			●	●		●	●	○		○		○	●	
3	Northeastern Minnesota					◉								◉				
2	Oklahoma	Jan		●	●	●	○			●	○			◉				
1	Northern & Central California			●	●	○	●			●	●			●		●		

Key:
- ● Key Species
- ◐ Probable Species
- ◉ Possible Species
- ○ Remotely Possible Species

Species Seen: date ___ place ___

Chapter	#	Month	Gray Partridge	Chukar	Ring-necked Pheasant	Spruce Grouse	Blue Grouse	Willow Ptarmigan	Rock Ptarmigan	White-tailed Ptarmigan	Ruffed Grouse	Sage Grouse	Greater Prairie-Chicken	Lesser Prairie-Chicken	Sharp-tailed Grouse	Wild Turkey	Montezuma Quail	Northern Bobwhite
The Baker's Dozen	20				A-I	A	F	A-G-I	F		G-H	A-G	B		B			
Niagara River Area	19	Dec	○		◉													
Maine to Nova Scotia	18	Sep			●	◉					●							
Central & Southern California	17			●												◉		
Southeastern Arizona	16	Aug														◉	◉	
W. Wash. & SW British Columbia	15	Jul			●	◉	●			◉	◉							
West Texas	14																●	
Colorado	13			●	●		●			●						●		◉
Minnesota & North Dakota	12	Jun	●		●	○					◉		○		●			
Alaska	11					●		●	▨	◉	○				○			
Southeastern Arizona	10	May														●	◉	
Coastal North Carolina	9				◉													◉
Florida Keys & Dry Tortugas	8	Apr																
Texas	7				◉							○				●	◉	●
Colorado	6	Mar			●		◉			●		●	●	●	●	◉		◉
South Florida	5															◉		●
Lower Rio Grande Valley	4	Feb														●		●
Northeastern Minnesota	3				◉	◉					●				◉			
Oklahoma	2	Jan			○									●		●		●
Northern & Central California	1		○	●												◉		
ABA Code			1	1	1	2	1	1	1	2	1	2	2	2	2	1	2	1

Key Species ●
Probable Species ●
Possible Species ⊙
Remotely Possible Species ○

chapter		Species Seen: date / place	Scaled Quail	Gambel's Quail	California Quail	Mountain Quail	Yellow Rail	Black Rail	Corn Crake	Clapper Rail	King Rail	Virginia Rail	Sora	Paint-billed Crake	Spotted Rail	Purple Gallinule	Azure Gallinule	Common Moorhen
20	The Baker's Dozen						A	A					F					
19	Niagara River Area	Dec																
18	Maine to Nova Scotia											⊙	⊙					○
17	Central & Southern California	Sep			●	●			○	●		●	●					●
16	Southeastern Arizona	Aug	●	●								●						●
15	W. Wash. & SW British Columbia	Jul			●	⊙						●	●					
14	West Texas		●										⊙					⊙
13	Colorado					●						⊙	●					
12	Minnesota & North Dakota	Jun						●				●	●					
11	Alaska																	
10	Southeastern Arizona	May	●	●														●
9	Coastal North Carolina								⊙	●	●	⊙	○					●
8	Florida Keys & Dry Tortugas	Apr							⊙			⊙				⊙		○
7	Texas		●				⊙	●		●	●	⊙	●			●		●
6	Colorado	Mar	⊙															
5	South Florida						○	○		⊙	⊙	⊙	●			●		●
4	Lower Rio Grande Valley	Feb	●								⊙		●					●
3	Northeastern Minnesota																	
2	Oklahoma	Jan																
1	Northern & Central California				●	●				⊙		●	●					○

| ABA Code | | | 1 | 1 | 1 | 2 | 3 | 3 | 5 | 2 | 2 | 1 | 1 | 5 | 5 | 1 | 5 | 1 |

Key Species ● **Probable Species** ◉ **Possible Species** ⊙ **Remotely Possible Species** ○

Location	chapter	date	Eurasian Coot	American Coot	Limpkin	Sandhill Crane	Common Crane	Whooping Crane	Double-striped Thick-knee	Northern Lapwing	Black-bellied Plover	Greater Golden-Plover	Pacific Golden-Plover	American Golden-Plover	Collared Plover	Mongolian Plover	Snowy Plover	Wilson's Plover
The Baker's Dozen	20					B-F											—	
Niagara River Area	19	Dec		○														
Maine to Nova Scotia	18	Sep		○							◉			◉				
Central & Southern California	17	Sep		◉							◉		⊙	○			◉	
Southeastern Arizona	16	Aug		◉														
W. Wash. & SW British Columbia	15	Jul		◉							◉			○			⊙	
West Texas	14			◉														
Colorado	13			◉														
Minnesota & North Dakota	12	Jun		◉		◉					○			○				
Alaska	11					◉					◉		◉	◉	▒			
Southeastern Arizona	10	May		◉														
Coastal North Carolina	9			○							◉							⊙
Florida Keys & Dry Tortugas	8	Apr		◉							◉			○			◉	◉
Texas	7			◉				●			◉		●				◉	◉
Colorado	6	Mar		◉		⊙												
South Florida	5			◉	●	◉					◉		⊙				◉	●
Lower Rio Grande Valley	4	Feb		◉		⊙					◉						◉	⊙
Northeastern Minnesota	3																	
Oklahoma	2	Jan		◉		○												
Northern & Central California	1			◉		◉					◉	●					◉	

Species	ABA Code
Eurasian Coot	5
American Coot	1
Limpkin	2
Sandhill Crane	1
Common Crane	5
Whooping Crane	2
Double-striped Thick-knee	5
Northern Lapwing	5
Black-bellied Plover	1
Greater Golden-Plover	5
Pacific Golden-Plover	1
American Golden-Plover	1
Collared Plover	5
Mongolian Plover	4
Snowy Plover	1
Wilson's Plover	1

Species Seen — place / date

Legend

●	Key Species
◉	Probable Species
⊙	Possible Species
○	Remotely Possible Species

chapter		Location	month	Common Ringed Plover	Semipalmated Plover	Piping Plover	Little Ringed Plover	Killdeer	Mountain Plover	Eurasian Dotterel	American Oystercatcher	Black Oystercatcher	Black-winged Stilt	Black-necked Stilt	American Avocet	Oriental Pratincole	Northern Jacana	Common Greenshank	Greater Yellowlegs
20		The Baker's Dozen						⌐						—	—				—
19		Niagara River Area	Dec					⊙											
18		Maine to Nova Scotia	Sep		◉			◉											◉
17		Central & Southern California	Sep		◉			◉	○			◉		◉	◉				◉
16		Southeastern Arizona	Aug					◉					⊙	◉					⊙
15		W. Wash. & SW British Columbia	Jul		◉			◉				◉	⊙	⊙					◉
14		West Texas	Jul					◉	○										
13		Colorado						◉	●					○	◉				
12		Minnesota & North Dakota	Jun		⊙	⊙		◉							◉				⊙
11		Alaska		(shaded)	◉			○				◉					(shaded)		◉
10		Southeastern Arizona	May					◉						◉	◉				
9		Coastal North Carolina	May		◉	◉		◉			◉			◉	◉				◉
8		Florida Keys & Dry Tortugas	Apr		◉	◉		◉		○				⊙	⊙				◉
7		Texas	Apr		◉	◉		◉	○		◉			◉	◉		○		◉
6		Colorado	Mar					◉	⊙						◉				◉
5		South Florida	Mar		◉	●		◉			●			◉	◉				◉
4		Lower Rio Grande Valley	Feb		◉	⊙		◉	○					◉	◉		○		◉
3		Northeastern Minnesota	Feb																
2		Oklahoma	Jan					◉											
1		Northern & Central California	Jan		◉			◉	⊙		●		◉	◉					◉

| ABA Code | 4 | 1 | 1 | 5 | 1 | 2 | 4 | 1 | 1 | 5 | 1 | 1 | 5 | 4 | 4 | 1 |

Key Species ● Probable Species ◉ Possible Species ◎ Remotely Possible Species ○

Species Seen — place — date

chapter	date	Region	Lesser Yellowlegs (1)	Marsh Sandpiper (5)	Spotted Redshank (4)	Wood Sandpiper (4)	Green Sandpiper (5)	Solitary Sandpiper (1)	Willet (1)	Wandering Tattler (1)	Gray-tailed Tattler (4)	Common Sandpiper (4)	Spotted Sandpiper (1)	Terek Sandpiper (4)	Upland Sandpiper (1)	Little Curlew (5)	Eskimo Curlew (5)	Whimbrel (1)
20		The Baker's Dozen	—												D			
19	Dec	Niagara River Area																
18	Sep	Maine to Nova Scotia	●					◎					●					◎
17		Central & Southern California	●					◎	●	●			●					●
16	Aug	Southeastern Arizona	◎					◎	◎				●					
15	Jul	W. Wash. & SW British Columbia	◎					○	◎	●			●					●
14		West Texas																
13		Colorado											●		○			
12	Jun	Minnesota & North Dakota	◎					◎	●				●		●			
11		Alaska	●		▓	▓		◎		●	▓		●		◎			●
10	May	Southeastern Arizona											●					
9		Coastal North Carolina	●					○	●				◎					●
8	Apr	Florida Keys & Dry Tortugas	●					○	●				●	◎				●
7		Texas	●					●	●				●	◎		○		●
6	Mar	Colorado	◎															
5		South Florida	●					●	●				●					●
4	Feb	Lower Rio Grande Valley	●					◎	●				●					○
3		Northeastern Minnesota																
2	Jan	Oklahoma																
1		Northern & Central California						●	●				●					●

ABA Code

Legend — Species Seen

●	Key Species
◉	Probable Species
⊙	Possible Species
○	Remotely Possible Species

Columns for recording: date / place

Location	Chapter	Month	Bristle-thighed Curlew (4)	Slender-billed Curlew (5)	Far Eastern Curlew (5)	Eurasian Curlew (5)	Long-billed Curlew (1)	Black-tailed Godwit (4)	Hudsonian Godwit (1)	Bar-tailed Godwit (3)	Marbled Godwit (1)	Ruddy Turnstone (1)	Black Turnstone (1)	Surfbird (1)	Great Knot (5)	Red Knot (1)	Sanderling (1)	Semipalmated Sandpiper (1)
The Baker's Dozen	20								F									
Niagara River Area	19	Dec																
Maine to Nova Scotia	18	Sep							○			◉				⊙	◉	◉
Central & Southern California	17	Sep					◉				◉	◉	◉	◉		◉	◉	⊙
Southeastern Arizona	16	Aug								○								
W. Wash. & SW British Columbia	15	Jul					⊙				⊙	◉	◉	◉		⊙	◉	⊙
West Texas	14	Jul																
Colorado	13						◉											
Minnesota & North Dakota	12	Jun									◉	○					○	⊙
Alaska	11		⊙		(shaded)			(shaded)	⊙	●	◉	⊙	⊙	○	○		⊙	●
Southeastern Arizona	10	May																
Coastal North Carolina	9	May							⊙		◉					◉	◉	◉
Florida Keys & Dry Tortugas	8	Apr									◉				○	◉	◉	◉
Texas	7	Apr					◉		●		◉	◉			●	◉	◉	◉
Colorado	6	Mar																
South Florida	5	Mar					⊙				◉	◉				⊙	◉	
Lower Rio Grande Valley	4	Feb					◉				◉	◉				⊙	◉	
Northeastern Minnesota	3	Feb																
Oklahoma	2	Jan																
Northern & Central California	1	Jan					◉				◉	◉	●	●		⊙	◉	

Key: ● Key Species ◉ Probable Species ⊙ Possible Species ○ Remotely Possible Species

chapter	month	Location	Western Sandpiper	Rufous-necked Stint	Little Stint	Temminck's Stint	Long-toed Stint	Least Sandpiper	White-rumped Sandpiper	Baird's Sandpiper	Pectoral Sandpiper	Sharp-tailed Sandpiper	Purple Sandpiper	Rock Sandpiper	Dunlin	Curlew Sandpiper	Stilt Sandpiper	Spoonbill Sandpiper
20		The Baker's Dozen	—	J				—	C-F-H	F-I			J	M			J	
19	Dec	Niagara River Area											●					
18	Sep	Maine to Nova Scotia	○					●	◉	○	◉		○		⊙		⊙	
17	Sep	Central & Southern California	●					●		⊙	◉				⊙		●	
16	Aug	Southeastern Arizona	⊙					○										
15	Jul	W. Wash. & SW British Columbia	●					●		⊙				○				
14		West Texas																
13		Colorado																
12	Jun	Minnesota & North Dakota						⊙	○	○	⊙						○	
11		Alaska	●	○		▓	▓	●		○	●	▓	●	●				
10	May	Southeastern Arizona																
9	May	Coastal North Carolina	⊙					●	●		○			●	○		⊙	
8	Apr	Florida Keys & Dry Tortugas	●					●	⊙	○	○			⊙		○		
7	Apr	Texas	●					●	●	⊙	●			●		●		
6	Mar	Colorado								●								
5	Mar	South Florida	●					●		⊙				●		⊙		
4	Feb	Lower Rio Grande Valley	●					●	○		○			●		⊙		
3		Northeastern Minnesota																
2	Jan	Oklahoma																
1	Jan	Northern & Central California	●					●			○			●				
ABA Code			1	4	4	4	4	1	1	1	1	3	1	1	1	4	1	5

Legend:
- ● Key Species
- ◉ Probable Species
- ⊙ Possible Species
- ○ Remotely Possible Species

Chapter	#	Month	Broad-billed Sandpiper	Buff-breasted Sandpiper	Ruff	Short-billed Dowitcher	Long-billed Dowitcher	Jack Snipe	Common Snipe	Pin-tailed Snipe	Eurasian Woodcock	American Woodcock	Wilson's Phalarope	Red-necked Phalarope	Red Phalarope	Pomarine Jaeger	Parasitic Jaeger	Long-tailed Jaeger
The Baker's Dozen	20						J		I				B-C	I	H-I	F	F-H	F-H
Niagara River Area	19	Dec							○									
Maine to Nova Scotia	18				⊙	○	●		●			⊙	○	●	●	⊙	⊙	○
Central & Southern California	17	Sep				○	●	●	●					●	●	●	●	⊙
Southeastern Arizona	16	Aug												●				
W. Wash. & SW British Columbia	15	Jul				●	●		●				⊙	○	●	●	●	⊙
West Texas	14																	
Colorado	13							○	●				●					
Minnesota & North Dakota	12	Jun					○	○	●			●	●	○				
Alaska	11				▨	●	●		●					●	●	●	●	●
Southeastern Arizona	10	May											●					
Coastal North Carolina	9					○	●	○					○	●	⊙	●	●	●
Florida Keys & Dry Tortugas	8	Apr					⊙	○					○	⊙	○	●	○	
Texas	7			●	○	●	●	●	●				●					
Colorado	6	Mar							●									
South Florida	5					○	●	●	●			○						
Lower Rio Grande Valley	4	Feb				⊙	●		●			○						
Northeastern Minnesota	3																	
Oklahoma	2	Jan						⊙				○						
Northern & Central California	1					○	●	●	●				○	●	⊙	○		

ABA Code: Broad-billed Sandpiper 5, Buff-breasted Sandpiper 1, Ruff 3, Short-billed Dowitcher 1, Long-billed Dowitcher 1, Jack Snipe 5, Common Snipe 1, Pin-tailed Snipe 5, Eurasian Woodcock 5, American Woodcock 1, Wilson's Phalarope 1, Red-necked Phalarope 1, Red Phalarope 2, Pomarine Jaeger 2, Parasitic Jaeger 2, Long-tailed Jaeger 2

Key:
- ● Key Species
- ◉ Probable Species
- ⊙ Possible Species
- ○ Remotely Possible Species

Species Seen (date / place) →	chapter	date	Great Skua	South Polar Skua	Laughing Gull	Franklin's Gull	Little Gull	Common Black-headed Gull	Bonaparte's Gull	Heermann's Gull	Black-tailed Gull	Mew Gull	Ring-billed Gull	California Gull	Herring Gull	Thayer's Gull	Iceland Gull	Yellow-legged Gull
The Baker's Dozen	20						I	M	M				I			F	M	
Niagara River Area	19	Dec			○	⊙	●	●	◉			○	◉	○	◉	◉	●	
Maine to Nova Scotia	18	Sep	○	⊙	⊙		○	○	◉				◉		◉			
Central & Southern California	17			⊙	◉	○			⊙	◉			◉	◉	⊙			
Southeastern Arizona	16	Aug																
W. Wash. & SW British Columbia	15	Jul		●					◉	◉		⊙	◉	◉				
West Texas	14																	
Colorado	13					⊙							◉	◉				
Minnesota & North Dakota	12	Jun				●			○				◉	◉	○			
Alaska	11								◉		●				◉	○		
Southeastern Arizona	10	May											○					
Coastal North Carolina	9		●	◉					○				◉		◉			
Florida Keys & Dry Tortugas	8	Apr		●									⊙		●			
Texas	7			●	⊙			⊙					◉		●			
Colorado	6	Mar						○					◉	◉	◉	○		
South Florida	5			●				●					◉		●			
Lower Rio Grande Valley	4	Feb		●				⊙					◉		●			
Northeastern Minnesota	3														⊙	⊙	○	
Oklahoma	2	Jan						⊙					◉		◉			
Northern & Central California	1						●	●		●		●	◉	●	◉	●		
ABA Code			3	3	1	1	3	3	1	1	5	1	1	1	1	2	2	5

Key (Species Seen — place / date):
- ● Key Species
- ◉ Probable Species
- ◎ Possible Species
- ○ Remotely Possible Species

Species (with ABA Code):
1. Lesser Black-backed Gull — 3
2. Slaty-backed Gull — 4
3. Yellow-footed Gull — 3
4. Western Gull — 1
5. Glaucous-winged Gull — 1
6. Glaucous Gull — 1
7. Great Black-backed Gull — 1
8. Black-legged Kittiwake — 1
9. Red-legged Kittiwake — 2
10. Ross's Gull — 3
11. Sabine's Gull — 2
12. Ivory Gull — 3
13. Gull-billed Tern — 1
14. Caspian Tern — 1
15. Royal Tern — 1
16. Elegant Tern — 2

Chapter	Place	Date	1	2	3	4	5	6	7	8	9	10	11	12	13	14	15	16
20	The Baker's Dozen								F-M	H	H	F.	F				—	
19	Niagara River Area	Dec	●						●	◉	◎		○	○				
18	Maine to Nova Scotia	Sep							●	●			○					
17	Central & Southern California	Sep			●	◉	◎			◎			●		◎	●	◎	●
16	Southeastern Arizona	Aug																
15	W. Wash. & SW British Columbia	Jul				◉	●			◎			●			●		
14	West Texas																	
13	Colorado													○				
12	Minnesota & North Dakota	Jun												○				
11	Alaska			○			●	●		◉			◎					
10	Southeastern Arizona	May																
9	Coastal North Carolina	May							●	○			○		●	●	●	
8	Florida Keys & Dry Tortugas	Apr	○										○		◎	◎	●	
7	Texas	Apr													●	●	●	
6	Colorado	Mar						○		○								
5	South Florida	Mar	○						○						●	●	●	
4	Lower Rio Grande Valley	Feb													●	●	◎	
3	Northeastern Minnesota	Feb						◎										
2	Oklahoma	Jan																
1	Northern & Central California	Jan				◉	●	○		●								

Key Species ● | **Probable Species** ◉ | **Possible Species** ⊙ | **Remotely Possible Species** ○

chapter	date	place — Species Seen	Sandwich Tern	Roseate Tern	Common Tern	Arctic Tern	Forster's Tern	Least Tern	Aleutian Tern	Bridled Tern	Sooty Tern	Large-billed Tern	Whiskered Tern	White-winged Tern	Black Tern	Brown Noddy	Black Noddy	Black Skimmer
20		The Baker's Dozen			H	F-H	−							J	J	−		
19	Dec	Niagara River Area																
18	Sep	Maine to Nova Scotia			●	⊙	○	○							○			
17	Sep	Central & Southern California			●	●	●	⊙							●			●
16	Aug	Southeastern Arizona																
15	Jul	W. Wash. & SW British Columbia			⊙	⊙	⊙								○			
14	Jul	West Texas																
13	Jun	Colorado					●	○							●			
12	Jun	Minnesota & North Dakota			○		●								●			
11		Alaska				●			●									
10	May	Southeastern Arizona																
9	May	Coastal North Carolina	●	○	●	●	●	●		⊙	⊙				○	○		●
8	Apr	Florida Keys & Dry Tortugas	●	●	⊙		⊙	●		●	●				⊙	●	⊙	⊙
7	Apr	Texas	●		●		●	●							●			●
6	Mar	Colorado																
5	Mar	South Florida	⊙	○	○		●											●
4	Feb	Lower Rio Grande Valley	⊙				●											●
3	Feb	Northeastern Minnesota																
2	Jan	Oklahoma																
1	Jan	Northern & Central California					●											
ABA Code			1	2	1	1	1	1	2	3	2	5	5	5	1	3	4	1

Legend — Species Seen:
- ● Key Species
- ◉ Probable Species
- ⊙ Possible Species
- ○ Remotely Possible Species

Place (Species Seen)	chapter	date	Dovekie	Common Murre	Thick-billed Murre	Razorbill	Black Guillemot	Pigeon Guillemot	Marbled Murrelet	Kittlitz's Murrelet	Xantus's Murrelet	Craveri's Murrelet	Ancient Murrelet	Cassin's Auklet	Parakeet Auklet	Least Auklet	Whiskered Auklet	Crested Auklet
The Baker's Dozen	20			M	H	M	H-M	H-M										
Niagara River Area	19	Dec																
Maine to Nova Scotia	18	Sep		⊙	○	●	●											
Central & Southern California	17	Sep		●	○			●	●		●	●	●					
Southeastern Arizona	16	Aug																
W. Wash. & SW British Columbia	15	Jul		●				●	●		○		●					
West Texas	14																	
Colorado	13																	
Minnesota & North Dakota	12	Jun																
Alaska	11			⊙	●		○	⊙	●	●			●	⊙	●			
Southeastern Arizona	10	May																
Coastal North Carolina	9	May																
Florida Keys & Dry Tortugas	8	Apr																
Texas	7	Apr																
Colorado	6	Mar																
South Florida	5	Mar																
Lower Rio Grande Valley	4	Feb																
Northeastern Minnesota	3	Feb																
Oklahoma	2	Jan																
Northern & Central California	1	Jan		●	○			●	●		○		⊙	●				
ABA Code			2	1	2	2	2	1	1	2	2	4	2	2	2	2	4	2

Key to symbols:
● Key Species
◉ Probable Species
⊙ Possible Species
○ Remotely Possible Species

Species Seen: date / place

#	Month	Chapter	Rhinoceros Auklet	Tufted Puffin	Atlantic Puffin	Horned Puffin	Rock Dove	Scaly-naped Pigeon	White-crowned Pigeon	Red-billed Pigeon	Band-tailed Pigeon	Oriental Turtle-Dove	Eurasian Collared-Dove	Spotted Dove	White-winged Dove	Zenaida Dove	Mourning Dove	Inca Dove
20		The Baker's Dozen				H												
19	Dec	Niagara River Area					◉								◉			
18	Sep	Maine to Nova Scotia				●	◉								◉			
17	Sep	Central & Southern California	◉	⊙			◉				◉			●	◉		◉	○
16	Aug	Southeastern Arizona					◉				◉				◉		◉	◉
15	Jul	W. Wash. & SW British Columbia	◉	◉			◉				◉				◉		◉	
14	Jul	West Texas					◉				◉				◉		◉	◉
13	Jun	Colorado					◉				◉				◉		◉	
12	Jun	Minnesota & North Dakota					◉								◉		◉	
11	Jun	Alaska	⊙	◉		◉	◉											
10	May	Southeastern Arizona					◉				◉				◉		◉	◉
9	May	Coastal North Carolina					◉								◉		◉	
8	Apr	Florida Keys & Dry Tortugas					◉		●				◉	⊙	◉		◉	
7	Apr	Texas					◉			⊙					◉		◉	◉
6	Mar	Colorado					◉								◉		◉	
5	Mar	South Florida					◉		⊙				●		◉	○	◉	
4	Feb	Lower Rio Grande Valley					◉			●					◉		◉	◉
3	Feb	Northeastern Minnesota					◉										◉	
2	Jan	Oklahoma					◉								◉		◉	
1	Jan	Northern & Central California	●	○		○	◉				◉				◉		◉	
		ABA Code	1	1	2	2	1	5	2	3	1	5	2	1	1	5	1	1

Legend:
- ● Key Species
- ◉ Probable Species
- ◎ Possible Species
- ○ Remotely Possible Species

Chapter	Month	Place	Common Ground-Dove	Ruddy Ground-Dove	White-tipped Dove	Key West Quail-Dove	Ruddy Quail-Dove	Budgerigar	Monk Parakeet	Thick-billed Parrot	Canary-winged Parakeet	Red-crowned Parrot	Common Cuckoo	Oriental Cuckoo	Black-billed Cuckoo	Yellow-billed Cuckoo	Mangrove Cuckoo	Greater Roadrunner
20		The Baker's Dozen																
19	Dec	Niagara River Area																
18		Maine to Nova Scotia													◎	◎		
17	Sep	Central & Southern California	●	○												●		●
16	Aug	Southeastern Arizona	●	○												●		●
15		W. Wash. & SW British Columbia																
14	Jul	West Texas	◎													●		●
13		Colorado														○		
12	Jun	Minnesota & North Dakota													●	○		
11		Alaska																
10	May	Southeastern Arizona	●	○											◎			●
9		Coastal North Carolina														●		
8	Apr	Florida Keys & Dry Tortugas	●											◎		●	●	
7		Texas	●		●							◎		◎		●		●
6	Mar	Colorado																◎
5		South Florida	●				○	●	●			◎					○	
4	Feb	Lower Rio Grande Valley	●	○	●						●							●
3		Northeastern Minnesota																
2		Oklahoma														●		
1	Jan	Northern & Central California														●		

ABA Code / Species:

ABA Code	Species
1	Common Ground-Dove
4	Ruddy Ground-Dove
2	White-tipped Dove
5	Key West Quail-Dove
5	Ruddy Quail-Dove
2	Budgerigar
2	Monk Parakeet
5	Thick-billed Parrot
2	Canary-winged Parakeet
2	Red-crowned Parrot
5	Common Cuckoo
5	Oriental Cuckoo
1	Black-billed Cuckoo
1	Yellow-billed Cuckoo
3	Mangrove Cuckoo
1	Greater Roadrunner

Legend:
- ● Key Species
- ◉ Probable Species
- ⊙ Possible Species
- ○ Remotely Possible Species

chapter	date	place / Species Seen	Smooth-billed Ani (2)	Groove-billed Ani (2)	Barn Owl (2)	Oriental Scops-Owl (5)	Flammulated Owl (3)	Eastern Screech-Owl (2)	Western Screech-Owl (2)	Whiskered Screech-Owl (2)	Great Horned Owl (1)	Snowy Owl (2)	Northern Hawk Owl (2)	Northern Pygmy-Owl (2)	Ferruginous Pygmy-Owl (3)	Elf Owl (2)	Burrowing Owl (1)	Mottled Owl (5)
20		The Baker's Dozen					A	I			A	M	F	A-I				
19	Dec	Niagara River Area						⊙			⊙	⊙						
18	Sep	Maine to Nova Scotia									●							
17	Sep	Central & Southern California			●				●		●			⊙			●	
16	Aug	Southeastern Arizona			●		●		●	●	●			●	○	●	⊙	
15	Jul	W. Wash. & SW British Columbia			●		○		⊙		●			⊙			⊙	
14	Jul	West Texas			⊙		○	○	●		●					●	○	
13	Jun	Colorado			⊙			⊙	●		●			⊙			●	
12	Jun	Minnesota & North Dakota						⊙			⊙							
11		Alaska									●	○	●					
10	May	Southeastern Arizona			●		●		●	●	●			●	○	●	●	
9	May	Coastal North Carolina						⊙			⊙							
8	Apr	Florida Keys & Dry Tortugas						⊙									●	
7	Apr	Texas		●	⊙			●			●				○	⊙	○	
6	Mar	Colorado			○			⊙	⊙		●			●				
5	Mar	South Florida	●		●			●			●						●	
4	Feb	Lower Rio Grande Valley		⊙	⊙			●			●			●	⊙	⊙		
3	Feb	Northeastern Minnesota						⊙			●	●	●					
2	Jan	Oklahoma			⊙			⊙			●						⊙	
1	Jan	Northern & Central California			⊙				⊙		⊙			⊙			⊙	

ABA Code

Legend:
● Key Species ◉ Probable Species ⊙ Possible Species ○ Remotely Possible Species

#	Location	Month	Spotted Owl (2)	Barred Owl (1)	Great Gray Owl (3)	Long-eared Owl (2)	Short-eared Owl (2)	Boreal Owl (3)	Northern Saw-whet Owl (2)	Lesser Nighthawk (1)	Common Nighthawk (1)	Antillean Nighthawk (3)	Pauraque (2)	Common Poorwill (2)	Chuck-will's-widow (2)	Buff-collared Nightjar (4)	Whip-poor-will (2)	Jungle Nightjar (5)
20	The Baker's Dozen		A			G	A-F	G										
19	Niagara River Area	Dec				⊙	⊙		⊙									
18	Maine to Nova Scotia	Sep		●		○	○		⊙		⊙						○	
17	Central & Southern California	Sep	⊙				●	⊙	⊙	◉				⊙				
16	Southeastern Arizona	Aug	⊙						◉	○				●		◉	●	
15	W. Wash. & SW British Columbia	Jul	⊙	⊙		○	⊙		⊙		⊙			○				
14	West Texas	Jul							●	●				●			⊙	
13	Colorado					⊙	⊙		○		●			●				
12	Minnesota & North Dakota	Jun			⊙	⊙	○	⊙	○		●						⊙	
11	Alaska				○		◉	●	○									
10	Southeastern Arizona	May	⊙				○			◉	○			●		●	●	
9	Coastal North Carolina			⊙							⊙				◉		⊙	
8	Florida Keys & Dry Tortugas	Apr									◉	●			◉			
7	Texas	Apr		●			○			●	●		⊙	⊙	●		●	
6	Colorado	Mar				⊙	⊙	○	○									
5	South Florida	Mar		●			○				⊙				⊙		⊙	
4	Lower Rio Grande Valley	Feb					○						●					
3	Northeastern Minnesota	Feb		⊙	●			○	○									
2	Oklahoma	Jan		⊙		⊙	⊙											
1	Northern & Central California	Jan	●			⊙	⊙	●										

Key Species ● **Probable Species** ◉ **Possible Species** ⊙ **Remotely Possible Species** ○

Chapter (location)	chapter	date	Black Swift	White-collared Swift	Chimney Swift	Vaux's Swift	White-throated Needletail	Common Swift	Fork-tailed Swift	White-throated Swift	Antillean Palm Swift	Green Violet-ear	Green-breasted Mango	Broad-billed Hummingbird	White-eared Hummingbird	Xantus's Hummingbird	Berylline Hummingbird	Cinnamon Hummingbird
ABA Code			2	5	1	1	5	5	5	1	5	4	5	2	4	5	4	5
The Baker's Dozen	20	—																
Niagara River Area	19	Dec																
Maine to Nova Scotia	18	Sep				⊙												
Central & Southern California	17	Sep	○				●			●								
Southeastern Arizona	16	Aug				○				●				●	⊙		⊙	
W. Wash. & SW British Columbia	15	Jul	●				●			⊙								
West Texas	14	Jul								●			○					
Colorado	13	Jun	●			●				●								
Minnesota & North Dakota	12	Jun				●												
Alaska	11																	
Southeastern Arizona	10	May								●				●				
Coastal North Carolina	9	May			●													
Florida Keys & Dry Tortugas	8	Apr			⊙													
Texas	7	Apr			●													
Colorado	6	Mar																
South Florida	5	Mar			⊙													
Lower Rio Grande Valley	4	Feb																
Northeastern Minnesota	3	Feb																
Oklahoma	2	Jan																
Northern & Central California	1	Jan								●								

Species Seen — date — place

Legend:
- ● Key Species
- ◉ Probable Species
- ◎ Possible Species
- ○ Remotely Possible Species

Chapter	#	Month	Buff-bellied Hummingbird	Violet-crowned Hummingbird	Blue-throated Hummingbird	Magnificent Hummingbird	Plain-capped Starthroat	Bahama Woodstar	Lucifer Hummingbird	Ruby-throated Hummingbird	Black-chinned Hummingbird	Anna's Hummingbird	Costa's Hummingbird	Calliope Hummingbird	Bumblebee Hummingbird	Broad-tailed Hummingbird	Rufous Hummingbird	Allen's Hummingbird
The Baker's Dozen (G-I)	20																	
Niagara River Area	19	Dec																
Maine to Nova Scotia	18	Sep								◎								
Central & Southern California	17	Sep									◎	●	◎				●	●
Southeastern Arizona	16	Aug		●	◉	◉	○		○		◉	◎	◎	◎		●	●	◎
W. Wash. & SW British Columbia	15	Jul									◎	◎		●			●	
West Texas	14	Jul			◉	◎			●		◉			●		●		
Colorado	13										◉					●		
Minnesota & North Dakota	12	Jun								●								
Alaska	11																●	
Southeastern Arizona	10	May		◎	●	●					◉	◎	●	○		●		
Coastal North Carolina	9	May								●								
Florida Keys & Dry Tortugas	8	Apr								●								
Texas	7	Apr	●							●	◉							
Colorado	6	Mar																
South Florida	5	Mar								●								
Lower Rio Grande Valley	4	Feb	●						◎		◎					◎		
Northeastern Minnesota	3																	
Oklahoma	2	Jan																
Northern & Central California	1	Jan										●						○

ABA Code: Buff-bellied 2, Violet-crowned 3, Blue-throated 2, Magnificent 2, Plain-capped Starthroat 4, Bahama Woodstar 5, Lucifer 2, Ruby-throated 1, Black-chinned 1, Anna's 1, Costa's 1, Calliope 1, Bumblebee 5, Broad-tailed 1, Rufous 1, Allen's 1

Key Species ● **Probable Species** ◉ **Possible Species** ⊙ **Remotely Possible Species** ○

Area	chapter	month	Elegant Trogon	Eared Trogon	Hoopoe	Ringed Kingfisher	Belted Kingfisher	Green Kingfisher	Eurasian Wryneck	Lewis's Woodpecker	Red-headed Woodpecker	Acorn Woodpecker	Gila Woodpecker	Golden-fronted Woodpecker	Red-bellied Woodpecker	Yellow-bellied Sapsucker	Red-naped Sapsucker	Red-breasted Sapsucker
The Baker's Dozen	20																	
Niagara River Area	19	Dec					●								⊙			
Maine to Nova Scotia	18						●									⊙		
Central & Southern California	17	Sep					●				⊙	●	⊙				○	⊙
Southeastern Arizona	16	Aug	●	⊙				⊙				●	●					
W. Wash. & SW British Columbia	15	Jul					●				⊙						⊙	●
West Texas	14						⊙					●		●				
Colorado	13						●			●	●						●	
Minnesota & North Dakota	12	Jun					●				●				●			
Alaska	11						⊙											
Southeastern Arizona	10	May	●					⊙				●	●					
Coastal North Carolina	9						○								⊙			
Florida Keys & Dry Tortugas	8	Apr					●								●			
Texas	7					⊙	●	⊙			●	○		●	●	●		
Colorado	6	Mar					●			⊙					○	○	⊙	
South Florida	5						●				●				●	●		
Lower Rio Grande Valley	4	Feb				●	●	●						●	⊙			
Northeastern Minnesota	3																	
Oklahoma	2	Jan					●				●	○		●	●	○		
Northern & Central California	1						●		●		●						●	

ABA Code: Elegant Trogon 3 · Eared Trogon 5 · Hoopoe 5 · Ringed Kingfisher 2 · Belted Kingfisher 1 · Green Kingfisher 2 · Eurasian Wryneck 5 · Lewis's Woodpecker 1 · Red-headed Woodpecker 1 · Acorn Woodpecker 1 · Gila Woodpecker 1 · Golden-fronted Woodpecker 1 · Red-bellied Woodpecker 1 · Yellow-bellied Sapsucker 1 · Red-naped Sapsucker 1 · Red-breasted Sapsucker 1

Key:
- ● Key Species
- ◉ Probable Species
- ◎ Possible Species
- ○ Remotely Possible Species

Species Seen →																		
chapter	#	date	Williamson's Sapsucker	Great Spotted Woodpecker	Ladder-backed Woodpecker	Nuttall's Woodpecker	Downy Woodpecker	Hairy Woodpecker	Strickland's Woodpecker	Red-cockaded Woodpecker	White-headed Woodpecker	Three-toed Woodpecker	Black-backed Woodpecker	Northern Flicker	Gilded Flicker	Pileated Woodpecker	Northern Beardless-Tyrannulet	Greenish Elaenia
The Baker's Dozen	20	G-I											G-I / H					
Niagara River Area	19	Dec					●	◎						●				
Maine to Nova Scotia	18						●	◎				○	◎	●		●		
Central & Southern California	17	Sep	◎		●	●	●	◎			●			●				
Southeastern Arizona	16	Aug			●			●	●					●	◎		●	
W. Wash. & SW British Columbia	15	Jul	◎				●	◎			◎	◎	◎	●		●		
West Texas	14				●									●				
Colorado	13		●				●	◎				○		●				
Minnesota & North Dakota	12	Jun					●	◎					○	●		●		
Alaska	11						●	◎				●	○	◎				
Southeastern Arizona	10	May			●			●	●					●	●		●	
Coastal North Carolina	9						◎	◎		◎				●		◎		
Florida Keys & Dry Tortugas	8	Apr												●				
Texas	7				●		●	○		●				●		●	○	
Colorado	6	Mar			◎		●	●			●			●		●		
South Florida	5						●	◎		●				●		●		
Lower Rio Grande Valley	4	Feb			●									●		○		
Northeastern Minnesota	3						●	◎				○	●			●		
Oklahoma	2	Jan			◎		●	◎						●				
Northern & Central California	1					●	●	◎						●				
ABA Code			1	5	1	1	1	1	2	2	1	2	2	1	1	1	2	5

Key Species legend

- ● Key Species
- ◉ Probable Species
- ⊙ Possible Species
- ○ Remotely Possible Species

Species Seen: date / place

chapter	Species (location)	month	Caribbean Elaenia	Tufted Flycatcher	Olive-sided Flycatcher	Greater Pewee	Western Wood-Pewee	Eastern Wood-Pewee	Yellow-bellied Flycatcher	Acadian Flycatcher	Alder Flycatcher	Willow Flycatcher	Least Flycatcher	Hammond's Flycatcher	Dusky Flycatcher	Gray Flycatcher	Pacific-slope Flycatcher	Cordilleran Flycatcher
20	The Baker's Dozen				G-H-I			H			H		H					
19	Niagara River Area	Dec																
18	Maine to Nova Scotia	Sep			⊙			⊙	⊙		⊙		⊙					
17	Central & Southern California	Sep			⊙		●							●	⊙	⊙	⊙	●
16	Southeastern Arizona	Aug				●	●							⊙				●
15	W. Wash. & SW British Columbia	Jul			●		●							●	●	⊙	⊙	●
14	West Texas	Jul					●											●
13	Colorado				●		●					●	○	●	●	●		●
12	Minnesota & North Dakota	Jun			⊙			⊙	●		●	⊙	●					
11	Alaska	Jun			⊙		⊙				●		⊙					
10	Southeastern Arizona	May			⊙	●	●				⊙		○	⊙	○			●
9	Coastal North Carolina	May						⊙		⊙								
8	Florida Keys & Dry Tortugas	Apr			○			⊙	○	○								
7	Texas	Apr			○		⊙	●	○	●	○	⊙						
6	Colorado	Mar																
5	South Florida	Mar									○							
4	Lower Rio Grande Valley	Feb																
3	Northeastern Minnesota	Feb																
2	Oklahoma	Jan																
1	Northern & Central California	Jan																
ABA Code			5	5	1	2	1	1	1	1	1	1	1	1	1	1	1	1

Legend:
- ● Key Species
- ◉ Probable Species
- ⊙ Possible Species
- ○ Remotely Possible Species

chapter	month	Location	Buff-breasted Flycatcher (3)	Black Phoebe (1)	Eastern Phoebe (1)	Say's Phoebe (1)	Vermilion Flycatcher (1)	Dusky-capped Flycatcher (2)	Ash-throated Flycatcher (1)	Nutting's Flycatcher (5)	Great Crested Flycatcher (1)	Brown-crested Flycatcher (1)	La Sagra's Flycatcher (5)	Great Kiskadee (2)	Sulphur-bellied Flycatcher (2)	Variegated Flycatcher (5)	Tropical Kingbird (2)	Couch's Kingbird (2)
20		The Baker's Dozen																
19	Dec	Niagara River Area																
18	Sep	Maine to Nova Scotia				⊙					○							
17	Sep	Central & Southern California		●			●	⊙	⊙			○					○	
16	Aug	Southeastern Arizona	●	●			●	●	●			●			●		●	
15	Jul	W. Wash. & SW British Columbia					⊙		○									
14		West Texas		●			●	●				●						
13		Colorado				○	●				●							
12	Jun	Minnesota & North Dakota			●	⊙					●							
11		Alaska				●												
10	May	Southeastern Arizona	●	●			●	●	●			●			⊙		●	
9		Coastal North Carolina									●							
8	Apr	Florida Keys & Dry Tortugas									●		○					
7		Texas		⊙	●	⊙	⊙		●		●	●		●			○	●
6	Mar	Colorado			○	⊙												
5		South Florida			●						●		○					
4	Feb	Lower Rio Grande Valley		○	●	⊙	⊙		○					●			○	⊙
3		Northeastern Minnesota																
2	Jan	Oklahoma																
1		Northern & Central California		●		●												

Key Species ●
Probable Species ◉
Possible Species ⊙
Remotely Possible Species ○

Species Seen — place / date

chapter	#	Month	Species / Place	Cassin's Kingbird	Thick-billed Kingbird	Western Kingbird	Eastern Kingbird	Gray Kingbird	Loggerhead Kingbird	Scissor-tailed Flycatcher	Fork-tailed Flycatcher	Rose-throated Becard	Masked Tityra	Eurasian Skylark	Horned Lark	Purple Martin	Cuban Martin	Gray-breasted Martin	Southern Martin
	20		The Baker's Dozen																
	19	Dec	Niagara River Area												⊙				
	18	Sep	Maine to Nova Scotia				●								⊙				
	17		Central & Southern California	●		●									●	○			
	16	Aug	Southeastern Arizona	●	●	●						●			●	⊙			
	15	Jul	W. Wash. & SW British Columbia			⊙	⊙							●	●	⊙			
	14		West Texas	●	○	●				⊙					●				
	13	Jun	Colorado	○		●	●								●	○			
	12		Minnesota & North Dakota			●	●								●	●			
	11		Alaska											▒	●				
	10	May	Southeastern Arizona	●	●	●						●			●	●			
	9		Coastal North Carolina				●								●				
	8	Apr	Florida Keys & Dry Tortugas			⊙	●	●		⊙						⊙			
	7		Texas			⊙	●			●	○				●	●			
	6	Mar	Colorado												●				
	5		South Florida				○	●	⊙	⊙						●			
	4	Feb	Lower Rio Grande Valley							⊙									
	3		Northeastern Minnesota																
	2	Jan	Oklahoma												●				
	1		Northern & Central California												●				
ABA Code				1	2	1	1	2	5	1	4	2	5	3	1	1	5	5	5

Legend: ● Key Species · ◉ Probable Species · ◎ Possible Species · ○ Remotely Possible Species

Chapter	Region	Species Seen (date / place)	Brown-chested Martin	Tree Swallow	Violet-green Swallow	Bahama Swallow	Northern Rough-winged Swallow	Bank Swallow	Cliff Swallow	Cave Swallow	Barn Swallow	Common House-Martin	Gray Jay	Steller's Jay	Blue Jay	Green Jay	Brown Jay	Western Scrub-Jay
20	The Baker's Dozen												—					
19	Niagara River Area	Dec													●			
18	Maine to Nova Scotia			◎				◎	◎		◎		●		●			
17	Central & Southern California	Sep		●	●		●	●	●		●			●				●
16	Southeastern Arizona	Aug		●	●		●	○	●		●			●				●
15	W. Wash. & SW British Columbia	Jul		●	●		●	◎	●		●		●	●				◎
14	West Texas			○	●		●	●	◎	◎	●							●
13	Colorado			●	●		◎	◎	●		●		●	●	●			●
12	Minnesota & North Dakota	Jun		●			●	●	●		●		○		●			
11	Alaska			●	●			●	●				●	●				
10	Southeastern Arizona	May			●		●		●		●			●				●
9	Coastal North Carolina						◎	○			●			●				
8	Florida Keys & Dry Tortugas	Apr		○			●	●	○	○	●							
7	Texas			●			●	●	●	●	●				●	●	◎	●
6	Colorado	Mar		◎	◎								●	●	●			●
5	South Florida			●		○	◎		○	◎	●				●			
4	Lower Rio Grande Valley	Feb		●			●			◎						●	●	
3	Northeastern Minnesota								●		●		●		●			
2	Oklahoma	Jan							●						●			
1	Northern & Central California			●	◎								●	●				●
ABA Code			5	1	1	4	1	1	1	1	1	5	1	1	1	2	2	1

Key (symbols):

- ● Key Species
- ◉ Probable Species
- ◎ Possible Species
- ○ Remotely Possible Species

Columns at right of chart: **Species Seen** — *date* / *place* (blank write-in columns).

Chapter	#	Month	Florida Scrub-Jay	Santa Cruz Island Scrub-Jay	Mexican Jay	Pinyon Jay	Clark's Nutcracker	Black-billed Magpie	Yellow-billed Magpie	Eurasian Jackdaw	American Crow	Northwestern Crow	Mexican Crow	Fish Crow	Chihuahuan Raven	Common Raven	Black-capped Chickadee	Carolina Chickadee
The Baker's Dozen	20																	
Niagara River Area	19	Dec									◉						◉	
Maine to Nova Scotia	18	Sep									◉					◉	◉	
Central & Southern California	17					●	◎	◉	◉		◉					◉		
Southeastern Arizona	16	Aug			◉										◉	◉		
W. Wash. & SW British Columbia	15	Jul					◉	◎			◉	◉				◉	◉	
West Texas	14				◉										◎	◉		
Colorado	13					●	◉	◉			◉				○	◉	◉	
Minnesota & North Dakota	12	Jun						◎			◉					◉	◉	
Alaska	11							◉				●				◉	◉	
Southeastern Arizona	10	May			◉										◉	◉		
Coastal North Carolina	9										◉			◉				◉
Florida Keys & Dry Tortugas	8	Apr																
Texas	7										◉		◎	◉	◉			◉
Colorado	6	Mar				○	●	◉			◉				◎	◉	◉	
South Florida	5		●								◉			●				◎
Lower Rio Grande Valley	4	Feb											●		●			
Northeastern Minnesota	3										◉					◉	◉	
Oklahoma	2	Jan									◉						●	
Northern & Central California	1								●		◉					◉		
ABA Code			1	2	2	2	1	1	1	4	1	1	3	1	1	1	1	1

Legend: ● Key Species ◉ Probable Species ⊙ Possible Species ○ Remotely Possible Species

Species Seen: date ____ place ____

Chapter	Month	Area	Mexican Chickadee	Mountain Chickadee	Siberian Tit	Boreal Chickadee	Chestnut-backed Chickadee	Bridled Titmouse	Plain Titmouse	Tufted Titmouse	Verdin	Bushtit	Red-breasted Nuthatch	White-breasted Nuthatch	Pygmy Nuthatch	Brown-headed Nuthatch	Brown Creeper	Red-whiskered Bulbul
20		The Baker's Dozen			—		H						—					
19	Dec	Niagara River Area								⊙			⊙	●			⊙	
18		Maine to Nova Scotia				●						○	●	⊙			⊙	
17	Sep	Central & Southern California		◉			●		●			●	●	●	●	●	●	
16	Aug	Southeastern Arizona	●					●	●			●	●		●	●	●	
15	Jul	W. Wash. & SW British Columbia		⊙		○	●						●	●	⊙	⊙	●	
14		West Texas								●	●	●	●	●				
13		Colorado		●					●			●	●	●	●		●	
12	Jun	Minnesota & North Dakota				⊙							●	●			⊙	
11		Alaska				●	●						●				●	
10	May	Southeastern Arizona	●					●	◉			●	●		●	●	●	
9		Coastal North Carolina								⊙						⊙		
8	Apr	Florida Keys & Dry Tortugas																
7		Texas								●	●	◉	○	○		●	⊙	
6	Mar	Colorado		●								○	⊙	⊙	⊙	●	⊙	
5		South Florida								⊙						⊙		●
4	Feb	Lower Rio Grande Valley								●	⊙							
3		Northeastern Minnesota				●							●	●				
2	Jan	Oklahoma								●	○	○	⊙				●	
1		Northern & Central California					●		●			●	●	●	●		●	
ABA Code			2	1	4	1	1	1	1	1	1	1	1	1	1	1	1	2

Legend:
- ● Key Species
- ◉ Probable Species
- ⊙ Possible Species
- ○ Remotely Possible Species

Chapter	#	Month	Species Seen (date / place)	Cactus Wren	Rock Wren	Canyon Wren	Carolina Wren	Bewick's Wren	House Wren	Winter Wren	Sedge Wren	Marsh Wren	American Dipper	Middendorff's Grasshopper-Warbler	Lanceolated Warbler	Wood Warbler	Dusky Warbler	Arctic Warbler	Golden-crowned Kinglet
The Baker's Dozen	20									—			E	—	G				—
Niagara River Area	19	Dec							⊙										⊙
Maine to Nova Scotia	18	Sep							○	●		⊙							●
Central & Southern California	17			●	●	●		●	●			●	⊙						⊙
Southeastern Arizona	16	Aug		●	●	●		●	●										⊙
W. Wash. & SW British Columbia	15	Jul			⊙	⊙		●	●	●		●	●						●
West Texas	14			●	●	●		●											
Colorado	13				●	●		⊙	●		⊙	●							⊙
Minnesota & North Dakota	12	Jun						●	⊙	●	●								●
Alaska	11							⊙			●						●	●
Southeastern Arizona	10	May		●	●	●		●	●										⊙
Coastal North Carolina	9						●		○			●							
Florida Keys & Dry Tortugas	8	Apr																	
Texas	7			●	⊙	⊙	●	●	●		●	●							
Colorado	6	Mar			⊙	⊙		○		○		○	●						⊙
South Florida	5						●		●		⊙	⊙							
Lower Rio Grande Valley	4	Feb		●	⊙		●	●	●		⊙	⊙							●
Northeastern Minnesota	3																		⊙
Oklahoma	2	Jan			⊙	⊙	●	●	○	○									●
Northern & Central California	1				●	⊙		●		●		●	○						●
ABA Code				1	1	1	1	1	1	1	1	1	1	5	5	5	5	2	1

Legend:
- ● Key Species
- ◉ Probable Species
- ⊙ Possible Species
- ○ Remotely Possible Species

chapter	month	Location	Ruby-crowned Kinglet (1)	Blue-gray Gnatcatcher (1)	Black-tailed Gnatcatcher (1)	California Gnatcatcher (2)	Black-capped Gnatcatcher (4)	Narcissus Flycatcher (5)	Mugimaki Flycatcher (5)	Red-breasted Flycatcher (5)	Siberian Flycatcher (5)	Gray-spotted Flycatcher (5)	Asian Brown Flycatcher (5)	Siberian Rubythroat (4)	Bluethroat (4)	Siberian Blue Robin (5)	Red-flanked Bluetail (5)	Northern Wheatear (3)
20		The Baker's Dozen																
19	Dec	Niagara River Area																
18		Maine to Nova Scotia	●															
17	Sep	Central & Southern California	⊙	◉	◉	●												
16	Aug	Southeastern Arizona	⊙	●	⊙		○											
15		W. Wash. & SW British Columbia	●															
14	Jul	West Texas		◉	◉													
13		Colorado	●	⊙														
12	Jun	Minnesota & North Dakota	●															
11		Alaska	●						▒	▒			▒	▒	⊙			●
10	May	Southeastern Arizona	⊙	●	●		○											
9		Coastal North Carolina		⊙														
8	Apr	Florida Keys & Dry Tortugas		⊙														
7		Texas	●	●	⊙													
6	Mar	Colorado	○															
5		South Florida	●	●														
4	Feb	Lower Rio Grande Valley	●	●														
3		Northeastern Minnesota																
2	Jan	Oklahoma	●															
1		Northern & Central California	●															

Species Seen — date, place

Key: ● Key Species ◐ Probable Species ⊙ Possible Species ○ Remotely Possible Species

Chapter	No.	Month	Species Seen – date	place	Stonechat	Eastern Bluebird	Western Bluebird	Mountain Bluebird	Townsend's Solitaire	Veery	Gray-cheeked Thrush	Bicknell's Thrush	Swainson's Thrush	Hermit Thrush	Wood Thrush	Eyebrowed Thrush	Dusky Thrush	Fieldfare	Redwing	Clay-colored Robin
The Baker's Dozen	20								—	—				—						
Niagara River Area	19	Dec				⊙									○					
Maine to Nova Scotia	18	Sep				●				⊙	⊙	⊙	⊙	●	⊙					
Central & Southern California	17						●	⊙	●					●	⊙					
Southeastern Arizona	16	Aug				●	●							●						
W. Wash. & SW British Columbia	15	Jul					⊙	⊙	⊙	⊙				●	●					
West Texas	14					○	⊙							○						
Colorado	13					○	●	●	●					⊙	●					
Minnesota & North Dakota	12	Jun				●				●				●	●	●				
Alaska	11								⊙		●			●	●	▨	▨			
Southeastern Arizona	10	May				●	●							●						
Coastal North Carolina	9					⊙														
Florida Keys & Dry Tortugas	8	Apr								●	●	⊙	●		●					
Texas	7					●			○	●	●		●	●	●					⊙
Colorado	6	Mar						●	⊙											
South Florida	5					●								●						
Lower Rio Grande Valley	4	Feb				●		○						●						●
Northeastern Minnesota	3																			
Oklahoma	2	Jan				●		⊙	○					⊙						
Northern & Central California	1						●	●						●						
ABA Code					5	1	1	1	1	1	1	2	1	1	1	4	4	5	5	4

Key:
- ● Key Species
- ◉ Probable Species
- ⊙ Possible Species
- ○ Remotely Possible Species

Column header blocks at top right (blank fill‑in columns): **Species Seen — date / place**

Area	Chapter	Month	White‑throated Robin	Rufous‑backed Robin	American Robin	Varied Thrush	Aztec Thrush	Wrentit	Gray Catbird	Northern Mockingbird	Bahama Mockingbird	Sage Thrasher	Brown Thrasher	Long‑billed Thrasher	Bendire's Thrasher	Curve‑billed Thrasher	California Thrasher	Crissal Thrasher
The Baker's Dozen	20																	
Niagara River Area	19	Dec			●					●								
Maine to Nova Scotia	18				●				●	⊙			⊙					
Central & Southern California	17	Sep			●			●		●		⊙				○	●	●
Southeastern Arizona	16	Aug		○	●		○			●					●	●		●
W. Wash. & SW British Columbia	15	Jul			●	●			⊙			⊙						
West Texas	14				⊙					●						●		⊙
Colorado	13				●				●	●		●	●					
Minnesota & North Dakota	12	Jun			●				●				●					
Alaska	11				●	●												
Southeastern Arizona	10	May			●					●					●	●		●
Coastal North Carolina	9				⊙				●	●			●					
Florida Keys & Dry Tortugas	8	Apr							●	●	○		⊙					
Texas	7				●				●	●		○	●	●		●		
Colorado	6	Mar			●											○		
South Florida	5				●				●	●			●					
Lower Rio Grande Valley	4	Feb			●				●	●				●		●		
Northeastern Minnesota	3				⊙													
Oklahoma	2	Jan			●					●		○	⊙			○		
Northern & Central California	1				●	●		●		●							●	

ABA Code (bottom row, per species column): White‑throated Robin 5 · Rufous‑backed Robin 4 · American Robin 1 · Varied Thrush 1 · Aztec Thrush 5 · Wrentit 1 · Gray Catbird 1 · Northern Mockingbird 1 · Bahama Mockingbird 5 · Sage Thrasher 1 · Brown Thrasher 1 · Long‑billed Thrasher 1 · Bendire's Thrasher 2 · Curve‑billed Thrasher 1 · California Thrasher 1 · Crissal Thrasher 1

Legend — Species Seen (date / place):

- ● Key Species
- ◉ Probable Species
- ⊙ Possible Species
- ○ Remotely Possible Species

Chapter	Month	Location	Le Conte's Thrasher	Siberian Accentor	Yellow Wagtail	Citrine Wagtail	Gray Wagtail	White Wagtail	Black-backed Wagtail	Brown Tree-Pipit	Olive Tree-Pipit	Pechora Pipit	Red-throated Pipit	American Pipit	Sprague's Pipit	Bohemian Waxwing	Cedar Waxwing	Gray Silky-flycatcher
20		The Baker's Dozen												—				
19	Dec	Niagara River Area														○	◉	
18	Sep	Maine to Nova Scotia												◉			◉	
17	Sep	Central & Southern California	●														⊙	
16	Aug	Southeastern Arizona	○															
15	Jul	W. Wash. & SW British Columbia												◉			◉	
14	Jul	West Texas																
13		Colorado												◉			○	
12	Jun	Minnesota & North Dakota													◉		◉	
11		Alaska			●			⊙					○	◉	●		◉	
10	May	Southeastern Arizona												⊙			◉	
9		Coastal North Carolina															○	
8	Apr	Florida Keys & Dry Tortugas																
7	Apr	Texas												⊙	○		◉	
6	Mar	Colorado												◉	○		◉	
5	Mar	South Florida												◉			◉	
4	Feb	Lower Rio Grande Valley												◉	●		◉	
3	Feb	Northeastern Minnesota														●	⊙	
2	Jan	Oklahoma												⊙	○		◉	
1	Jan	Northern & Central California												◉			◉	
ABA Code			2	5	3	5	5	3	4	5	4	5	3	1	2	1	1	5

Key Species ● **Probable Species** ◉ **Possible Species** ⊙ **Remotely Possible Species** ○

Chapter	Month	Location	Phainopepla	Brown Shrike	Northern Shrike	Loggerhead Shrike	European Starling	Crested Myna	White-eyed Vireo	Thick-billed Vireo	Bell's Vireo	Black-capped Vireo	Gray Vireo	Solitary Vireo	Yellow-throated Vireo	Hutton's Vireo	Warbling Vireo	Philadelphia Vireo
20	A-M	The Baker's Dozen																
19	Dec	Niagara River Area			⊙		●											
18		Maine to Nova Scotia					●							●	○		⊙	⊙
17	Sep	Central & Southern California	●			●	●				⊙		○	●		●	●	⊙
16	Aug	Southeastern Arizona	●			●	●				●		⊙	●		●	●	
15	Jul	W. Wash. & SW British Columbia				⊙	●	●						●		⊙	●	
14		West Texas	●			●	⊙				●	⊙	●	⊙		●	○	
13		Colorado				●	●						⊙	●			●	
12	Jun	Minnesota & North Dakota				⊙	●								●		●	○
11		Alaska			●		○											
10	May	Southeastern Arizona	●			●	●				●		⊙	●		●	●	
9		Coastal North Carolina					●		●						⊙			
8	Apr	Florida Keys & Dry Tortugas					●		●								○	○
7		Texas				●	●		●		●	●	○	●	●		●	●
6	Mar	Colorado			○	●	●											
5		South Florida				●	●		●					●	⊙			
4	Feb	Lower Rio Grande Valley				●	●		●					●	⊙			
3		Northeastern Minnesota			●		●											
2	Jan	Oklahoma				●	●											
1		Northern & Central California	⊙		○	●	●									●		

Species	ABA Code
Phainopepla	1
Brown Shrike	5
Northern Shrike	1
Loggerhead Shrike	1
European Starling	1
Crested Myna	2
White-eyed Vireo	1
Thick-billed Vireo	5
Bell's Vireo	1
Black-capped Vireo	2
Gray Vireo	1
Solitary Vireo	1
Yellow-throated Vireo	1
Hutton's Vireo	1
Warbling Vireo	1
Philadelphia Vireo	1

352 BIRDFINDER

Legend (Species Seen — date / place):
- ● Key Species
- ● Probable Species
- ◉ Possible Species
- ○ Remotely Possible Species

Chapter	Month	Place	Red-eyed Vireo	Yellow-green Vireo	Black-whiskered Vireo	Yucatan Vireo	Blue-winged Warbler	Golden-winged Warbler	Tennessee Warbler	Orange-crowned Warbler	Nashville Warbler	Virginia's Warbler	Colima Warbler	Lucy's Warbler	Northern Parula	Tropical Parula	Crescent-chested Warbler	Yellow Warbler
20		The Baker's Dozen					C	C										
19	Dec	Niagara River Area																
18	Sep	Maine to Nova Scotia	●							◉	●				●			◉
17		Central & Southern California	○							●	●	◉		◉				●
16	Aug	Southeastern Arizona								○	●		●					●
15	Jul	W. Wash. & SW British Columbia	●							●	◉							●
14		West Texas											●	◉				
13		Colorado	◉							◉		●						●
12	Jun	Minnesota & North Dakota	●					●	◉		●				●			●
11		Alaska								●								●
10	May	Southeastern Arizona								●		●	●					●
9		Coastal North Carolina	◉											○				◉
8	Apr	Florida Keys & Dry Tortugas	●		●		◉	○	◉	○					●			◉
7		Texas	●	◉			●	●	●	●	●				●	○		●
6		Colorado																
5	Mar	South Florida	◉		○					●					●		◉	
4	Feb	Lower Rio Grande Valley								●	●			○	●			
3		Northeastern Minnesota																
2		Oklahoma																
1	Jan	Northern & Central California								●								
ABA Code			1	3	2	5	1	1	1	1	1	1	3	1	1	3	5	1

Legend: ● Key Species ◉ Probable Species ◎ Possible Species ○ Remotely Possible Species

Columns at right (blank form fields): Species Seen — date — place

chapter	month	Location	Chestnut-sided Warbler (1)	Magnolia Warbler (1)	Cape May Warbler (1)	Black-throated Blue Warbler (1)	Yellow-rumped Warbler (1)	Black-throated Gray Warbler (1)	Townsend's Warbler (1)	Hermit Warbler (1)	Black-throated Green Warbler (1)	Golden-cheeked Warbler (2)	Blackburnian Warbler (1)	Yellow-throated Warbler (1)	Grace's Warbler (1)	Pine Warbler (1)	Kirtland's Warbler (3)	Prairie Warbler (1)
20		The Baker's Dozen	C	C-H	C	C				H			C-H			D	D	
19	Dec	Niagara River Area																
18	Sep	Maine to Nova Scotia	◎	●	◎	◎	●				●		◎			◎		◎
17		Central & Southern California					●	●	●	●								
16	Aug	Southeastern Arizona					●	●	●	●					●			
15	Jul	W. Wash. & SW British Columbia					●	●	●	◎								
14		West Texas																
13		Colorado					●	●										
12	Jun	Minnesota & North Dakota	●	●	●	○	●				●		●			◎		
11		Alaska					●		●									
10	May	Southeastern Arizona					●	●	●	◎					●			
9		Coastal North Carolina												◎		●		●
8	Apr	Florida Keys & Dry Tortugas	◎	●	●	●	◎				◎		◎	◎		○		●
7		Texas	●	●	◎	○	●	○	○		●	●	●	●		●	○	
6	Mar	Colorado					○											
5		South Florida		◎	◎		●	◎			◎			◎		●		●
4	Feb	Lower Rio Grande Valley					●	○			○			○		○		
3		Northeastern Minnesota																
2		Oklahoma					●											
1	Jan	Northern & Central California					●		●	●								

ABA Code

Key:
- ● Key Species
- ◉ Probable Species
- ◎ Possible Species
- ○ Remotely Possible Species

chapter	date	Location / Species Seen	Palm Warbler	Bay-breasted Warbler	Blackpoll Warbler	Cerulean Warbler	Black-and-white Warbler	American Redstart	Prothonotary Warbler	Worm-eating Warbler	Swainson's Warbler	Ovenbird	Northern Waterthrush	Louisiana Waterthrush	Kentucky Warbler	Connecticut Warbler	Mourning Warbler	MacGillivray's Warbler
20		The Baker's Dozen	C-H								H					C	C-H	I
19	Dec	Niagara River Area																
18	Sep	Maine to Nova Scotia	●	◉	●		●	●				◉	◉				◉	
17		Central & Southern California			◎		◎	◎				○						●
16	Aug	Southeastern Arizona					○											
15		W. Wash. & SW British Columbia						◎				○						●
14	Jul	West Texas																
13		Colorado						○										●
12	Jun	Minnesota & North Dakota	○	○			●	●				●	●			●	●	
11		Alaska			●								●					
10	May	Southeastern Arizona					○											◎
9		Coastal North Carolina							●		◎							
8	Apr	Florida Keys & Dry Tortugas	●	○	●	○	●	●	◎	◎		●	●	◎	◎	○		
7		Texas	○	●	●	●	●	●	●	●	●	●	●	●	●		○	○
6	Mar	Colorado																
5		South Florida	●				◉	◎				●	◎	◎				
4	Feb	Lower Rio Grande Valley	◎				◉											
3		Northeastern Minnesota																
2	Jan	Oklahoma																
1		Northern & Central California	○															
ABA Code			1	1	1	1	1	1	1	1	2	1	1	1	1	2	1	1

Key:
- ● Key Species
- ◉ Probable Species
- ⊙ Possible Species
- ○ Remotely Possible Species

Chapter	#	Month	Common Yellowthroat (1)	Gray-crowned Yellowthroat (5)	Hooded Warbler (1)	Wilson's Warbler (1)	Canada Warbler (1)	Red-faced Warbler (2)	Painted Redstart (1)	Slate-throated Redstart (5)	Fan-tailed Warbler (5)	Golden-crowned Warbler (5)	Rufous-capped Warbler (4)	Yellow-breasted Chat (1)	Olive Warbler (2)	Bananaquit (4)	Stripe-headed Tanager (4)	Hepatic Tanager (2)
The Baker's Dozen	20						H											
Niagara River Area	19	Dec																
Maine to Nova Scotia	18		●			⊙	⊙							⊙				
Central & Southern California	17	Sep	●			●								⊙				
Southeastern Arizona	16	Aug	●			●		●	●				○	●	●			●
W. Wash. & SW British Columbia	15	Jul	●			●								⊙				
West Texas	14		⊙						⊙				○	●				●
Colorado	13		●			●								●				
Minnesota & North Dakota	12	Jun	●				●											
Alaska	11					●												
Southeastern Arizona	10	May	●			●		●	●					●	●		●	
Coastal North Carolina	9		●		⊙									●				
Florida Keys & Dry Tortugas	8	Apr	●		⊙	○	○							○		○		
Texas	7		●		●	●	⊙							●				
Colorado	6	Mar																
South Florida	5		●			⊙											○	
Lower Rio Grande Valley	4	Feb	●	○								○						
Northeastern Minnesota	3																	
Oklahoma	2	Jan																
Northern & Central California	1		●															

Key:
- ● Key Species
- ◉ Probable Species
- ⊙ Possible Species
- ○ Remotely Possible Species

chapter	Species Seen (location)	date	Summer Tanager	Scarlet Tanager	Western Tanager	Flame-colored Tanager	Crimson-collared Grosbeak	Northern Cardinal	Pyrrhuloxia	Yellow Grosbeak	Rose-breasted Grosbeak	Black-headed Grosbeak	Blue Bunting	Blue Grosbeak	Lazuli Bunting	Indigo Bunting	Varied Bunting	Painted Bunting
20	The Baker's Dozen														G			
19	Niagara River Area	Dec						●										
18	Maine to Nova Scotia	Sep		⊙				⊙			⊙					⊙		
17	Central & Southern California		○		●							●		⊙	●	⊙		
16	Southeastern Arizona	Aug	●		●	⊙		●	●	○		●		●	○	●	●	○
15	W. Wash. & SW British Columbia	Jul			●							●			●			
14	West Texas		●		●			●	●			●		●			●	⊙
13	Colorado				●							●		●	●	⊙		
12	Minnesota & North Dakota	Jun		●							●				●			
11	Alaska																	
10	Southeastern Arizona	May	●		●	○		●	●	○		●		●	○	○	●	
9	Coastal North Carolina		⊙	○				●			○			⊙		●		
8	Florida Keys & Dry Tortugas	Apr	⊙	⊙				●			⊙			●		●		⊙
7	Texas		●	●				●	●		●			●		●		●
6	Colorado	Mar																
5	South Florida							●							⊙			⊙
4	Lower Rio Grande Valley	Feb					○	●	●				○					
3	Northeastern Minnesota																	
2	Oklahoma	Jan						●										
1	Northern & Central California																	
ABA Code			1	1	1	5	5	1	1	5	1	1	4	1	1	1	2	1

Key:
- ● Key Species
- ◉ Probable Species
- ◉ Possible Species
- ○ Remotely Possible Species

chapter	month	Chapter	Dickcissel	Olive Sparrow	Green-tailed Towhee	Rufous-sided Towhee	Spotted Towhee	California Towhee	Canyon Towhee	Abert's Towhee	White-collared Seedeater	Yellow-faced Grassquit	Black-faced Grassquit	Bachman's Sparrow	Botteri's Sparrow	Cassin's Sparrow	Rufous-winged Sparrow	Rufous-crowned Sparrow
20		The Baker's Dozen					G											
19	Dec	Niagara River Area																
18		Maine to Nova Scotia				○												
17	Sep	Central & Southern California			◉		●	●		●								●
16	Aug	Southeastern Arizona				○	●		●	●					●	●	●	●
15	Jul	W. Wash. & SW British Columbia				○	●											
14		West Texas				○	●		●							●		●
13		Colorado		○		●	●									◉		
12	Jun	Minnesota & North Dakota		◉		◉												
11		Alaska																
10	May	Southeastern Arizona			◉		●		●	●					●	●	●	●
9		Coastal North Carolina				●								◉				
8	Apr	Florida Keys & Dry Tortugas	◉															
7		Texas	●	●	○	●	◉		●		◉			●	◉	●		●
6	Mar	Colorado					◉		◉									○
5		South Florida				●								●				
4	Feb	Lower Rio Grande Valley		●	◉	●	◉				●				◉	◉		
3		Northeastern Minnesota																
2	Jan	Oklahoma			◉	●											●	
1		Northern & Central California					●	●									●	

| ABA Code | 1 | 2 | 1 | 1 | 1 | 1 | 1 | 1 | 4 | 5 | 5 | 2 | 2 | 1 | 2 | 1 |

Legend:
- ● Key Species
- ◉ Probable Species
- ⊙ Possible Species
- ○ Remotely Possible Species

Species Seen — date / place

#	Chapter (place)	Month	American Tree Sparrow	Chipping Sparrow	Clay-colored Sparrow	Brewer's Sparrow	Field Sparrow	Black-chinned Sparrow	Vesper Sparrow	Lark Sparrow	Black-throated Sparrow	Sage Sparrow	Five-striped Sparrow	Lark Bunting	Savannah Sparrow	Baird's Sparrow	Grasshopper Sparrow	Henslow's Sparrow
20	The Baker's Dozen		B	—	D	G			—									C-D-E
19	Niagara River Area	Dec	⊙															
18	Maine to Nova Scotia	Sep		●			⊙		⊙						●			
17	Central & Southern California	Sep		●	○		⊙		⊙	●	⊙	●			●		○	
16	Southeastern Arizona	Aug		⊙				⊙	◉	●	●		⊙	⊙	●			
15	W. Wash. & SW British Columbia	Jul		●		⊙			⊙	◉	○	⊙			●	⊙		
14	West Texas	Jul		⊙				⊙	●	●	●							
13	Colorado			●		●			●	●	●	⊙	●	●	●			
12	Minnesota & North Dakota	Jun		◉	◉		○		●	⊙				⊙	●	●	●	○
11	Alaska		●	⊙											●			
10	Southeastern Arizona	May		●		○		●	●	●			●	⊙	●			
9	Coastal North Carolina						●											
8	Florida Keys & Dry Tortugas	Apr																
7	Texas			●	●		●		●	●	⊙			⊙	●		⊙	○
6	Colorado	Mar	●						○									
5	South Florida			●	○		●		⊙	⊙					●		●	
4	Lower Rio Grande Valley	Feb			⊙		●		●	●	●			⊙	●		●	
3	Northeastern Minnesota																	
2	Oklahoma	Jan	●				●							⊙	●			
1	Northern & Central California								●			●			●			
	ABA Code		1	1	1	1	1	2	1	1	1	1	3	1	1	2	1	2

Legend
- ● Key Species
- ◉ Probable Species
- ⊙ Possible Species
- ○ Remotely Possible Species

Species Seen — date — place

Chapter	Month	Location	Le Conte's Sparrow	Salt-marsh Sharp-tailed Sparrow	Nelson's Sharp-tailed Sparrow	Seaside Sparrow	Fox Sparrow	Song Sparrow	Lincoln's Sparrow	Swamp Sparrow	White-throated Sparrow	Golden-crowned Sparrow	White-crowned Sparrow	Harris's Sparrow	Dark-eyed Junco	Yellow-eyed Junco	McCown's Longspur	Lapland Longspur
1	Jan	Northern & Central California					●	●	●		⊙	●	●		●			
2	Jan	Oklahoma	○				⊙	●	⊙	○	⊙		●	●	●		●	●
3	Feb	Northeastern Minnesota													⊙			
4	Feb	Lower Rio Grande Valley	⊙		○	○	●	●	●	●	●							
5	Mar	South Florida		○		○	●	○	●	○	○		○					
6	Mar	Colorado					●	●	⊙	⊙	●	●	●				⊙	○
7	Apr	Texas	⊙		●	●	○	●	●	●	●		●		○			
8	Apr	Florida Keys & Dry Tortugas																
9	May	Coastal North Carolina			○	●	●											
10	May	Southeastern Arizona						●					⊙		●			
11	Jun	Alaska					●	●	●			●	●					◉
12	Jun	Minnesota & North Dakota	●		●			●	●	●	●				○			
13	Jul	Colorado					⊙	●	●		●		●		●		●	
14	Jul	West Texas																
15	Jul	W. Wash. & SW British Columbia						●	●	●			●		●			
16	Aug	Southeastern Arizona						●								●		
17	Sep	Central & Southern California						●	●	●		⊙	●		●			
18	Sep	Maine to Nova Scotia				●	⊙	●	●	●	●		⊙		●			
19	Dec	Niagara River Area						⊙			⊙		⊙		●			
20		The Baker's Dozen		M-J	H	J							—		B-F	—		B-M

ABA Code: Le Conte's Sparrow 2; all others 1.

Key:
● Key Species
◉ Probable Species
◉ Possible Species
○ Remotely Possible Species

chapter / region	#	date	Smith's Longspur (2)	Chestnut-collared Longspur (1)	Pine Bunting (5)	Little Bunting (5)	Rustic Bunting (4)	Yellow-breasted Bunting (5)	Gray Bunting (5)	Pallas's Reed-Bunting (5)	Common Reed-Bunting (5)	Snow Bunting (1)	McKay's Bunting (3)	Bobolink (1)	Red-winged Blackbird (1)	Tricolored Blackbird (1)	Tawny-shouldered Blackbird (5)	Eastern Meadowlark (1)
The Baker's Dozen	20	F										B-M						
Niagara River Area	19	Dec										◉			◉			
Maine to Nova Scotia	18	Sep										●			◉			◉
Central & Southern California	17														●	●		
Southeastern Arizona	16	Aug													●			●
W. Wash. & SW British Columbia	15	Jul										◉			●			
West Texas	14														●			●
Colorado	13				●							○			●			
Minnesota & North Dakota	12	Jun			●							●			●			◉
Alaska	11		◉								●	◉			◉			
Southeastern Arizona	10	May													●			●
Coastal North Carolina	9											○			●			●
Florida Keys & Dry Tortugas	8	Apr										●			●			
Texas	7											○			●		●	
Colorado	6	Mar		○											●			
South Florida	5														●		●	
Lower Rio Grande Valley	4	Feb													●		●	
Northeastern Minnesota	3										●							
Oklahoma	2	Jan	●	●											●		●	
Northern & Central California	1														●	●		

Legend:
- ● Key Species
- ◉ Probable Species
- ⊙ Possible Species
- ○ Remotely Possible Species

#	Date	Chapter	Western Meadowlark	Yellow-headed Blackbird	Rusty Blackbird	Brewer's Blackbird	Great-tailed Grackle	Boat-tailed Grackle	Common Grackle	Shiny Cowbird	Bronzed Cowbird	Brown-headed Cowbird	Black-vented Oriole	Orchard Oriole	Hooded Oriole	Streak-backed Oriole	Spot-breasted Oriole	Altamira Oriole
20		The Baker's Dozen				—		—										
19	Dec	Niagara River Area				⊙						●						
18		Maine to Nova Scotia				⊙			●			●						
17	Sep	Central & Southern California	●	◉		●	●	●				●			●			
16	Aug	Southeastern Arizona		○	○			●			●	●			●	○		
15	Jul	W. Wash. & SW British Columbia	●	⊙		●						●						
14		West Texas		⊙			●				●	●		●	●			
13		Colorado	●	◉		●		○	●			●		●				
12	Jun	Minnesota & North Dakota	●	●	○	●			●			●		●				
11		Alaska				●												
10	May	Southeastern Arizona	⊙					●			●	●			●	○		
9		Coastal North Carolina					●	●				●		⊙				
8	Apr	Florida Keys & Dry Tortugas						⊙	●			○		⊙				
7		Texas	⊙	⊙		●	●	●	●		●	●		●	⊙			●
6	Mar	Colorado	●	⊙	○	⊙	○		●			○						
5		South Florida						●	●	⊙	○	●					●	
4	Feb	Lower Rio Grande Valley	●			●	●				⊙	●						●
3		Northeastern Minnesota																
2	Jan	Oklahoma	●		○	●	●		●		⊙	●						
1		Northern & Central California	●	⊙		●						●						
ABA Code			1	1	1	1	1	1	1	4	1	1	5	1	1	5	2	2

Key:
- ● Key Species
- ◉ Probable Species
- ⊙ Possible Species
- ○ Remotely Possible Species

Species Seen: place / date

Chapter	Location	Month	Audubon's Oriole	Baltimore Oriole	Bullock's Oriole	Scott's Oriole	Brambling	Gray-crowned Rosy-Finch	Black Rosy-Finch	Brown-capped Rosy-Finch	Pine Grosbeak	Common Rosefinch	Purple Finch	Cassin's Finch	House Finch	Red Crossbill	White-winged Crossbill	Common Redpoll
20	The Baker's Dozen							G-I			I		H	G-I		G-I	H	
19	Niagara River Area	Dec											⊙		●	⊙	⊙	⊙
18	Maine to Nova Scotia	Sep			⊙						○		●			○	⊙	⊙
17	Central & Southern California	Sep			●	○							●	●	●	⊙		
16	Southeastern Arizona	Aug			●	●									●	⊙		
15	W. Wash. & SW British Columbia	Jul			⊙			⊙			⊙		●	⊙	●	●	○	
14	West Texas	Jul			⊙	●									●			
13	Colorado				●	○				●	●		●	●	⊙			
12	Minnesota & North Dakota	Jun		●									●		●	○	○	
11	Alaska						⊙				⊙					○	●	●
10	Southeastern Arizona	May			●	●								○	●	⊙		
9	Coastal North Carolina				○										⊙			
8	Florida Keys & Dry Tortugas	Apr			⊙													
7	Texas		⊙	●	⊙									○	●			
6	Colorado	Mar						●	●	⊙	●		○	●	●	⊙		○
5	South Florida				⊙	○												
4	Lower Rio Grande Valley	Feb	●			○												
3	Northeastern Minnesota										●		⊙			⊙	⊙	●
2	Oklahoma												⊙					
1	Northern & Central California	Jan											●		●			
ABA Code			2	1	1	1	4	1	1	1	1	5	1	1	1	1	1	1

Key Species ● **Probable Species** ● **Possible Species** ◉ **Remotely Possible Species** ○

chapter	date	Species Seen / place	Hoary Redpoll	Eurasian Siskin	Pine Siskin	Lesser Goldfinch	Lawrence's Goldfinch	American Goldfinch	Oriental Greenfinch	Eurasian Bullfinch	Evening Grosbeak	Hawfinch	House Sparrow	Eurasian Tree Sparrow
20		The Baker's Dozen (F … E)												
19	Dec	Niagara River Area			◉			●			◉		●	
18	Sep	Maine to Nova Scotia			●			●			●		●	
17		Central & Southern California			◉	●	●	●					●	
16	Aug	Southeastern Arizona			○	●					○		●	
15	Jul	W. Wash. & SW British Columbia			●			●			●		●	
14		West Texas				●							●	
13		Colorado			●	●		●			●		●	
12	Jun	Minnesota & North Dakota			●			●			○		●	
11		Alaska	●		●				▨			▨		
10	May	Southeastern Arizona			●	●		●			○		●	
9		Coastal North Carolina											●	
8	Apr	Florida Keys & Dry Tortugas											●	
7		Texas					◉	●					●	
6	Mar	Colorado			●			●			●		●	
5		South Florida						●					●	
4	Feb	Lower Rio Grande Valley			◉	○		●					●	
3		Northeastern Minnesota		◉	●						●		●	
2	Jan	Oklahoma			◉			●					●	
1		Northern & Central California			●	●	○	●					●	
ABA Code			2	5	1	1	1	1	5	5	1	4	1	2

Nomenclature Changes and the Index

The bird names used in this book basically follow those of the American Ornithologists' Union (AOU) and the American Birding Association (ABA). Below are also some names which differ from those used in older field guides, or which yet to appear in even the most recent field guides.

Names Used in this Book	Former Name or Derivation
Neotropic Cormorant	Neotropical or Olivaceous Cormorant
Green Heron	Green-backed Heron
Tundra Swan	Whistling Swan
Common Moorhen	Common Gallinule
Pacific Golden-Plover	split from Lesser Golden-Plover
American Golden-Plover	split from Lesser Golden-Plover
Gilded Flicker	split from Northern Flicker
Pacific-slope Flycatcher	split from Western Flycatcher
Cordilleran Flycatcher	split from Western Flycatcher
Western Scrub-Jay	split from Scrub Jay
Florida Scrub-Jay	split from Scrub Jay
Santa Cruz Island Scrub-Jay	split from Scrub Jay
Mexican Jay	Gray-breasted Jay
Bicknell's Thrush	split from Gray-cheeked Thrush
American Pipit	Water Pipit
Spotted Towhee	split from Rufous-sided Towhee
California Towhee	split from Brown Towhee
Canyon Towhee	split from Brown Towhee
Salt-marsh Sharp-tailed Sparrow	split from Sharp-tailed Sparrow
Nelson's Sharp-tailed Sparrow	split from Sharp-tailed Sparrow
Baltimore Oriole	split from Northern Oriole
Bullock's Oriole	split from Northern Oriole

The index below does **not** include bird species; the index is basically for locations in this book. To find where individual species appear in the book, refer to the Birdfinder Chart. The chart indicates not only the location of the species as to chapter, but also the status of the species in the chapter. In this way, the Birdfinder Chart functions as a species index.

INDEX

Austin 103
Austwell 96
Averill Park 228
Avon Park 70

B

Bahia Honda 116
Bahia Honda State Park 114
Bake Oven Knob 299
Bald Mountain 286
Bangor 242, 246
Bar Harbor 241-242
Barfoot Peak Trail 146
Barrow 164
Bay of Fundy 239, 244
Beach
 Dillon 21
 Drake's (Point Reyes) 19
 First Encounter 301
 Matagorda 95
 Nude 193, 301
Bear River Migratory Bird Refuge 285

Bear Valley National Wildlife Refuge 259
Beaumont 86
Belle Glade 71
Bellingham 208
Ben Walters Park 156
Bentsen-Rio Grande Valley State Park 49-55, 88, 90, 93, 100
Big Bend National Park 197, 200
Big Morongo Canyon Preserve 231
Big Pine Key 113
Big Sandy Lake 175
Big Sur 233
Big Thicket 86, 90, 92, 105
Bill Baggs Cape Florida State Park 72
Bisbee 143
Blue Creek Trail 201
Boca Chica 54, 99
Bodega 23
Bodega Bay 17, 19-21, 23
Bodie Island 123
Bolinas Lagoon 19-21, 25
Bolivar Flats 89, 94, 105
Bolivar Peninsula 85, 88, 93
Bombay Hook National Wildlife Refuge 291
Bonny State Recreation Area 81
Boot Spring 199, 201
Borrego Springs 230
Bradenton 64, 70
Brawley 230
Brewster 303
Brier Island 239, 241, 243
Briggsdale 189
Brownsville 51, 54, 58, 88, 99
Brownsville City Dump 52, 54, 99
Brush 81
Buffalo 251
Buffalo River State Park 175
Burlington, ON 254
Burlington, WA 207
Bush Key 111, 114

C

Cache la Poudre River 77-78, 80
Cahokia Mounds State Historical Site 272
California Gulch 132, 134, 140
Cameo 186, 193
Cameron Pass 77, 80
Campground
 Adolph Thomae Jr. County Park, TX 99
 Bahia Honda State Park 114
 Bog Springs 139
 Cape Hatteras Point 124
 Catalina State Park 136-137
 Clear Lake 79
 Cuyamaca Rancho State Park 229
 Endovalley 191
 Falcon State Park 101
 Fort Anahuac Park 104
 General Hitchcock 136

Abbreviated Table of Contents

M

N

Abbreviated Table of Contents

Abbreviated Table of Contents

Abbreviated Table of Contents

Other Birdfinding Guides in ABA/Lane Series

A Birder's Guide to Southeastern Arizona
by Richard Cachor Taylor
1995, $16.95

A Birder's Guide to Arkansas
by Mel White
1995, $16.95

A Birder's Guide to Eastern Massachusetts
by Bird Observer
1994, $16.95

A Birder's Guide to Churchill (Manitoba)
by Bonnie Chartier
1993, $14.95

A Birder's Guide to Wyoming
by Oliver K. Scott
1993, $16.95

A Birder's Guide to the Texas Coast
by Harold R. Holt
1993, $14.95

A Birder's Guide to the Rio Grande Valley of Texas
by Harold R. Holt
1992, $16.95

A Birder's Guide to Southern California
by Harold R. Holt
1990, $14.95

A Birder's Guide to New Hampshire
by Alan Delorey
1996 (in preparation), $16.95

A Birder's Guide to Florida
under revision

A Birder's Guide to Colorado
under revision

These and many other birdfinding and bird identification publications are available from:

ABA Sales

P.O. Box 6599
Colorado Springs, CO 80934
Toll-free (US and Canada): phone 800/634-7736
fax 800/590-2473

AMERICAN BIRDING ASSOCIATION
Membership Application

The American Birding Association is *the* organization of North American birders dedicated to being the main source for up-to-date information on bird identification, birdfinding, and bird conservation. The ABA gives active birders what they want.

All memberships include six issues of **Birding** magazine, monthly issues of **Winging It,** ABA's newsletter, member discounts offered by ABA Sales, and full rights of participation in all ABA activities.

Membership classes and dues:

❑ Individual - US	$36/yr	❑ Family - US	$43/yr
❑ Individual - Canada	$45/yr*	❑ Family - Canada	$52/yr*
❑ Individual - Int'l	$45/yr	❑ Family - Int'l	$52/yr
❑ Century Club	$100/yr	❑ Life Membership	$1,200

All membership dues include $27 for **Birding** magazine and $9 for **Winging It** newsletter;
* = includes GST

Application Type   ❑ New Membership ❑ Renewal

Member Information

Name _____

Address _____

_____

_____

Phone _____

Payment Information

❑ Check or Money Order enclosed (US funds only)

❑ Charge to VISA / MasterCard (circle one)

Account Number _____

Exp Date _____ Signature _____

Sent this completed form with payment to: **ABA Membership**
PO Box 6599
Colorado Springs, CO 80934

BF 10/95